Introducing Communication Research

Third Edition

For Joseph, Luke, Owen, and James—now on their own paths of inquiry.

Introducing Communication Research

Paths of Inquiry

Third Edition

Donald Treadwell

Los Angeles | London | New Delhi
Singapore | Washington DC

Los Angeles | London | New Delhi
Singapore | Washington DC

FOR INFORMATION:

SAGE Publications, Inc.
2455 Teller Road
Thousand Oaks, California 91320
E-mail: order@sagepub.com

SAGE Publications Ltd.
1 Oliver's Yard
55 City Road
London EC1Y 1SP
United Kingdom

SAGE Publications India Pvt. Ltd.
B 1/I 1 Mohan Cooperative Industrial Area
Mathura Road, New Delhi 110 044
India

SAGE Publications Asia-Pacific Pte. Ltd.
3 Church Street
#10-04 Samsung Hub
Singapore 049483

Printed in the United States of America

ISBN 978-1-4833-7941-8

Acquisitions Editor: Matthew Byrnie
Development Editor: Eve Oettinger
Editorial Assistant: Janae Masnovi
eLearning Editor: Gabrielle Piccininni
Production Editor: Olivia Weber-Stenis
Copy Editor: Melinda Masson
Typesetter: C&M Digitals (P) Ltd.
Proofreader: Ellen Brink
Indexer: Diggs Publication Services
Cover Designer: Candice Harman
Marketing Manager: Ashlee Blunk

This book is printed on acid-free paper.

Certified Chain of Custody
Promoting Sustainable Forestry
www.sfiprogram.org
SFI-01268

SFI label applies to text stock

17 18 19 10 9 8 7 6 5 4 3

Brief Contents

List of Exhibits   xviii

Preface   xx

Chapter 1: Getting Started: Possibilities and Decisions   1

Chapter 2: First Decisions: What, Why, How?   21

Chapter 3: Ethics: What Are My Responsibilities as a Researcher?   40

Chapter 4: You Could Look It Up: Reading, Recording, and Reviewing Research   58

Chapter 5: Measurement: Research Using Numbers   80

Chapter 6: Summarizing Research Results:
Data Reduction and Descriptive Statistics   96

Chapter 7: Generalizing From Research Results: Inferential Statistics   117

Chapter 8: Sampling: Who, What, and How Many?   138

Chapter 9: Surveys: Putting Numbers on Opinions   157

Chapter 10: Experiments: Researching Cause and Effect   177

Chapter 11: Watching and Listening:
Qualitative Research for In-Depth Understanding   195

Chapter 12: Content Analysis:
Understanding Communication Content in Numbers   216

Chapter 13: Rhetorical and Critical Analyses, and More:
Understanding Communication Content in Words   234

Chapter 14: Writing and Presenting Research   255

Glossary   273

Index   287

About the Author   296

Detailed Contents

List of Exhibits   xviii

Preface   xx

Chapter 1: Getting Started: Possibilities and Decisions   1

  Chapter Overview   1
  Chapter Objectives   1
  Getting Started in Research   1
  The Situation   2
    Interaction I—The Couple: Romance, "Just Friends," or Doing Business?   3
    Interaction II—The Group: Collaboration or Conflict? Business or Pleasure?   4
    Interaction III—The Topic Turns to the Media   5
  Basic Assumptions Behind Communication Research   6
    Observations Capture/Do Not Capture an Underlying Reality   6
    Theories About Human Behavior Can/Cannot Be Generalized   7
    Researchers Should/Should Not Distance Themselves From Their Research Participants   7
    Research Should/Should Not Be Done for a Specific Purpose   7
    There Is/Is Not One Best Position From Which to Observe Human Behavior   8
  Some Research Possibilities: What Can We Do With an Ad?   8
    Does the Ad Work?   9
    What Can Readers and Viewers Tell Us?   10
    What Can the Content Tell Us?   10
    What Can the Creators of the Ad Tell Us?   11
  Some Research Possibilities: Beyond the Ad   11
  A Series of Unavoidable Decisions   12
    The Field of Study—Wide or Narrow?   12
    The Researcher—Dispassionate or Involved?   12
    The Approach—Objective or Subjective?   13
    The Priority—Your Questions or Their Answers?   14
    The Sample—Large or Small?   14
    The Data—Quantitative or Qualitative?   14
    The Report—Subjective or Objective?   15
  Problem Posing, Problem Solving, Peer Persuasion   16
    Problem Posing   16
    Problem Solving   16
    Peer Persuasion   16
  Ethics Panel: A Health Communication Dilemma   17

Chapter Summary   17
Key Terms   17
Application Exercises   18
    Exercise 1. Finding Research Questions   18
    Exercise 2. Exploring Communication Interest Areas   18
    Exercise 3. Researching Internet Communication   18
Recommended Reading   19
    General   19
    Mass Communication   19
    Organizational Communication   19
    Group Communication   19
    Interpersonal Communication   19
    Social Media   20
Recommended Web Resources   20
References   20

Chapter 2: First Decisions: What, Why, How?   **21**

Chapter Overview   21
Chapter Objectives   21
Starting With the "What" Question: Ideas and Observations   22
    Induction   23
    Deduction   23
    Abduction   24
Starting With the "Why" Question: Goals and Values   24
    Exploration   24
    Description   25
    Explanation   25
    Prediction   25
    Control   26
    Interpretation   27
    Criticism   27
Starting With the "How" Question: Methods and Epistemologies   28
Starting With a Worldview: Basic Beliefs   28
Starting From the Work of Others   30
Firming Up Questions   30
    Hypotheses: Making Predictions   32
    Research Questions: Less Certainty; More Room to Move   32
Questioning the Questions   33
Starting With No Questions   33
Moving in a Hermeneutic Circle   34
Ethics Panel: Do Some Research Methods
   Have More Ethical Implications Than Others?   34
Chapter Summary   35
Key Terms   35
Application Exercises   36
    Exercise 1: Identifying Your Interests   36
    Exercise 2: Finding Your Worldview   36
    Exercise 3: Starting From Published Research   37
    Exercise 4: Pew Research Center Internet, Science &
       Tech Project   38

Recommended Reading   38
Recommended Web Resources   38
References   39

Chapter 3: Ethics: What Are My Responsibilities as a Researcher?   40

Chapter Overview   40
Chapter Objectives   40
Introduction: Some Ethical Decisions   41
    Sex, Violence, and Deception   41
    Money and Relationships   42
Ethics Issues in Communication Research   42
    Honesty   42
    Confidentiality and Anonymity   43
    Making Generalizations   43
    Debriefing   43
    The Literature Review   44
    Acknowledging Others   44
    Appropriate Language   44
    Plagiarism   45
Some Classic Ethical Positions   45
Two Brief Histories—Or Why We Care About Research Ethics   46
Contemporary Codes of Ethics   46
    The Nuremberg Code   46
    The Declaration of Helsinki   46
    The Belmont Report   47
Regulations   48
Peer Review and Institutional Review Boards   48
What Should I Call You? The Ethics of Involvement   48
The Internet and Research Ethics   49
    What Is the Internet?   49
    Anonymity and Identification on the Internet   50
    Privacy on the Internet   50
    Informed Consent and Debriefing on the Internet   51
    Guidelines and Questions for Internet Research   52
Ethics Panel: Facebook Faces a Furor   53
Chapter Summary   53
Key Terms   54
Application Exercises   54
    Exercise 1: The Ethics of Content Analysis   54
    Exercise 2: Ethics and Virtual Respondents   54
    Exercise 3: The Ethics of Internet Research   54
    Exercise 4: The Ethics of Public Opinion Polling   55
Recommended Reading   55
Recommended Web Resources   55
References   56

Chapter 4: You Could Look It Up: Reading, Recording, and Reviewing Research   58

Chapter Overview   58
Chapter Objectives   58

Library Research: Why Bother?   59
 Methods   59
 Ethics   60
 Language and Style   60
 Inspiration   60
Finding Relevance, Finding Quality   60
 Identifying Relevant Information   60
 Identifying Quality Information   61
Scholarly Databases Versus Search Engines   61
 Search Engines   61
 Databases   61
Scholarly Journals: A Good Starting Point   62
 Assessing Scholarly Journals   63
Scholarly, Popular, and Trade Publications:
 What Is the Difference?   63
 How Will I Know a Scholarly Article When I See One?   63
Primary Versus Secondary Sources   64
Search Strategies: General to Specific and Specific to General   65
Search Terms and Search Fields   65
How Can the Library of Congress Help My Literature Search?   67
Other Resources   67
How to Be Skeptical About Information, Especially Web Information   67
 Stage 1: Think Book or Journal   67
 Stage 2: Additional Questions for Websites   68
Mr. Boole and the Three Bears   68
Saving Your Search Results   69
 Information You Must Record   69
 Information You Should Record   70
 Citation Management Software   71
Reviewing the Literature   72
The Literature Review: Writing Your Search Results   73
 Structuring the Literature Review   73
 Questions of Style   74
Ethics Panel: Politics and Publication   75
Chapter Summary   75
Key Terms   75
Application Exercises   76
 Exercise 1: APA Style   76
 Exercise 2: Comparing Primary and Secondary Sources   76
 Exercise 3: Search Terms and Boolean Operators   76
 Exercise 4: Writing a Literature Review   76
Recommended Reading   77
Recommended Web Resources   77
 APA, Chicago, and MLA Style Guides   78
 Evaluating Websites   78
 Citation Management Software   78
 Journal Impact Sites   78
 Miscellaneous   78
 What Is Everybody Else Searching For?   78
References   79

Chapter 5: Measurement: Research Using Numbers　　　　　80

　　Chapter Overview　80
　　Chapter Objectives　80
　　What Do Your Head Size, Attitudes, and Readability Have in Common?　81
　　An Introduction to Scales　82
　　Research NOIR　82
　　　　Nominal Measurement　83
　　　　Ordinal Measurement　83
　　　　Interval Measurement　83
　　　　Ratio Measurement　84
　　　　Why Do We Care?　84
　　　　NOIR in Action　85
　　To NOIR Is Not Enough: Reliability and Validity　85
　　Reliability　85
　　　　Test-Retest　86
　　　　Intercoder or Observer Reliability　86
　　　　Inter-Item or Internal Reliability　87
　　　　Established Measures Reliability　87
　　Validity　88
　　　　Content Validity: Looks OK　89
　　　　Construct Validity: Theoretically OK　89
　　　　Criterion Validity: Tests OK　90
　　　　Who Wins in the Reliability–Validity Shootout?　90
　　Two Common Measurement Scales　90
　　　　The Likert Scale　90
　　　　The Semantic Differential Scale　91
　　Ethics Panel: The Ethics of Measurement Scales　93
　　Chapter Summary　93
　　Key Terms　94
　　Application Exercises　94
　　　　Exercise 1. NOIR Revisited　94
　　　　Exercise 2. The Web at 25　94
　　　　Exercise 3. Parlez-moi d'amour　94
　　Recommended Reading　95
　　References　95

Chapter 6: Summarizing Research Results:
　　　　Data Reduction and Descriptive Statistics　　　　96

　　Chapter Overview　96
　　Chapter Objectives　97
　　Introduction　97
　　Preliminary Considerations: Missing Data and Anomalous Data　99
　　Data Reduction　100
　　　　Data Reduction and Univariate Data　100
　　　　Data Reduction and Bi-variate Data　102
　　　　Data Reduction and Multivariate Data　104
　　Measures of Central Tendency: Mean, Median, and Mode　105
　　Measures of Dispersion: Minimum, Maximum, Range, Interquartile Range,
　　Variance, and Standard Deviation　106

Minimum, Maximum, Range, and Interquartile Range 106
Variance and Standard Deviation 106
Variance: Formula 106
Standard Deviation: Formula 107
Variance and Standard Deviation: Example 107
z Score 109
z Score: Formula 109
z Score: Example 109
The Chi-Square Test 110
Chi-Square: Formula 111
Chi-Square: Example 111
Ethics Panel: Can Rankings Be Misleading? 112
Chapter Summary 113
Key Terms 113
Application Exercises 114
Exercise 1: Basic Statistics 114
Exercise 2: Brand, Color, and Gender Preferences 114
Exercise 3: "The Internet of Things" 114
Exercise 4: A Social Media Study 114
Recommended Reading 115
Recommended Web Resources 115
College Rankings 116
References 116

Chapter 7: Generalizing From Research Results: Inferential Statistics   **117**

Chapter Overview 117
Chapter Objectives 117
Introduction 118
The Language of Curves 118
Generalizing From Data: Inferential Statistics 119
The Normal Curve and the Central Limit Theorem 119
The Normal Curve, z Scores, and the Return of Standard Deviation 120
Calculating Probabilities Based on the Normal Distribution 122
z Scores, Hypotheses, and Decision Making 123
Confidence Level and Sample Size 124
Testing for Differences Between and Among Groups 125
The t Test 125
t Test: Formula 126
t Test: Example 127
Another Type of *t* 129
Analysis of Variance 129
ANOVA: Formula 130
ANOVA: Example 130
Testing for Relationships Between and Among Variables 131
Correlation 131
Regression 132
Paths, Partials, and Parts 132
Two Final Decisions 132
Accept or Reject My Findings? 132
If It's Significant, Is It Significant? 133

Ethics Panel: A Communicative Tension   134

Chapter Summary   135

Key Terms   135

Application Exercises   136

    Exercise 1: Predicting Group Wealth   136

    Exercise 2: Generalizing From a Sample to a Population   136

    Exercise 3: Gender and Beverage Preferences   136

    Exercise 4: "The Internet of Things" Revisited   136

Recommended Web Resources   137

References   137

Chapter 8: Sampling: Who, What, and How Many?   **138**

Chapter Overview   138

Chapter Objectives   138

Introduction   139

Nonprobability Sampling   139

    Convenience Sampling   139

    Purposive or Judgmental Sampling   140

    Quota Sampling   140

    Network or Snowball Sampling   140

    Volunteer Sampling   141

Probability Sampling   142

    Random Sampling   143

    Stratified Random Sampling   144

    Systematic Sampling   144

    Multistage Cluster Sampling   146

How Big Does My Sample Have to Be?   148

Some Issues With Sampling Frames   149

    Postal Sampling Frames   149

    Telephone Sampling Frames   149

    Internet Sampling Frames   150

    Special Population Sampling   152

    The Future of Survey Sampling   152

Ethics Panel: Checking the Ethics of Survey Research   153

Chapter Summary   153

Key Terms   153

Application Exercises   154

    Exercise 1. Systematic Sampling   154

    Exercise 2. How Does Sampling for

       One Variable Affect Another Variable?   154

    Exercise 3. Multistage Cluster Sampling   154

    Exercise 4. Pew Research Center Internet Knowledge Survey   154

Recommended Reading   155

Recommended Web Resources   155

    Sample Size Calculators   155

References   156

Chapter 9: Surveys: Putting Numbers on Opinions   **157**

Chapter Overview   157

Chapter Objectives   157

Introduction: Advantages and Disadvantages of Surveys   158
Types of Surveys   159
 Cross-Sectional   159
 Trend   159
 Panel   159
 Cohort   159
 Cross-Lagged   160
Writing and Formatting Questions   160
 Open-Ended Questions   161
 Dichotomous Questions   161
 Multiple-Choice Questions   162
 Likert Scale   162
 Semantic Differential Scale   163
Survey Wording: "If It Can Be Misinterpreted, It Will Be"   163
 Common Problems With Wording   164
  Leading Questions   164
  Double-Barreled Questions   165
  Framing Questions   165
  Negative Wording   165
  The Double Negative   165
 Language   165
 Guiding Respondents Through Surveys   166
 Filter Questions and Instructions   166
Online Surveys   167
 Online Survey Design   167
  Involvement   167
  Control   167
  Privacy   167
  Technology   168
 Mobile Surveys   168
Improving Survey Response Rates   168
Capturing and Processing Survey Data   171
Using Other People's Surveys   171
Ethics Panel: Clients and Methods as Ethical Decisions   172
Chapter Summary   173
Key Terms   173
Application Exercises   174
 Exercise 1. Survey Wording   174
 Exercise 2. Survey Method   174
 Exercise 3. Mobile Technologies   174
 Exercise 4. Survey Mode   174
Recommended Reading   175
Recommended Web Resources   175
References   176

Chapter 10: Experiments: Researching Cause and Effect   177

Chapter Overview   177
Chapter Objectives   177
Introduction: Advantages and Disadvantages
 of Experiments   178
Field Experiments and Ex Post Facto Designs   179

Basic Experimental Design   181
    One-Group Pretest–Posttest Design   181
Designing for Control   181
    Two-Group Pretest–Posttest Design   182
Designing for Random Assignment   182
    Two-Group Random Assignment Pretest–Posttest Design   183
    The Solomon Four-Group Design   183
Time Series Analysis   184
Factorial Designs   184
Between-Subjects and Within-Subjects Design   186
Validity and Experimental Design   187
    Internal Validity   187
    External Validity   188
    Manipulation Checks   189
Ethics Panel: Two Famous and Controversial Experiments   190
    Stanley Milgram's Experiments on Authority   190
    Philip Zimbardo's Stanford Prison Experiment   191
Chapter Summary   191
Key Terms   191
Application Exercises   192
    Exercise 1. Further Adventures With Study Conditions   192
    Exercise 2. An Experiment in Persuasion   192
    Exercise 3. Hybrid or Regular?   192
    Exercise 4. Assessing the Effect of an Instructional Program   193
Recommended Reading   193
Recommended Web Resources   194
References   194

Chapter 11: Watching and Listening:
    Qualitative Research for In-Depth Understanding   **195**

Chapter Overview   195
Chapter Objectives   195
Introduction: Advantages and Disadvantages of Watching and Listening Methods   196
Qualitative and Quantitative: Similarities and Differences   196
Researcher–Participant Relationships   197
Watching and Listening Methods   198
    Interviews   199
        Interview Structure   199
        Interview Persona   200
        Interview Setting   200
        Interview Sensitivities   201
        Interview Recording   201
        Interview Sequence   201
        Interview Question Types   201
        Interview Question Prompts   202
    Focus Groups   202
        Online Focus Groups   203
    Ethnographic Methods   204
        Ethnographic Starting Points   206
        Online Ethnography   206

        Observational Studies   207
        Unobtrusive Measures   207
        Conversation Analysis   208
    Making Sense of Qualitative Data   208
        Fixed Coding   208
        Flexible Coding   209
    Drowning in Data? CAQDAS to the Rescue   210
    Ethics Panel: In Which a Professor Becomes a Student   211
    Chapter Summary   212
    Key Terms   212
    Application Exercises   213
        Exercise 1: An Ethnographic Study   213
        Exercise 2: An Interview   213
        Exercise 3. Understanding Social Media Stress   213
    Recommended Reading   213
    Recommended Web Resources   214
    References   215

**Chapter 12: Content Analysis: Understanding
Communication Content in Numbers**   **216**

    Chapter Overview   216
    Chapter Objectives   216
    Introduction: Advantages and Disadvantages of Content Analysis   217
    A Basic Content Analysis   218
        Research Questions   219
        Define the Content to Be Analyzed   219
        Sample the Content   219
        Select Units for Coding   219
        Develop a Coding Scheme   219
        *Assign Each Occurrence of a Unit in the Sample to a Code
           in the Coding Scheme*   220
        Count Occurrences of the Coded Units   220
        Report Results, Patterns of Data, and Inferences From Data   221
    An Expanded Content Analysis   222
        Define the Content to Be Analyzed   223
        Sample the Content   223
        Select Units for Coding   224
        Develop a Coding Scheme   225
        *Assign Each Occurrence of a Unit in the Sample to a Code in the Coding
           Scheme*   226
        Count Occurrences of the Coded Units   227
        Report Results, Patterns of Data, and Inferences From Data   227
    Content Analysis of Human Interaction   227
    Content Analysis Software   229
    Ethics Panel: Could Analyzing Media Content Result in Harm?   230
    Chapter Summary   230
    Key Terms   231
    Application Exercises   231
        Exercise 1. Sampling   231
        Exercise 2. News Media Bias   231

     Exercise 3. Stereotyping in Entertainment Media and Advertising   231
     Exercise 4. Analyzing Online Harassment: Quantitatively   231
Recommended Reading   232
Recommended Web Resources   232
References   232

Chapter 13: Rhetorical and Critical Analyses, and More:
           Understanding Communication Content in Words   **234**

Chapter Overview   234
Chapter Objectives   234
Introduction: Advantages and Disadvantages
   of Qualitative Analyses of Content   235
Rhetorical Analyses   235
     Aristotelian Analysis   235
     Dramatistic Analysis   236
     Fantasy Theme Analysis   237
Narrative Analysis   238
Metaphor Analysis   238
Discourse Analysis   239
Conversation Analysis   240
     Utterances   241
     Adjacency Pairs   241
     Turn Taking   241
     Repair Mechanisms   242
Semiotics   242
     Semiotic Thinking: The Tobacco King,
       Restrooms, and Sleeping Policemen   242
     Roman Jakobson Visits Sam's Car Lot   244
Critical Analyses   246
Ethics Panel: Research as Manipulative Practice   248
Chapter Summary   249
Key Terms   249
Application Exercises   250
     Exercise 1. Discourse Analysis   250
     Exercise 2. Matching Method With Interest   250
     Exercise 3. Analyzing Organizational Stories   250
     Exercise 4. Analyzing Online Harassment: Qualitatively   250
Recommended Reading   251
     Aristotle   251
     Bormann   251
     Burke   251
     Conversation Analysis   251
     Discourse Analysis   252
     Metaphor   252
     Narrative Analysis   252
     Semiotics   252
Recommended Web Resources   253
References   253

Chapter 14: Writing and Presenting Research   **255**

Chapter Overview   255
Chapter Objectives   255
Introduction   256
Writing for Scholarly Publics: Voices in the Conversation   256
 The Voice of Scholarly Publication   257
 The Voice of the Author   259
 The Voices of Research Participants   259
 Qualitative and Quantitative Writing   260
Writing for Interest Groups and News Media: Answering the "So What?"
Question   261
 Interest Groups   261
 News Media   262
Editorial Processes   263
The Interplay of Style and Accuracy   264
Presenting for Scholarly Publics: Conferences and Panels   265
An FYI on PPT   266
Writing and Presenting With the Web   267
Some Communication Guidelines   269
Ethics Panel: Balancing Between Scholarly and Popular Writing   269
Chapter Summary   270
Key Terms   270
Application Exercises   270
 Exercise 1. Readability   270
 Exercise 2. Slideware Presentation   270
 Exercise 3. Writing Styles   271
 Exercise 4. Assessing Researchers' Community Engagement   271
Recommended Reading   271
Recommended Web Resources   271
References   272

Glossary   **273**

Index   **287**

About the Author   **296**

List of Exhibits

Exhibit 1.1	Communication Research Interest Areas	13
Exhibit 2.1	Operationalizing Constructs	31
Exhibit 2.2	Assumptions About Human Communication and Their Research Implications	34
Exhibit 3.1	The Belmont Report—Principles, Applications, and Questions for Internet Research	47
Exhibit 3.2	Researcher–Participant Relationships in Communication Research	49
Exhibit 4.1	Focusing Search Results by Combining Search Terms and Search Fields	62
Exhibit 4.2	The Champagne Glass Model of Bibliographic Research	65
Exhibit 4.3	Use of Boolean Search Terms	69
Exhibit 4.4	One Way to Summarize Your Bibliographic Research	71
Exhibit 4.5	Reviewing Scholarly Literature as Investigative Journalism	72
Exhibit 4.6	Literature Review Checklist	74
Exhibit 5.1	Example of Likert Question, Responses, and Basic Descriptive Statistics	92
Exhibit 6.1	Survey Results for 20 Respondents	99
Exhibit 6.2a	Data Reduction: Hours of Internet Use per Week (HWI) Initial Data	101
Exhibit 6.2b	Data Reduction: Frequency of Individuals Reporting Hours of Internet Use per Week (HWI) in Five Categories	101
Exhibit 6.2c	Data Reduction: Frequency of Individuals Reporting Hours of Internet Use per Week (HWI) in Two Categories	101
Exhibit 6.3	Distribution of Individuals Reporting Hours of Internet Use per Week (HWI)	102
Exhibit 6.4	Distribution of Individuals Reporting Hours of Internet Use per Week (HWI) by Male (M) and Female (F)	102
Exhibit 6.5	Summary Table of Hours of Internet Use per Week (HWI) by Gender	103
Exhibit 6.6	Summary Table of Knowledge of World Affairs (KWA) by Hours of Internet Use per Week (HWI) by Gender	104
Exhibit 6.7	Measures of Central Tendency for Hours of Internet Use per Week (HWI)	105
Exhibit 6.8	Computing Variance and Standard Deviation for Hours of Internet Use per Week (HWI)	108
Exhibit 6.9	Measures of Dispersion for Males and Females on Hours of Internet Use per Week (HWI) Variable	108
Exhibit 6.10a	Observed Values (O) of Political Affiliation by Gender	110
Exhibit 6.10b	Expected Values (E), Assuming No Difference Between Groups	110

Exhibit 6.11   Part of Chi-Square Table   111

Exhibit 7.1   Distribution of Means of Knowledge of World Affairs
(KWA) for Samples of Three With Increasing Number of Samples   120
Exhibit 7.2   Normal Curve Showing Two z Scores   121
Exhibit 7.3   Percentage Distribution of Values Under the
Normal Curve by Standard Deviation (SD) From the Mean   122
Exhibit 7.4   Part of a Table of z Scores   123
Exhibit 7.5   Relationship of Sample Size to Standard Deviation
for Hours of Internet Use per Week (HWI) Variable   124
Exhibit 7.6   Distribution of Scores on Knowledge of
World Affairs (KWA) by Political Preference (POLP)   125
Exhibit 7.7   Calculation of t for the Variable Knowledge of
World Affairs (KWA) on Liberal and Conservative Groups   127
Exhibit 7.8   Part of a Table of t Values   128
Exhibit 7.9   Type I and Type II Error   133

Exhibit 8.1   Population   142
Exhibit 8.2   Convenience Sample   143
Exhibit 8.3   Stratified Random Sample   145
Exhibit 8.4   Systematic Sample   146
Exhibit 8.5   Advantages and Disadvantages of Sampling Methods   147
Exhibit 8.6   Relationships Among Standard Error, Homogeneity, and Sample Size   148
Exhibit 8.7   Some Distinguishing Characteristics of Social Media Users   151

Exhibit 9.1   Advantages and Disadvantages of Specific Survey Methods   170

Exhibit 10.1   Solomon Four-Group Design   184
Exhibit 10.2 2×2 Factorial Design, Test Results by Gender
by Study Condition, Showing Hypothetical Results   185
Exhibit 10.3 $2 \times 2 \times 2$ Factorial Design, Test Results by Gender
by Residence Status by Study Condition, Showing Hypothetical Results   186

Exhibit 11.1   Sample Analysis Sheet for Qualitative Data: Predetermined Categories   209
Exhibit 11.2   Sample Analysis Sheet for Qualitative Data: Categories Emerge From Data   210

Exhibit 12.1   Data Coding Sheet for Content Analysis of Political Campaign Stickers   220
Exhibit 12.2   Summary Data From Exhibit 12.1   221
Exhibit 12.3   Sample Coding Sheet for Content Analysis of Comic Strips   226
Exhibit 12.4   Sample Coding Sheet for Group Behaviors Over Time   228

Exhibit 13.1   Example of Conversation Analysis Transcript   243
Exhibit 13.2   Jakobson's Semiotic Functions   245

Exhibit 14.1   Scholarly and Professional Report Formats   258
Exhibit 14.2   Summary Guidelines for Scholarly, News, and Web Formats   268

Preface

For Students

Let's imagine that you are just finishing a tough semester or you are looking forward to a well-deserved midsemester break. Imagine it is now time for that trip you have been dreaming about. Two inescapable questions come to mind immediately. Where will you go, and how will you get there?

Generally, you will have some goal in mind. Perhaps, as a music lover, you will be thinking about a great concert experience somewhere. Perhaps you have always been intrigued by the cultures of Asia and think of Asia as a destination. Or perhaps you really want to visit Great-Aunt Minerva, who was an endless source of funny stories when you were young and whom you have not seen in years. Your trip is triggered by some basic interest, but interest alone is not enough to make it happen. To get to your destination, you must have a specific address, and you must decide how you will get there.

Two further questions will shape the nature of your trip: What is my budget, and how much time do I have? Then there's the question of how you will experience your destination when you get there. Some of us like to "put down roots" and stay in one area to experience it as fully as possible. Others are movers—every day a new attraction. The first approach gives you an in-depth experience; the second gives you a broad experience.

Of course, you will want to record your trip and share your experiences with others, so questions of recording and communication arise. What will you record at your destination—local music, architecture, interesting people, food, and/or landscapes? How will you record this content—video, audio, photography, drawings, and/or written notes? How will you share this content with others—blog, social media postings, e-mail, postcards, and/or Internet chat?

Most journeys are fun, interesting, and intellectually and emotionally satisfying, but you had better know where and how you are going or you won't get there.

Researching human communication is very similar. At heart, it is simply a journey from not knowing something to knowing something or to knowing something more about human communication. Certainly it is interesting and intellectually rewarding. Virtual realities, love affairs, employee morale, social networking, web chat, soap operas, family dynamics, podcasts, advertising, tweets, and group decision making are just a few manifestations of the complex interactions that we call human communication and that we can research.

Other travel analogies apply. Because it is difficult to take two journeys simultaneously, most researchers opt to study one area at a time. They also have a specific "travel plan" in the form of decisions about the phenomena they will study, the method(s) they will use, and the people they will invite to be in their study. They will undoubtedly seek advice from those who have been there before to help them avoid the pitfalls and to maximize the return on the time, effort, and intellectual energy that good research demands. Their research reports may well be the only insight that others will have on the phenomena being studied. This means that their reports must be carefully written to provide accurate information and to identify any possible shortcomings and biases in the research.

Much of the above introduction is clearly a metaphor for the research process. Other metaphors, perhaps more accurate ones, are possible. We might, for instance, recast research as a fight against ignorance, as a contest between what we intuit and what we can demonstrate, or between fact and sentiment. You will find other such tensions as you read through the text; for example, should the researcher be a dispassionate observer of communication phenomena or an individual with biases and preferences for viewing the world in a particular way?

Becoming comfortable with research is therefore not just a matter of mastering method; it is also a matter of identifying and understanding the assumptions and uncertainties that underpin the methods.

Just as maps, websites, and guidebooks can help optimize your travel experiences, this book will guide you through the basics of communication research design while pointing out many of the "fork in the road" decisions that will need to be made en route.

Chapters 1 through 3 begin the journey by examining some of the basic assumptions and disagreements about human communication, how best to understand it, and the ethical implications of becoming involved in people's lives as you study them. These chapters give you the language and customs of the territory you will be visiting—scholarly research in communication.

Chapter 4 will help you identify your areas of interest and how to find out more about them. It will help you identify the detailed reading and recording you will need to do in order to get a good working knowledge of the specific area you will be researching.

Chapters 5 through 13 discuss statistics and sampling and the qualitative and quantitative research methods you will most likely encounter in a career in communication. Metaphorically, these chapters will help you with your mode-of-travel decision. Automobiles can stop anytime you need them to; trucks consume more fuel but carry more weight. Planes are fast and can provide a wonderful overview of the territory but may not take you exactly where you want to go. So it is with research methods. There is no such thing as one best method, only a most appropriate method.

We finish with a chapter on writing and presenting your research results in traditional and web media so that others can get a good picture of where and how you went, what you discovered, and how you have chosen to interpret it.

Throughout this edition, you will find an emphasis on the Internet and the problems and challenges the Internet presents as both topic of and tool for research.

Each chapter has learning objectives to highlight the skills and knowledge you should get from the chapter, a summary of key ideas, and an ethics panel to help you think about the ethical implications of your research. The application exercises in each chapter will help you think about research design in practice or have you explore a relevant resource. Terminology that may be new to you is shown in boldface **like this**. The glossary at the end of the book defines each highlighted term.

Communication research is almost inescapable in a communication career. If you are not involved in initiating research at some level, you will almost certainly be in the position of having to interpret the research of others. Therefore, I suggest that you keep this book and find a place for it on your office bookshelf. The ideas and questions that you run into in your research courses will almost certainly come back to visit you in your professional career.

Welcome to that most fascinating of journeys—research in human communication.

For Faculty

This text aims to provide a reader-friendly, inexpensive introduction to the basics of communication research and to some of the assumptions and questions behind research practice.

My experiences in teaching communication research have led me to believe that an introductory text should give students looking at either academic or professional careers

- a basic mastery of communication research methods,
- an understanding of the assumptions and questions behind research methods,
- an enthusiasm for research that will continue on into advanced research,
- an appreciation of the relevance of communication research to communication practice, and
- a sense of why we find human communication so fascinating as a research field.

I hope you will find that this text achieves these aims in your research courses.

Chapters 1 through 3 examine some of the basic assumptions and disagreements about human communication. Chapter 4 centers on bibliographic research and the literature review. Chapters 5 through 13 discuss research methods, statistics, and sampling. Chapter 14 covers the basics of research writing as well as the challenges and potential of writing for multimedia and hypermedia.

This edition has

- an expanded section on the art of the literature review in Chapter 4;
- a new section on online surveys in Chapter 9;
- a new section on online ethnography in Chapter 11;
- a new section on online focus groups in Chapter 11;
- a new section on writing and presenting for the web in Chapter 14;
- an emphasis throughout on social media and the Internet as subjects of, and tools for, communication research; and
- new learning objectives at the beginning of each chapter to help identify key competencies students should get from the chapter.

Support for student learning in each chapter includes

- learning objectives to highlight the skills and knowledge students should get from the chapter;
- a chapter summary that provides an overview of chapter content;
- an ethics panel with questions to facilitate discussion of research ethics in practice;
- highlighted vocabulary words, which are defined and explained in the glossary at the end of the text; and
- application exercises to help students learn to make decisions about research practice.

Each method chapter has a practice-based organizing example that guides students through the practical and theoretical decisions a researcher faces when designing and implanting research.

The instructor website has a new section on APA style as well as the updated ancillary material listed below.

I hope that this text will make a useful contribution to your research courses, and I welcome your thoughts on it. Thank you for adopting it.

Ancillaries

⑤SAGE edge™

The password-protected Instructor Teaching Site at **edge.sagepub.com/treadwell3e** gives instructors access to a full complement of resources to support and enhance their courses. The following assets are available on the site:

- **Test Bank:** This Word test bank offers a diverse set of test questions and answers for each chapter of the book. Multiple-choice, true/false, short-answer, and essay questions for every chapter help instructors assess students' progress and understanding.
- **PowerPoint® Slides:** Chapter-specific slide presentations offer assistance with lecture and review preparation by highlighting essential content, features, and artwork from the book.
- **Lecture Notes:** Carefully crafted chapter summaries, outlines, and learning objectives help with preparation for lectures and class discussions.
- **Sample Syllabi:** A sample quarter and semester syllabus covering both regular and online classes is provided to help professors structure their courses.
- **Discussion Questions:** Chapter-specific questions help launch discussion by prompting students to engage with the material and by reinforcing important content.
- Carefully selected chapter-by-chapter **video and multimedia content** which enhance classroom-based explorations of key topics
- **Chapter Activities:** These lively and stimulating exercises and assignments for group or individual activities help structure class time and enhance student learning.
- **Recommended Readings:** Suggested readings are provided for additional resources in key subject areas.
- **Case Studies:** The industry case studies from previous editions have been added to the ancillaries website and can be used as a basis for "research in practice" discussions.
- **Tables and Figures:** All exhibits from the book are available in an easily downloadable format for use in papers, handouts, and presentations.

The open-access Student Study Site available at **edge.sagepub.com/treadwell3e** is designed to maximize student comprehension of the material and to promote critical thinking and application. The following resources and study tools are available on the student portion of the book's website:

- A customized online **action plan** includes tips and feedback on progress through the course and materials, which allows students to individualize their learning experience.
- **E-flashcards:** These study tools reinforce students' understanding of key terms and concepts that have been outlined in the chapters.
- **Web Quizzes:** Flexible self-quizzes allow students to independently assess their progress in learning course material.
- Carefully selected chapter-by-chapter **video and multimedia** content enhance classroom-based explorations of key topics.
- **SAGE Journal Articles:** Access to full-text SAGE journal articles exposes students to important research and scholarship tied to chapter concepts.

Acknowledgments

Every text benefits from rigorous and informed criticism, and I have benefited from the thoughtful input provided by

Jessica J. Rack, University of Cincinnati;

Heidi L. Muller, University of Northern Colorado; and

Carolyn Cunningham, Gonzaga University.

The following reviewers are gratefully acknowledged for providing an accuracy check of the final manuscript:

Paula Soder, California Polytechnic State University, San Luis Obispo, and

Carmen Stitt, California State University, Sacramento.

I thank them for their time and patience, and hope that they will recognize the results of their advice in this final product.

Thanks go to the students who thoughtfully critiqued the text for understanding and interest as it evolved into this edition.

I am grateful for the resources available from the Pew Research Center Internet, Science & Tech Project—a valuable source of method discussions and raw data as well as the frequent research reports on how we use the Internet and other communication technologies.

Thanks go to the SAGE editorial, production, marketing, and ancillaries teams for bringing this project to fruition and, once again, to Melinda Masson for her editorial insight and skills.

Special thanks go to Brian Hubbard for his professional presence as reference librarian; to Dr. Diane Prusank for her input as "adopter in residence"; and to a friendly avatar, Jill Student, whose questions helped focus each chapter on student learning.

I am especially grateful to Dr. Andrea Davis for developing the ancillary resources.

Above all, thanks once again go to Jill Treadwell—textbook veteran, editor, muse, critic, and sounding board. Without her conceptual, creative, and culinary input, the text would be a lesser work.

Donald Treadwell

CHAPTER 1

Getting Started
Possibilities and Decisions

Basic research is what I am doing when I don't know what I am doing.

—Wernher von Braun (1912–1977)

Chapter Overview

Welcome to communication research. This chapter introduces some of the many ways scholars of human communication think about research, their main interest areas, and some of their research methods. It will help you with the often-difficult process of getting started and getting focused on a research project, and introduce you to some of the assumptions and decisions that every researcher makes, consciously or unconsciously.

Chapter Objectives

This chapter will help you

- Identify several basic assumptions behind human communication research.
- Identify several research questions that might be asked about advertising content.
- Describe some of the initial, unavoidable decisions required when planning communication research.
- Identify basic steps in the process of communication research.

Getting Started in Research

Any day or any journey requires that you first wake up and then make a series of decisions to get started. Stay in bed or get up? Gym first and then breakfast? Or breakfast first and hang out with friends? Bike, bus, or walk to work, or work online from home? Each day requires that you get oriented in some direction and decide on the priorities for that day.

Similarly, any research project requires that you start by getting yourself oriented toward an area of interest. Then you will need to decide what questions, assumptions, and methods will best get you the answers to your interest questions.

A glance at the communication research literature will show you that communication researchers have interests ranging from interpersonal communication on up to web media reaching millions of people worldwide. Researchers often may specialize in areas defined by the numbers of people they are studying, as in interpersonal communication, groups, organizations, or social media. But many research interests transcend such categories. For example, rhetoricians, those who study the use of language and argumentation, may do so in all of these areas.

Potential topics for research in human communication are all around us. Why do people prefer some music genres over others? What is the best way to deliver instructional content—the web, readings, seminars, lectures, or hands-on experience? What websites are seen as the most credible sources of advice for students downloading new "apps"? Do student behaviors in class influence instructor behavior? Do blockbuster movies shape public opinion or follow it? What can we say about the effects of violent or sexually explicit media content on people exposed to such content? What predicts whether an online video will "go viral"?

The next step after finding questions of interest is deciding how best to get an answer to these questions. You will find from the scholarly literature that this can be a hotly contested issue. Choosing a research method or methods unavoidably requires making assumptions and decisions about the nature of human behavior, such as whether people are basically all alike or are unique individuals. These assumptions and decisions will help you prefer some methods over others, but you may well find that for every researcher going down your road, there is another researcher opting for a different route to answering essentially the same question.

Every research question has assumptions behind it that reflect the researcher's view of communication and how to study it. These assumptions about human communication, how best to study it, and why we study it are discussed more in Chapter 2.

For example, let's take a look at three examples of communication interactions with which you will likely be familiar. The interactions are quite innocuous, but as we shall demonstrate, each one could lead to many interesting research projects.

The Situation

It is a Friday afternoon at a campus coffee bar. As a casual observer, you notice the ambience—carpet, comfortable chairs, cable news running silently on television, indie fusion rock on the sound system, a continuing traffic of people lined up for coffee and snacks, the hiss of espresso machines, and the overall buzz of conversation.

You decide to listen in on one couple more specifically. (Of course, in itself that has ethical implications that we will explore more in Chapter 3.) A casual listener might be interested just to hear the conversation, but a communication scholar interested in interpersonal communication would take a keen interest in the interaction and think about specific questions that might be raised, research methods that might best get answers to those questions, and some of the assumptions behind the questions and methods.

The dialogue below records part of the interaction. This is followed by a very brief summary that a researcher might write down to remind herself of the interaction and some questions that she might ask based on the observations. In Chapter 2, we shall explore turning these casual questions into formal research questions and hypotheses.

INTERACTION I—The Couple:
Romance, "Just Friends," or Doing Business?

Caroline: Wow, am I happy this week's over! I've got three courses I don't like, this project in a group that's just about nonfunctional, and more assignments than I can handle. I'll be working all weekend.

Brian: Same here. I'll be chained to the keyboard for the weekend, what with online courses and all. But what are you doing outside of that? Party time somewhere? Driving home to do the laundry?

Caroline: None of the above. It'll be work, work, work!

Brian: Ooh, Babe! Not good for body or soul. Gotta look after the old mental health, you know. How about we take a break Saturday night? You could come around for a movie, maybe a "golden oldie." I volunteer to make that cheese popcorn you like.

Caroline: OK. Well, yeah, maybe. I'll text you Saturday afternoon.

Brian: Great! Hey, it's nearly 3 o'clock. I thought the rest of the group promised to be here by now.

Following is a brief summary that the researcher might write about the above conversation:

> Looks like two study buddies, meeting casually, perhaps accidentally. It turns out to be a planned encounter that is supposed to include others in a group. Is it the group Caroline described as nonfunctional? Are these two more than friends? It appears that Brian thinks so, or wants it to be so. Not sure about Caroline. Why are they meeting face-to-face instead of just texting each other?

The above summary should bring to mind many general questions about communication and communication behaviors. For example:

- Questions about relationships: How do we identify relationships? How do people express their relationships? What do language and behavior tell us about relationships? Do romantic couples develop vocabulary unique to themselves?
- Questions about decision making: Are decisions by a romantic couple made using different criteria than decisions made by friends? Are individuals in a romantic relationship more likely to compromise on a decision than individuals in a work relationship?
- Questions about technology and relationships: How does intimacy in a relationship affect the nature and frequency of contacts using communication technologies? Why does Caroline propose "texting" rather than a phone call?

Now let's move on to what is about to become a more complex set of interactions as three more students join the conversation. There are only five students, but the possibilities for different interactions and subgroups forming obviously increase significantly.

INTERACTION II—The Group: Collaboration or Conflict? Business or Pleasure?

Brian: Hey, Tshinta. Wassup?

Caroline: About time you showed up. We've got to get this media effects project under way.

Tshinta: I couldn't help it; I had to talk with Prof. Thomas about the midterm.

Caroline: I hope you convinced him to cancel it.

Tshinta: No such luck.

Elizabeth: Sorry I was late, but practice ran overtime.

Mike: Yeah. Me too. Sorry . . . I was waiting for Elizabeth. By the way, I have class in 15 minutes.

Brian: Geez! Our group can't even get together, much less get a project organized.

Elizabeth: Why do we even have to meet? Can't someone just divide up the work and e-mail me what I have to do?

Mike: OK by me as long as I don't have to do the oral presentation . . .

Tshinta: . . . or be responsible for the paper.

Brian: Caroline's pretty good at deciding who does what best. Let's appoint her the group leader and take it from there.

Caroline: Leader? Who me? I don't think so. I don't want responsibility for this. Besides, part of the purpose is that we're supposed to work together.

Tshinta: Caroline's right. Looks like we'll be here awhile. In that case, I need a coffee . . .

Following the format we used for Interaction I, below is a brief summary that the researcher might write about the above interaction:

> Five students . . . a small group. Participants arrive late making excuses and showing little enthusiasm for the project or the group. The dynamics look grim. It appears that no one wants to lead or to follow. No evidence that they have a procedure for making decisions. Who will emerge as leader? Will the group hold together? What will happen as they get closer and closer to the project deadline? How should I interpret Tshinta's comment about Mike not being responsible for the paper—sarcasm, sympathy, or an objective assessment of his abilities? Ends with a move toward consensus building. Need to get involved with this group if I'm going to understand them better.

As with the previous example, this summary might lead to many questions about group behavior and communication. Following are some broad areas under which these questions might be grouped. Some are the same as in the previous example; others are new.

- Questions about relationships: What are the relationships among these people? How do we identify relationships among group participants? How does group size affect communication content? How does group size affect interactions among individuals?
- Questions about decision making: How will this group make a decision? How do groups make decisions? How do personal relationships influence decision making?
- Questions about leadership: What makes a leader? How can you identify a group leader? How are leaders chosen? Are effective leaders always respected?
- Questions about technology and group interactions: What effects might communication technologies such as social media have on group processes? Do social media support or hinder group interactions? How might the participants' performance change if they used web conferencing instead of meeting face-to-face?

Adding more students to this conversation has opened up many questions related to group size, status, decision making, leadership, and communication technologies. From a researcher's viewpoint, this is good news because there is so much more to discover but perhaps bad news in that a focus on one topic of interest may be at the cost of other equally interesting topics.

We will now move on to a final "burst" of conversation. The group remains the same, but the topic shifts to mediated communication such as social media, broadcast media, and newspapers—the channels or media by which people communicate other than face-to-face. This time, the research questions will focus on the content of the conversation rather than on personal interactions or group dynamics.

INTERACTION III—The Topic Turns to the Media

Brian: . . . Speaking of coffee, did anyone see that great new animated coffee ad? With the cartoon cat drinking coffee?

Caroline: Brian's a foodie. Remembers every food ad but can't remember anything else . . . like today's news.

Brian: Maybe. But I'm in good company. Ask them over there at the next table. No two people will agree on what they remember as today's news, but all six of them will tell you about that rip-off cats-drinking-coffee video that went viral. And who watches newscasts anymore anyway? If I want news, I'll go online and find it somewhere when I feel like it.

Caroline: I've watched you, and I don't think the websites you use for news are very credible.

Brian: So television or radio or newspapers are better? Why should I trust them? Any news source is just someone's version of the news. That's why I watch all over the place. I get balance—multiple perspectives. You can't get well informed from just one source.

Tshinta: But good news sources have trained journalists, more journalists, dedicated newsrooms, professional standards—all that stuff.

Brian: Doesn't matter. They're all corporate spin. You know they all accept advertising, and they're not going to say anything that will turn an advertiser off. They might not be politically biased, but they're corporately biased. They're all pushing consumerism. You can't trust them.

Elizabeth: So who *do* you trust?

Brian: You—to buy me another mocha latte!

Elizabeth:	Generic or brand name?
Brian:	Brand name, of course.
	(laughter)
Tshinta:	Behold—the power of advertising!
Brian:	No! It's the other way around. Manufacturers know they need to reach people like me to keep me buying their product. I influence their advertising!
Mike:	Yeah right!

> The group is still together. Discussion is casual, but the topic seems to have shifted from group process to the media effects topic of their class project. Brian is the catalyst for the discussion. He sneers at traditional news media and claims to be immune to media influence. The others refute his statements on both issues. Seems to be a tension here between what's popular and what's credible; also a question of causality—does advertising influence consumers, or vice versa?

It looks as if we have some serious media-related questions here . . . and this time it is your turn to identify them. Go to the "Application Exercises" section at the end of this chapter for guidance on this task and how to approach it.

Basic Assumptions Behind Communication Research

So far, we have looked at specific situations that might lead to specific research questions that point to specific research methods. There are, however, several basic assumptions that underpin all communication research. Consciously or implicitly, researchers bring these assumptions to their research. Several major assumptions—each of which can be contested—are outlined below.

Observations Capture/Do Not Capture an Underlying Reality

One such assumption is that what we choose to look at—dress or language, for example—tells us something about an underlying reality we cannot see but assume to exist. For example, "power" is not something we can actually see. When you think about it, what we see is not power as such but rather someone behaving or dressing in a particular way and other people responding. Nonetheless, "power" seems like a useful concept in our efforts to understand human communication, and generally we elect to study it by looking at behaviors that we assume represent power.

Similarly, no one has ever actually "seen" an attitude. What people have actually seen is someone behaving in a particular way or responding to a set of survey questions designed to capture this thing called "attitude." Once again, "attitude" seems too useful a concept to discard from our thoughts about human behavior, and so we research attitudes on the assumption that they exist or at least that the concept of attitude provides a useful tool for thinking about communication processes.

Theories About Human Behavior Can/Cannot Be Generalized

A second assumption is that theories about human behavior can be generalized. It may be insightful to discover that your grandfather has a LinkedIn account and that your little sister has a Twitter account. But your research would be much more useful and rewarding if you were able to make a general statement such as "Young people are more likely than older people to have a Twitter account." If true, this statement would be of interest to advertisers, educators, and disaster management agencies, the last of which might need to reach large numbers of people rapidly in an emergency. However, to make this statement, you basically have to assume that your grandfather is like other grandfathers and your little sister is like other little sisters, at least with respect to social media use.

Probably, though—and correctly—your grandfather and sister regard themselves as unique individuals, so to what extent can we assume people are basically like other people? It is an important question because if our world is full of unique individuals, we are not entitled to make any generalizations about them (except, of course, that each of them is unique!). Nonetheless, researchers using survey or experimental methods typically will want to assume that the results of their research will apply to people who are similar to the study participants but not in the study. That is to say, there is an assumption that people are similar in the way they behave.

Researchers Should/Should Not Distance Themselves From Their Research Participants

A third assumption relates to the researchers' level of engagement with their research participants. In the researcher's notes above, you will notice a thought about getting more involved with the students in the conversation—perhaps by sitting in on the conversation or interviewing some of them. This brings up a fundamental choice in research design. The more distant the observer becomes, the more neutral or dispassionate she can be in reporting a group's behavior, but she will be unable to get the insights she would get if she were closer to the group. In fact, her observations might actually be wrong, such as deciding that Elizabeth and Mike have a social relationship. On the other hand, moving closer to the group will provide her with insight, but she then becomes open to influencing the group dynamics or to seeing only the group's view of the world and becoming biased in her reporting as a result.

Research Should/Should Not Be Done for a Specific Purpose

A fourth assumption is about the purpose or reason that should underlie research. Most scholarly researchers probably began their careers with a simple curiosity about some aspects of human behavior, and it is that curiosity and the pleasure of discovery for its own sake that continues to drive them. Scratch the surface of that interest, though, and we will find other purposes or motivations that come into play. At a personal level, it may be need for fame or funding. At another level, researchers may see the purpose of their research as helping to solve society's problems or refining a highly theoretical model of human interaction. As we will see in Chapter 2, researchers may be content if their studies lead to accurate descriptions or an understanding of human behavior, but they are more likely to see their research as worthwhile if it explains or predicts that behavior.

Researchers whose work is funded by a corporation or foundation looking for specific answers to a question as quickly as possible may find that their personal motivations for research and their preferred direction for the research take second place relative to the needs and motivations of the funding agency.

There Is/Is Not One Best
Position From Which to Observe Human Behavior

A fifth assumption is simply that some aspects of a question are more important to look at than others and, related, that there is one best standpoint from which to observe human communication. A simple way to understand this is to consider an early telecommunications-based model of human communication (Shannon & Weaver, 1949). Given the complexities of human communication, it is an overly simplistic model, but it does identify major components in any human interaction as follows:

- Source—the provider or initiator of content
- Message or messages—the content of communication
- Channel or medium—the vehicle for communication content; for example, social media
- Receiver or receivers—the recipients or consumers of information
- Noise—extraneous information or distractions that can disrupt an interaction

In human interaction, communication gets more complicated. Source and receiver may swap roles as a discussion proceeds. What is noise to one party may be useful information to another and so on. Nevertheless, this basic source–message–channel–receiver–noise model does indicate some possible major entry points into the study of human interaction.

For example, a major area of research on the first component of the model is source credibility. For example, why do some online news consumers find *The Huffington Post* more credible than, say, *The New York Times*, or *The New York Times* more credible than *Al Jazeera* or vice versa? The "message" component raises any number of questions about communication content—how best to present complex scientific information to a lay public, for example. The "channel" component raises questions about the impact of process on human behavior. For example, what are the circumstances in which personal, face-to-face instruction should be preferred to online learning for students? Or what happens to a recipient's understanding when complex message content is reduced to 140-character tweets? The "receiver" component often raises questions about how the demographic, cultural, and psychological characteristics of people influence their comprehension of messages, willingness to engage with others, and receptiveness to persuasive messages.

You will likely have already decided that none of these components can be studied in isolation. Receiver and sender interact and swap roles in many interactions. In the case of advertising research, receiver characteristics affect message content and channel selection. But researchers will typically find one of these components of the communication process more interesting than others and will give that component priority in their investigations.

By way of example, let's look at how researchers might approach a specific piece of communication content—an advertisement. We shall see that there are many possible approaches to studying such advertising.

Some Research Possibilities:
What Can We Do With an Ad?

Let's explore how a single situation can lend itself to many research questions, using public service advertisements (PSAs) as the basis for our discussion. PSAs are targeted communications designed specifically to promote positive attitudes and behaviors. They focus on public interest topics such as health, education, safety, environment, and other social causes. Many of them are likely to be familiar to you. Most PSAs are produced under the auspices of the Ad Council, a body that links nonprofit organizations with professional agencies that produce advertisements as a public service. For this discussion, we will focus on recent PSAs that tackle the problem of impaired or distracted driving. You can find the ads mentioned in this section, as well as many others, at AdCouncil.org.

PSAs are typically based on a strong, often alarming, fact or statistic, such as "In 2012, 10,322 people were killed in alcohol-impaired-driving crashes—that's one person every 51 minutes" or "A texting driver is 23 times more likely to get into a crash than a non-texting driver." The creative challenge is to relate these often "remote" statistics to individual audience members. This relevance is usually achieved by a tagline that makes the message personal and/or encourages a behavior or attitude change. This tagline usually becomes the overall campaign theme.

For example, the first statistic mentioned above resulted in the following anti–drunk-driving campaign themes, which you will likely find familiar:

"Friends don't let friends drive drunk."

"Drinking and driving can kill a friendship."

"It's easy to tell if you've had way too many. But what if you've had just one too many? Buzzed driving is drunk driving."

The second statistic inspired the themes of two anti–texting-while-driving messages.

The Ad Council's anti-texting print PSA features the image of an ambulance with the message "You don't want them responding to your text." The organization's television PSA puts the viewer in the car with a teen driver while she checks a text message . . . and subsequently crashes. You can view this ad at www.adcouncil.org/Our-Campaigns/Safety/Texting-and-Driving Prevention.

These are hard-hitting, "pull-no-punches" messages that have the potential to grab attention and, perhaps, shock the target audience into a behavior change.

Communication researchers may be interested in answering a number of questions about any of these PSAs. Does it work or doesn't it? How or why does it work? Whose interests are being advanced by the ad? Does the medium itself (radio, magazine, television, newspaper, Internet) have an effect on how the content is understood? The following sections introduce several approaches to evaluating advertising using these PSAs as examples.

Does the Ad Work?

This is a question that, essentially, focuses on the receivers of the message. We want to know what they did or how they felt as a result of exposure to the message. Applied communication researchers, and certainly advertising executives and their clients, want to know how many people adopted the recommended behavior or at least changed their attitudes as a result of exposure to this ad. The question is not that readily answered.

Clearly, the police have statistics on driving infractions, and if accidents associated with texting, for example, decreased, we could assume that the anti-texting advertisement was effective. Correct? Not necessarily. There could be many other explanations for such a decrease, and these would need to be ruled out before we could conclude that the ad had a significant effect.

One way to assess the effectiveness of these advertisements is to take a scientific approach. Two characteristics of scientific method are observation or empiricism and the attempt to rule out alternative explanations. From a scientific point of view, we might measure how much advertising time or space the campaign received and the number of texting citations issued and then look for a relationship between the two. We would hope to discover that as the amount of advertising increased, the number of citations decreased. But we would also need to be sure that any observed decrease was related to our advertising and not to an increase in the number of police on the highways or to a new ad that was launched before assessing whether the old one was working effectively. All possible causes would need to be identified and ruled out before we could assume that the anti-texting advertisement and *only* the advertisement caused the decrease.

What Can Readers and Viewers Tell Us?

This question also focuses on the receivers of the message, but with a shift in emphasis toward understanding the "whys" of human behavior. Establishing that the advertisement did influence behavior or attitudes provides no insight on why it did so. One way to answer this question would be to conduct a survey, asking questions based on what you suspect made the advertisement effective—the celebrity spokesperson, the animation showing how distractions affect reaction time, or the real-life story of an "innocent victim" of a texting-related crash, for example.

It is likely that an advertising agency would ask such questions before the advertisement was released in order to know in advance that the ad was going to be as effective as possible. Of course, the audience may have totally different perceptions of what is important about the ad; for example, viewers may decide that the catchy soundtrack is really what grabbed their attention. It is important, therefore, to capture what people have to say in their own words as well as to ask the questions that you think are important.

For such public opinion research, surveys are typically used to ask questions the researcher thinks are important, and focus groups are used to capture opinions that the audience thinks are important. Historically, surveys have used mail, phone, or personal interviews (such as in a shopping mall) to present a series of specific, predetermined questions to a predetermined group of respondents, but today the Internet and social media are equally likely vehicles, depending on the target audience. Focus groups involve bringing together maybe 6 to 12 people and asking them to discuss their reactions to an advertisement, issue, or product. The essential focus group strategy is listening to people in order to capture their responses in their own words.

Surveys generally produce quantitative results (48% did not like the spokesperson); focus groups generally produce qualitative results in that they capture people talking ("I really did not like the spokesperson because . . ."). Surveys and focus groups both have their advantages and limitations, as we will see in later chapters.

What Can the Content Tell Us?

This question clearly focuses on message content. So far we have analyzed the texting campaign largely in terms of audience response, but what could we learn from the ad content itself? There are many angles from which to study media content, including rhetoric, content analysis, and critical theory. These angles share an interest in media content, but take different approaches for different reasons.

Rhetoricians are essentially interested in the **appeals** or persuasive tactics the advertisement uses to persuade an audience to adopt the behavior. For example, if you look at the Ad Council's anti-texting campaign, two appeals are apparent: the appeal of the ambulance EMTs as authority figures (in the print ad) and the real-life experience of being in the car with a driver who cannot resist just a quick look at the text that has just come in (in the TV ad). As with many commercial ads, this shows a "typical" teenager in a "typical" texting situation, leading to a further appeal that "people just like us" are guilty of dangerous texting behavior.

Rhetoricians using theory developed by Aristotle (384–322 BCE) might search for appeals based on *logos* (logic), in this case the logic of "texting + driving = crash"; *ethos*, (character), in this case the use of a typical teenager with typical reactions to a text; or *pathos* (emotion), in this case the tragic consequences of a crash.

Kenneth Burke, a 20th-century theorist who analyzed human communication in terms of drama, offered a set of analytical questions that ask, essentially, "What is the act, the scene, the people, and the purpose of the act?" We could analyze our ad using Burke's questions. Looking at the ad content, we could describe the setting, the teenager, and the mini-drama of a person becoming absorbed in a text, losing control, and crashing.

Rhetorical approaches to researching advertising content are essentially qualitative; they analyze the use of language.

Content analysis, by contrast, is primarily a quantitative method for assessing media content. For example, looking at ads for distracted driving, including drunk driving, buzzed driving, and texting and driving, a content analyst might set up categories of content based on her interest in representations of gender in advertising. The analyst counts the number of appearances in the ads of men and women and compares them. She could also compare her results to a known distribution of these categories in accident records. She might then be able to conclude that the advertisements overrepresent women as buzzed drivers and underrepresent them as texting drivers, for example. She would be comparing advertising's world with what we know of the real world.

Critical analysis works from a basic assumption that communication maintains and promotes power structures in society. Essentially, the focus is on the relationship, explicit or implied, between message source and recipient rather than just one component of the communication process. With that as a basis, the critical researcher asks "Whose interests are being served by advertising, and more specifically, how exactly do language and representations maintain the interests of such entities as corporations, colleges, or governments?" Unlike the content analyst, who looks for what is explicit and observable, the researcher may look as much for what is implicit or unsaid.

For example, the researcher may discover that anti-texting advertising more frequently portrays young women as more likely to text while driving than young men. This is a conclusion that our content analyst might also have arrived at. But the researcher's question becomes "Whose interests are advanced by such portrayals?"

What Can the Creators of the Ad Tell Us?

This question focuses on the source of the message rather than the recipient, message, or communication medium. Our understanding of the advertisement would, of course, be enhanced if we could talk with the client, and with the producers, directors, and writers in the agencies that produced the ads. In this case, we would probably be interested in finding out how and why decisions about content and production were made.

Researchers interested in organizational dynamics and decision making might want to know whether the basic creative approach was worked out over the course of extended meetings involving large numbers of people or if it came about as a directive from a client or creative director. Researchers interested in decision making would want to interview members of the creative team individually so that each person feels free to talk. They might also want to interview the team as a group and probably would want to get permission to videotape the creative meetings as they take place. Such research could give us insight on how communication facilitates or discourages creativity, decision making, and client-agency relationships, or how professional communicators build an image of the consumers they are trying to reach.

Some Research Possibilities: Beyond the Ad

The above discussion centers on advertising by way of example, but analogous questions can also be asked of interpersonal, group, or organizational communication. For example, suppose your academic department has a Facebook page and/or tweets its student community to keep it apprised of relevant news such as new course offerings, faculty changes, scholarship opportunities, and the like.

We might, again, ask the "Did it work?" question. For example, can we observe that the tweets triggered additional numbers of students to register for the new course offerings or apply for scholarship(s)? We might, by using surveys, interviews, or focus groups, determine how students feel about this use of social media to provide them with departmental information. We could analyze this social media content to see what appeals are used to promote new courses and scholarships. We might even take the perspective of a critical organizational theorist and examine how such social media content encourages student compliance with the departmental "way of doing things."

With interpersonal communication, we might be interested in tracking how communication changes as two people move from acquaintances to friends to romantic partners. Again, similar questions apply. The "Did it work?" question might be reframed in terms of trying to observe what vocabulary or behaviors work to strengthen or weaken the relationship, or we could interview the two individuals themselves to see what they have to say about their communication and why it works, or doesn't. Similarly, we could examine the content of their text messages or transcripts of their phone calls to relate the content to key events in the relationship.

A Series of Unavoidable Decisions

Communication researchers have different agendas, methods, and assumptions behind what they do. One reason for this is the complexity of human communication. Because it is almost impossible to examine and explain a communication event in its totality, researchers focus on a part of that totality and choose a method for investigating it with which they have a comfort level, be it methodological or ideological.

For example, even though the research approaches outlined above share a common focus on understanding public service advertising, researchers clearly differ in what exactly they choose to research and the reasons for doing their research.

In addition to their theoretical priorities, all researchers have to face the reality of limited time, limited resources, and an inability to be in more than one place at a time (web conferencing excepted). Following are some of the choices that are almost inevitable for all types of researchers, based on their theoretical predispositions and resources.

The Field of Study—Wide or Narrow?

Time is short, the topic vast, and, realistically, we must research the available and the achievable. Methodological preferences aside, communication scholars typically divide communication studies into a number of specific interest areas such as those shown in Exhibit 1.1. This list is compiled from listings of divisions and interest groups of the National Communication Association and the International Communication Association.

The Researcher—Dispassionate or Involved?

To what extent should researchers get involved with their human "subjects"? The scientific tradition values objectivity and dispassionate observation. The "reward" to the researcher is the satisfaction of a new finding, the development of a new theory, or the confirmation or disconfirmation of an existing theory.

By contrast, **action research** engages in research specifically to improve people's lives. Whereas the scientific tradition is to remain detached from one's subjects, the action tradition

EXHIBIT 1.1   **Communication Research Interest Areas**

Applied Communication	Instructional/Developmental Communication
Argumentation and Forensics	Intergroup Communication
Children, Adolescents, and the Media	International and Intercultural Communication
Communication and Technology	Interpersonal Communication
Communication and the Future	Journalism Studies
Communication Apprehension and Avoidance	Language and Social Interaction
Communication Ethics	Mass Communication
Communication History	Nonverbal Communication
Communication Law and Policy	Organizational Communication
Critical and Cultural Studies	Peace and Conflict Communication
Environmental Communication	Performance Studies
Ethnicity and Race	Philosophy of Communication
Family Communication	Political Communication
Feminist Scholarship	Popular Communication
Freedom of Expression	Public Address
Game Studies	Public Relations
Gay, Lesbian, Bisexual, and Transgender Studies	Rhetoric
Global Communication and Social Change	Semiotics
Group Communication	Spiritual Communication
Health Communication	Theatre
Information Systems	Training and Development
	Visual Communication Studies

is to be closely involved with them in order to better people's lives. One school sees research as a quest for knowledge, and the other sees research as an engaged contribution to engineering a better society. In both cases, the researcher's behavior has ethical implications, as we shall see in Chapter 3.

The Approach—Objective or Subjective?

Can research be objective? **Social scientists** often bring the assumption of an external "real" world that can be observed, understood, and agreed on to the study of human interaction. For example, they assume that concepts such as intelligence or loyalty can be found across all people and measured objectively with an "instrument" that will apply universally and perhaps predict human behavior.

By contrast, phenomenologists and ethnographers try to understand people's subjective worlds. They have an interpretive perspective in that they seek to understand how humans interpret or make sense of events in their lives. They assume that concepts such as intelligence or loyalty are indeed just concepts, and that such concepts are defined subjectively by the people they are researching, not to mention the researchers themselves. Such concepts vary from culture to culture, and from individual to individual. For example, simple interpersonal behaviors such as holding hands, kissing, or embracing may have widely different interpretations from culture to culture. The phenomenologist may observe a behavior such as kissing but really want to know what that action means for the individuals involved. There is no assumption that such behavior has a universal meaning.

The Priority—Your Questions or Their Answers?

All researchers have a basic question that frames their research, for example "Do men and women view social media differently?" To get an answer to such a question, researchers have two basic options. The first is to ask men and women a series of specific questions that together will provide an answer to the researcher's question. Often, these might be survey-type questions such as "On a scale of 1 through 10, where 1 is not at all important and 10 is extremely important, how would you rate the importance of social media in your life?" Typically, this would be one of many such questions aimed at assessing how or why social media is used, how many hours a day participants spend on social media, and so on.

This approach may well answer the researcher's question but completely fail to capture how users feel about social media. For example, if users see social media primarily as entertainment, it may never occur to them to describe social media as "important." A basic research decision, then, is whether to get answers to specific questions you have or whether to elicit people's views in their own language—not quite knowing what you might get.

The Sample—Large or Small?

How many people do you need to talk to in order to know that you have "an accurate picture" of a communication phenomenon? Public opinion researchers can answer that question: For an accurate view of adult public opinion in the United States, you need about 1,200 randomly selected people—as long as you can live with something like plus or minus 3% error.

"True enough," the small-sample people might reply, "but counting gives you only numbers and knowledge, not understanding. Will a survey of the thousands of people affected by weather, hunger, or a down-sliding economy give us any more understanding of how people communicate about such events than an in-depth interview with one family? You know what's going on, but you don't know why or how people feel about it or explain it. That is why one solid series of interviews with a few people can give a better grasp on a situation than all of the thousand-people surveys that the big-sample people can conduct."

The Data—Quantitative or Qualitative?

Are humans storytelling animals, counting animals, or both?

Numbers are important; they are how democracies and committees make decisions. Count the vote; majority wins. While the ultimate truth may never be known, many researchers accept that the current "best" truth of a phenomenon may be what a majority of researchers currently believe it to be. Numbers and counting are important to scientific methods. Not only are counting and statistics an important part of such methods, but the number of researchers in agreement on a particular finding also helps to suggest the "truth" of a finding.

Researchers with interests in human subjectivity, motivation, and aesthetics respond that the complexities and subtleties of interpersonal attraction, responses to modern art, or the critical approaches to understanding media cannot be captured in mere numbers. The "truth" can best be understood by listening to the stories that research participants and researchers themselves have to tell us.

Few of the above "either-or" distinctions are clear cut. For example, a passionately involved action researcher may use objective social science methods to study a problem. Or the survey questions that a numbers-oriented methodologist asks may be based on extensive initial qualitative interviewing. The above ideas have been presented as "either-or" to help you think about where you stand on such issues. In practice, many of the seeming opposites blend together. The most obvious blending is in the approach called **triangulation** in which researchers use multiple methods providing multiple perspectives to ensure that they have a good "fix" on a problem.

For example, in trying to understand how family life interacts with television viewing, a researcher might survey several families on their use of and attitudes toward television, interview a few family members in depth, live with one family as they watch television, and conduct a content analysis of television content to determine how content shapes the family's interactions and vice versa. Advertising executives will frequently pretest or pilot a commercial with a focus group before running the advertisement and then assessing results with a large-scale survey.

Approaches such as **Q-Methodology** assume that it is respondents' subjective views of the world that are of interest but combine that research focus with quantitative, computational approaches to recording and assessing these views.

The Report—Subjective or Objective?

Just as there are different ways of doing research, there are different ways of writing research. Researchers interested in interpreting the subjective world of their informants may use the primarily qualitative languages of ethnomethodology and phenomenology. In most cases, they report what their informants have to tell them in their informants' own words. By contrast, social science researchers typically use statistics to report and interpret the data they have collected.

The involved researcher may unabashedly use "I" writing as in "I lived with Thomas and his two children for three months, and we formed a warm social bond that had us eating together, watching movies together, and exchanging seasonal gifts." Dispassionate researchers will report in a language that strives for neutrality and that removes them from the narrative altogether—thus, "Subjects were recorded on video and their facial expressions subsequently analyzed for changes as visual stimuli were presented to them." And the critics of this style will point out that such a dispassionate style is in itself a persuasive strategy aimed at convincing the reader of the author's credibility as a researcher!

The subjectively involved researcher believes that credibility and reporting are enhanced by including personal experiences and reactions. We are getting "the truth, the whole truth, and nothing but the truth." The dispassionate researcher believes credibility is maximized by objective reporting "uncontaminated" by sentiment and value judgments (ignoring perhaps the idea that to adopt this style of writing is in itself a value judgment).

Research and research reporting both are communication activities framed by disciplinary standards and expectations, ethical decisions, and personal motivations. As critical theorists would point out, published and topical research carries a "meta-message" about what research topics are "hot," what approaches are in vogue, and who the current "stars" are.

The fact that research has an argumentative component does not necessarily mean it is adversarial. The academic journals in which research is published reflect ongoing discussions about research. A research study may be followed by responses, critiques, and other studies that change our thinking about it. You can think of articles in the scholarly communication journals (some listed at the end of this chapter) as a considered, continuing worldwide conversation among researchers on how best to understand human communication.

Problem Posing, Problem Solving, Peer Persuasion

Borrowing a model from the biological sciences, communication research can be regarded as having three main components—problem posing, problem solving, peer persuasion ("A 3P's Approach to Science Education," n.d.).

Problem Posing

Research questions do not arrive "pre-posed." You have to decide what the question is. This can be the hardest part of the research process. Once you have clearly defined the question, the rest of your research often seems to fall into place. Defining "the question" is a very human process involving personal interest in the topic, the feasibility of doing a study, and the rewards, tangible and intangible, of completing it. The three interactions we looked at earlier in this chapter illustrate the first, general steps in posing the question. In Chapter 2, we shall look at the important process of getting general questions and observations written as specific research questions and hypotheses.

Problem Solving

Having posed a question, we face the problem of how best to answer it. In many respects, this is what this book is primarily about. But problem solving is more than selecting a research method and using it. It can involve amending your methods as they prove to be inappropriate, discovering other questions that must be answered before your "real" question can be answered, finding new questions opening up, or changing your research altogether when someone publishes a "breakthrough" study that gives you a whole set of new ideas about your research.

Peer Persuasion

Research has no value to the world unless the world knows about it. Research must be published (literally, be made public) if others are to benefit from it. Academic publication is a process of persuasion. Journal and book editors and reviewers must be persuaded that yours is a worthwhile project with worthwhile results, and readers must be similarly convinced if your research is to gain recognition. Publication is a process of persuasion and argumentation even though it is couched in the language of scholarship and conducted via the printed or electronic page.

For most scholarly journals, your research report will go through a process of peer review in which scholars in your field assess your work and suggest ways you could improve your report before it is accepted for publication. This process can be time-consuming and painful to the ego, but research progresses on challenges and rigorous examination of ideas, and these challenges are simply another part of "research as conversation." Assertions about communication must be defensible if they are to be accepted. Publication in particular gets you into the cut and thrust of debate about communication and how best to study it.

As the news from time to time reminds us, researchers can be prone to error and to ethical lapses. Publication and peer review are also ways of monitoring the ethics of research, a topic addressed in Chapter 3.

Increasingly, researchers recognize that communicating the results of any research goes far beyond the peer persuasion of other researchers. For example, where research is funded by a government agency, a corporation, or a foundation, there will be a need to adapt research findings and for an explanation of the research processes to politicians, department managers, boards of directors, news media, and interest groups. This means that research reports in practice can range from a multivolume set of documents detailing the processes and outcomes of a 10-year study on social media to a one-line tweet summarizing the study's results. You will find some of the writing conventions for reporting research discussed in Chapter 14.

One proposition raised at the beginning of this book was that communication research inescapably involves ethical decisions. This ethics panel, and the ones in following chapters, will give you a sense of the ethical decisions you may face as a researcher. You should try to reason through to a decision for each of the ethics problems as they are typical of the decisions you may face when doing your own research. For help with these ethics panels, read Chapter 3, "Ethics: What Are My Responsibilities as a Researcher?"

Ethics Panel: A Health Communication Dilemma

Suppose that a public health agency wants to determine the best way to help people identify the symptoms of diabetes so they can take preventive measures and better deal with the condition if they are diagnosed as diabetic.

To do this, the agency hires your research firm to find out how best to get messages about diabetes to the public. You decide to run a three-group experiment in which people in county A will receive messages about diabetes by traditional mass media (newspapers, television, and radio). People in county B will receive intensive interpersonal communication about diabetes through neighborhood meetings, counseling, and their workplaces. People in county C will receive no messages because you need a "baseline" against which to measure whether your interventions in counties A and B have any effect. As a result of this study, you will be able to develop effective communication programs for your region.

What are the ethical implications, if any, of not providing people in county C with information that might save a life?

CHAPTER SUMMARY

This chapter introduced the ways scholars think about communication research, their main areas of research, and the methods they use. In summary:

- Communication research is a systematic process of posing questions about human communication, designing and implementing research that will answer those questions, and then persuading other researchers that your results are valid.
- Communication researchers typically specialize in one aspect of communication.
- Researchers may use qualitative methods, quantitative methods, or both.
- Researchers have empirical, interpretive, or critical perspectives on communication.

KEY TERMS

action research

appeals

Q-Methodology

social scientists

triangulation

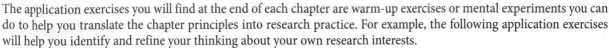

APPLICATION EXERCISES

The application exercises you will find at the end of each chapter are warm-up exercises or mental experiments you can do to help you translate the chapter principles into research practice. For example, the following application exercises will help you identify and refine your thinking about your own research interests.

There is much more to research than simply finding a topic area and questions that interest you. You must also, for example, choose a research method or methods that will give you the data you need to answer your research questions.

For example, observing people, interviewing them, and analyzing message content are all valid research methods, but we must also consider the positives and negatives of each method in order to choose the one most likely to provide credible, complete data. For example, in relation to the student conversations earlier in this chapter, you might consider such issues as these:

- If you interview a couple, won't each partner tell you only what he or she wants the other partner to hear? Would you be better off interviewing them separately?
- Would individual questionnaires give you more "honest" answers because you are not interviewing face-to-face? Or could the time required to complete a questionnaire mean that you would get less than full answers?
- Does listening in on a private conversation raise ethical issues? If so, shouldn't you introduce yourself and ask permission to listen in? Might your presence then change the nature of the conversation?

Exercise 1. Finding Research Questions

Earlier in this chapter, we presented three interactions among students in a campus coffee bar. In the first two cases, we presented a dialogue followed by a researcher's summary and some questions the interaction raised. In the third case, Interaction III—The Topic Turns to the Media, we left it up to you to identify research questions that the example brought to mind. Identify as many media-related questions as possible. Think freely and broadly. No question is irrelevant at this stage of your thinking, and one may well be the spark that ignites a long-term research interest for you.

Exercise 2. Exploring Communication Interest Areas

One way to develop your own interests is to go to two of the major communication research interest groups—the National Communication Association (NCA) and the International Communication Association (ICA), listed in this chapter's recommended web resources. At the NCA site, on the About menu, look for "What is Communication?" At the ICA site, look for "Divisions & Interest Groups." In both cases, you will find a list of the specific interest groups for each association. The interest areas that overlap will give you a sense of the "mainstream" interest areas, and either list may spark your interest in an area that perhaps you were not previously aware of.

Exercise 3. Researching Internet Communication

Access the website for the Pew Research Center Internet, Science & Tech Project, listed below. (This site was previously known as the Pew Research Center Internet & American Life Project.) Locate a February 27, 2014, survey report titled "The Web at 25 in the U.S." At the report site, you will find the full report, the questionnaire, and the data from which the report was compiled. From the questionnaire, select three questions that interest you, ask the same questions of 10 people you know, convert your answers into percentages, and compare your results with the Pew Research Center results. For example, the first question, with response options, is as follows:

Do you use a computer at your workplace, at school, at home, or anywhere else on at least an occasional basis? Yes / No / Don't Know / Refused

Do your results differ from those reported by the Pew Research Center? If so, how? Why do you think your results differ? What might you do to improve the credibility of your results?

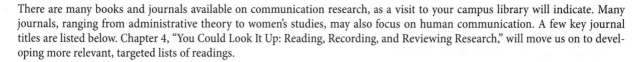

RECOMMENDED READING

There are many books and journals available on communication research, as a visit to your campus library will indicate. Many journals, ranging from administrative theory to women's studies, may also focus on human communication. A few key journal titles are listed below. Chapter 4, "You Could Look It Up: Reading, Recording, and Reviewing Research," will move us on to developing more relevant, targeted lists of readings.

General

Communication Monographs

Communication Research

Human Communication Research

Journal of Applied Communication Research

Quarterly Journal of Speech

Mass Communication

Critical Studies in Media Communication

Journal of Public Relations Research

Journalism and Mass Communication Quarterly

Quarterly Review of Film and Video

Television and New Media

Organizational Communication

Academy of Management Review

Administrative Science Quarterly

Business and Professional Communication Quarterly

Journal of Organizational Culture, Communications and Conflict

Management Communication Quarterly

Group Communication

Conflict Studies

Group and Organization Management

Group Dynamics: Theory, Research, and Practice

Group Processes and Intergroup Relations

Small Group Research

Interpersonal Communication

Human Relations

Journal of Applied Psychology

Journal of Family Communication

Journal of Research in Personality

Journal of Social and Personal Relationships

Social Media

Convergence: The International Journal of Research Into New Media Technologies

Cyberpsychology, Behavior, and Social Networking

Journal of Computer-Mediated Communication

Journal of Magazine and New Media Research

New Media and Society

RECOMMENDED WEB RESOURCES

Association for Education in Journalism and Mass Communication (AEJMC)..www.aejmc.org

Canadian Communication Association...www.acc-cca.ca

Human Communication Research Centre (HCRC), University of Edinburgh ....www.hcrc.ed.ac.uk

International Communication Association (ICA) ....www.icahdq.org

National Communication Association (NCA) ....www.natcom.org

Defining the boundaries of human communication studies is difficult and a debate in its own right. The ICA, NCA, and AEJMC are three of several U.S. academic associations devoted to the study of communication. Looking at their websites (above) will give you an idea of the many areas of research specialization under the "communication umbrella." By contrast, the HCRC site shows one of many institutions where communication studies are being reconceptualized by bringing together such fields as computing, philosophy, psychology, and language studies.

Pew Research Center Internet, Science & Tech Project ....www.pewinternet.org

The Pew Research Center Internet, Science & Tech Project studies how Americans use the Internet and how their online activities affect their lives. The project uses nationwide random phone surveys, online surveys, and qualitative research, along with data from government agencies, technology firms, academia, and other expert venues. You should become familiar with this site, and the Pew Research Center more generally, as we will refer to it throughout this book.

REFERENCES

A 3P's approach to science education: Problem-posing, problem-solving and peer persuasion. (n.d.). Retrieved from http://bioquest .org/index3ps.html

Fox, S., & Rainie, L. (2014, February 27). The web at 25 in the U.S. Retrieved from http://www.pewinternet.org/2014/02/27/the-web-at-25-in-the-u-s/

Shannon, C. W., & Weaver, W. (1949). *The mathematical theory of communication.* Urbana: University of Illinois Press.

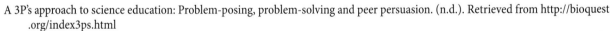

$\circledS$ SAGE edge™

Want a better grade?

Get the tools you need to sharpen your study skills. Access practice quizzes, eFlashcards, video, and multimedia at **edge.sagepub.com/treadwell3e**

CHAPTER 2

First Decisions

What, Why, How?

It seems to me what is called for is an exquisite balance between two conflicting needs: the most skeptical scrutiny of all hypotheses that are served up to us and at the same time a great openness to new ideas.

—Carl Sagan

ᐧᐧᐧ

Chapter Overview

"How do I get started?" may be the most difficult question of all for the beginning researcher. As we explored in Chapter 1, the problem is that there are so many possible starting points. Think how many questions could be generated from even the most casual overheard conversation. Of course, this is also the good news. Research questions are indeed all around us, and identifying some questions about topics that interest you is a good start. You might even have good ideas about how to answer those questions, especially if you have jumped ahead to some other chapters in this book.

This chapter is about moving from those general questions that interest you to thinking about more specific questions and about well-designed research that will provide credible answers and contribute to the general body

Chapter Objectives

This chapter will help you

- Define the terms *induction*, *deduction*, and *abduction*.
- Identify key reasons for doing research.
- Discuss the various ways we "know what we know."
- Describe two major worldviews in human communication research and how each shapes the nature of research.
- Identify the advantages and disadvantages of basing your work on the work of other researchers.
- Explain with examples the difference between a research question and a hypothesis and the advantages of one relative to the other.

of knowledge about human communication. It is a process of moving from casual questions to more formal research questions and hypotheses that will launch a planned, structured, and defensible set of activities that let you collect, analyze, and interpret data. Appropriate research methods are those that best match your theories about human communication and the type of data you intend to collect. Behind every research project are assumptions and first decisions that you cannot escape about the nature of human communication and of research.

This chapter discusses some of these assumptions and basic starting points that underpin communication research and finishes with a discussion of how to write the questions we hope to get answers to.

Starting With the "What" Question: Ideas and Observations

The most obvious starting question is "What shall I study?"

Listening to the Rolling Stones' "Start Me Up" probably won't help a lot unless you have a specific interest in rock lyrics. But communication phenomena in the form of song lyrics, interpersonal behavior, group dynamics, social media, news coverage, and virtual realities are all around us. So a good starting point is to observe the communication phenomena you are interested in.

"Communication" is a large umbrella under which many research interests find a home. As noted in Chapter 1, many researchers may specialize at the level of mediated, organizational, group, or interpersonal communication, but others have interests such as social media and rhetoric and argumentation that transcend these interest areas. Your career interests and academic electives likely already have you heading toward a general interest area. You may find a more specific focus by looking at the websites of the scholarly communication associations listed at the end of this chapter and of Chapter 1 and revisiting the communication research interest areas shown in Chapter 1, Exhibit 1.1.

Reading relevant scholarly articles is a "must." See Chapter 4, "You Could Look It Up: Reading, Recording, and Reviewing Research," for a discussion of one of your most important starting points—your academic library. Often, our interest may be triggered by a news item, a casual observation, or an occupational interest. For example, the following scholarly research may have been triggered by a casual question—"Why do people use online dating sites?"

Kang, T., & Hoffman, L. H. (2011). Why would you decide to use an online dating site? Factors that lead to online dating. *Communication Research Reports, 28*(3), 205–213.

The following research may have been triggered by the casual observations that more women than men appear to blog, and that physically attractive politicians seem to get more TV coverage.

Chen, G. M. (2015). Why do women bloggers use social media? Recreation and information motivations outweigh engagement motivations. *New Media & Society, 17*(1), 24–40. doi:1461444813504269

Waismel-Manor, I., & Tsfati, Y. (2011). Why do better-looking members of Congress receive more television coverage? *Political Communication, 28*(4), 440–463.

While popular news and entertainment media and events plus your own observations and experiences might trigger a research interest, your academic library will provide the best examples of research based on serious, systematic observation using research methods appropriate to the task and reviewed by other researchers before publication. As Chapter 4 explains, the scholarly articles you find in academic databases will give you ideas about appropriate research methods, point you to other relevant articles, and help you decide whether your research could lead to new understandings or would be merely "reinventing the wheel."

A theory or generalization about communication is weak if not supported by evidence, so researchers move between theory and observation. They may start with a theory that needs testing with observations, or they may have observations that lead them to construct or reconstruct a theory. Three thought processes that link observations with theories are induction, deduction, and abduction.

Induction

Induction is reasoning from observations to a theory that might explain your observations. Let's go back to Chapter 1, in which we dropped in on students drinking coffee and socializing. As an observer, you might make a note of communication behaviors such as the following:

- Gender clustering—males are more likely to sit with males, and females to sit with females.
- Class distinction—upper-class students are more likely to be found socializing in the coffee bar than first- or second-year students.

What theories might explain these observations? You might think of several. For your gender-clustering observation, you might theorize that

- Students have a greater comfort level with same-sex than with opposite-sex conversations.
- Male students have more classes in common with each other than they do with female students, and vice versa.
- Male and female students have already formed separate social groups by virtue of being in separate campus housing units.

For your class-distinction observation, you might theorize that

- Upper-class students are more likely to have jobs, grants, and fellowships, and can afford to socialize and drink handcrafted coffees.
- Upper-class students are more likely to live off campus, and meeting on campus is the only way to get group projects done.
- Upper-class students are more stressed as graduation approaches and feel a greater need to "unwind" by socializing with friends.

Having generated several such theories, you could then design a study that would help you decide which theory offers the best explanation of the phenomenon.

Deduction

By contrast, **deduction** moves from a theory to defining the observations you will make to test the theory. For example, you might have some reason to theorize that women are more likely than men to discuss grades and academic performance. You would then design a study to capture the observations that would test this idea. In this case, your research might involve recording the conversations of both men and women and counting for each group the number of times words such as *grade*, *grade point average*, or *assignment* occur. If you could then show that the frequency of these words is greater in women's conversations than in men's, your theory would be supported—except for two big "ifs."

First, if you want to make a general statement about women discussing their academic performance more frequently than men, you will want to be confident that your statement is true for all female students, not just the small group of communication majors you have observed. Second, you will want to know that this pattern you observed is true at all times, not just for the one discussion you happened to observe, perhaps as final examinations were approaching. This is where appropriate sampling (Chapter 8) can help us.

Deduction is in a sense more efficient than induction in that it leads to a specific observation that will test your **hypothesis**—the statement about the relationships you expect to find. Having done so, you can then move on to another test. With induction, you have a further step: finding a way to decide which of the many possible theories you induced from your observations are correct. Induction requires the confidence that you have enough observations to support your conclusion and that you can rule out all the other conclusions that might also be derived from your observations.

Abduction

In the context of research, **abduction** refers not to being kidnapped by aliens from the planet Zog but rather to reasoning from an effect to possible causes. For example, a large group of young children in the campus coffee bar would be an unusual sight. That occurrence might raise some questions, but a perfectly plausible answer might be that university employees are participating in a "bring your children to work" day. With abduction, your starting point is an effect from which you reason back to possible causes. In this example, your research project would be to find out whether there is such an event on campus that explains your observation or if there are other events that offer a more plausible explanation.

Starting With the "Why" Question: Goals and Values

"Why research?" is perhaps a more philosophical starting point. Most scholars are ultimately motivated by curiosity and, more specifically, by the desire to understand human communication. The specific "whys" of research can be as varied as human motivations. Every research study starts with a purpose, be it an interest in testing a sophisticated theoretical concept or attempting to get an A in a research course. Peer pressure, ego, or financial incentives may also motivate researchers.

Generally, though, research has several purposes—exploration, description, explanation, prediction, control, interpretation, and criticism.

Exploration

Exploration is curiosity-based research. You start down a path that may lead who-knows-where, but that's OK. You have a commendable curiosity to learn more. Good starting points here will be targeted library research so you don't "reinvent the wheel," discussions with those who share your interests, and your own initial observations.

"I wonder why the residents of two dorms have such different lifestyles" or "Students don't watch broadcast television nearly as much as they used to" may be the beginning of your research career in organizational culture or media use, respectively.

Exploratory research typically results in descriptions of what you are interested in. The description may be quantitative or qualitative. For example, based on observations and surveys of a student group, we might summarize them statistically in terms of gender, major, class year, choice of drink, topic of conversation, or campus address. But the study could also be qualitative as we interview each person and report, in the students' own words, what it means to be a student, what it means to socialize with others, or how the ambience of a preferred coffee bar helps them socialize or get work done.

Following are two broad research questions that might arise from a researcher's initial, exploratory interest in student social behavior and media use. At this beginning phase of a research program, a researcher is more likely to be writing broad questions than specific hypotheses. Specific hypotheses will come later as the researcher gathers the data that will form the basis for a specific statement about what he or she expects to find. In this text, we follow a style of *RQ* and *H* to denote research questions and hypotheses, respectively.

RQ_1: How do the patterns of social life on campus differ from dorm to dorm?

RQ_2: What factors explain students' use of social media?

Description

Description, especially rich descriptions of people's lives, can be compelling reading. Indeed, one test of a good description of human behavior is that it *is* compelling reading. But description does tend to leave us wanting more—in particular wanting an answer to the "why" question. For example, reporting that women are more likely than men to discuss their grades or to blog regularly is informative but does leave us wondering why.

Explanation

Studies focused on **explanation** attempt to answer the "why" question. For example, your observations might indicate that women are more likely than men to socialize over coffee after class. Your interviews with them might lead you to the discoveries that more women than men live off campus and that socializing after class is the easiest way to get group projects organized. Thus what was observed to be a primarily female social behavior is explained in terms of housing status and face-to-face as a preferred way of getting work organized.

Following are a research question and a hypothesis that a researcher might use to focus her energies on an explanation of student social behavior. In both cases, the wording has become more specific than that of the questions asked above under "Exploration." Exploratory questions are of necessity rather general, but with explanatory research, the researcher may be in a position to propose possible explanations, as in the research question below, before the research begins.

RQ_1: Are patterns of student social life on campus related primarily to the residence status of the student?

H_1: Female students differ from male students in the language used to explain their use of social media.

Prediction

Generally, our explanations have greater credibility if they are capable of **prediction**. There is an intellectual satisfaction in obtaining research results that predict human behavior and confirm a theory. There is also an understandable demand from almost every sector of society for research that allows prediction of human behavior. Political communication consultants want to know what appeals will predictably move swing voters toward a particular candidate. Faculty teaching online courses want to know whether reticent students will be more or less likely to engage in online discussion. And so on.

The conclusion we arrived at about female students drinking coffee is reasoned and verifiable based on observation, but our theory would be even more impressive if it could predict this behavior. In principle, this is easily done. We could devise an experiment in which we give the same group project to equal numbers of on- and off-campus students. If our theory is correct, we should see more off-campus students in the coffee bar, discussing how to get the project done. Note, though, that this design is weak because it does not rule out other explanations. For example, we cannot rule out the possibility that the students we see meeting have bad Internet access, and it is this rather than housing status per se that explains their need to meet in person. We discuss how to strengthen such experimental designs in Chapter 10.

Sample hypotheses we might write if our research goal is prediction are

H_1: Patterns of interaction within student work groups are predicted primarily by the residence status of the students in the group.

H_2: Swing voters will vote for the political candidate who most emphasizes local issues.

H_3: Students who rate themselves as introverted will be more active in online discussions than in in-class discussions.

Notice that each of the above hypotheses could also be written as a research question. They have been formulated as hypotheses because an attempt at prediction is an attempt to relate two or more variables, which need to be specified in advance of the research.

Control

Another goal of research may be **control**. In the physical world, control means researching with a view to being able to predict and manipulate physical processes such as digital recording, combustion, or space flights. In the case of human communication, advertisers, for example, want to be able to control audience responses to advertising, broadcasting, or direct mail. Their interest is in knowing how best to motivate viewers to watch a particular program, purchase a product, or open a piece of direct mail. Industry journals such as *Advertising Age*, *Broadcasting & Cable*, and *Adweek* contain such advice on how to "control" audiences, frequently in the form of "if–then" ideas. "If you make your direct mail piece an unusual shape, then it will attract more readers" is the generic nature of this advice.

The research questions and hypotheses written with control as a primary research interest will generally be as specific as those written under the umbrella of prediction. For example:

H_1: Direct mail recipients are more likely to open mail pieces that resemble official government mail.

H_2: Students are more likely to attend early morning classes if a tuition discount is offered for those classes.

The problem with basing expensive direct mail programs or educational policy on such research is that hypotheses often may specify only one influence on human behavior (the appearance of direct mail and the cost of academic credits in the above two cases). Obviously, human behavior is a function of many influences, as your own voting behavior, social behavior, course scheduling, and responses to direct mail will tell you. The reason we use sophisticated research designs is, essentially, to help eliminate the influences that are not important in explaining a specific behavior.

Interpretation

Interpretive studies are best understood as attempts to place yourself "in the other person's shoes." In other words, the researcher attempts to understand human communication from the point of view of the people doing it. For example, what does meeting with student colleagues to get coffee really mean for those doing it? Is this an opportunity to set up dates for the weekend, to engage in intimate conversation with significant others, to clarify a difficult concept in the communication theory, to get work organized, or some combination of these? Our interest as researchers is not to impose our own interpretation but to capture the interpretations of those involved in a way that our readers will get an accurate understanding. Almost by definition, this will mean reporting the results of your research in the language of your research participants.

In the case of a student group working on a class project, the research interest thus becomes "What does the group mean by 'meeting for coffee'?" Obviously, a campus coffee bar provides a common meeting place and the coffee provides a social lubricant, but tea, fruit juice, and soda will also be on the drinks list, so "meeting for coffee" is to be understood not literally as a thirst-quenching experience, but most likely as a metaphor for something else. What is that something else?

Careful listening of the type discussed in Chapter 11 will tell us.

In the interpretive frame of mind (see, for example, Fish, 1990), the researcher's questions become more focused on language in use and its meaning and might include such research questions as these:

RQ_1: What metaphors and analogies are most commonly used by students to describe and explain classroom assignments?

RQ_2: What stories told by students about assignments have most credibility with other students?

RQ_3: How do students and instructors differ in their explanations of what assignments mean in the curriculum?

Under the interpretive umbrella, we could write specific hypotheses but are more likely to write open-ended research questions because we need to be open to whatever our research participants may want to tell us rather than seeking a simple confirmation or disconfirmation of a hypothesis generated by the researcher.

Criticism

The basic quest of critical theorists is to understand and explain the way in which communication is used to exercise and maintain power in groups, organizations, and societies. To this end, critical researchers might look, for example, at the way in which organizational structures and processes prevent or facilitate the progress of certain groups within the organization. For example, in the case of our campus coffee bar, do coffee-drinking rituals perpetuate and reinforce class or gender distinctions? Can males join a female discussion group? Are there informal rules that say first-year students cannot mix with senior students? Does an individual's language define him or her as a member of an in-group or an out-group?

The basic starting point of critical research is the assumption of power structures in society or organizations that are reinforced and perpetuated by behavior and language. This basic assumption allows the critical researcher to start with general exploratory questions or to propose specific hypotheses about communication behavior and language. For example:

RQ₁: What rhetorical strategies are used in employee magazines and newsletters to promote loyalty to the organization? (The assumption here is that the content of employee communications is controlled by management.)

H₁: Leaders perceived as democratic will use the term *we* more frequently than the term *I* in addressing employees.

The above starting points may mix to a greater or lesser degree. As Kaplan (1964) points out, it is possible to have explanation without prediction, and vice versa. For example, we may have a very good understanding of the dynamics of small groups but be unable to predict whether a new group will be a success or not. Or we may be able to predict the changes in language that a couple uses as they become more intimate, without necessarily understanding why this change is taking place.

Starting With the "How" Question: Methods and Epistemologies

Many researchers start with a method preference. For example, a political communication consultant may know that monitoring Twitter or Facebook postings is the best way to track rapid changes in voter preferences and to make some generalizations about them. Or a brand consultant consulting on what a new product should be named may know that focus groups offer the best chance of capturing all the (mis)understandings that a new product name is capable of generating.

As such, this "method start" is really not intellectually defensible. It is the equivalent of saying you will video-record human behavior because you know how to do video recording. For experienced researchers, however, a method start is grounded in a concept of what about human communication is important to know and how best to know it. It is the track record of the method and its "fit" to the researcher's interests that make the method start defensible.

Method decisions are rooted in **epistemology**—the question of how we know what we know. We might know as a result of **tenacity**—we've always done it or understood it that way; **intuition**—the hunch or the gut instinct; **authority**—because a credible source said so; **rationalism**—logical reasoning; or **empiricism**—observation.

Scientific methods typically combine empiricism, rationalism, and **positivism** (the idea that phenomena are governed by, and can be explained by, rules). Two strengths of this approach are openness and self-correction. Openness means that a researcher's methods and data are open to inspection by other researchers, most typically in peer-reviewed publications. Self-correction means that other researchers can replicate a study. If a second study supports the first, researchers can have increased confidence in the findings.

Starting With a Worldview: Basic Beliefs

What do we really believe about human behavior? Are people basically all alike or fundamentally different; predictable or unpredictable; predisposed to cooperation or to conflict; living in a shared, tangible world or their own internal, subjective worlds?

The argument for reality as an underlying, objective, concrete entity versus reality as no more than a product of our senses is almost as old as human thought. Generalizations or predictions about human behavior often can be made with some success, but it is equally true that many predictions fail—as political pollsters can find to their dismay. We tend to have more success with larger numbers of people than we do with individuals. Faculty can be quite confident predicting that most students will attend class on a given day. Predicting that a specific student will attend a specific class on a specific day is a different matter altogether.

As evidence supports any and all such views, ultimately we are obliged to decide which basic beliefs will inform our research, and to live with them, based on our own best judgment. From a research point of view, basic assumptions about human behavior coalesce into broad **worldviews**.

Worldview I is that human behavior is predictable, objectively measurable, and generalizable. Worldview I researchers aim to make generalizations about human communication that will hold true across space and time. This emphasis on measurement and generalization is called a **nomothetic** approach.

Advertising and audience research subscribe to Worldview I. Researchers seek to find rules that will predict the success of interpersonal relationships, direct-marketing or broadcast content, or cat videos on social media, or the ability of group members to work together or how to increase sales or hold a broadcast audience. Television infomercials, for example, are presumably based on research indicating that using a particular type of spokesperson plus showing the product plus repeated exposure of the 1-800 phone number will maximize the number of consumer call-ins. In principle, such a generalization would apply to most products and most television audiences.

Worldview II, by contrast, sees human behavior as individualistic, unpredictable, and subjective. This view assumes that knowledge is socially constructed out of interaction between people and is subjective. Research based on these assumptions attempts to describe and assess the subjectivity and individuality of human communication, rather than aiming to discover universal laws. This emphasis on individual understanding is called an **idiographic** approach.

Worldview I privileges the researcher's perspectives; Worldview II privileges participants' perspectives. For example, the student discussions recorded in Chapter 1 are what we might call "naturally generated" or "participant generated." An external observer or researcher has had no influence on this content. However, as soon as a researcher decides to impose a method such as a survey on the group members, the research data are researcher generated and may have little or no resemblance to the participant-generated data.

Thus, researchers who are interested in how consumers respond subjectively to media content will spend time listening to individuals, with a view to capturing this subjectivity. Their goal might be, for example, to understand why some television viewers develop a close relationship to soap opera characters or a Second Life avatar and how they describe those relationships. Researchers make no assumption that their findings will be generalizable and typically reject counting or measuring in favor of reporting what their interviewees said. They may take an interest in the overall organizational culture of a campus but may become even more interested in how residence life cultures vary from dorm to dorm within a campus. Their overall goal is understanding rather than generalization or prediction.

There is no inherent reason that one aspect of human communication should be privileged over others for research anymore than one specific research method should be privileged. Rather, the focus and the method of research are the outcome of the researchers' interests and the environments in which they are doing research. The research method you select should logically follow from the basic assumptions you have made about human behavior. For example, a Worldview I researcher who believes that people's thinking can be measured and that careful sampling will allow her to generalize results from a small sample to a large number of people may ask "What type of survey can I run?" A Worldview II researcher interested in hearing people's subjective experiences in their own words is more likely to ask "What focus groups or interviews will I need?" The first researcher will use quantitative methods by virtue of her worldview; the second will prefer qualitative measures.

An ethnographic study aimed at uncovering the hidden metaphors of organizational life implies that experimental design and scaled survey questions would not be appropriate. There must be a logical match among theory, method, and data. The researcher in this instance therefore will prefer in-depth interviews and perhaps focus group–type discussions in order to be able to report organizational imagery and metaphor in organization members' own words.

The first question for researchers, then, is not whether to prefer qualitative over quantitative methods. Rather, it is "What are my basic assumptions about human behavior?" It is the answer to this question that will drive the decisions about the nature of the research data to be gathered and therefore the research methods to be employed.

These foundational beliefs and arguments about human behavior are issues ultimately of **ontology**, which addresses the nature of what we study.

Ontological questions deal with the nature of existence and what language actually refers to. In communication studies, ontology wrestles with assumptions about the nature of human communication and what we "really" observe when we observe it.

For example, have you ever seen someone's attitude? You might answer "Yes, many times." But what have you really seen? What you have really seen is someone behaving in a particular way, being verbally aggressive perhaps. Or perhaps all you saw was check marks on an attitude rating scale, from which you infer an attitude. Where is the attitude itself? Is there, in fact, such as thing as an attitude?

Ontological questions for communication scholars include "To what extent do we make real choices?" For example, is your decision to attend class voluntary or not? Is human experience primarily individual or societal—what would you know of the world and of yourself if you had no interaction with other people? Is communication contextual or universal—does a smile always mean the same thing, or does the meaning depend on who is smiling and under what conditions?

Starting From the Work of Others

Starting a research project without regard to the work of others is risky business. You run the risk of doing research that has already been done and therefore making no new contribution to knowledge. You will also miss out on knowing about especially relevant research methods, advances in research, and findings that might help you. Most importantly, perhaps, you will miss out on knowing about "good research"—the research that most scholars agree is well designed, is professionally executed, and makes a significant contribution to knowledge.

The easiest way to join the community of scholars who share your interests is to use your academic libraries regularly. Academic journals (**serials**) record in the form of articles and letters ongoing conversations among researchers. They are admittedly conversations punctuated by lengthy periods of silence as we wait for the next issue of a journal to come out, but browsing communication journals regularly will keep you up to speed with current research and ideas in your interest area.

Chapter 4 discusses this essential starting point in more detail.

Firming Up Questions

Getting started often requires that you identify key **constructs** and **operationalize** them. Constructs are ideas or concepts. Operationalizing them means to define them in such a way that they can be measured. For example, let's suppose that you are interested in the relationship between playing video games and academic performance. You observe individuals who are heavily involved in such games. You conclude inductively that such people keep weird hours and some have peculiar personal habits, but that could be true for any group of people, gamers or not.

Deductively, you reason through to two contrary conclusions. First, time spent on gaming must detract from time spent on studying. Therefore, gaming must be detrimental to academic performance. On the other hand, gaming appears to need mental agility, the ability to think fast and to make decisions, and imagination. Deductively, it seems that gaming ought to have a positive effect on academic performance.

You have identified two important ideas or constructs—involvement in gaming and academic performance. You think that there is a relationship between them; you're just not sure what that relationship is.

To operationalize these constructs means to define them in a way that other researchers could replicate your study. Now comes a question of professional judgment: How could we operationalize these constructs—that is, define what they mean in practice?

EXHIBIT 2.1   Operationalizing Constructs

CONSTRUCT	
INVOLVEMENT IN GAMING	**ACADEMIC PERFORMANCE**
OPERATIONALIZING THE CONSTRUCTS	
Time spent on gaming	Class rank
Money spent on gaming	Number of academic awards
Number of memberships in gaming clubs	Current grade point average
Number of online "personas" or avatars	Cumulative grade point average
Percent of time spent with other gamers	Class participation as rated by faculty
Number of gaming software titles owned	Class attendance as recorded by faculty
Percentage of gaming terms used in conversation	Number of memberships in academic honor societies

Exhibit 2.1 shows some of the ways the two constructs could be operationalized or made measurable. We have taken ideas (mental constructions or "constructs") and translated them into observable operations that can be measured.

At the heart of many studies is a decision as to what measures will be used. Intuitively, some of the measures shown in Exhibit 2.1 appear to do a better job than others. Grade point average, for example, is a widely, though not totally, accepted measure of academic performance. On the other hand, membership in a gaming club or amount of money spent on games may have little or no relationship to whether an individual is an active game player. Of all the options, a best guess might be that time spent on gaming is the best measure of involvement as long as we can measure it accurately. (Note, however, the assumption that objective measurement of time spent is going to be the most relevant or useful measure. It could well turn out that gamers' subjective ratings of time spent ["not much time," "most of my time," etc.] have greater explanatory power than an objective measure such as "hours per week.")

These constructs or concepts have now been operationalized into **variables**. Variables are the aspects of a construct that are capable of being measured or taking on a value. In other words, they can vary. The constructs "gaming" or "academic performance" cannot be measured; the variables "time spent on gaming" and "grade point average" can.

Hypotheses: Making Predictions

A statement about the relationship that we expect to find between variables is a hypothesis. Hypotheses can state simply that there will be a relationship, specify the direction of the relationship, or state that no relationship is expected.

Two-tailed hypotheses state that there is a relationship between two variables but do not specify the direction of the relationship. For example:

H_1: There is a relationship between level of involvement in video gaming and academic performance.

One-tailed hypotheses require extra confidence because you commit to predicting the direction of the relationship between the variables. For example:

H_2: As time spent in video gaming increases, academic performance decreases.

Null hypotheses, usually symbolized as H_0, specify that there is no relationship between variables. For example:

H_0: There is no relationship between level of involvement in video gaming and academic performance.

Isn't a null hypothesis self-apparent? Yes and no. Basically, the null hypothesis makes explicit the notion that we are always working with two hypotheses—the first that the relationship we suspect exists; the second that it does not (the null hypothesis). The null hypothesis proposes there is no relationship between variables other than what we would find by chance. The probability of getting the results we did can be calculated, as we shall see in Chapter 7. Based on that probability, we can then decide which of these two hypotheses to accept, and which to reject.

Research Questions: Less Certainty; More Room to Move

Hypotheses specify the results you expect to find from your research. But suppose that your preliminary reading and research do not give you the certainty to make a prediction? In that case, you are left with not a prediction but a research question.

Open-ended research questions ask simply whether there is a relationship between variables. For example:

RQ_1: Is there a relationship between involvement in video gaming and academic performance?

Closed-ended research questions focus on a direction of relationship. For example:

RQ_2: Does academic performance decline as involvement in video gaming increases?

Starting with an open-ended research question, such as RQ_1 above, is appropriate for the exploratory study you would conduct when you don't have a lot of evidence as to what might be going on. With additional evidence, you can question the direction of the relationship between variables as in RQ_2 above. With even more evidence, you may be able to predict a relationship and to write that prediction in the form of a hypothesis.

Preferring a hypothesis over a research question gives you the advantage of focusing your study because you have said with some level of confidence "I know what's going on." Your study then simply becomes an exercise in determining whether or not your hypothesis is supported.

A research question, on the other hand, is more speculative. You sense that something is going on, but you may need to be more open-minded in your research design in order to capture relationships you had not anticipated.

Questioning the Questions

Hypotheses have the advantage of focusing your research, but you may not be able to focus your research initially, or indeed want to. For some researchers, the specificity of hypothesis testing is its own weakness. Researchers out of the **ethnomethodology** and **phenomenology** traditions especially would argue that complex human behavior cannot be simplified into variables as we did with our hypothetical video game study. They may further argue that finding a relationship between two variables provides no explanation of why the relationship exits and oversimplifies complex relationships by focusing on a few variables rather than on the multitude of influences on human behavior. Fundamentally, they are interested in rich description that provides understanding rather than a simple "yes, there is a relationship" answer to their questions. We will examine such approaches to communication more fully in Chapter 11.

Starting With No Questions

A specific question or hypothesis focuses your study and helps define your research priorities and methods, but it may blind you to relevant phenomena outside your immediate focus. Another approach, therefore, is to begin your study with no prior assumptions (in itself an assumption that you have selected an appropriate starting point). For example, as organization culture researchers Evered and Reis (1981) describe their process of finding out about a new organization, "We were 'probing in the dark' into the hidden organizational realities around us, in many directions simultaneously. . . . We did not form and test explicit hypotheses, we did not do a literature search, we had no elaborate instruments, and we did not use sample statistics or draw inferences at the '.05 level of significance.' In comparison to the idealized scientific method, the process we used to make sense of our organization was a messy, iterative groping through which we gradually, though quite rapidly, built up a picture of the organizational system of which we were a part" (p. 387).

This approach is the complete reverse of designing a study to test a specific idea. It is an approach that builds a picture of human communication, impression by impression, until the researchers have a full picture that allows them to confidently make statements about the topic that interests them.

"My method beats your method" arguments take place repeatedly and heatedly in research circles, but your reading of this chapter should have you understanding that one method never "beats" another method except in the context of the research. The real question is "Is your research method theoretically and practically appropriate for the research you want to do?" Or, to put it another way, "Can you make defensible connections among your theory, your method(s), and the data you plan to collect?"

As you will see from Exhibit 2.2, there should be a match between assumptions about human communication and the most appropriate approaches to studying it. You will also discover from your reading of scholarly research reports that researchers may "mix and match" assumptions and methods. For example, researchers in health communication may spend a great deal of time with adolescents who drive and text in order to fully understand what texting means in the adolescents' own terms. This subjective information may then be used to develop **scaled questions** for quantitative analysis in a broader survey of young people's risky driving behavior.

Moving in a Hermeneutic Circle

Hermeneutics may be understood as a theory of text interpretation. In essence, it holds that the part may not be understood without reference to the whole, and vice versa. It also cautions us that no observation or interpretation is free from the effects of an observer's own experiences, values, and expectations.

In the context of getting started, the theory suggests that by moving back and forth between the specific and the general, we gain a better understanding of both. For example, suppose you develop an interest in how and why individuals purchase new technologies such as smart watches.

A study of how and why people adopt new technologies might be theoretically informed by earlier studies on how farmers adopt new agricultural technologies (for example, Rogers, 1983). But your study of how and why people adopt smart watches may reshape our initial understanding of the concept of adoption itself. This new way of thinking about adoption may then (re)frame research questions about new wearable technologies, and so on.

EXHIBIT 2.2   **Assumptions About Human Communication and Their Research Implications**

Assumptions About Human Communication	Research Implications
People are generally similar, predictable, and motivated by events, personality type, and other people. We can make generalizations about their behavior.	Surveys, experiments, and other quantitative methods allow for precision in reporting and generalizations to populations from smaller samples.
Each person is unique, unpredictable, and self-motivated. We cannot make generalizations about his or her behavior.	Ethnography, interviews, and observations allow for insight, understanding, and the authenticity of the research participants' own language.

Ethics Panel: Do Some Research Methods Have More Ethical Implications Than Others?

The subjectivity in human communication requires that you explore the subjective life of individuals as they report it. Typically, this means interviewing people and "probing" as to why they see things the way they do. To facilitate this process, you assure your interviewees that their confidences will be respected and that nothing you report will identify them.

As you explore the complexities of organizational culture in a major corporation, one informant, based on your assurances of confidentiality, "lets loose." You hear all about his unsatisfactory working conditions, personal life, and prospects in general. The veiled threats that emerge from the informant's interview suggest that he may become a danger to his colleagues, if not himself. What do you do?

As you walk away with a voice recorder full of statements that you have chosen to interpret as veiled threats, you contemplate the fact that had you asked simple yes/no− or multiple-choice−type questions, the troubling information you now have may never have surfaced.

Could it be that some research methods raise more ethical problems than others?

What is your obligation to those who might be harmed in some way if the threats you detect were to translate into action?

What is your obligation to the individual you interviewed?

What is your obligation to the research process in general? For example, should you stay away from such research because of its potential complications or be prepared to break your assurances of confidentiality when you detect potential danger to your participants or others?

You can jump ahead to Chapter 3 for some help with these questions.

CHAPTER SUMMARY

- Communication researchers differ in ontology (how to define communication) and in epistemology (how best to understand communication).
- Generally, researchers assume either that human communication is objectively measurable and can be summarized in rules and generalizations or that communication is subjective and individualistic and must be described as such.
- The processes of induction, deduction, and abduction link observations to theory.
- Ways of understanding communication include tenacity, intuition, authority, and empiricism.
- The general purposes of research are description, explanation, prediction, control, interpretation, and criticism.
- Research may begin with specific hypotheses, general research questions, or no specific questions at all.
- Credible research must have a logical link between the methods chosen and the assumptions that underpin them.

KEY TERMS

abduction

authority

closed-ended research questions

constructs

control

deduction

description

empiricism

epistemology

ethnomethodology

explanation

exploration

hermeneutics

hypothesis

idiographic

induction

intuition

nomothetic

null hypotheses

one-tailed hypotheses

ontology

operationalize

open-ended research questions

phenomenology

positivism

prediction

questions

rationalism

research questions

scaled questions

scientific methods

serials

tenacity

two-tailed hypotheses

variables

worldviews

APPLICATION EXERCISES

Exercise 1: Identifying Your Interests

In practice, research is often an intersection of topic interest and the appropriate method(s) for that topic. Use the following checklist to identify your broad topic interests and the types of research that most appeal to you.

Context	
(a) Mass media and social media	
(b) Organizations	
(c) Groups	
(d) Interpersonal	
(e) Other (name it)	
Data Collection	
(a) Count behaviors or media content.	
(b) Observe behaviors.	
(c) Interview and listen.	
Reason for Research	
(a) Get practical results that can be used.	
(b) Get results that test ideas and theories.	
Relationship to Research Participants	
(a) Observe objectively from a distance.	
(b) Engage closely with people.	
Focus of Research	
(a) Study large numbers of people or media.	
(b) Study a few people or media in depth.	
Level of Research	
(a) Study messages at "face value."	
(b) "Unpack" hidden meanings behind messages.	

Exercise 2: Finding Your Worldview

As discussed in this chapter, all researchers bring to their research a worldview or basic assumptions about human communication and therefore how best to study and report it.

This exercise is an opportunity for you to explore and identify your own worldview. Following are a number of statements about human behavior and ways of understanding it formatted as polar opposites. Think through each pair of statements and put a check mark on the line next to the statement with which you most agree. If you cannot decide, put a check mark in the middle column (B).

When finished, total the number of check marks for each column. If you have the most check marks in column A, you have a Worldview I perspective; if most marks are in column C, you have a Worldview II perspective. Having the most marks in column B suggests that you see advantages to both perspectives or have yet to take a position. In this case, you might try the exercise again, this time forcing yourself to select from either column A or column C. Review this chapter for a discussion of each worldview and its implications for research.

Worldview I	A	B	C	Worldview II
People are basically alike.				Each person is unique.
People are predictable.				People are not predictable.
It is possible to make generalizations about human behavior.				It is not possible to make generalizations about human behavior.
People's behavior is determined by events and circumstances.				People's behavior is determined by the choices and decisions they make.
People live in an objective world that makes sense to any observer.				People live in an objective world that makes sense only to the individual.
Human communication is best understood by examining one aspect at a time, in depth.				Human communication is best understood by examining all aspects simultaneously, or holistically.
The best understanding of human communication comes from keeping an objective distance from participants.				The best understanding of human communication comes from getting as close as possible to participants.
The most accurate reports of human communication come from quantitative methods such as surveys and experiments.				The most accurate reports of human communication come from qualitative methods such as interviews and observations.
The best understanding of human communication comes from reports written in the scholarly language of research.				The best understanding of human communication comes from reports written in the language of the research participants.
TOTALS				

Exercise 3: Starting From Published Research

This exercise anticipates the bibliographic research discussed in Chapter 4.

1. Find an area of interest from the list of interest groups to be found at either the International Communication Association or the National Communication Association, listed below under "Scholarly Organizations."

2. Use your academic library to search for recent research using the name of the interest area as your search term.

3. Read two or three of the scholarly articles you find interesting. What further research do these articles suggest is needed? Typically, these suggestions will be in the "discussion" section of the article. Having read the articles, what further research do you see as necessary?

HINT: For example, look at the International Communication Association's list of divisions and interest groups and select "Interpersonal Communication." Go to an academic database such as "Communication & Mass Media Complete" (www.ebscohost.com/academic) and search for articles with "interpersonal communication" in the title and/or the abstract.

Exercise 4: Pew Research Center Internet, Science & Tech Project

Go to the Pew Research Center Internet, Science & Tech Project website at www.pewinternet.org and click on "Publications" to get a list of Pew research projects. What projects appear dated enough that they should be updated? What projects suggest a research gap that needs to be filled? For example, you should find a 2015 Pew report titled "U.S. Smartphone Use in 2015." Can you find projects focused on, for example, workgroups, religion, and social media or couples and social media?

RECOMMENDED READING

Anderson, J. A., & Baym, G. (2004, December). Philosophies and philosophic issues in communication, 1995–2004. *Journal of Communication, 54*(4), 589–615.

A review of many of the issues discussed in this chapter.

Becker, H. S. (1998). *Tricks of the trade: How to think about your research while you're doing it.* Chicago, IL: University of Chicago.

Discusses ways of thinking about research in practice.

Littlejohn, S. W., & Foss, K. A. (2011). *Theories of human communication* (10th ed.). Long Grove, IL: Waveland Press.

Provides coverage of major communication theories, their intellectual origins, and their relationships.

Lowery, S., & DeFleur, M. L. (1995). *Milestones in mass communication research: Media effects* (3rd ed.). New York, NY: Longman.

Summarizes major breakthroughs in conceptualizing and answering major questions about mass communication.

Pirsig, R. M. (1974). *Zen and the art of motorcycle maintenance: An inquiry into values.* New York, NY: Morrow.

A best seller that documents one individual's personal journey through the nature of knowing.

Powdermaker, H. (1967). *Stranger and friend.* New York, NY: Norton.

Hortense Powdermaker is known for her ethnographic studies of African Americans in the rural United States and of Hollywood. Her book title captures the balancing act that communication researchers must often adapt when working with research participants.

Trent, J. S. (1998). *Communication: Views from the helm for the 21st century.* Boston, MA: Allyn & Bacon.

An overview of where the field of communication is heading, from the points of view of a diversity of communication scholars.

RECOMMENDED WEB RESOURCES

Communication Research (SAGE Publications) . . . . .http://crx.sagepub.com

You can sign up for free content alerts from this journal at this site.

Idea Monkey . . . . www.cios.org

Idea Monkey, a creation of the Communication Institute for Online Scholarship (CIOS), works by pairing key concepts identified by the CIOS in its analyses of the communication literature. Concepts with high prominence in the field are paired, and the pairings are rated for originality.

Visual Communication Concept Explorer . . . . .www.cios.org

You can use the CIOS Visual Communication Concept Explorer (VCCE) to explore related concepts from the communication literature and to learn what communication concepts are related to other concepts.

Scholarly Organizations

Association for Education in Journalism and Mass Communication . . . . www.aejmc.org

International Communication Association . . . . www.icahdq.org

National Communication Association . . . . www.natcom.org

The above sites are for three of the many academic interest groups in communication. Visit them to explore the diversity of academic research areas and method interests.

Pew Research Center Internet, Science & Tech Project . . . . www.pewinternet.org

See Chapter 1.

Applied Communication Research

American Association of Advertising Agencies . . . . www.aaaa.org

American Marketing Association . . . . www.marketingpower.com

Direct Marketing Association . . . . www.the-dma.org

National Association of Broadcasters . . . . www.nab.org

Public Relations Society of America . . . . www.prsa.org

The above five websites are for major communication industry groups. You will not be able to access all aspects of these sites, but you will be able to browse for insights on current research, research issues, and possible careers.

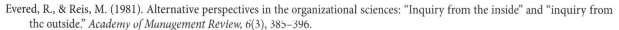

REFERENCES

Evered, R., & Reis, M. (1981). Alternative perspectives in the organizational sciences: "Inquiry from the inside" and "inquiry from the outside." *Academy of Management Review, 6*(3), 385–396.

Fish, S. L. (1990). Interpretive research: A new way of viewing organizational communication. *Public Administration Quarterly, 14*(1), 67–74.

Kaplan, A. (1964). *The conduct of inquiry: Methodology for behavioral science.* San Francisco, CA: Chandler Publishing.

Rogers. E. M. (1983). *Communication of innovations* (3rd ed.). New York, NY: Free Press.

⑤SAGE edge™

Want a better grade?
Get the tools you need to sharpen your study skills. Access practice quizzes, eFlashcards, video, and multimedia at **edge.sagepub.com/treadwell3e**

CHAPTER 3

Ethics

What Are My Responsibilities as a Researcher?

Ethics are complex it's true
With many a rule to think through
But there's one easy guide.
Keep this by your side—
"Would you do what you're doing to you?"

❧ ❧ ❧

Chapter Overview

Researching human communication means interacting with people, and there is no escaping the fact that this has ethical implications. Your relationship with research participants will be guided by your personal ethical standards, by organizational and sector standards, and by codes of ethics and laws designed to protect research participants from psychological and physical harm. This chapter focuses on some of the ethical issues in human communication research, codes of ethics that govern research on human subjects, approval procedures for human communication research in a scholarly setting, and some of the many issues and problems that arise with research on the Internet.

Chapter Objectives

This chapter will help you

- Identify major ethics issues in human communication research.

- Explain some of the classic ethical positions that inform communication research.

- Describe some of the major contemporary codes of ethics.

- Discuss the concepts of peer review and of institutional review boards.

- Describe how the level of involvement with research participants can shape a researcher's relationship with them.

- Identify some of the ethical issues unique to researching human communication on the Internet.

Introduction: Some Ethical Decisions

You will recognize the verse at the beginning of this chapter as a loose interpretation of the "do unto others" rule. If only specific ethical decisions in human communication research were that simple. Consider the decisions that might need to be made in the course of designing communication research. For example, would you expose research participants to sexually explicit or violent material? Deliberately deceive participants? Ensure that some people receive important information while denying it to others? Accept research funding from a source that hopes your research results will help promote its products or services? Start false rumors? Monitor people's behavior without their knowledge or consent?

The following sections set out some of the ethical issues for communication researchers, some of the "classic" ways of resolving ethical dilemmas, and some specific ethical standards and practices that anyone researching human communication should be aware of.

Sex, Violence, and Deception

Sex, violence, and deception may sound like the elements of a reality show, but each can be the focus of serious research in communication, and each clearly has ethical implications.

Debates, often politically fueled, rage over sexually explicit and violent media content, and over the nature of their effects. From a research point of view, there are two major questions: First, what are the effects (if any) of viewing such content, and second, what causes these effects? In other words, can we claim that exposure to such content causes some condition, or is it possible that the condition itself leads to voluntary exposure to such content?

Many studies and research designs have addressed these two questions, but suppose there comes a point in your own research at which you decide that you need to expose participants to explicit content so that you can assess their responses(s) to it. With respect to minors, this could well become a legal question, the answer to which is "you can't." For adults, you may be able to, but should you? Specific answers will be determined by the age and other characteristics of the research participants, the specific research experiences that the participants will be going through, the sponsoring agency behind the research, and, of course, the personal values and ethical standards of the researcher.

You may be interested in how audience feedback influences a speaker. For example, does a supportive audience improve a speaker's performance? Can a hostile audience weaken a speaker's performance? To answer such questions, you decide to expose speakers participating in your study to an audience made up of **confederates**. Confederates are participants in a study who have been briefed to behave in a particular way. In other words, they are "faking it" and deceiving the speaker. The speakers then address audiences who are faking a response such as enthusiasm or disinterest. Legal? Sure. Ethical . . . ?

Or perhaps you are interested in how information travels in organizations. The only way you can study this in a controlled fashion is to start a rumor, ask around to find out who heard it, and then "back track" to see from whom individuals first heard the rumor. This allows you to track the speed and the patterns of informal communications in an organization. To begin the experiment, you sit with a couple of strangers in your campus coffee bar and, conversationally, let out the information that your university's trustees are planning a 30% hike in student fees and tuition effective next semester. You are, of course, lying. Does the value of your research outweigh the need to deceive people?

Many health communication studies seek to establish the most effective means of getting health information to groups of people. One basic research design is to provide information to one community by interpersonal means, to another by social media, and to a third by a combination of the two. In order to establish that there have been any effects at all, you need a fourth, control, community that receives no information. As part of your study, then, you deny the control community information that could perhaps save or extend a life. Legal? Sure. Deceptive? Maybe. Ethical . . . ?

Money and Relationships

If sex, violence, and deception can feature in our list of ethical considerations, can money and relationships be far behind?

Let's take look at the hypothetical ClickAQuiz educational technology company. The company makes software that allows multiple-choice quizzes to be downloaded to smartphones; students can answer the questions in their own time and space and then upload their answers for grading. Your interest is in how such technology affects academic performance, and you have designed survey questions that focus on technology and academic performance. ClickAQuiz has a keen interest in your research in interactive technologies. In fact, the company offers to write a check to support your research. In return for the check, ClickAQuiz wants you to include several additional questions about how and where students might use this technology, what they would be willing to pay for the service, and how they feel about banner advertising on their phones. Do you incorporate these questions into your research or reject them as an unnecessary commercial "intrusion" unrelated to the focus of your research? Could the ClickAQuiz questions, if used, affect student responses to the questions you want answered by, for example, "framing" the technology as "user pays" rather than free? On what basis might you change or drop any of the ClickAQuiz questions?

In the "relationships" department, researchers may relate to their research participants in ways that range from dispassionate observation to psychologically close.

Unobtrusive measures is an approach that by definition observes people's behavior without their being aware of it. This approach is often used to check on the reliability of information people provide. For example, most people would probably say when interviewed that they wear seat belts when driving. One unobtrusive measures check on this is simply to observe people driving and to record the percentage you see wearing seat belts.

At the other extreme, as someone researching family dynamics and how parents and siblings interact across generations, you may find that you need in-depth face-to-face interviews to gain an understanding of a family's culture and communication patterns. As you question family members in depth, you may find that the questions you ask are distressing to your interviewees. Or you may find that they are revealing confidences about other members of the family, who would be hurt if they knew that this information was going outside the family to a stranger—you.

Less dramatic decisions such as simply listening in on a conversation also have an ethical component. In Chapter 1 of this book, you were invited to listen in on a discussion among a group of students and asked the question "Should you?" From a straight research point of view, this might be an interesting thing to do, but it seems intuitive that just as we would ask permission to physically join the group, so also would we ask permission to record, and in due course publish, our report and interpretation of their discussions. This becomes an especially important issue when studying human communication on the Internet and is discussed more fully later in this chapter.

The overriding question in all the hypothetical cases outlined above is "What standards of behavior should apply to my research?" Typical issues in communication research are discussed in the following section. These issues relate to your relationships with research participants and/or the readers who will depend on you for an accurate account of your research. Both are important to your career as a researcher.

Ethics Issues in Communication Research

Honesty

It seems axiomatic that honesty is always the best policy, but honesty in practice can be difficult. Deception can be part of legitimate and professional research studies. To be honest and reveal the deception "up front" may be to weaken the whole research design. Professional codes of ethics generally address this dilemma by allowing deception in some research designs as long as the participants are made aware of the deception immediately after the study is concluded.

Researchers have an ethical responsibility to their readers as well as to their research participants. In this case, this means reporting possible flaws in your research and negative results as well as the good news. Most research papers have a section where the author discusses possible weaknesses in the study. Such a section is helpful, not an embarrassment, because it provides a launchpad for further research. Finding "nothing" or results that are counterintuitive may not do a lot for your ego, but it does not invalidate your study. Obviously, a significant finding is more likely to be published, but the fact that something you expected to find was not found still contributes to our knowledge, and you can honestly report that finding.

Confidentiality and Anonymity

To protect the individuals who may be giving you personal information, it is customary to assure them of **confidentiality**. This means that you will not release any information that identifies your participants even if as the researcher you know what information each participant provided you.

To fully protect and reassure participants, you may need to offer **anonymity**. Anonymity goes a step further in protecting people in that the data you collect from them absolutely does not identify them. Even you do not know which participant provided the information you collected. Typically you ensure anonymity by instructing respondents not to put their names on any information they provide. Any consent forms that they sign are turned in separately so that there is no link between those documents that identify them and any other document.

Violation of any anonymity or confidentiality agreements when reporting your research results is an ethical issue and may well become a legal one. Researchers usually protect their respondents' anonymity in qualitative studies by referring to them as "Respondent A," or by using a false and typically neutral name such as "Bob Smith" or "Jane Jones." Quantitative studies typically report statistical summaries for a group of people, so there is no need to identify specific individuals.

Making Generalizations

The professional codes of practice discussed below require that research participants be volunteers. If only willing volunteers are recruited to your study, you will be recruiting individuals who have a bias toward your study in the sense that they are willing to participate in it. Generalizations from your study, then, can be made only to this type of individual. Because you recruited volunteers for your study, you cannot make statements about the likely effect of these materials on the "nonvolunteer" type.

Debriefing

If your participants have been exposed to deception, you have an ethical obligation after the study is over to ensure that you contact them, explain the deception, and invite any follow-up questions they may have. Failure to do so means that your participants will leave the research assuming that they have been involved in a real event when in fact they have not. The American Psychological Association (APA) Ethical Principles of Psychologists and Code of Conduct calls for any deception to be revealed to participants no later than at the conclusion of data collection.

More generally, researchers should respond promptly to participants' requests for information about the nature, results, and conclusions of the research. Most researchers need to ask their participants to document their agreement to be in a research study by signing a consent form. Consent forms typically describe the nature of the study and emphasize the right of participants to leave the study at any time and to access the results of the study. Because consent forms must be signed in advance of a study, they will not explain any deceptions that are a part of it. As noted above, participants who have been subject to deception should be made aware of that deception as soon as possible, and readers of your research report will want to know that your results were obtained under conditions of deception.

The Literature Review

A large part of any research project is the literature review—discussed in Chapter 4. This is your summary and evaluation of what other researchers working on your topic have published. You review this literature to get ideas on how best to do your own research and, importantly, to demonstrate to others how your own research will contribute to our shared knowledge.

There is a voluminous literature on communication research. You will have to read and report it selectively. This means that your readers' view of the field, as well as your own, will be shaped by what you choose to write and how you write about it. Following are some of the questions you might have about a literature review.

How far back in time should I review? Can I use secondary (summary) articles rather than primary (original) sources? Should I report articles that do not support my viewpoint?

Can I report research that is relevant but proprietary (i.e., "owned" and I do not have permission to publish it)?

Views about communication change over time, as they should. Just as it is possible to misrepresent the current state of knowledge by selecting only certain authors to review, so is it possible to misrepresent by selecting particular time periods for review. Reviewing summaries of research rather than the original reports can give you an initial overview of the field, but summarizing summaries may lead to dangerous oversimplifications and further magnify any biases of interpretation in the summaries you are reading. Articles that do not support your ideas and methods should be reported because your readers need to be aware of any debates and controversies in your area of interest and you have a responsibility to summarize the debates.

Proprietary information is information that is owned, typically, by corporations and may not be published without their permission. As a researcher, you may have access to proprietary information, but publishing that information may be both an ethical and a legal violation.

In summary, your writing may accurately represent the work of other researchers or misrepresent it and therefore requires that you be ethically sensitive.

Acknowledging Others

It is rare for one individual to be able to take full credit for a research project, especially in the physical and biological sciences where a team of technicians and colleagues may be needed to bring a project to successful fruition. Authorship of a published paper implies more than just writing it; it implies taking responsibility for the project reported. To the extent that others contributed to your project, it may be appropriate to list them as coauthors or at least to acknowledge their contributions.

The basic decision is what constitutes "others." Researchers reporting summary data for hundreds of survey respondents are unlikely to acknowledge specific individuals. Researchers who work closely with one or two collaborators may well want to acknowledge them but may be unable to do so if they have been promised anonymity.

Appropriate Language

Members of the research community who share your interests will want to see your literature review, research methods, results, and conclusions all written in a professional scholarly style.

Scholarly writing may become ethically problematic, however, if your research participants cannot understand it. Seeking permission from, and communicating results to, participants needs to be done at their level of understanding. The Office for Human Research Protections (OHRP) of the U.S. Department of Health and Human Services (U.S. DHHS, 1993) recommends that informed consent documents "be written in 'lay language', (i.e. understandable to the people being asked to participate)."

"Understandable to the people being asked to participate" implies not only language but also level of the language. In other words, consent documents may need to be written in the language best understood by the participant (not necessarily English) and at the level of comprehension of that participant.

Plagiarism

There are a number of reasons to dislike plagiarism. Primarily, of course, it is an unethical (and may well be an illegal) representation of others' work as your own. From the point of view of your busy research colleagues, however, plagiarism also represents the problem of "used goods." Representing others' work as your own means that readers may end up reading both the original research and the plagiarist's version of that research. It does a disservice to researchers trying to stay current because they may be misled into reading two different versions of the same research. Of course, if the plagiarist is publishing proprietary research, the issue also becomes one of copyright violation (at least).

Some Classic Ethical Positions

All the above issues pose questions that must be answered in order to design ethically defensible research studies. For many researchers, the answers come in the form of specific ethical codes that must be followed, with penalties such as loss of funding if they are not.

More generally, researchers may turn to one or more of the following "classic" ethical positions for guidance.

The **Judeo-Christian ethic** is the basis of the verse at the beginning of this chapter. Its test of ethical behavior is a simple one. Would you be willing to be a participant in your own study? If not, your project may be ethically suspect as it affects other people.

Philosopher Immanuel Kant proposed a **categorical imperative**—that a behavior is valid if you are willing to see it applied as a universal rule. For example, if you are willing to use deception as part of a research design, then you ought to be prepared to accept deception as a universal value.

The **principle of utilitarianism**, associated with philosophers Jeremy Bentham, John Stuart Mill, and David Hume, argues for the greatest good for the greatest number. It suggests that research designs that may hurt a minority of people are justified if there is an overall greater good. For example, we might argue in communication research that misinforming a few people via a false rumor is defensible if out of that research emerges a fuller understanding of how best to use informal communication networks in an emergency.

Philosopher John Rawls's "**veil of ignorance**" approach asks us to take a dispassionate approach, reviewing all sides of a decision equally. We are asked to wear a veil that blinds us to all information about ourselves that might cloud our judgment. For example, suppose our research design has the potential to cause severe psychological distress to our research participants. We need an ethical decision as to whether this is acceptable or not. The "veil of ignorance" blinds us to the role we would be playing in the research; that is, we could be the researcher, or we could be participants. Recognizing that psychological distress is undesirable and could happen to us, we would probably decide that our research ought not to cause any distress to our research participants.

Two Brief Histories— or Why We Care About Research Ethics

It's a long way from Nazi Germany to monitoring people's behavior on the Internet, but Nazi medical experiments during World War II were the 20th-century impetus for codes of ethics covering research on human **subjects**. After the war, at the Nuremberg trials, a number of Nazi physicians and administrators were charged with crimes against humanity, more specifically with conducting without consent medical experiments that caused death and inflicted injury on concentration camp inmates.

From 1932 to 1972, the U.S. Public Health Service ran a study in Tuskegee, Alabama, to learn more about syphilis. In doing so, it withheld adequate treatment from a group of Black men who had the disease and were participants in the study. In 1972, a panel reviewing the study concluded that it was ethically unjustified and that the knowledge gained was sparse compared with the risks the study posed for its subjects. The review of the study led to the 1979 **Belmont Report**, discussed below, and to the establishment of the OHRP. Remarks made by President Bill Clinton in 1997 when apologizing for the Tuskegee study are referenced under "Recommended Web Resources" at the end of this chapter.

Contemporary Codes of Ethics

Professional concern for human subjects dates back to at least the 4th century BCE oath of Hippocrates, and the above two brief histories indicate why such a concern is still warranted. It is unlikely that most communication research would have the potential for physical harm. However, there is always the possibility of psychological harm, for example as a result of exposure to graphic violence or from requiring participants to behave in a way contrary to their beliefs. Codes of ethics seek to protect research participants from any form of harm by prescribing professional standards of behavior for researchers.

The Nuremberg Code

One outcome of the Nuremberg trials was the 1948 **Nuremberg Code**, the first international code to emphasize that

- Research subjects must consent to the research in which they are involved.
- The benefits of the research must outweigh the risks.

The Declaration of Helsinki

In 1964, the World Medical Association's **Declaration of Helsinki** established international ethical guidelines for medical professionals researching human subjects. The Declaration of Helsinki continues to be revised and emphasizes that

- Research protocols must be reviewed by an independent committee prior to the research.
- **Informed consent** must be obtained from research participants.
- Research must be conducted by medically or scientifically qualified individuals.
- Research risks should not exceed the benefits.

The Belmont Report

The National Commission for the Protection of Human Subjects of Biomedical and Behavioral Research prepared the Belmont Report in 1979. The report outlines three basic ethical principles surrounding research with human subjects. These are **autonomy**, **beneficence**, and **justice**. The principles and their applications in practice are summarized in Exhibit 3.1.

EXHIBIT 3.1   **The Belmont Report—Principles, Applications, and Questions for Internet Research**

Principle	Application	Questions Related to Internet Research

Autonomy
 	
Individuals should be treated with respect.
 	
Persons with diminished autonomy are entitled to protection.
	Informed Consent
	
	Subjects must be given the opportunity to choose what shall or shall not happen to them.
	
	The consent process must include three elements:
	
	• Information
	• Comprehension
	• Voluntariness
		• Are avatars human subjects?
		• How do researchers verify:
		
		  ○ The identity of participants?
		  ○ Participants' understanding of informed consent?
		  ○ The validity of "signed" consent forms?
		
		• Could pseudonyms "mask" vulnerable individuals such as minors?
		• Should consent forms inform participants about special risks from Internet research (e.g., anonymity may not be guaranteed)?
		• How can researchers debrief all participants and do long-term follow-up when the online population is constantly changing?

Beneficence Human subjects must not be harmed, and efforts should be made to secure their well-being. Research should maximize possible benefits and minimize possible harm.	**Assessment of Risks and Benefits** The nature and scope of risks and benefits must be assessed systematically.	• Are all possible risks and benefits to research participants actually known? • Can researchers guarantee anonymity? • How can long-term risks and benefits be assessed when the online population is constantly changing?
Justice The benefits and risks of research must be distributed fairly.	**Selection of Subjects** There must be fair procedures and outcomes in the selection of research subjects. For example: • Subjects ought not to be recruited simply on the basis of accessibility. • Some individuals and groups must not bear disproportionate risks while others reap the benefits of research.	• The Internet population is different from the population at large, so how can the risks and benefits of online research be distributed equitably?

Regulations

Many nations have regulations that implement principles such as those set out above. In the United States, DHHS regulations that implement these principles have been adopted by many other agencies that fund or conduct research on human subjects. These shared standards are known as the Federal Policy for the Protection of Human Subjects, or "**Common Rule**."

The Common Rule addresses requirements for ensuring compliance by research institutions, requirements for obtaining and documenting informed consent, **institutional review boards (IRBs)** (see below), and special protections for vulnerable research subjects such as pregnant women, prisoners, minors, and participants with disabilities.

Peer Review and Institutional Review Boards

Peer review at its simplest consists of qualified researchers with similar interests assessing each other's work.

Informally, researchers brainstorm over coffee cups, swap ideas at conferences, and put together research teams for major projects. Such interactions can provide an informal peer review of ethics and research design more generally before any project is launched. This, of course, can be a hit or miss operation, depending on how actively the researcher networks.

Formal review is required when researchers undertake any human subjects research for the federal government or are employed by any institution that receives federal funding.

The most typical method of formal peer review with respect to ethics and treatment of human participants is the IRB. The IRB is a panel established to review research proposals specifically for their impact on any human participants. There is an IRB in some form on almost every campus where human subjects research is conducted.

The fact that most communication research does not involve physical impact on participants does not exempt it from IRB review. Protection involves psychological protection as much as physical protection. As you saw from examples at the beginning of this chapter, subjects could potentially suffer psychological distress from exposure to explicit materials, from having been deceived, or from being asked to behave in a way contrary to their beliefs.

What Should I Call You? The Ethics of Involvement

While researchers are generally known as researchers or investigators, the individuals participating in the research may be known as subjects, informants, participants, or collaborators.

Traditionally, researchers used the term *subjects*, with the connotation of an omniscient white-coated professional observing an acquiescent group of human subjects in the cause of a greater good. *Informant* and *collaborator* may have negative connotations outside research, but within it both terms recognize that researchers would be nowhere without the information provided by research participants. *Participant* recognizes the active and voluntary role that research participants play in making research possible.

As you can see from Exhibit 3.2, terminology, research design, and the nature of the relationship with research participants are closely related. All researchers are bound by relevant regulations and professional codes, but as research participants move from being subjects to being collaborators, the ethical dilemmas can increase. It is unlikely that a researcher out of the "let's survey 1,200 people" school of thought would need to be professionally concerned with

EXHIBIT 3.2   Researcher–Participant Relationships in Communication Research

		Researcher's Involvement With Participants	
		Low	**High**
Researcher's Orientation to Participants	Dispassionate observer: "Stranger"	Measure people objectively	Explore people's subjective views
		Not involved	Involved in order to elicit subjective information
		Behavior motivated by regulations and ethical codes	Behavior motivated by regulations, ethical codes, and need to establish trusting relationship
		People: "Subjects"	People: "Informants"
	Involved in participants' condition: "Friend"	Involved in lives only as a means of observing them	Involved, with participants' views driving research design and implementation
		Behavior motivated by regulations, ethical codes, and need to successfully access participants	Behavior motivated by regulations, ethical codes, and research goals important to participants
		People: "Participants"	People: "Collaborators"

each subject's private life. At the other extreme, a researcher working with a small group of collaborators is more likely to assume an ethical responsibility for their well-being because they are part of the team that has shaped the nature of the research from the beginning and may well continue to do so.

The Internet and Research Ethics

Research on the Internet can be an ethical gray area, complicated by the fact that relevant human subjects regulations were written essentially for biomedical research, and long before virtual realities and avatars came into existence. It is probably fair to summarize the ethics of Internet research as a debate generating more questions than answers—as we shall see. The following sections set out some of the theoretical and practical issues with Internet research, and their ethical implications.

What *Is* the Internet?

The big theoretical question that shapes thinking about research ethics on the Internet is "What is the Internet?" The ambiguity in the very term *Internet research* captures the basic definitional problem.

Internet research may include research on Internet content with no direct human subjects interaction, research that uses the Internet as a tool for recruiting subjects, research about the Internet itself and how it affects people, research about Internet users, and research that uses the Internet as an intervention tool. It is a tool for research and a venue of research, with social media blurring the distinction between tool and venue (U.S. DHHS, 2013).

Simplistically, the Internet can be regarded as both process and content. If it is regarded as a process of interaction or a virtual space within which human interaction occurs, then the argument has to be made that social science research standards apply because the communication behaviors of individuals are being studied. That obligates researchers to respect that human subjects are being studied and to seek the institutional approvals outlined earlier in this chapter.

However, the case can also be made that the Internet is fundamentally text or visual content and that researchers studying web behavior are simply studying published content. The notion that the web is nothing more than content raises the proposition that because individuals are not being studied directly, the researcher has no impact on their lives and therefore no research approvals are required. Internet research in this light becomes essentially a type of content analysis.

The issues are more complicated than the simple process-versus-content distinction sketched out above. Even if the view is taken that the Internet is fundamentally content, an issue that remains is that much Internet content is intellectual property and subject to copyright law.

Anonymity and Identification on the Internet

An important issue with respect to human subjects research is that Internet content may have the names of identifiable individuals attached to it. Sometimes this is unavoidable—witness Facebook's policy that requires members to provide their real names; pretending to be anything or anyone isn't allowed. In other instances, an individual's identity may not be immediately obvious but can be found or deduced by a determined "web sleuth."

A dismissive response might be that if individuals choose to paint their names on a billboard or to stick bumper stickers on their vehicles, then they ought reasonably to expect that a researcher or the news media might publicly report on their Internet postings and who produced them. However, many Internet residents post content on the assumption that they are doing so anonymously or are posting to a discussion area that is not open to the public.

There is also an issue of what we might call intentionality of publication. Bumper stickers, billboards, and newspaper articles are all produced with the intention of publication. It is difficult to publish any of them accidentally, and almost any publication goes through some kind of review process before "going public."

The same cannot, however, be said of Internet content. "Public" does not mean the same as "publication," and while much Internet content is public and planned in the way billboard content is, much of it can be closer to informal "thought this yesterday; don't think it today" ephemeral discussion than to planned publication content.

Questions related to Internet research rapidly become much more complex than whether the Internet is a tool such as a **search engine**, or a medium such as a newsgroup, blog, or tweet. The same issues that arise with non-Internet studies—privacy, consent, participant risk, method appropriateness, sampling, recruitment, and anonymity—are all compounded by the sheer size of the Internet, its ever-shifting population, and its special problem areas of authenticity and security.

The U.S. DHHS (2013) notes that while the regulatory definition of "human subjects" has not changed, new forms of identity such as avatars exist in the Internet, and personally identifiable information about living individuals may be obtainable through such virtual representations. The DHHS identifies the verification of identity as a major issue in Internet research. While low-risk studies may require only minimal identity verification, high-risk studies involving sensitive information may call for "multiple-factor authentication."

Privacy on the Internet

The regulatory definition of "private information" means "information about behavior that occurs in a context in which an individual can reasonably expect that no observation or recording is taking place, and information which has been provided for specific purposes by an individual and which the individual can reasonably expect will not be made public" (U.S. DHHS, 2013, p. 5).

The DHHS notes that all information that is legally available to any Internet user could be considered public information. Alternatively, the privacy policy created by the site could be used to establish whether its online information is public or confidential, with investigators operating in accordance with the privacy expectations that the site offers and requests from members. Another approach would be to consider as private any venue where authorization for membership or participation is necessary.

Thelwall (2010) argues that academic researchers should not have any restrictions placed on the kinds of (legal) data that they investigate on the public web and that they should be able to do so without obtaining informed consents, if the information researched is on the public web. He argues that the web is a venue where individuals may expect that their postings are private but ought not to assume that their privacy is protected. For example, a posting to a work group of colleagues may be regarded as private to that group, but the group has no reason to assume a guarantee of privacy given the rights and abilities of employers to monitor employee e-mail.

A further privacy issue is cross-national data storage. For example, Canadian research ethics boards may include a statement that SurveyMonkey survey data are held in the United States and are subject to U.S. law, in particular to the USA PATRIOT Act that allows U.S. authorities to access the records of Internet service providers.

A 1999 report on the relationship between Internet research and the Belmont Report discussed previously remains valid today. Frankel and Siang (1999) reiterate the basic considerations addressed by the Belmont Report—autonomy, beneficence, and justice. Issues in addressing these requirements of ethical research on the Internet include the following.

The Internet has a fluid population, meaning that individuals may move from web address to web address or maintain multiple web addresses, unlike most people owning or renting a residence. The Internet population is skewed in terms of gender, race, income, and geographical distribution, and people may be more or less open to disclosure based on the Internet environment they are in than when they respond to other individuals in person. By analogy, you can see that what you might be prepared to "go public" with depends very much on whether you are in your physician's office, at a restaurant with friends, or in a job interview.

Surveys, at first sight easily done via web survey software, cannot guarantee survey respondents anonymity because identifying information may be linked to documents they are transmitting and to their e-mail addresses.

Informed Consent and Debriefing on the Internet

Informed consent becomes a much more complex issue because the individuals providing that consent cannot necessarily be easily identified. For example, two or more people may share one e-mail address. Which person at that address agreed to participate in the survey, and is that the same person who actually answered the survey questions? Similarly, how is the researcher to determine and verify that any person answering the survey is a minor? (You will recall that research on minors and other special groups particularly requires IRB approval.)

The informed consent process requires that participants be informed about the research and that the researcher ensures that participants comprehend the research and obtains their signed voluntary agreement to the research. Each of these steps presents a difficulty on the Internet. For example, risks to the participants may not be fully known to researchers because they do not know what effect participating in the research will have on a respondent's relationship with other individuals in cyberspace. While in principle the researcher is available to answer any questions about the research, knowing that respondents fully comprehend the research can be made more difficult by the fact that "signing" consent forms often means that respondents use electronic signatures or click an "agree" box on an online form. This gives researchers less confidence, perhaps, that the respondent is fully aware of the research and its implications than a signed document would provide. A further question related to informed consent is "From whom?" A participant in a discussion group may agree to make his contributions accessible to a researcher, but do not other participants in the group also have the right to decide that this content can be made available?

Lawson (2004) proposes that some of the problems associated with obtaining informed consent might be addressed by obtaining consent at different levels as appropriate. For example, web content and its associated author(s) might be used for data analysis and reporting only, with no identification of the authors. Alternatively, the name(s) of the author(s) might be published but not linked to their content so that the content would have no identifiable author. Another option would be to publish the content and link it to the name(s) of the author(s). The latter two options could be done with or without the prior approval of participants.

Kozinets (2013) argues that for research that involves no risk to participants an "implied consent" may be appropriate. Implied consent occurs online when a participant agrees to continue in a study by clicking an "accept" button on a web page or by providing information.

Then comes the problem of **debriefing**. How to ensure that everyone who participated in a study receives a follow-up explanation of the study? In principle, this can be done by e-mailing a debriefing document to every participant, but again the researcher cannot know exactly who has access to an e-mail account and therefore who such a mailing will reach. Releasing sensitive or controversial material to an e-mail address may place participants in an emotionally difficult situation the researcher is unaware of.

Guidelines and Questions for Internet Research

To address many of the questions outlined above, the Association of Internet Researchers (AoIR) proposes guidelines for Internet research rather than a specific code that may not fit every eventuality (Markham & Buchanan, 2012). Because the ethical questions may be different at different stages of the research process, the AoIR recommends a process approach, that is to say posing different questions at each stage of the research. These questions include those below.

How is the research context defined and conceptualized? How is the context (venue/participants/data) being accessed? Who is involved in the study? What is the primary object of the study? How are data being managed, stored, and represented? How are texts/persons/data being studied? How are findings presented? What are the potential harms, risks, and potential benefits associated with this study? How are we recognizing the autonomy of others and acknowledging that they are of equal worth to ourselves and should be treated so? What particular issues might arise around the issue of minors or vulnerable persons?

An AoIR summary chart that presents commonly asked ethical questions for different types of Internet contexts such as direct contact, special interest forums, and avatar-based social spaces is listed under "Recommended Web Resources" below.

In summary, the AoIR and DHHS both remind us that the Belmont Report's fundamental principles of respect for persons, beneficence, and justice apply to Internet research as much as to any other form of human subjects research. As the DHHS report reminds us, adherence to these fundamental principles is important to encouraging public trust in the ethical conduct of Internet researchers.

Dr. Mary Gray, a senior researcher at Microsoft Research and associate professor at Indiana University's Media School, proposes a simple test for researchers: "If you're afraid to ask your subjects for their permission to conduct the research, there's probably a deeper ethical issue that must be considered" (Goel, 2014). The AoIR summary, the DHHS "Considerations and Recommendations" document, and the classic ethical positions and codes of ethics outlined in this chapter will help you with research ethics and with this chapter's application exercises.

Ethics Panel: Facebook Faces a Furor

The following looks like a typical scholarly research paper, so why did it make headlines when published in 2014?

Experimental evidence of massive-scale emotional contagion through social networks.
Adam D. I. Kramer, Jamie E. Guillory, and Jeffrey T. Hancock
8788–8790 | PNAS | June 17, 2014 | vol. 111 | no. 24

The basic summary from the above paper is "In an experiment with people who use Facebook, we test whether emotional contagion occurs outside of in-person interaction between individuals by reducing the amount of emotional content in the News Feed."

The research question, in essence, is whether there is a relationship between Facebook content to which you are exposed and your emotional status.

Let's look at the research method—experiment.

As we shall see in Chapter 10, the classic experimental design consists of two groups of participants, with each group exposed to different conditions.

In the Facebook study, 698,003 users were randomly assigned to two experimental groups. One group had its News Feed manipulated so that it saw fewer positive posts than usual, while the other group saw fewer negative posts. This is a classic experimental design with perhaps predictable results. "When positive expressions were reduced, people produced fewer positive posts and more negative posts; when negative expressions were reduced, the opposite pattern occurred."

The furor over the study stems from the apparent disregard of many of the ethical considerations outlined in this chapter. For example, individuals in the study did not know they were in the study; their consent was not sought; and they were not debriefed after the study. Conceivably, they could have had adverse psychological reactions to a reduction in their positive news content.

A defense of the study might include the following arguments. Only 0.04% of Facebook users were involved (Kramer, 2014). Participant consent was obtained by virtue of users having agreed to Facebook's terms of service, which allow for use of users' personal data for research. A further argument might be that most social media platforms and news sites manipulate their interfaces to improve user experience and to increase the relevance of their offerings and advertising. The effect on those in the experiment was small. "At the end of the day, the actual impact on people in the experiment was the minimal amount to statistically detect it—the result was that people produced an average of one fewer emotional word, per thousand words, over the following week" (Kramer, 2014).

Evaluate this study in light of the principles set out in the Belmont Report and the specifics you can find about IRB approvals for human subjects research. Questions you might think about include the possible presence of minors in the Facebook samples, the principle of informed consent, debriefing, and whether the presence or absence of federal funding makes a difference to your evaluation.

CHAPTER SUMMARY

- Ethics is the study of right and wrong; responsibility; and, in the context of this chapter, appropriate behavior toward research participants.
- Communication research ethics share with medical and psychological ethics a basic concern to protect the well-being of human participants.

- The formal mechanism for reviewing the protections for human subjects at most institutions is an institutional review board.
- Peer review and publication also provide a check on the ethics of research.
- Ethical decisions are involved in treatment of human participants, in research design, and in research reporting.
- Formal codes of ethics include the Nuremberg Code, the Declaration of Helsinki, the Belmont Report, the Common Rule, and the APA's Ethical Principles of Psychologists and Code of Conduct.
- The Internet as both research site and research tool raises questions and challenges related to participant selection, anonymity, informed consent, and debriefing.

KEY TERMS

anonymity

autonomy

beneficence

Belmont Report

categorical imperative

Common Rule

confederates

confidentiality

debriefing

Declaration of Helsinki

informed consent

institutional review board (IRB)

Judeo-Christian ethic

justice

Nuremberg Code

peer review

principle of utilitarianism

proprietary

search engine

subjects

unobtrusive measures

veil of ignorance

APPLICATION EXERCISES

Exercise 1: The Ethics of Content Analysis

A student wishes to analyze the content of student blogs posted to the web and to publish the results of her analysis.

List the reasons why she should seek IRB approval for her research and the reasons an IRB approval is not necessary. Come to a conclusion as to whether an IRB approval is needed or not. Identify the web resources that would be most helpful to her in deciding whether to seek IRB approval. Should the fact that these blogs are part of an online class in which she is participating affect her thinking about IRB approval?

Exercise 2: Ethics and Virtual Respondents

You are a member of Second Life—the virtual world populated by avatars. For a research project, the results of which will be published, you seek to interview two other members: Princess Morag the Malevolent, mighty slayer of dragons, and her associate, Vangoth the Vulgarian, on whether their attitudes toward dragon extermination are influenced by high levels of exposure to *Harry Potter* movies.

Identify any research approvals you think you would need to obtain for this research.

Exercise 3: The Ethics of Internet Research

You have been asked to advise your campus IRB on whether campus-based Internet research implies a special set of "e-ethics" specific to research on and of the Internet. There is some thinking that the basic principles of human subjects research protections cover Internet research adequately and that no specific guidelines for such research are required. List the sources of information you might go to in order to write a report and recommendations for your board.

Exercise 4: The Ethics of Public Opinion Polling

Many research firms do survey work for clients other than the federal government and therefore may not require IRB approvals. This does not mean that such organizations lack a code of ethics. For example, you can find the codes under which the Pew Research Center operates at its "FAQ" page: www.people-press.org/methodology/frequently-asked-questions/.

Under "Do pollsters have a code of ethics? If so, what is in the code?" Pew links to two codes—those of the American Association for Public Opinion Research (AAPOR) and the Council of American Survey Research Organizations (CASRO).

Examine these two professional codes of practice and note where they do and do not overlap with respect to (a) underlying principles set out in the Belmont Report and (b) specific issues addressed in this chapter, such as parental consent for researching minors, verification of participant identities, informed consent, and debriefing.

RECOMMENDED READING

Hamilton, A. (2005). The development and operation of IRBs: Medical regulations and social science. *Journal of Applied Communication Research, 33*(3), 189–203.

An overview of IRBs, the most common means of reviewing research on human subjects.

RECOMMENDED WEB RESOURCES

Formal Ethics and Codes of Practice

American Association for Public Opinion Research
Code of Professional Ethics and Practices . . . . www.aapor.org/AAPORKentico/Standards-Ethics.aspx

Council of American Survey Research Organizations Code of
Standards and Ethics for Market, Opinion, and Social Research . . . . www.casro.org/?page=TheCASROCode

Direct Marketing Association Ethical Guidelines . . . . www.the-dma.org/guidelines

The above three websites provide the codes of ethics for two areas of applied communication—public opinion research and direct marketing.

American Psychological Association Ethical Principles
of Psychologists and Code of Conduct . . . . www.apa.org/ethics/code/index.aspx

Many of the ethical principles set out by the APA apply to communication research. APA style is the publication style used to format many communication research papers.

Association of Social Anthropologists of the U.K. and
Commonwealth Ethical Guidelines for Good Research Practice . . . . www.theasa.org/ethics/guidelines.shtml

This site, in addition to providing ethical guidelines, sets out all the parties that can impact and be impacted by human subjects research—research participants; sponsors, funders, and employers; colleagues and the discipline; governments and society at large.

Illinois Institute of Technology Center for the Study of Ethics in the Profession . . . . http://ethics.iit.edu

This site has hundreds of codes of ethics from a variety of disciplines, including communication. In addition to the codes, you can find discussion on the value of having such codes and guidelines on constructing a code for your own organization.

National Communication Association Code of
Professional Responsibilities for the Communication Scholar/Teacher . . . . www.natcom.org/publicstatements

The above code of professional responsibilities for one of the major U.S. academic communication associations sets out professional standards for research, teaching, and publication.

National Institutes of Health (NIH) Bioethics Resources ....www.bioethics.nih.gov/resources/index.shtml

This central site provides information on a variety of topics related to research on human subjects in the United States.

Presidential Commission for the Study of Bioethical Issues ....www.bioethics.gov

This site provides information on human subjects research and research ethics.

U.S. Department of Health and Human Services, Office of Human Research Protection ....www.hhs.gov/ohrp

U.S. Department of Health and Human Services: Informed Consent ....www.hhs.gov/ohrp/policy/consent/index.html

U.S. Public Health Service Syphilis Study at Tuskegee ....www.cdc.gov/tuskegee/index.html

This site at the U.S. Centers for Disease Control and Prevention provides a timeline and information on the Tuskegee study.

Remarks by the President [Bill Clinton] in Apology for Study Done in Tuskege ....www.cdc.gov/tuskegee/clintonp.htm

Internet Research Ethics

American Association for the Advancement of Science (AAAS) Report
on Ethical and Legal Aspects of Human Subjects Research in Cyberspace www.aaas.org/sites/default/files/migrate/uploads/report2.pdf

This report of a 1999 workshop lists specific recommendations related to Internet research, ranging from setting up a website of sample informed consent forms to the possibility of special certification for online researchers.

Association of Internet Researchers (AoIR) ....http://aoir.org

The AoIR is a cross-disciplinary association of scholars and students and the source of the AoIR guide on ethical decision making and online research, at aoir.org/ethics.

Charting Ethical Questions by Data and Type—
a summary table to help decision making http://ethics.aoir.org/reports/2012aoirgraphic.pdf

The above site presents commonly asked ethical questions for different Internet contexts, such as special interest forums and avatar-based social spaces.

eResearch Ethics ....http://eresearch-ethics.org

This site is a source of papers and ongoing discussions about "e-research."

International Journal of Internet Research Ethics ....http://ijire.net

This cross-disciplinary journal publishes theoretical and practical articles on Internet research ethics.

O'Riordan, K. (2010). Internet research ethics: Revisiting the relations between
technologies, spaces, texts and people. *eResearch Ethics*................ http://eresearch-ethics.org/position/internet-research-ethics-
revisiting-the-relations-between-technologies-spaces-texts-
and-people/

Discusses the differences between the Internet as social text and as social space, and the notion that new media genres may not sit neatly under either the assumption of informed consent or the assumption that there are no human subjects.

REFERENCES

Frankel, M. S., & Siang, S. (1999). *Ethical and legal aspects of human subjects research on the Internet.* A report from the Scientific Freedom, Responsibility and Law Program, Directorate of Science and Policy Programs, American Association for the Advancement of Science, Washington, DC. Retrieved from http://www.aaas.org/sites/default/files/migrate/uploads/report2.pdf

Goel, V. (2014, August 12). As data overflows online, researchers grapple with ethics. *The New York Times.* Retrieved from http://www.nytimes.com/

Kozinets, R. V. (2013). *Netnography: Doing ethnographic research online.* London: Sage Publications.

Kramer, A. D. I. (2014, June 29). OK so. A lot of people have asked me about my and Jamie and Jeff's recent study published in PNAS, and I wanted to give a brief public explanation [Facebook post]. Retrieved from https://www.facebook.com/akramer/posts/10152987150867796

Lawson, D. (2004). Blurring the boundaries: Ethical considerations for online research using synchronous CMC forums. In E. Buchanan (Ed.), *Readings in virtual research ethics: Issues and controversies* (pp. 80–100). Hershey, PA: Information Science.

Markham, A., & Buchanan, E. (2012). *Ethical decision-making and Internet research: Recommendations from the AoIR ethics working committee* (Version 2.0). Retrieved from http://aoir.org/reports/ethics2.pdf

Thelwall, M. (2010, July 12). Researching the public web. *eResearch Ethics.* Retrieved from http://eresearch-ethics.org/position/researching-the-public-web/

U.S. Department of Health and Human Services. (2013, March 12–13). *Considerations and recommendations concerning Internet research and human subjects research regulations, with revisions.* Retrieved from http://www.hhs.gov/ohrp/sachrp/mtgings/2013%20March%20Mtg/internet_research.pdf

U.S. Department of Health and Human Services, Office for Human Research Protections, Office for Protection From Research Risks. (1993, March 16). *Tips on informed consent.* Retrieved from http://www.hhs.gov/ohrp/policy/ictips.html

U.S. Food and Drug Administration. (2014, June 25). *A guide to informed consent—Information sheet.* Retrieved from http://www.fda.gov/regulatoryinformation/guidances/ucm126431.htm#general

Ⓢ**SAGE** edge™

Want a better grade?

Get the tools you need to sharpen your study skills. Access practice quizzes, eFlashcards, video, and multimedia at **edge.sagepub.com/treadwell3e**

CHAPTER 4

You Could Look It Up
Reading, Recording, and Reviewing Research

In his student days, he had won several retrieval championships racing against the clock while digging out obscure items of information on lists prepared by ingeniously sadistic judges. ("What was the rainfall in the capital of the world's smallest national state on the day when the second-largest number of home runs was scored in college baseball?" was one that he recalled with particular affection.)

—Clarke, 1984, p. 136

Chapter Overview

All good research is built on a foundation of previous research. Reviewing and synthesizing this research is an essential start to any scholarly paper. Your review of the research literature should suggest research topics, ways of doing research, and most importantly how your proposed research will contribute to our collective understanding of human communication. Finding relevant information may be easy, but scholarly research requires that you prefer information that is credible as well as relevant. This chapter will help you identify the most credible sources of information and discusses how to search for them in a way that gets you the most relevant and credible results.

Chapter Objectives

This chapter will help you

- Explain why library research is a necessary preliminary to your own research.
- Illustrate the difference between relevant information and quality information.
- Describe with examples the difference between search engines and databases.
- Summarize the difference between scholarly, popular, and trade publications.
- List the differences between primary and secondary sources.

- Summarize the difference between search terms and search fields.

- Identify key questions you might ask to assess whether an item of information is credible.

- Discuss the concept of Boolean logic and its use in researching databases.

- Explain the purpose and nature of a scholarly literature review.

Library Research: Why Bother?

If I have seen further than other men it is by standing upon the shoulders of giants.

This quote, attributed to Sir Isaac Newton (1642–1727), the British physicist and mathematician, refers to his dependency on Galileo's and Kepler's previous work in physics and astronomy.

The purpose of any research is to add to knowledge. The operative word is *add*. Unless you know what has gone before, you cannot know if your research will add to knowledge or merely replicate what others have already done. You must know the past if you are to contribute to the future.

Knowing the published scholarly research in your area—or, in research jargon, "the literature"—will stimulate your own research, give you a broader vision of your field, suggest appropriate research methods, and show where your own research fits into the broader body of knowledge.

Once you know what has been researched, you will be able to assess what needs to be researched and be confident that your efforts will result in a further contribution to our knowledge of human communication. You will also be able to identify other people working in your area of interest, the research methods used, and the debates surrounding your interest area and how best to research it. By synthesizing and thinking about previous and current research in your field, you will be able to see much farther than you ever would have seen on your own.

In most cases, the place to find published relevant literature is your academic library—your one-stop shop for scholarly research reports. Academic libraries will also have other material such as newspaper and video archives of potential relevance to communication researchers. You may want to look at such resources to identify the breadth of material that may be relevant to you. Ultimately, though, you will want to focus on "the literature"—the published scholarly research that has been done to academic standards and is available most typically through the databases in academic libraries.

A thorough review of the scholarly literature will help you in the following specific areas.

Methods

Focus group or field interview? Ethnography or experiment? Your readings of the literature will identify accepted methods of research in your area of interest. A good review of the literature should also reveal methods that challenge conventional wisdom and the debates about how best to do the research that interests you.

Ethics

Most communication research is research on human subjects. As discussed in Chapter 3, how people are recruited, treated, and debriefed is important to them psychologically and to you professionally. The research literature can suggest how to ensure your research is conducted ethically.

Language and Style

Each research specialization is a community defined by its own language and way of writing. From your own readings, you will see the somewhat formulaic format that most research papers have and the language that typifies each subfield and its specific style for citations, abbreviations, and use of tables and graphics. Just as reading generally is a good way to develop your general vocabulary and writing skills, so reading research is a good way to develop your research vocabulary and writing skills.

Inspiration

An unpredictable but joyous outcome of a literature search is discovering that one great "breakthrough" paper that suddenly makes a difficult concept clear, shows precisely how to use a specific method, or takes you off in a whole new direction. You will know it when you see it. You may find it out of a random search, but a systematic, thorough search will maximize your chances of finding it.

In summary, a targeted, systematic search for relevant journal articles, books, and other media will have you "standing on the shoulders of giants and able to envisage your research project, how to go about it, and the contribution it will make to our collective understanding of human communication.

Finding Relevance, Finding Quality

We want two things from a literature search—relevance and quality. The two are not the same.

Relevant information is information that is immediately useful to you. Quality information is information that is credible, can be relied on, and, in the case of scholarly research, meets the standards of the research community. Information can be highly relevant but not of any academic quality, or it can be highly credible but irrelevant. For example, you may find that the *National Enquirer* has information about communication with extraterrestrials that is highly relevant to your interests but not of any scholarly merit. The *New England Journal of Medicine* publishes research that is highly credible but probably irrelevant to your interest in corporate rhetoric. The art and science of a good literature search is finding out how to overlap relevance and quality.

Identifying Relevant Information

"Out there" is a lot of information that will be highly relevant. There is also a significantly larger volume of information that is irrelevant. Example? Use *communication* as a **search term**, and you will get material on mass, group, interpersonal, and organizational communication. You will also get information on telecommunications, animal communication, and communication with extraterrestrials. If your interest is in, say, rhetoric and public address, you will drown in information you don't need even though it all relates to communication.

The strategy of the search for relevance is simple. You want to find all relevant information—only. You do not want to find irrelevant information, and you do not want to miss relevant information.

In communication research, this can be difficult because many other fields ranging from evolutionary psychology and web design to computer systems and marketing could be relevant to your interests. One key to obtaining relevant information is to develop a good vocabulary and to appreciate the difference in results that different search terms may bring. For example, *groups* and *teams*, though similar in concept, may produce quite different results when used as search terms.

Identifying Quality Information

Quality information means information that has been obtained in a way that meets scholarly standards. These standards include a clear, defensible, ethical research design, data collection methods and analyses that logically fit the research design, and results and conclusions that make an original contribution to our understanding of communication. Academic journals put all the research reports they receive through a process of peer review or **refereeing**. A refereed article is one that has been reviewed or refereed by other researchers in the author's field (peers) before being accepted for publication. Academic journals by definition contain refereed articles that meet scholarly standards; most other journals do not.

Scholarly Databases Versus Search Engines

Search Engines

Search engines such as Google, Yahoo, Bing, Lycos, and Dogpile are popular if for no other reason than their elegantly simple interfaces. A one-line box allows you to type in search terms and get results, usually far more than you can cope with. The pluses of search engines are ease of use, ease of access, and a simple interface. The minuses can be a totally unmanageable number of search results, many of questionable quality.

Search engines can be useful in giving you a sense of what's "out there" and what's popular. For example, the web resources listed at the end of this chapter include the Google Trends site, which allows you to monitor Google searches by topic area, by country, or by time period. This can be one way of accessing what is of current interest to Internet users, but any understanding of Internet users based on these rankings will obviously be superficial.

Databases

With the important caveat that not all scholarly and relevant research findings are online, the place to find scholarly research is scholarly **databases**, typically hosted by academic libraries.

Databases have a defined number of entries, and many databases consist of scholarly articles that have been peer reviewed. You will not get millions of irrelevant hits as the result of a search, and your research results should have a high level of credibility. You can automatically improve the quality of your search results simply by preferring databases to search engines. Proof? A search using the Google search engine for *communication* resulted in over one thousand million hits. Now look in the "All Fields" column of Exhibit 4.1, which shows the results of using different search terms in the scholarly database Communication & Mass Media Complete (CMMC). Just by preferring this database to Google, we reduced the number of hits for *communication* from millions down to about 230,000.

Databases are similar to phone directories in that a wrong search term or misspelling will give you the "wrong" results, or no results.

Exhibit 4.1 Focusing Search Results by Combining Search Terms and Search Fields

Search Terms	Search Fields		
	All Fields	Subject Search	Title Search
Communication	232,171	77,552	27,400
Communication in organizations	2,771	2,466	27
Communication in nonprofit organizations	5	5	2

Scholarly databases have more sophisticated interfaces than search engines. Their **search fields** allow you to search for an article by author, date of publication, title, subject matter, or any combination thereof, resulting in a much more targeted search. A well-executed database search should give you the results you want and none of the results you don't want.

Because different databases contain different content, you can make your search for relevant literature even more focused simply by selecting the most relevant database. For example, CMMC might be a good starting point for a literature review unless you are specifically interested in business communication, in which case a database such as Business Source Premier may be preferable.

Don't forget CIOS, the Communication Institute for Online Scholarship, introduced in Chapter 2. You can use a key word system, the Visual Communication Concept Explorer, or the Idea Monkey to get started on your research project.

By combining relevant academic databases with a focus on refereed articles, you can maximize your chances of getting relevant, quality search results. Two cautions are in order, though. First, you should not restrict yourself to refereed journals exclusively. Books, news media, and websites may all be relevant—especially, perhaps, in communication research. Second, communication studies are wide ranging. You may find the articles you need in political science, international affairs, psychology, journalism, or business databases. Your initial searches will require both a broad vision and a narrow focus.

Again, with a reminder that not all relevant scholarly information is necessarily online, you should be able to optimize your research results simply by preferring specific search terms in a scholarly database to general search terms in a search engine.

Scholarly Journals: A Good Starting Point

Scholarly journals will give you a more specific start on a search because most of them focus on a specific area of interest. Once you find one issue of a journal with a high percentage of articles that are relevant to you, you may well find that other issues of the same journal will also have relevant content.

Communication Research could be a good general starting point because it reports research in a variety of fields.

More focused sources might include, for example,

Journal of Applied Communication Research, if you are interested in applying research in a campus or workplace setting;

Critical Studies in Media Communication, if you are interested in communication as an expression of power; or

Convergence: The International Journal of Research Into New Media Technologies, if you are interested in social media.

Revisit Chapter 1 for a nonexhaustive list of communication journals you might select as a starting point for your literature review.

Assessing Scholarly Journals

One way to assess scholarly journals is to look at each journal's **impact factor**. In essence, the impact factor is a measure of the number of times the articles in a journal are cited by other scholarly articles. An impact factor of two would indicate that, on average, the articles in a journal were cited twice by other authors; a factor of three indicates that on average the articles were cited three times. The impact factor is the subject of debate, as with any such **metric**, but journals with a high impact factor can be regarded at least as publishing articles that are influential in their field.

The impact factor is, of course, irrelevant if the journal's content is irrelevant to your interests. Given two journals covering essentially the same interest area, though, you may decide to focus on the one with the higher impact factor.

Examples of sites that list journal impact factors or allow you to search for them are listed under "Recommended Web Resources" at the end of this chapter.

Scholarly, Popular, and Trade Publications: What Is the Difference?

What is the difference between scholarly and popular material? **Scholarly articles** go through a process of peer review before publication. Peer review means that before journal editors will accept an article for publication, they will seek the opinions of other scholars doing the same kind of research as the author of the article. These reviewers read the article to determine whether the research has been done to professional standards, that the article makes a contribution to knowledge, and that there are no apparent ethical violations such as plagiarism.

How Will I Know a Scholarly Article When I See One?

The title *Journal of . . .* is one good clue but does not automatically flag a journal as refereed. Another clue is the format of the article. If you see headings such as "Abstract," "Method," and "Literature Review" and a list of references at the end of the article, there is a good chance that the article is refereed. Frequency of publication is also a clue. Refereed publications are typically quarterly, perhaps monthly, but not daily or weekly.

By contrast, **popular articles** are published without a refereeing process, typically in daily or weekly media, and are targeted to a lay audience. They do not have the formal subheadings noted above or a list of references as scholarly articles do. Newspaper and magazine stories are typical examples of popular articles.

Between these two extremes are the so-called **trade publications**. Trade publication articles, like academic articles, are written by experts, but the experts are more likely to be practitioners than academics and their articles are not usually peer reviewed or refereed.

Articles in the trade press are more topical than academic articles because they appear daily, weekly, or monthly and do not get held up by a review process. However, information important to you as a researcher such as a literature review, method description, and references will not be included.

One reason to prefer scholarly, refereed journals and books is that they give you access to primary (original) research. Popular and trade articles may give you a summary of other authors, but you will need to go to scholarly sources to read what the original author wrote. Scholarly articles always provide **citations** ("cites") at the end of the article to let you find out what their sources wrote. Popular and trade articles do not do this; you have to accept what one author is telling you about other authors.

Primary Versus Secondary Sources

A **primary source** is an original article; a **secondary source** is another author's summary of the primary source. Consider the two articles referenced below on "sexting." If you go to the first, the primary source, you will find that it is several pages in length and has the subheadings typical of scholarly research papers—"Abstract," "Methods," "Results," "Discussion," "Conclusions," and "References." By contrast, the second article, from *The New York Times*, is a secondary source. It summarizes the 10-page primary source in a relatively short newspaper column with no subheadings. (Both articles appear at the end of this chapter in the list of references.)

Prevalence and Characteristics of Youth Sexting: A National Study

Kimberly J. Mitchell, David Finkelhor, Lisa M. Jones and Janis Wolak
Pediatrics 2012;129;13; originally published online December 5, 2011;
DOI: 10.1542/peds.2011–1730

Sending of Sexual Images by Minors Isn't as Prevalent as Expected, Study Finds

By ANAHAD O'CONNOR

Published: December 5, 2011

Note that the secondary source gets right to the point with the heading "Sending of Sexual Images by Minors Isn't as Prevalent as Expected" because the author is summarizing the essence of the primary source as far as possible.

Secondary sources may be credible, as with the *New York Times* article shown above, or, from a research point of view, have no credibility whatsoever. What all secondary sources have in common is that they summarize other people's research. They therefore omit detail that other researchers may need if they are to fully understand the research as well as specific details that the original authors might have wanted published in order for an audience to fully understand their work.

Secondary sources can be a quick way to get an overview of research, but making your own summary based on secondary sources is a bad idea because your summary of the summaries can magnify any biases and misinterpretations in the secondary sources. You can use secondary sources as a starting point, but as a professional, scholarly researcher, you will want and need to go to the primary sources and write your own summaries of this research.

Search Strategies: General to Specific and Specific to General

Often, your **bibliographic** research will take the profile of a champagne glass, as shown in Exhibit 4.2. You start with a wide-ranging search and a large number of search results. You then narrow down your findings to a few highly relevant sources whose reference lists then provide a larger number of relevant sources.

EXHIBIT 4.2   **The Champagne Glass Model of Bibliographic Research**

(1) Wide-ranging findings from your initial search

should lead you to

(2) very specific

citations,

which

generate

(3) still more highly relevant readings.

On the other hand, you may start by finding or being assigned one "breakthrough" article that summarizes the history of a topic, explains how to research it, and inspires you to research it further. From the citations in that one article, or by searching a relevant database for the author, you will be able to generate a bigger set of relevant readings.

Search Terms and Search Fields

Search terms are the logical start to a search. They are also an exercise in using your vocabulary to expand or refine your search, for example trying the search term *virtual world* or *hyperreality* if the term *fantasy world* does not produce credible results.

Another way to expand or refine a search is to use the search fields in scholarly databases. Typically, you will be able to search by name of author, title of article, subject, and many other fields. You can search for these alone or in combination. The results for any given search term will vary according to whether you do a general search of the database or restrict the search to the title or the subject of articles.

Subject terms such as *health communication* are assigned by authors and publishers to help the search process. They are important because they help locate an article in an area of interest but are not necessarily words that appear in the title. Think of a title as the name or label of an article. The subject is what the article is about, so a subject search will capture more articles than a title search because it is less specific and is likely to be a better starting point for a search.

An example of combining search terms and search fields to get more and more specific is shown in Exhibit 4.1. Note how selecting a specific search field such as "Subject" or "Title" makes a difference in search results. The "All Fields" column of the exhibit shows how the number of results becomes smaller as the search term becomes more and more specific.

You can see from Exhibit 4.1 that a general search using a broad search term such as *communication* produces an unmanageable number of results. On the other hand, the very specific search term *communication in nonprofit organizations* in a title search produced only two scholarly articles. The five results from using this search term in a search of all fields in the CMMC database were

- Two conference papers given at annual meetings of the International Communication Association.
- An article from the serial publication *Communication Arts* on the design and printing of nonprofit publications.
- Two scholarly journal articles, cited below, that together list 73 references. If you had a specific interest in nonprofit communications, this search would give you 73 immediately relevant references, at least according to these articles:

When the "Stakes" are Communicative.

By: Lewis, Laurie K.; Richardson, Brian K.; Hamel, Stephanie A. Human Communication Research. Jul2003, Vol. 29 Issue 3, p400. 31p. 6 Charts.

Subjects: COMMUNICATION; STOCKHOLDERS; NONPROFIT organizations; ORGANIZATIONAL change; STOCKS (Finance)

Discourse, Identity, and Power in International Nonprofit Collaborations.

By: Murphy, Alexandra G.; Dixon, Maria A. Management Communication Quarterly. Feb2012, Vol. 26 Issue 1, p166–172. 7p. DOI: 10.1177/0893318911424374.

Subjects: FIRST person narrative; UGANDA; KENYA; GROUP identity; POWER (Social sciences); NONPROFIT organizations

Obviously, some judgment is required here; two seems a suspiciously small number of results. A search that is too specific may be "overfocused" and miss articles that might have been relevant to your interests.

Note that the above citations are reproduced from the original search result. They are not formatted in the American Psychological Association (APA) style frequently used to cite communication research materials. Also, the examples presuppose that we were looking for scholarly articles. Scholarly databases may also let you search for other types of material such as editorials; books, or magazines; or nontext resources such as photographs, maps, and graphs.

How Can the Library of Congress Help My Literature Search?

The answer is subject headings. You will want to be familiar with Library of Congress (LOC) Subject Headings. The source is a standard reference item in academic libraries. The subject headings show you how information is categorized by the LOC, but more to the point, they give you alternative search terms and perhaps a reminder of how your own vocabulary can limit or expand your search. To use the LOC's own example (n.d.):

> If you search the Library's online catalog for the keywords "battered women," you find more than one hundred entries and may be perfectly satisfied. But by not identifying the Library's correct subject headings—"Abused women," "Abused wives," and "Wife abuse"—you may miss the best materials for your topic. A search combining these three terms yields more than one thousand records.

In other words, thinking of alternative words to *women* and to *battered* can substantially multiply the number of relevant "hits" you get.

Other Resources

Journals, books, and databases are not the only resources available. Other resources include catalogs, dictionaries, encyclopedias, indexes, annuals, yearbooks, handbooks, and abstracts. Some of these are listed as resources at the end of this chapter.

How to Be Skeptical About Information, Especially Web Information

Your initial search results may vary in quality between refereed journal articles and web sources of extremely variable quality. When anyone with a website can post to the world the "fact" that his or her parents were Martians, a touch of skepticism is required in evaluating websites. The following questions will help you identify good scholarship in web as well as print formats.

Stage 1: Think Book or Journal

Ask of the website the same questions you would ask of a book or journal.

- Author's credentials (e.g., Prof., Dr., PhD, MD)
- Author's affiliation (e.g., university, college, corporation, think tank)
- Date of publication and edition or revision

Remember that a book that has been frequently reprinted and is now into its 20th edition may have scholarly credibility or may simply be popular.

- Publisher

University presses and academic associations are academically respectable, as are academic publishers. This does not mean that their books and journals are unbiased; it means merely that there is a level of credible scholarship behind them.

- Title

"Lost tribes of Israel found at South Pole" versus "Conceptualizing and assessing organizational image: Model images, commitment, and communication" will give you some clue as to academic credibility.

- Intended audience

From the style of writing (word and sentence length and language), you will be able to guess at the intended audience and also whether the author's intent is persuasive or informative.

- Objectivity–subjectivity. What biases can you discover?
- Coverage—comprehensive or selective?
- Writing style—popular, technical, or academic?
- Reviews (if any). Use the name of the author or title of the article as search terms; you may pick up reviews of the article that will give you some critical insight on it.
- Citations. What references (credible or otherwise) are drawn on by the author(s)?

Stage 2: Additional Questions for Websites

- What does the URL tell you? Is it .com, .edu, .org, .mil, .gov, or another extension?
- Does the site tell you the criteria by which information is accepted or rejected? Does it accept all contributions, or is there some review process?
- What people or organization wrote the page? Do they have demonstrable expertise? Note that *expert* does not have to mean *unbiased*. We expect the XYZ company's website to be an authoritative source of information on XYZ products and predictably biased toward them.
- Could the page be a satire or comedic? It doesn't happen often in academia, but it does happen. Check out the *Journal of Irreproducible Results* by way of example (www.jir.com).
- Is contact information provided?
- Can you verify what is said or shown on the website? If not, it is academically suspect.
- Are documents in the site dated, and when was the site last updated?
- Comparable sites: If you do a web search for sites with a similar name, URL, or content, what is the quality of the information you get?

Many library websites demonstrate with examples how to distinguish quality sites from the more suspect ones. Some of these are listed at the end of this chapter.

Mr. Boole and the Three Bears

One way to reduce the number of search results to something manageable is to ask the right combination of questions.

George Boole (1815–1864), an English mathematician, invented a type of linguistic algebra, the three most basic operations of which are AND, OR, and NOT. The relevance of these "**Boolean operators**" is this. Suppose you were unwise enough to use the search term *communication* in a search. As we have seen, you would likely drown in the number of largely irrelevant results, even from a database. You might similarly drown in the results of using the term *Smith* for an author search. But if you search for "*communication* AND *Smith*" you will reduce the number of results significantly. Similarly, "*communication* OR *telecommunication*" will expand your search results if you need to, and "*communication* NOT *telecommunication*" will narrow your search.

Exhibit 4.3 demonstrates the use of Boolean operators on a search of the CMMC database using all fields. You can see that combining search terms with the AND operator can reduce the number of search results significantly.

EXHIBIT 4.3   **Use of Boolean Search Terms**

Search Term	Number of Results
communication	232,236
feminist	3,228
Search Term Combinations	
communication OR *feminist*	234,044
communication NOT *feminist*	230,816
communication AND *feminist*	1,510

As with the story of Goldilocks and the three bears, literature searches can produce results that are too big, too small, or just right. Mr. Boole's operators can help you fine-tune a search to "just right."

Saving Your Search Results

Ways of recording your search results include pen and paper, dumping everything to print or "flash drive," bookmarking websites, and using citation management software, discussed below. Saving search results electronically saves trees and makes sense because you will record citations accurately and you can edit your saved content as necessary for your literature review. Note, however, that recording citations accurately does not necessarily mean that you will be recording them in the style that you will need for writing your report. Most scholarly databases will allow you to select the style in which you want citations saved (APA, Chicago, or MLA), and you should check for this option. Old-fashioned pen and paper still are helpful because they allow you to sketch out and visualize relationships that may be important in your search, as well as summarize details that are important to you.

Information You Must Record

Record *full* bibliographic information. Bibliographic information is information that uniquely identifies a specific book, journal or newspaper article, website, or specific quotation so that your readers can immediately locate it. For print media, bibliographic information includes the following items. Make sure to record them all; you will need them for your literature review and list of references at the end of your research report.

- Author—full name. Note that APA citation style uses author first initials and last name; other styles use the author's full first name. Play it safe and record full names initially so that you have them if you need them. Keep in mind that other citation styles may use first names, so it is always better to record first names than not.
- Title of book, or of article and journal in which it appears.
- Date of publication, and volume and issue number if a journal.
- Edition, if a book.
- Page numbers that locate a journal article in a periodical.
- Page numbers that locate any direct quote that you wish to reproduce from a book or periodical.
- For websites, additionally record the URL (web address), the **DOI** (digital object identifier) if available, and the date you downloaded the information. Style guides are becoming less insistent on reporting the download date for documents because the DOI or URL will adequately identify many Internet resources. For example, the article on sexting from the journal *Pediatrics* has its own DOI. When appended to http://dx.doi.org/ in the address bar of an Internet browser, the DOI will lead to the source document or object.

Information You Should Record

The information that you should record is in some respects the information that most interests you. It is the information that explains why and how the research was done and the results and conclusions from the research.

In addition to author, title, and publication details, you will typically want to record the following:

- Method—how the research was conducted
- Results and conclusions—the results of and conclusions from the research

Results are the qualitative or quantitative new information generated by the research. Conclusions are how the researcher opts to interpret that information.

- Participants and/or media content—who or what (in the case of critical analyses or content analyses) was studied
- Unique aspects of the study—what is special about it

Exhibit 4.4 shows one possible design for summarizing and recording the results of your searches. The example is based on an interest in searching for research on news media bias.

When starting your search, you might prefer to use such headings until you have a more specific sense of the headings you will need to best summarize your findings. Setting up the form as shown in Exhibit 4.4 or your own version as a table or a database will allow you to sort your records by author, date, or title and search for words just as you would in an online database search. Many database services allow you to build your own portfolio of search results online and to format the results of your research in a particular scholarly style, such as APA.

Bookmarking articles and websites is another way to organize and retain information although that process provides no summary of the information you have identified. For some people, handwritten notes of the type shown in Exhibit 4.4 are helpful because the writing process helps them think about the content of the material and its implications. Others find that an effective way of summarizing information is to type their research notes into a personally constructed database and to flag their own searchable key words for easy retrieval.

EXHIBIT 4.4   **One Way to Summarize Your Bibliographic Research**

Title	Author(s)	Publication Details
Objective Evidence on Media Bias: Newspaper Coverage of Congressional Party Switchers	Niven, David	*Journalism & Mass Communication Quarterly*; Summer 2003, Vol. 80, Issue 2, pp. 311–326. From CMMC database, March 27, 2015.

Summary

Examined newspaper articles on congressional party switchers or members who left their political party in midterm, in order to find objective evidence on media bias. Basically found Democrats and Republicans who leave their parties get very similar coverage.

Method

Looked at newspaper coverage of four members of congress (Democratic and Republican) who switched parties. Examined coverage of the members beginning 7 days before they switched and for 30 days after they switched. Analysis based on coders' estimate of the "tone" (positive or negative) of newspaper paragraphs.

Participants and/or Media Content

Newspapers from Nexis major newspapers database and from politicians' home states.

Results/Conclusions

When Democrats and Republicans engage in the same behavior, they get the same media coverage. No support for claim of liberal pro-Democratic bias in newspaper coverage.

My Notes/Unique Aspects of Study

Looks exactly like what I want. Presents an objective basis for studying bias, although still depends on coders' judgments. Content analysis good idea—more objective than interviewing journalists about bias. Should also look for interviews with news professionals to find out *why* editorial or journalistic bias might occur. Follow up on the citations in this article.

Typically, resources such as scholarly databases will allow you to set up a personal file in which you can collect selected resources at the click of a "save" button. Often you will be able to save your search history, which is useful in reviewing what combination of search terms did or did not work for you and which journals provided the most relevant content. An important bonus for many users is the ability to view and save the citation for any article in the scholarly style you need— APA, MLA, or Chicago, for example. Online tools may or may not let you record your own notes and interpretations of what you are reading. Ensuring you have some mechanism that lets you record your own notes is therefore essential.

Citation Management Software

Citation management software lets you organize and retrieve citations for books, articles, websites, and the like, by interfacing with library databases. The software can then work with word processing software to insert properly formatted citations into your paper and create a properly formatted reference list. Examples include EndNote, Mendeley, RefWorks, and Zotero. You can find out more about each of these from the websites listed at the end of this chapter.

Reviewing the Literature

It is useful to make a distinction between reviewing the literature and the literature review. Reviewing the literature is the process by which you get from a perhaps mind-numbingly large number of relevant scholarly materials to a final product—a literature review.

Reviewing the literature means assessing the results of your literature search item by item and deciding which items will be in your literature review and what you will write about each item. This means assessing each of your search results for its theoretical and methodological relevance to your research question and its importance with respect to the other items in your search results. Exhibit 4.5 shows the questions an investigative journalist might ask when reading a research report. They will help you to assess scholarly literature and develop your own sense of what articles are credible and relevant to your own needs.

EXHIBIT 4.5   Reviewing Scholarly Literature as Investigative Journalism

General Question	Specific Questions	Why Ask?
WHO	did the research?	A literature search using the author(s) names may generate more relevant articles. Authors' credentials and institutional affiliations provide clues to credibility of the research.
	was researched?	The number and nature of the research participants will indicate the sampling strategy and whether the research was done with a large sample with a view to making generalizations or small sample and focused more on in-depth understanding.
	published the research?	University, think tank, interest group, advocacy group, commercial organization, or political party? The publisher provides clues to credibility, expertise, and possible bias of the study.
WHAT	was researched?	For communication content studies, the media, the content, and how they were selected and analyzed will provide insight on the generalizability of the findings and the researcher(s)' theoretical framework.
	were the results?	Qualitative, quantitative, empirical, critical, generalizable? The nature of the results reported, independent of the specific findings, provides insight on the assumptions behind the research.
WHEN	was the research done?	The date of the research tells you whether you are looking at current research, research that may be outdated because of advances in the field, or a "classic" well worth reading and reviewing even though dated.
	was the research published?	Many scholarly journals publish their articles' editorial histories. The time between the date of acceptance and the date of publication of an article may indicate whether the original paper needed substantial revision or had questionable content that required further research to clarify.
WHERE	was the research done?	This question should have you thinking generalizability. For example, would research done in a college classroom be generalizable to a factory workforce or a military setting?

General Question	Specific Questions	Why Ask?
WHY	was the research done?	To test a theory? Explore a new concept? Solve a marketing problem? Thinking about the "why" question may help identify bias and strengths and weaknesses in the study.
HOW	was the research done?	This is basically a method question—focus group, survey, ethnography, observation, data mining? Answering the "how" question will give you insight on the assumptions behind the research. In the case of human subjects research, you should also get insight into the ethical standards influencing the research.
	important is this research, theoretically and methodologically?	Relative to other articles, does this paper stand out in terms of helping you theorize about a research topic or design a research project?
HOW WELL	was the research done?	Answering all of the above questions will help you decide whether the research merits inclusion in your literature review, and what and how much you need to write about it.

The Literature Review: Writing Your Search Results

You are now poised to write your literature review—your organized synthesis, analysis, critique, and summary of the literature most relevant to your research. This means turning your bibliographic notes into a summary and review of relevant literature that will convince readers that your own research is built on a sound theoretical foundation and will advance our comprehension of human communication.

A literature review may be very brief or constitute an entire paper, the purpose of which is to capture the history and current status of a discipline or a research method.

Generally, a literature review is a prelude to a research report. When you come to write up your research, your readers will first want to know your justification for doing the research and how it contributes to existing knowledge. In both cases, this means summarizing your search results in the form of a literature review.

The literature review is more than a summary of the relevant literature; it is also your assessment of each article and its significance. A well-written literature review will support your own research while at the same time demonstrating gaps in our knowledge, some of which your own research demonstrably will fill. The literature review is just one part of a research proposal or a research report, but it is an essential part in that it should lead readers to understand that the methods you have used or propose to use are appropriate to your research question and that the results of using those methods do indeed contribute to our knowledge of human communication.

Structuring the Literature Review

There are several ways to structure a literature review.

Many reviews are written as a history; that is, they describe and evaluate selected research reports in order from oldest to most recent. This gives the reader a sense of how thinking about the topic has changed over time.

If there is little consensus among scholars, a review might be written with a "pro–con" structure, analyzing where the research articles agree and disagree and then coming to a conclusion. You could, for example, base your review on method, discussing all the studies that were done as surveys and all those done as experiments and then coming to conclusions about why your proposed method will be the most appropriate to answer your research question.

Most likely you will use one of the above two structures for your literature review, but other structures are possible. For example, a study of censorship internationally might be prefaced by a literature review that reviews current research country by country rather than chronologically or with a pro–con structure.

Questions of Style

Scholarly papers have specific ways of setting out information or styles that clearly mark them as scholarly and not as trade or popular publications. The most common style in the social sciences is **APA** (American Psychological Association) style, the style used in this book for formatting references. Two others that you may encounter are **Chicago** and **MLA** (Modern Language Association).

All styles agree on the requirement for specific subheadings that flag the literature review, research method(s), results, discussion, conclusions, and a listing of other people's work. They also all insist on consistency of language and style so that readers are not confused and on accurate citation so that readers can easily find the cited works.

For specifics of APA style, see the APA style resources listed at the end of this chapter under "APA, Chicago, and MLA Style Guides." You should consult the websites and stylebooks available in any academic library for specific guidance in all three styles.

Use the checklist shown in Exhibit 4.6 to help ensure that your literature review meets scholarly standards.

Exhibit 4.6   Literature Review Questions

1. Does your review:

   - Explain how your readings agree and disagree?
   - Identify gaps in our knowledge of human communication?
   - Summarize the current status of research on the topic being reviewed?

2. Does your review have a logical structure that helps the reader understand it?

3. Does your review set the scene for readers to understand that a logical next step would be one or more of the following?

   - Test a hypothesis.
   - Describe or explain a phenomenon.
   - Develop a critical insight.
   - Replicate previous research in a different setting.
   - Explore a new research method or combination of methods.

4. Are all the reviewed articles cited accurately in an appropriate scholarly style?

Ethics Panel: Politics and Publication

In July 2009, *The New York Times* revealed that officials at the National Highway Traffic Safety Administration had withheld hundreds of pages of research about the hazards of using cell phones while driving (Richtel, 2009).

Critics say that this decision cost lives and has allowed a culture of driving while multitasking to blossom. Research suggests that motorists talking on a phone are four times as likely to crash as other drivers (Richtel, 2009). We might therefore wonder why this research was not released in a more timely fashion.

There appear to be two answers. First, the then head of the agency was apparently urged to withhold the research to avoid antagonizing members of Congress who did not want the agency lobbying states about legislative solutions to the problem. Second, the research data were considered preliminary rather than conclusive.

This story reminds us that not all research data on human communication can be found within academic libraries. Such data may also be found in businesses and government agencies. More to the point, the story raises important ethical questions.

Are there circumstances under which control of research publication by political, academic, or corporate institutions is justified? If so, what are they?

Can research ever be "final"? For example, in communication research, at what point could a researcher recommend with absolute confidence that action video games not be sold to children under a certain age?

CHAPTER SUMMARY

Library research, well done, will guide you on

- What other researchers in your field have discovered
- Research methods
- Research ethics
- Language and style

You should know:

- The difference between databases and search engines
- The difference between primary and secondary sources
- The difference between scholarly, trade, and popular publications
- How to focus your library research by using appropriate databases, search terms, and search techniques
- The basics of formatting and style for scholarly papers

KEY TERMS

APA

bibliographic

Boolean operators

Chicago

citations

databases

DOI	refereeing
impact factor	scholarly articles
literature	search fields
metric	search term
MLA	secondary source
popular articles	trade publications
primary source	

APPLICATION EXERCISES

Exercise 1: APA Style

Under the heading "Primary Versus Secondary Sources" above, locate the referenced article "Prevalence and Characteristics of Youth Sexting" taken from the journal *Pediatrics*. Rewrite the citation so that it conforms to APA style.

Exercise 2: Comparing Primary and Secondary Sources

Locate the original *Pediatrics* and *New York Times* articles on sexting cited above under the heading "Primary Versus Secondary Sources." Carefully compare these two articles and answer the following questions:

- What information in the original *Pediatrics* article is missing from the *New York Times* article? What content, if any, in the *New York Times* article cannot be found in the *Pediatrics* article?
- Assuming the *New York Times* article is written to help and inform parents, what writing techniques can you identify that are used to interest and motivate such readers and maintain their interest?

Exercise 3: Search Terms and Boolean Operators

Write down all of the search terms you might use to get a comprehensive listing of scholarly papers on social media. Combine these search terms using Boolean operators to then focus your research on

- Social media and youth
- Social media and romantic relationships
- Social media and public relations

Note that this is not just an exercise in Boolean operators; it is also an exercise in vocabulary. For example, *social media* may prove to be too broad a search term. What terms other than *social media* could you use to narrow your search? Note also that *youth*, *romantic*, and *public relations* all have analogous terms that might give you better or worse search results. For each of these three terms, identify an alternative word or words that you might substitute to narrow or expand your search.

Exercise 4: Writing a Literature Review

Search the Pew Research Center Internet, Science & Tech Project website—www.pewinternet.org—for the topic "elections and campaigns." You will find a series of reports on U.S. elections for the years 2000 through 2015. Write a brief literature review summarizing how the role of the Internet and social media in U.S. elections has changed since 2000. Cite all sources correctly using APA style. For most years, you will find several different reports, so you will need to be selective in your reading and writing.

RECOMMENDED READING

Communication Yearbook

An annual review of communication research, published by the International Communication Association. The series provides in-depth articles on research on such aspects of communication as interpersonal, health, organizational, intercultural, international, technology, politics, and rhetoric.

Cull, N. J., Culbert, C., & Welch, D. (2003). *Propaganda and mass persuasion: A historical encyclopedia, 1500 to the present.* Santa Barbara, CA: ABC-CLIO.

Surveys key propaganda campaigns, people, concepts, techniques, and current research.

Danesi, M. (2000). *Encyclopedic dictionary of semiotics, media, and communications.* Toronto, ON: University of Toronto Press.

Describes the terms, concepts, personages, schools of thought, and historical movements related to these fields.

Lievrouw, L. A., & Livingstone, S. (Eds.). (2009). *New media.* Thousand Oaks, CA: Sage.

Covers historical, economic, social, and behavioral issues related to new media.

Rubin, R. B., Rubin, A. M., & Haridakis, P. M. (2010). *Communication research: Strategies and sources* (7th ed.). Belmont, CA: Wadsworth.

This book will help you learn library research skills, scholarly writing, and the basics of APA style.

The above resources provide an overview of some key areas in communication. Use your own academic library to find more specialized resources such as *Broadcasting and Cable Yearbook* or the *Handbook of Political Communication Research*.

RECOMMENDED WEB RESOURCES

Academic Serials in Communication . . . . www.ascus.info

Academic Serials in Communication—Unified System (ASCUS) is a not-for-profit, society-governed, full-text database of academic publications in communication. ASCUS is a collaboration between academics, societies, and publishers in which content is widely distributed at low cost.

American Psychological Association . . . . www.apa.org

Provides insights and resources on psychological aspects of human communication and on APA style.

The Electronic Journal of Communication . . . . www.cios.org/www/ejcmain.htm

One of the first peer-reviewed and electronically distributed scholarly journals.

Library of Congress Subject Headings . . . . www.loc.gov/catdir/cpso/lcco

This site shows the Library of Congress' classification outline. Clicking on any category will show you potential search terms in that category.

Voice of the Shuttle: Media Studies . . . . http://vos.ucsb.edu

Provides annotated links to resources in media theory and theorists, media histories, TV, film/video, new media, popular music, journalism, radio, comics, telecom issues, consumerism and advertising, censorship, journals, and departments, programs, and professional associations (Alan Liu, University of California, Santa Barbara).

APA, Chicago, and MLA Style Guides

APA style resources . . . . www.apastyle.org

Chicago style . . . . www.chicagomanualofstyle.org/home.html

MLA style . . . . www.mla.org/style

Evaluating Websites

Cornell University "Evaluating Web Sites: Criteria and Tools" . . . . http://olinuris.library.cornell.edu/ref/research/webeval.html

New Mexico State University Library "Evaluation Criteria" . . . . http://lib.nmsu.edu/instruction/evalcrit.html

Purdue University "Evaluating Print vs. Internet Sources" http://owl.english.purdue.edu/owl/resource/553/04/

Citation Management Software

EndNote . . . . http://endnote.com

Mendeley . . . . www.mendeley.com

RefWorks . . . . www.refworks.com

Zotero . . . . www.zotero.org

Journal Impact Sites

CiteFactor . . . . www.citefactor.org

Impact Factor Search . . . . www.impact-factor.org

Miscellaneous

Code of Ethics of the American Library Association . . . . www.ala.org/advocacy/ proethics/codeofethics/codeethics

What Is Everybody Else Searching For?

You can find out the most popular nonacademic search terms by time, category, or country at www.google/trends.

REFERENCES

Clarke, A. C. (1984). *The fountains of paradise.* New York, NY: Ballantine Books.

Library of Congress. (n.d.). *The library's catalogs.* Retrieved from http://memory.loc.gov/ammem/awhhtml/awsearchcat.html

Mitchell, K. J., Finkelhor, D., Jones, L. M., & Wolak, J. (2011). Prevalence and characteristics of youth sexting: A national study. *Pediatrics, 129*(1), 13–20. doi:10.1542/peds.2011–1730.

O'Connor, A. (2011, December 5). Sending of sexual images by minors isn't as prevalent as expected, study finds. *New York Times.* Retrieved from http://www.nytimes.com

Richtel, M. (2009, July 20). U.S. withheld data on risks of distracted driving. *New York Times.* Retrieved from http://www.nytimes.com

⑤SAGE edge™

Want a better grade?

Get the tools you need to sharpen your study skills. Access practice quizzes, eFlashcards, video, and multimedia at **edge.sagepub.com/treadwell3e**

CHAPTER 5

Measurement
Research Using Numbers

I often say that when you can measure what you are speaking about, and express it in numbers, you know something about it; but when you cannot measure it, when you cannot express it in numbers, your knowledge is of a meagre and unsatisfactory kind.

Lord Kelvin (William Thomson, 1st Baron) (1824–1907), English physicist and mathematician, in *Popular Lectures and Addresses*, Vol. I (London, 1889, p. 73)

❧ ❧ ❧

Chapter Overview

This chapter introduces quantitative approaches to the study of human communication. If we are to have faith in research numbers, however obtained, they must measure what they are supposed to measure (validity) and do so consistently (reliability). This chapter introduces these two important concepts; the nominal, ordinal, interval, and ratio levels of measurement; and two scales commonly used in communication research—the Likert and semantic differential scales.

Chapter Objectives

This chapter will help you

- Discuss the concept of measurement and its use in communication research.

- Differentiate, with examples, nominal, ordinal, interval, and ratio measurement.

- Explain the concepts of validity and reliability.

- Identify ways of assessing reliability.

- Identify ways of assessing validity.

- Compare and contrast, with examples, Likert and semantic differential scales.

What Do Your Head Size, Attitudes, and Readability Have in Common?

Nineteenth-century **phrenologists** argued that there was a relationship between cranial size and shape and mental attributes such as, perhaps, the ability to comprehend language or mathematical concepts. After all, if you have a big head, you must be brainy, right? Twenty-first-century wisdom rejects such a connection, but head size, readability, and attitudes do have one thing in common. They have all been subject to measurement, the focus of this chapter.

As we will see in Chapter 11, Lord Kelvin's quote at the beginning of this chapter is open to refutation by qualitative researchers, but most of us have an intuitive sense that measuring and assigning numbers to phenomena are good ways to make sense of the world even if numbers perhaps leave us short of fully understanding it. Think of the numbers in your life. Vehicles are advertised on the basis of miles per gallon. Committees make decisions on a "six for; two against" basis. Academic careers and financial aid are predicated on such numbers as grade point average (GPA) and GRE and SAT scores. Broadcast programs live or die on audience share and ratings. Politicians live or die on approval ratings, opinion polls, and of course the vote count. Web advertisers count click-throughs. You buy clothes and shoes based on a measurable body size. And then, of course, there's hang time, yardage, RBIs, assists, and handicaps.

Assigning numbers to things seems to lend precision to an imprecise world and is of course the basis of all statistical analysis.

This chapter discusses **measurement** as it is understood in communication research. To begin with, a couple of definitions:

- **Numerals** are labels. On their own, "13," "2013," and "64" are not numbers but labels for phenomena. They could be street addresses, a brand name, a commuter jet, or a cologne.
- **Numbers** assign value and relativity to phenomena. For example, the numbers 1 through 5 indicate increasing levels of agreement with a statement where people are asked to rate their agreement on a scale where 1 = strongly disagree and 5 = strongly agree. As an age, "64" signifies that someone has been on this earth longer than someone who is "13."

Numbers give us the ability to make accurate discriminations and to generalize. That ability is important when trying to decide whether there are "real" differences between groups. For example, a survey shows that 48% of a group of women and 52% of a group of men prefer candidate X. Can we assume that in the wider voting population candidate X would win the male vote and lose the female vote, or is there a probability that both groups are much the same in their attitudes?

Numbers and statistical methods can allow us to generalize with varying levels of confidence. Intuitively, if the above groups consisted of 10 men and 10 women, we would have some difficulty predicting the outcome of a national election. If the groups were each 100 people, we would feel more confident, and if 1,000 people, perhaps more confident still. Statistical calculations, as we will see, allow us an ability to generalize based on numbers, and tell us the level of confidence that we are entitled to in those generalizations.

One major advantage of numbers in applied communication fields such as marketing, political communication, advertising, employee communication, and public opinion tracking is the ease of processing the answers. If 2,000 people each write one page explaining their views on media violence, you are in for a lot of reading. If the same 2,000 people each position themselves on a scale between 1 (*strongly disagree*) and 5 (*strongly agree*), with respect to a statement about media violence, their responses can be readily collected by e-mail, phone, website, or optical scanners and, once collected, computer-analyzed in seconds.

Of course, those who disagree with Lord Kelvin would argue that adopting a "numbers only" approach ignores qualitative information and therefore loses a great deal of information and the potential for in-depth understanding of human communication. They are correct. We will explore the advantages of qualitative methods more fully in Chapter 11.

An Introduction to Scales

Measurement is essentially the process of finding out whether people or media content have more or less of an attribute we are interested in. For example, we might be interested in whether people have 5 or 500 social media contacts, whether they score high or low on a measure of religious intolerance, or whether they are rich or poor. It is clear that these questions vary in the level of precision with which they can be answered, and in the extent to which the answer requires a subjective judgment by the researcher.

For example, it is conceptually easy to measure how much time a person spends online. You could simply record his or her time online (ignoring, for the moment, how exactly we might do that) and get an answer. If two independent observers did this and agreed on their results, we could have even more confidence in the measurement.

On the other hand, measuring whether someone is rich or poor is problematic. We could measure the person's wealth, but that raises two questions. First, how do we measure wealth precisely? Second, assuming we have a good measure of wealth in, say, dollars, how do we decide what counts as rich and what counts as poor? The number of dollars in a bank account can be counted and verified. *Rich* and *poor* are relative terms. Even though the criteria may be clear, for example earning over or under $50,000 a year, the decision to establish such categories and to assign individuals to them is ultimately a subjective, and perhaps political, one.

Measurement requires answers to three questions:

What exactly shall we measure and record?

Does the measure capture what we're interested in?

Can we be sure that our measurements, when repeated, will give the same results?

For example, communication researchers often record demographic information such as political affiliation, level of education, or gender. These are legitimate and common "measurements," but what is it that Republicans have more of than Democrats, seniors more than sophomores, females more than males? The questions are not that readily answered, and some of these demographic variables are really little more than labels—a very low level of measurement, as we will see.

Research NOIR

We don't cover film noir in this book, but research NOIR is a handy acronym to help you remember the basic levels of measurement. NOIR stands for four basic levels of measurement—nominal, ordinal, interval, and ratio.

Measures can be nominal—essentially labels; ordinal—allow rank ordering; interval—allow statistical calculations; or ratio—allow more sophisticated statistical operations.

Nominal Measurement

Examples: New York, Nevada, Idaho, California, Ontario, Quebec

Newspapers, radio, television

Baseball, softball, cricket

Facebook, Twitter, Instagram, Tumblr

Nominal measurement is really nothing more than labeling or classification. For example, male, female; Buddhist, Christian, Muslim, Hindu; and 413, 508, 415, 775 are all sets of nominal "measures." Even when *male* and *female*, for example, are **coded** or transformed into numbers for computer processing, they remain nominal. Coding *male* into "1" and *female* into "2" does no more than substitute labels because in this instance 1 and 2 are numerals, not numbers. Similarly, the 413, 508, 415, and 775 characters are area codes. They also are numerals, not numbers. They don't "measure" anything. You can't add them up or come up with an "average area code." The 775 area code is not inherently bigger or better than the 413 area code (except perhaps subjectively to those who live in Nevada).

The only numbers we can really generate from nominal variables are counts or percentages, as in "75 respondents (30%) were female; 175 (70%) male."

Ordinal Measurement

Examples: Freshman, Sophomore, Junior, Senior

First, second, third place

BS, MS, PhD

Private, Corporal, Sergeant

Ordinal measures indicate some level of progression; in some sense, one category has "more" of something than another. Second graders have "more" education than first graders. Sophomores have "more" education than freshmen. Generally, parents, faculty, and students are comfortable with such a ranking, but it is imprecise. Is the difference between freshmen and sophomores time at school, number of credits, or a combination of the two? If the difference is credits, how many credits make a difference—one, three, six, nine? The distinction is not a clear one. We cannot say that a sophomore has X times more education than a freshman; we can say only in some less than precise way that a sophomore has been at school "longer" and/or has "more" credits.

In public opinion polling, **rank order questions** are an example of ordinal measurement. If you rank order restaurants on some attribute such as value for money, convenience, or hygiene, you are telling the researcher that you believe that your top-ranked restaurant has "more of" but not "how much more of" that attribute. As researchers, we get a sense of difference or proportion, but we still have no numbers with which we can compute. You cannot determine from such a ranking that restaurant X is twice as good as restaurant Y; you can determine only that X is "better than" Y.

Interval Measurement

The basic characteristic of interval measures is the assumption of equal intervals between points on a scale. In our NOIR hierarchy, we finally have instruments to which we can attach numbers rather than numerals, and results we can quantitatively analyze.

Two classic interval scales in communication research are the **Likert scale,** named after its developer, Rensis Likert; and the **semantic differential** scale, pioneered by Osgood, Suci, and Tannenbaum (1957). Examples of both are shown later in this chapter. Interval measurement is common in quantitative communication research. You will almost certainly be familiar with such scales from completing course evaluation forms at the end of each semester.

Ratio Measurement

Ratio scales contain a "true" zero that captures the absence of an attribute. There are authentic zeros, for example zero speed on a speedometer, zero heartbeat or brain activity, and an absolute zero temperature. There are some authentic zeros in human communication as well. Class attendance or going to the movies, for example, can both be zero if they never happened. It is possible to have zero income, zero employment, or zero formal education if you never attended school.

Why Do We Care?

The reason we care about these types of data is that the type of data determines what we can or cannot do with the data statistically. Nominal data limit us to reporting only numbers and percentages. We can do nothing more than report, for example, that in a sample of 20 individuals, 12 (60%) were female and 8 (40%) were male, or that 3 (15%) preferred print news, 7 (35%) preferred radio, and 10 (50%) preferred television.

The same is true for ordinal data. We cannot calculate an average of private, corporal, and sergeant anymore than we can calculate an average of freshman, sophomore, junior, and senior. Again, we can really only report the numbers and percentages of each class year. Note, however, that if we defined class status in terms of number of years at college, we could use that number from each individual in our sample to get an average number of years for the sample.

There are two broad categories of variables (attributes that vary) within the NOIR family. Nominal and ordinal data fall into the category of "discrete" variables; interval and ratio data fall into the category of "continuous" variables.

Discrete data "jump" from category to category. That is, a person is either a freshman or in another class year, a sergeant or another rank, a graduate or not a graduate, and so on.

Continuous variables change incrementally. Age, for example, changes by the day, the hour, the minute, the second, and the fraction of a second; income changes by the dollar or cent; speed changes by miles per hour, feet per second, and inches per second. It is obvious that continuous variables offer a greater level of precision in measurement and therefore can capture more subtle differences and changes than do discrete variables. Importantly, they also permit the use of the most sophisticated statistical tools. With ratio and interval data, we can explore relationships and differences in ways that are not possible with discrete variables.

Typically, we need questions that use interval or ratio scales because attitudes are rarely expressed in black-or-white, yes-or-no terms. We need to give people the opportunity to express the strength of their feelings in more graduated terms using, for example, a Likert scale—discussed below.

Ratio scales are at the top of our NOIR hierarchy for these reasons. Note that while discrete variables cannot be treated as continuous variables, it is possible to treat continuous variables as discrete ones. For example, a researcher may collect demographic data such as age but decide that he is really only interested in whether students are over or under the legal drinking age. In this case, the age of each individual would be examined, and each person would be labeled as either "over the drinking age" or "under the drinking age" on that basis. In effect, there are now two discrete groups—"over" and "under." We now have an ordinal scale, and the continuous variable, "age," has disappeared.

The advantage of converting a continuous variable—age in this case—into a discrete variable is that the original age variable remains available if the researcher needs to do more sophisticated analyses related to age in years. The technique works in only one direction, though; discrete variables cannot be converted into continuous variables.

In practice, researchers are likely to default to continuous variables whenever possible because they allow the most sophisticated statistical analyses. In principle, we should be thinking about getting the best match of theory (what ideas we are exploring), method (how we can best capture the data we are interested in), and data (what data best provide insight on our research problem). If categorical variables suffice, there is no theoretical reason to use continuous variables, but the latter often offer "the best of both worlds."

NOIR in Action

The following shows how the variable of age might be measured at the four different levels of NOIR:

Nominal: Parent, child (note that *a* child could be older than *a* parent)

Ordinal: Child, adolescent, adult

Interval: Age (years): __ 0–4 __ 5–9 __ 10–14 __ 15–19

Ratio: Age in years _____

The reason to remember NOIR is that statistical calculations assume a particular type of underlying measurement. To revisit an example, you cannot code *male* as "1" and *female* as "2," discover that you have seven women and three men in your sample, average the scores, and report that the average gender for the group was 1.3. "Gender" as a variable is nominal. It lends itself to classification but not to computation.

This is not a mistake most people make, but the danger comes with the use of statistical analysis software, which by and large requires information to be coded numerically. While it is possible to code *male* as M and *female* as F, the temptation is to use numbers for everything and code *male* and *female* as 1 and 2, respectively. Computers do exactly what they are told to do and will "average" men and women together and report a "mean" of 1.3 if you ask them to do so.

To NOIR Is Not Enough: Reliability and Validity

Credible research results demand the use of credible research instruments. *Credible* in a general sense means trustworthy or believable. You must use instruments that you and the readers of your research can have confidence in. In research, confidence is maximized, though never ensured, by knowing that your measures have both **reliability** and **validity**.

Reliability

Imagine the frustration of having an erratic watch. You arrive at 9:59 a.m. for a 10 a.m. class, to discover that the time on everyone else's watch is 10:15. You set your watch correctly and arrive in class the following day at 9:59 to discover that everyone else thinks the time is 9:45. This brings up the epistemological question of whether or not truth is ultimately that which most of us agree on;

perhaps everyone else is wrong. But the important issue for now is that your watch appears to be unreliable; you cannot trust it.

Obviously, we cannot rely on the results this watch is giving us, and equally we cannot rely on the data provided by a research device that is not reliable. We will trust the 10:00 a.m. time displayed by this watch when every other timekeeping device we can access also tells us it is 10:00 a.m., when independent observers each looking at the watch agree that it says 10:00 a.m., and when an agreed-on independent standard such as official "atomic time" says it is 10:00 a.m. when the watch is reporting 10:00 a.m. In other words, we want to see and hear again and again from multiple sources that it is 10:00 a.m. when the watch is reporting 10:00 a.m.

Reliable instruments are a must. Unreliable speedometers can get you into trouble, and so can unreliable measures of communication. A measure of interpersonal intimacy that captures a couple in love on Monday, mutually homicidal on Tuesday, and indifferent on Wednesday may be capturing the natural swings in any relationship, but assuming some level of steadfast mutual regard, it appears that the measure is behaving unreliably.

As researchers, we work toward eliminating errors of reliability in measurement as far as possible. If we can reach that ideal state, we will know that any variations in our research data are due to variations in the phenomena we are measuring and not to instability in our measuring instruments. The tests for reliability described below check for reliability across time and across space. For example, a **test-retest** check seeks to establish that a measure of communication will produce the same results at two different times, all other things being equal. A test for **intercoder or observer reliability** seeks to establish that two observers of the same phenomenon at the same time will record the same results, all other things being equal.

Conceptually, the reliability of a measure is established by repeating measurements on the same phenomenon and looking for similar results each time. If this does not happen, the reliability of the measure is questionable. The following paragraphs outline ways of assessing reliability.

Test-Retest

A common test for reliability is test-retest. A test is administered to a group of people and then repeated with the same group a week or two later. Their test scores are then compared using a process called **correlation**. Correlation scores in this particular case are referred to as **reliability coefficients** and range between 0 and 1.0, with 1.0 being perfect and, typically, unobtainable. Most communication researchers regard anything over 0.95 as close to perfection, a score over 0.85 as acceptable, and anything under 0.75 as perhaps indicating questionable reliability.

The administration, timing, and interpretation of test-retest scores are matters of judgment. Retesting within 24 hours of the first test can result in a high correlation because people probably remember how they replied the first time around and will repeat that. They will also find the retest easier to do because they have already done the test. Retesting a month later, we may find that a number of people will have changed their minds, will have developed other priorities, or will find the test a challenge because they don't recall how to answer. Thus, most test-retests typically take place within a week or two.

Intercoder or Observer Reliability

Just as you want a measure to be reliable over time, so you would want different observers to agree that they are observing the same thing and are consistent in their observations. In other words, we want to be assured that Observer A and Observer B are recording the same thing if they are both observing it.

Two typical research scenarios that require observer reliability are the observation of human interaction and the content analysis of news media. Let's say that in both cases you are interested in measuring aggression. As a starting point, you need to define aggression in a way that all observers can agree that they have or have not seen it. This is the process of operationalization introduced in Chapter 2. You might then develop two broad categories of aggression, armed and unarmed, and instruct your observers to classify each incident of aggression they see as either armed or unarmed. Armed aggression seems obvious enough. Assertive behavior with firearms or knives would count—once you have an agreed-on, operational definition of *assertive*. But how about a kitchen situation where your observers see aggressive domestic behavior involving a pan full of hot spaghetti sauce? Observers could easily disagree on whether the gesture is armed or unarmed, or even whether it is or is not aggressive.

The secret to high intercoder or observer reliability is thorough training of observers and clear definitions and classifications of behavior. That done, you will still want to know that your observers are categorizing the same content in the same way, and so you calculate a correlation between the coding of observers to see whether this is happening.

Two other checks are needed if we are to have full confidence in the reliability of our measures. These are a check on the **internal reliability** of our measures, and a check against other established measures that measure the phenomena we are interested in.

Inter-Item or Internal Reliability

Typically, we need more than one question to capture a concept because one question may not fully capture what the researcher is trying to ask or it may oversimplify the concept. For example, asking a question about war specifically may not capture attitudes toward the more general concept of violence or perhaps vice versa.

A check on **inter-item reliability** is a check that the individual questions in a question set are consistent in their results and capture the same concept. We need a check on internal reliability because we want to be as sure as possible that all the questions basically operationalize the same concept. If the questions operationalize different concepts, then any variation we see in our results may be a result of question design and not of variation in the attitudes of individuals in our sample.

Suppose, for example, we had a set of questions that were designed to capture attitudes toward social media. We might develop questions that ask individuals how they feel about using generic social media such as blogs, wikis, and photo sharing and perhaps specific media such as Facebook, Twitter, and Second Life. If we developed a set of 12 such questions, we should expect each question to elicit approximately the same level of response; that is, there should be a strong correlation among the 12 items. One way to check on this is the "**split half**" technique, in which the results from 6 of our 12 questions would be correlated with the results from the other 6. If the measure has an overall high level of reliability, there should be a high split-half reliability. Another way is to compute the correlation between scores from randomly selected pairs of questions in the measure.

Computing inter-item reliability allows researchers to modify their question sets to the point where they can be sure that each question is addressing the same concept but is not duplicative to the point that each individual respondent is scoring identically on every question. At that point, they can be comfortable that any variation in scores they see from a sample of people is due to the group's variation in attitudes toward the same concept and not a variety of responses to different concepts.

Established Measures Reliability

Established measures reliability is simply a comparison of the results obtained from the measure you are developing with the results obtained from a known, tested measure that has been designed for the same purpose. A high correlation between your measure and an established, credible measure should add to the level of confidence you can have in your measure.

So why not just use an existing measure? Perhaps you should if it appears to address your needs. You will know its history and its reported reliabilities from published research that has used the measure. By using such a measure, you may also be able to directly compare your results with those from earlier research or across different cultures. Often, though, a measure may not successfully cross cultural boundaries, and yesterday's measures may not be an exact match for today's research. For example, questions designed for use in the United States may need serious rewording for use in other countries. A measure designed to capture attitudes toward online banking, movie viewing, dating, or working in virtual organizations will almost inevitably need changing, and testing, as Internet technology changes.

You can improve the reliability of measures by rewording specific questions, adding or dropping questions based on inter-item correlations, pretesting instructions for observers, training observers, and trying to ensure that a measurement, when repeated, is repeated under the original conditions as far as possible.

Validity

A 100% reliable instrument that measures the wrong thing is 100% useless. This is obvious in the physical sciences. We do not expect barometers to measure wind direction or thermometers to measure air pressure, but life is not so simple in the social sciences. Take a simple Likert question such as the following:

	Strongly Agree	Agree	Neutral	Disagree	Strongly Disagree
I enjoy watching television.	_____	_____	_____	_____	_____

If respondents reply to this by marking their answers on paper, all that you have actually recorded are marks on paper. Because you have used an interval-level measure, you can make some summary statements such as "13% disagreed or disagreed strongly, 50% were neutral, and 37% either agreed or strongly agreed." But what has the question actually captured?

Enjoyment could mean enjoyment of content. So while 37% agree or strongly agree that they like watching television, in fact some are really telling you that they like watching football, others cooking shows, and others 24-hour news or weather. *Enjoyment* could also mean enjoying the television process in that these viewers don't really care what's showing. Just having another voice and maybe some background music in the house while they do something else altogether (maybe even reading a book) counts as their definition of television viewing. Some research suggests that people may be attracted to television by production values such as cuts, zooms, and changes in volume, voices, or lighting. In other words, there is a vaguely hypnotic quality to television that attracts some people quite independent of content.

What, then, has the "I enjoy watching television" question captured? If the question was intended to capture the television-viewing experience and instead captured a content preference, it has little validity. It is in a sense "misreporting" a communication phenomenon.

This is why it is important that we be confident that our measures really do capture what we set out to capture, and that readers of our research reports can be assured that, for example, we really are capturing attitudes toward a political candidate and not toward the candidate's party. This match between the measure and the concept it attempts to capture is called validity.

There are several kinds of validity. The literature has somewhat different names for them and ways of classifying them, but we can think basically of three kinds of validity—content validity, construct validity, and criterion validity.

Content Validity: Looks OK

A measure has **content validity** if it matches or covers all aspects of the concept under investigation. For example, the above "I enjoy watching television" question and other questions centered on the word *television* could be faulted for lacking content validity if the question set was actually designed to capture individuals' responses to viewing video content. As video content is increasingly viewed on smartphones and tablets, the question set does not cover all video-viewing scenarios and therefore lacks content validity.

Content validity is something of a judgment call. It might be established by the reviewer as the result of an extensive literature review, or by pretesting with research participants—for example, asking a group of web designers if the questions appear to fully capture the concept of "interactivity" if interactivity is the concept being researched. A determination by experts gives the questions "**expert validity**" or "**panel validity**." Expert validity is preferred because it means that your questions have passed the test of peer approval. Other experts in the field agree with what you are doing.

Face validity, a closely related concept, means basically that the questions appear to measure what they measure. Face validity can, however, vary from group to group. For example, a nonexpert might regard the above question about television viewing as having face validity. A group of communication theorists might disagree and decide that "I enjoy watching television" is really measuring a level of desire for escapism and fantasy.

However, face validity can be important. A series of questions about people's attitudes to sex may have no face validity to respondents who think they have been recruited to answer questions about romance; they may not see the two as related. The politics of research may also require face validity. For example, you may suspect that a high level of involvement in online chat rooms negatively affects students' academic performance, and you want a whole series of questions exploring that aspect of student lifestyle. However, agencies or foundations funding your research may expect to see questions that directly capture classroom activity. Your "chat" questions may have little face value to them and render the relevance of your study suspect to them.

Construct Validity: Theoretically OK

Construct validity means that there is a demonstrable agreement between the concept or construct you are trying to measure and other related concepts. In organizational communication studies, for example, one would expect employees to show a high correlation between their scores on measures of identification, loyalty, and commitment. This is **convergent validity**. Each of these measures captures somewhat different concepts, but all live under one broad conceptual umbrella called something like "willingness to stay with my organization."

Conversely, we might expect employees who score highly on measures of loyalty to score low on measures of individuality or independence. The theory is that highly individualistic, self-centered individuals are not attracted to the group ethos required by many organizations. If scores on commitment to an organization have a low correlation with the scores on individuality, we can argue that we have good **divergent validity**. In other words, valid measures should not only have a close relationship to similar measures (convergent validity); they should not show any relationship to dissimilar measures (divergent validity).

Criterion Validity: Tests OK

Criterion validity relates your measures to other specific measures in two ways.

You have high **concurrent validity** if scores on your measure correlate highly with other measures designed to measure exactly the same construct. If you construct a measure of political alienation, for example, you would expect scores on your measure to correlate highly with other measures of political alienation.

You have high **predictive validity** if your measures predict "real-world" outcomes. For example, SAT scores should predict success in college; GRE scores should predict success in graduate school; vocational preference tests should predict comfort if not success in a particular career field. If they do, they have high predictive validity. The personal interests questionnaire you filled out when applying for college or university may have been used to match you with a roommate. If the relationship is still flourishing, the questionnaire had good predictive ability (maybe!).

Frequently, the reason for such tests is to predict outcomes in the workplace and in relationships. Private enterprise, government agencies, schools, career and psychological counselors, dating services, and the military all use tests with presumably high predictive validity to help identify people who will perform in a particular way. Implicitly, there is another reason for testing, and that is to rank order people on their scores in an attempt to predict who will be most or least successful in a particular job, graduate school, or profession. There are many proprietary tests available, each marketed on the basis of its predictive validity.

Who Wins in the Reliability–Validity Shootout?

An ideal instrument has both reliability and validity. It should measure what it measures well and consistently. But validity has a theoretical priority. It does not matter how reliable an instrument is; if it is measuring something other than what you have in mind, it is, in a sense, capturing irrelevant data and has no value. That said, reliability has a claim also because if an instrument is unreliable, you can never properly assess its validity.

Two Common Measurement Scales

There are many ways of capturing human communication behavior that will be discussed in subsequent chapters. In terms of scaled measurements, you should know two scales commonly used in attitude research in academia and industry—the Likert scale and the semantic differential scale. There are many other types of scale, but these two are common in scholarly and applied research, as you may have discovered if you have ever filled in a class evaluation form or participated in a market research study. In this chapter, we introduce these two scales as measurement devices. In Chapter 9, we will revisit these scales and their construction in more detail.

The Likert Scale

Note, as in the following examples, that the Likert scale is framed as a statement, not a question. Each statement has its own scale.

The scale may vary between 5 and 7 points. It most commonly has 5 points, and the response options are always the same—"strongly agree" through "strongly disagree." Respondents are asked to check the answer that best describes their level of agreement with the statement. Each answer is given a numerical value between 1 and 5 for a 5-point scale, and the answer from each person for each question is recorded as a score.

Suppose, for example, we are interested in consumers' attitudes toward social media. We might ask Likert-formatted questions such as the following:

	Strongly Agree	Agree	Neutral	Disagree	Strongly Disagree
1. Social media are essential.	_____	_____	_____	_____	_____
2. Social media are secure.	_____	_____	_____	_____	_____
3. Social media content can be trusted.	_____	_____	_____	_____	_____
4. Social media violate people's privacy.	_____	_____	_____	_____	_____

The Semantic Differential Scale

The semantic differential scale pairs opposite ideas toward a concept or object and invites respondents to decide where between the two opposites their opinion lies. There may be multiple-word scales for each concept.

The semantic differential shown below explores attitudes to social media, capturing concepts similar to those in the Likert example above. It has a 5-point scale, and each point is assigned a value between 1 and 5. Scores are recorded for each person for each question after the respondents have marked a position representing their opinion on each scale.

Social Media

Positive influence on users					**Negative influence on users**
Friendly	_____	_____	_____	_____	_____ Unfriendly
Expensive	_____	_____	_____	_____	_____ Cheap
Safe	_____	_____	_____	_____	_____ Dangerous
Trustworthy	_____	_____	_____	_____	_____ Untrustworthy

A semantic differential scale can be more difficult to construct in that words that form authentic opposites have to be found and pretested for meaning before use. For example, how do people see the opposite of *expensive*? *Cheap*, *inexpensive*, or *affordable*? Likert statements require no such effort. Of course, neither type of question is exempt from the requirement that it have good reliability and validity. Significant pretesting time and effort may be required to establish these.

Both the Likert and semantic differential scales have "steps," to which we can assign numbers that will allow us to make some summary claims about the data.

For example, Exhibit 5.1 shows a basic Likert-scale question, the answers from five respondents, and, in a sneak preview of Chapter 6, the simple descriptive statistics that summarize those answers. Looking at the five responses we received, we can say from inspection and some elementary calculations that

- Scores ranged between 1 and 5.
- The most frequent score was 5.
- The average score is 3.2, or $(1 + 2 + 3 + 5 + 5) / 5$.

We can summarize these data by saying that while there is some collective disagreement with the statement, the average score of 3.2 is closer to agreement than disagreement and therefore, overall, our respondents are more likely to agree than disagree with the statement.

EXHIBIT 5.1   **Example of Likert Question, Responses, and Basic Descriptive Statistics**

(Statement) Social media are essential.					
	Strongly Disagree	Disagree	Neutral	Agree	Strongly Agree
Score	1	2	3	4	5
Value assigned to statement by respondents					
Respondent 1		X			
Respondent 2			X		
Respondent 3					X
Respondent 4	X				
Respondent 5					X
Descriptive Statistics					
Sample size					5
Minimum score					1
Maximum score					5
Range of scores				(5 − 1) = 4	
Average score (sum of scores / sample size)					3.2

While we can make statements about the distribution of results with nominal and ordinal variables (for example, 65% of respondents were male; 35% female), interval measures allow us for the first time to make summary statements such as "The average score was 3.2."

Note that the assumption of equal distances between points on a Likert or semantic differential scale is just that—an assumption. Mathematically, the distance between any two adjacent points on the scale is the same. Psychologically, however, this may not be the case for respondents. People can be reluctant to take extreme positions and may be more likely to favor middle-ground positions such as "agree" more than "strongly agree." There is also a question of what precisely the midpoint of a Likert scale means to the respondent. It may mean "undecided," "don't know," "neutral," or "both agree and disagree." Related is the broader question of whether a respondent's complex feelings on such issues as reproductive rights, same-sex marriage, or freedom of speech can ever be adequately captured in the form of a check mark on a 5-point or a 7-point scale.

In summary, measuring communication phenomena at the nominal and ordinal levels allows us to classify and rank communication phenomena. Measuring at the interval and ratio levels allows us to use statistics as a reporting and decision-making tool.

The downside of such quantification is the loss of all information that cannot be turned into a number and the danger of **reification** or turning the measure itself into the reality it is supposed to measure. As evolutionary scientist Stephen Jay Gould (1996) pointed out in his excoriating review of attempts to measure human attributes, the first problem is that scales and tests can lead us to assume that the test is the thing. The map is not the territory, but the fact that there is an IQ test leads us to assume, unwisely, that there is a single measurable entity called "intelligence." The second problem is the danger of ranking based on such scales. Given the existence of an IQ scale that is supposed to measure a unitary entity called intelligence, how wise is it to rank people on the basis of a single score?

This question is the focus of this chapter's Ethics Panel.

Ethics Panel: The Ethics of Measurement Scales

Stephen Jay Gould (1996), in his book *The Mismeasure of Man,* discusses the major problems with the development of measures such as the IQ test: first, the assumption that there is a single human ability or entity called intelligence; second, the related assumption that a test can be devised to assess it; and third, that individuals can be accurately ranked and their futures perhaps determined on the basis of such a test. A familiar example is the SAT, intended to predict (academic) success in college. In a general sense, academic success is a product of many factors—the quality of high school preparation, socioeconomic status, personal "drive," study habits and ambition, and of course the college environment itself. On what basis, then, should a student with high SAT scores be preferred for college admission over another student with lower scores?

Questions

- How ethical is it to rank or evaluate students based only on the results of a single set of tests such as the SATs?

- More generally, how wise is it to classify people on the basis of any single measure such as authoritarianism, conservatism, loyalty, commitment, or dogmatism?

- What nonscaled methods might you propose that capture, for example, intelligence, conservatism, or loyalty?

CHAPTER SUMMARY

Measures of communication must have:

- Validity—measure what they are supposed to measure.
- Reliability—produce the same results consistently.

Measures exist at four levels:

- Nominal—essentially labels.
- Ordinal—allow rank ordering.
- Interval—allow statistical calculations.
- Ratio—allow more sophisticated statistical operations.

Two frequently used scales in communication research are the

- Likert scale—ranges between "strongly disagree" and "strongly agree."
- Semantic differential scale—ranges between polar opposites such as "strong" and "weak."

KEY TERMS

coded	measurement
concurrent validity	nominal
construct validity	ordinal
content validity	panel validity
convergent validity	phrenologists
correlation	predictive validity
criterion validity	rank order questions
demographic	ratio
divergent validity	reification
established measures reliability	reliability
expert validity	reliability coefficients
face validity	scales
intercoder or observer reliability	semantic differential
inter-item reliability	split half
internal reliability	test-retest
interval	validity
Likert scale	

APPLICATION EXERCISES

These application exercises ask you to develop questions in nominal, ordinal, interval, and ratio formats so that you can develop an understanding of the strengths and weaknesses of each format. They will also have you thinking about how best to operationalize the concept you are hoping to measure and the relationships among concepts.

Exercise 1. NOIR Revisited

Under "An Introduction to Scales," the perhaps-questionable statement was made that it is relatively easy to measure how much time a person spends online. List as many ways you can think of to measure time spent online; then identify each measure as nominal, ordinal, interval, or ratio. Which of these measures do you consider to be most valid, and which do you consider most reliable?

Exercise 2. The Web at 25

At www.pewinternet.org, locate a February 27, 2014, survey report titled "The Web at 25 in the U.S." Click on the "Topline Questionnaire" icon to access the specific questions asked in this survey. You can also click on the "Complete Report" icon and find them at the end of the report. Categorize each question as nominal, ordinal, interval, or ratio. You will find that one level of measurement is predominant. What are the advantages and disadvantages of operating at this level of measurement? What types of information about Internet users might not be available as a result of operating at this level of measurement?

Exercise 3. Parlez-moi d'amour

Let's consider love. Generally, love is held to be a good thing. We might expect people in love to be happy, considerate of others, altruistic, and motivated and generally to have a positive outlook on life. A reliable and valid measure of love might allow us to predict, for example, individuals' success in romantic relationships, their success as members of a team, or their willingness to engage in antisocial behavior. There are good theoretical and practical reasons that a researcher might want to measure love.

- Develop a set of nominal, ordinal, interval, and ratio questions that measure love.

- Assess the validity and reliability of your measures.

- Identify other measures and other concepts.

Identify specific reasons you might want to measure an individual's level of love. For example, might a high level of love of country predict willingness to enlist for military service, to be active in politics and civic affairs, to be caring of one's fellow citizens, and more generally to be willing to contribute time and resources to building a better nation? Intuitively, this seems like a concept of love that is different from the passionate love for a significant other, warm familial love, the gourmet's love of fine food, or the extreme-sports enthusiast's love of rock climbing.

Given the reasons you identified for wanting to research love, would questions that focus not on love as you first operationalized it but on another concept such as patriotism be more appropriate to your research interest? Can measures that capture love of food, one's country, or rock climbing be used successfully to establish the validity of measures of romantic love? How likely is it that your questions developed in response to the first assignment in Exercise 3 will work successfully as a measure of love in a different culture?

RECOMMENDED READING

Gould, S. J. (1996). *The mismeasure of man*. New York, NY: Norton.
   Gould's book discusses the problems with the development and use of unitary measures such as the IQ test.

Rubin, R. B., Palmgreen, P., & Sypher, H. E. (Eds.). (2004). *Communication research measures: A sourcebook*. Mahwah, NJ: Erlbaum.
   This book shows many scales used in communication research and discusses scale development.

REFERENCES

Gould, S. J. (1996). *The mismeasure of man*. New York, NY: Norton.
Osgood, C. E., Suci, G. J. & Tannenbaum, P. H. (1957). *The measurement of meaning*. Urbana: University of Illinois Press.

⑤SAGE edge™

Want a better grade?
Get the tools you need to sharpen your study skills. Access practice quizzes, eFlashcards, video, and multimedia at **edge.sagepub.com/treadwell3e**

CHAPTER 6

Summarizing Research Results

Data Reduction and Descriptive Statistics

Whenever you can, count.

—Sir Francis Galton (1822–1911)
Statistician

❧❧❧

Chapter Overview

As the above quote from statistician Sir Francis Galton suggests, counting and statistics can be applied in a wide range of research settings. The word **statistics** refers generally to the formulae that help us process and understand the raw data of research and more specifically to the resulting numbers that summarize the raw data, the relationships among variables, and the differences among groups.

Descriptive statistics, introduced in this chapter, describe and summarize the data from a research sample. **Inferential statistics**, discussed in Chapter 7, help us make probability-based inferences about the wider population from which we obtained our sample.

This chapter focuses on understanding and describing research data. **Data reduction** is basically a process of reducing the raw data of research—perhaps hundreds or thousands of individual responses—into a much smaller number of categories to make the research data more comprehensible. Descriptive statistics help us describe the distribution of data in a **data set**, look for relationships within those data, and understand the numbers we have in front of us.

We begin this chapter with a discussion of data reduction and then move on to descriptive statistics. But first, a quick vocabulary check. A **sample** consists of individuals selected by the researcher to represent a much larger group. This larger group is referred to as the **population**. A population is defined simply as all of the individuals who fall into the category the researcher ideally wishes to research. A population by definition is larger than a sample, but is not necessarily immense. In fact, it could be relatively small, such as Asian special education teachers working in private schools.

Statistical formulae help us process the raw data of research into summary numbers that can tell us a lot about the raw data, the relationships among variables, and the differences among groups. Strictly speaking, statistics describe a sample. The numbers that describe a population are referred to as **parameters**. As we will see in Chapter 7, one important use of statistics is to estimate a population's parameters.

Chapter Objectives

This chapter will help you

- Describe the concept of descriptive statistics and provide examples.

- Describe the concept of data reduction and provide examples.

- Explain and calculate the following statistical measures:

  ○ Mean, median, and mode

  ○ Minimum, maximum, range, variance, and standard deviation

  ○ *z* score

  ○ Chi-square

Introduction

The data from a research project can be unwieldy and incomprehensible without some form of processing. A 20-question survey of 50 people means 1,000 answers to be analyzed. The same survey administered in a typical national opinion poll of 1,200 people will result in 24,000 answers that have to be analyzed, summarized, and understood. If each question were formatted as a 5-point scale, we would have $1,200 \times 20 \times 5 - 120,000$ possible answers to be examined

There are two major ways of reducing such data to comprehensible terms—**tables** and descriptive statistics. Tables summarize the data and relationships within the data. Descriptive statistics describe the distribution of data in summary numbers that will tell you a lot about the nature of the raw data if you have a basic understanding of statistics.

It is wise to understand the concept behind any statistic so that you can select the statistic(s) most relevant to your research questions. Even though most statistical calculations are done with calculators or data-processing software, you should work through the calculations shown in this chapter to get an understanding of what each statistic is trying to capture. To this end, the data in Exhibit 6.1 are much simplified relative to the data you would normally capture in a quantitative study. For example, the gender (GEND) and political preference (POLP) questions each limit respondents to only two choices—male/female and liberal/conservative, respectively.

Data, by the way, is a plural—as in "the data are," not "the data is."

In this chapter, we will examine the communication behaviors of 20 people. We have gathered data on their use of the Internet and social media, their political orientation, their knowledge of world affairs, and their gender.

Our results are shown in Exhibit 6.1. The columns, in order, show the names of respondents (NAME), an identifying number we have assigned them (ID), their gender (GEND), their political preference (POLP), a measure of the number of hours per week they spend on the Internet (HWI), their estimate of the percentage of their time they spend on the Internet (PTI), their score on a test of knowledge of world affairs (KWA), and their self-reported number of social media contacts (SMCS).

Note that the columns are numbered to facilitate chapter discussions; such numbering does not normally appear in research reports.

Exhibit 6.1 shows a small number of people and variables, simple data, and some numbers that may appear anomalous because they have been selected to illustrate some specific points. Otherwise, this set of raw data, or data set, is typical for a social science study in which we measure a number of variables and look for relationships among them.

Typically, we would start with a hypothesis or with research questions linking these variables, such as:

H_1: Women spend more time than men using the Internet.

H_2: Individuals with more social media contacts will score higher on a test of world affairs knowledge than those with fewer social media contacts.

In conducting such a study, our first step would be to gather data from each respondent and to record it in the form shown in Exhibit 6.1. We would then input the data into a computer for statistical analysis using **proprietary** software such as **IBM SPSS® Statistics**, open source software such as **R**, or a spreadsheet such as Excel. Normally letters such as M/F for male/female or L/C for liberal/conservative would be replaced by numerals (not numbers—remember Chapter 5) in the coding process. We would also be dealing with thousands of units of information, or **data points**, rather than the few shown here.

Preliminary Considerations: Missing Data and Anomalous Data

The first step in data analysis is to decide what data to use. The fact that you have it does not necessarily mean that you must or should use it. There are several reasons you might not use data you have. For example, ethically you may need to exclude data from individuals from whom you have not obtained a consent to participate in research.

Missing data is a problem. Suppose we have respondent X, who we know from information she provided is female, is politically liberal, and has a score of 4 on her knowledge of world affairs. However, we have no data related to her use of the Internet.

If our theoretical interest is in the relationship between gender and political orientation, we obviously have relevant data. If our data have been collected as part of a study related to Internet use and political orientation, the data become problematic for two reasons. If the data are missing—no response—obviously we cannot use them. If, however, the Internet data exist but are all zeros—that is, the respondent shows "0" for the variables HWI, PTI, and SMCS—we have the more difficult judgment of whether to use the data or not. It is possible that respondent X truly never uses the Internet, in which case her zeroes can be analyzed as valid data. On the other hand, if she never uses the Internet, why would we analyze her data as part of a project on Internet users? While there is no black-or-white answer to this dilemma, one possible solution is to analyze our data set excluding her data, and then to consider her data separately as an "outlier" case. This may prove to be theoretically interesting and provide new insights, especially if we also have comments from her—perhaps from a follow-up interview—about why she is not an Internet user.

Anomalous data are those that appear "out of line." For example, Exhibit 6.1 shows that Louise and Caroline both spend 80 hours a week on the Internet—a suspiciously large but not impossible amount of time. Louise estimates this as 80% of her time whereas Caroline estimates this as only 20% of her time. Such responses should trigger some questions. Did respondents misunderstand our questions, or might we be looking at an interesting new

EXHIBIT 6.1   **Survey Results for 20 Respondents**

1	2	3	4	5	6	7	8
Name (NAME)	ID Number (ID)	Gender* (GEND)	Political Preference* (POLP)	Hours per Week Internet (HWI)	% Time on Internet (PTI)	Knowledge World Affairs (KWA)	Social Media Contacts (SMCS)
Helen	01	F	L	07	1	4	2
Kiri	02	F	L	100	90	6	450
Lin	03	F	L	30	25	4	150
Miriam	04	F	C	40	20	10	250
Lakesha	05	F	L	60	10	2	350
Marie	06	F	L	60	5	6	250
Louise	07	F	L	80	80	6	350
Bonnie	08	F	L	40	60	8	150
Caroline	09	F	C	80	20	10	250
Elizabeth	10	F	C	10	10	2	100
Thomas	11	M	L	20	40	6	100
Harry	12	M	L	60	60	4	150
Wiremu	13	M	C	40	20	8	130
Jacques	14	M	C	80	80	4	350
Carlos	15	M	C	60	40	8	130
Gordon	16	M	C	40	40	6	100
Alfonso	17	M	L	60	60	4	100
Rafael	18	M	C	90	20	8	90
Joseph	19	M	C	80	80	4	350
Joseph	20	M	C	60	40	4	130

*F = female; M = male; L = liberal; C = conservative

theory here? For example, if Louise hates working online and Caroline loves it, is it possible they will each estimate the percentage of their time online differently? We may then be looking at a possible new measure of job satisfaction. Possibly, though, our measurement tools need closer examination. For example, an app that records the amount of time a device is connected to the Internet may well measure time online as a full 168 hours a week whether there is a human operator at the device or not.

Such questions may arise from an initial inspection of data or become apparent in the course of data analysis, the first step of which is data reduction.

Data Reduction

As shown in Exhibit 6.1, we have data for 20 respondents on eight variables ("NAME" through "SMCS") for a total of 160 data points.

How can these data be summarized so they are easily understood?

The first basic approach is to do data reduction using summary tables. The second is to compute summary statistics such as the measures of central tendency and measures of dispersion described later in this chapter.

The goal of data reduction is to present data in summary form. In survey and experimental research in particular, we are interested in groups more than we are in individuals. To select a couple of names at random from Exhibit 6.1, we have little theoretical interest in Lakesha or Gordon as individuals. What we are interested in is if and how males as a group and females as a group differ in Internet use, political preference, and knowledge of world affairs or in how such variables relate to each other.

Hard-hearted though it may be, Lakesha, Gordon, and 18 other individuals effectively disappear from our thinking when it comes to data analysis.

One clue to this "people as data" approach is the fact that in most data analyses the names of individuals (Column 1) disappear, to be replaced by a code number (Column 2). Our sample has two "Josephs," so one good reason for providing a unique identification number for each individual is to avoid the problem of duplicate names. Another function of an ID number is to provide some anonymity to individuals.

Typically, data for one individual would not be reported from such a data set unless he or she had such a unique combination of characteristics that the researcher saw a truly compelling reason to report them—for example, respondent X discussed above. The first step in data reduction, then, is simply to see what the data look like at the level of the group rather than the individual. (Compare this with the view you will find in Chapter 11 that the best insights on human communication come from an in-depth understanding of one individual or a small group.)

Research data such as those given in Exhibit 6.1 show that the researcher is specifically interested in six variables—gender through number of social media contacts—and has captured data about each of them. Statistical software will compute both descriptive and inferential statistics on request. In this chapter, we work through the thinking behind descriptive statistics.

Data Reduction and Univariate Data

Typically, researchers will start by looking at each variable on its own. This approach is called **univariate analysis**, as in one variable at a time.

A first step when inspecting data is to sort the values from lowest to highest as shown in Exhibit 6.2a for the variable HWI and then to establish the frequency with which each score occurs.

The term **frequencies** refers to the number of times or the frequency with which a particular value occurs. To produce **frequency tables**, we construct categories that include all the values we expect to find on a test or a survey and then report the number of values that fall in each category.

EXHIBIT 6.2a   **Data Reduction: Hours of Internet Use per Week (HWI) Initial Data**

HWI (Raw Scores)
7, 10, 20, 30, 40, 40, 40, 40, 60, 60, 60, 60, 60, 60, 80, 80, 80, 80, 90, 100

EXHIBIT 6.2b   **Data Reduction: Frequency of Individuals Reporting Hours of Internet Use per Week (HWI) in Five Categories**

HWI	0–20	21–40	41–60	61–80	81–100
Frequency of Responses	3	5	6	4	2

EXHIBIT 6.2c   **Data Reduction: Frequency of Individuals Reporting Hours of Internet Use per Week (HWI) in Two Categories**

HWI	0–50	51–100
Frequency of Responses	8	12

Exhibit 6.2b shows an intermediate stage in data reduction. Rather than reporting individual values as in Exhibit 6.2a, we have set up categories of values—0–20, 21–40, and so on to a category of 81–100—so that we now can assign each individual value to one of five categories and count the number of values in each category.

The number of categories is a judgment on the part of the researcher. Exhibit 6.2b shows five categories, and Exhibit 6.2c shows further data reduction down to two categories. We could equally well have had 10 categories ranging from 0–9, 10–19, and so on to 90–100. The fewer categories we have, the more data reduction or simplification we have, but the more information is lost in the process. Three would be a defensible number of categories if you wanted to capture and differentiate only low, midrange, and high values.

Sometimes the number of categories will be self-apparent. For example, categorizing people as male or female, or Democrat or Republican, means that there will be only two categories.

Presenting tables for variables such as gender and political preference are usually unnecessary. For example, gender data from Exhibit 6.1 would simply be reported as "Ten (50%) respondents were female, and 10 (50%) were male." However, when we move on to **bi-variate** analysis and want to show how gender interacts with another variable, gender will become part of a bi-variate table. See Exhibit 6.5 for an example.

Note that the numbers in Exhibits 6.2a–6.2c are not the actual values obtained from individuals but rather the number or frequency of these values. Exhibit 6.2b, for example, simply shows that three people had values between 0 and 20, and five people had values between 21 and 40. Do not make the mistake of reading such a table as people with values between 0 and 20 having an average value of 3. Carefully constructed and labeled tables indicate what their content represents, but research papers may report frequencies of values, such as shown above, as well as summary statistics, such as means, so it is wise to read tables carefully.

The distribution of values can also be plotted graphically; one such plot for the distribution of HWI values is shown in Exhibit 6.3.

Exhibit 6.3   **Distribution of Individuals Reporting Hours of Internet Use per Week (HWI)**

	7	10	20	30	40	50	60	70	80	90	100
							x				
							x				
Frequency of Values					x		x		x		
					x		x		x		
					x		x		x		
	x	x	x	x	x		x		x	x	x
Values	7	10	20	30	40	50	60	70	80	90	100

Data Reduction and Bi-Variate Data

Communication research is ultimately the study of relationships, be it among people or among variables. So researchers, typically, are more interested in how two or more variables relate to each other than in the nature of one variable on its own. Take, for example, one hypothesis set out at the beginning of this chapter:

H_1: Women spend more time than men using the Internet.

Here, the hypothesis frames our data reduction. Implicitly, we are interested in only two variables—gender and time spent on the Internet (the variables GEND and HWI in Exhibit 6.1)—so for the moment we can ignore the other variables and concentrate on the relationship between these two. Exhibit 6.4 shows the HWI data from Exhibit 6.1 plotted to show the results for males and females separately.

Exhibit 6.4   **Distribution of Individuals Reporting Hours of Internet Use per Week (HWI) by Male (M) and Female (F)**

	7	10	20	30	40	50	60	70	80	90	100
							M				
Frequency of Values							M				
					F M		F M		F M		
	F	F	M	F	F M		F M		F M	M	F
Values	7	10	20	30	40	50	60	70	80	90	100

Now we can start to explore the relationship between two variables. We can see, for example, that females' values on HWI range between 7 and 100 whereas males' values range between 20 and 90.

With the values plotted from lowest to highest, Exhibit 6.4 shows that our respondents appear to cluster into two or perhaps three separate groups. Assuming two groups for purposes of discussion, we see that the first group has values ranging between 7 and 40; the second group's values range between 60 and 100. Inspection also indicates while females are equally represented in both groups, more males are in the group with the higher values. Possibly, males and females are two separate groups with respect to time spent on the Internet, or, to rephrase it as a tentative hypothesis, level of Internet use can be predicted by gender.

To make this more apparent, we can do further data reduction and make a simple "two by two" summary table that summarizes the relationship between gender and HWI. Such tables are also known as **cross-tabs** because the values of one variable are cross-tabulated against the values of another variable or as **contingency tables** because their formatting shows how the values of one variable are contingent on another. Such tables can become more complex than a simple "two by two," as we shall see.

Exhibit 6.5 shows a simple summary table with the summary data highlighted. Here, we have defined low values for HWI as anything 50 or less and high values as anything 51 or more. Gender has the two categories of male and female.

EXHIBIT 6.5   **Summary Table of Hours of Internet Use per Week (HWI) by Gender**

HWI Values	Male (Out of 10)	Female (Out of 10)	Total (Out of 20)
0–50	3 (30%)	5 (50%)	8 (40%)
51–100	7 (70%)	5 (50%)	12 (60%)
Total	10 (100%)	10 (100%)	20

There are several things to remember about tables such as Exhibit 6.5. First, the numbers in the body of the table are not values for HWI; they are the count or frequency of values. To some extent, this is self-apparent; we know that the HWI values range between 7 and 100, so it is unlikely that we would look at the category labeled 0–50 and interpret a 3 or a 5 as an average for HWI.

In effect, we have reduced our HWI values to **categorical data**—high and low. This means that we can use only the statistical formulae that apply to categorical data. Using formulae that apply to **continuous data** such as age or grade point average (GPA) would be inappropriate. We will look more closely at how we examine relationships between such continuous variables as knowledge of word affairs and Internet use in Chapter 7.

A second point to be aware of is that any table can be rotated; that is, Exhibit 6.5 could have been set up with Male and Female as rows and HWI values as columns. This raises the question of how to read such tables. Because the initial research hypothesis proposed a difference between males and females in terms of Internet use, we need to read across the table to get that difference. Line 2 of the table compares the number of low HWI values by gender, and Line 3 compares the number of high HWI values by gender. Obviously, we would examine the overall distribution of values in determining how males and females differ in terms of time spent on the Internet, but looking at males only by reading down Column 2 and discovering that they have more high values of HWI than low values, and similarly looking down Column 3 for the distribution of values for females, is a secondary interest.

Note also that the table shows both row totals and column totals. Most statistical software will report both sets of totals by default, but you are likely to have some control over which of these totals are reported. If you look at percentages rather than raw numbers in Exhibit 6.5, you will see that they add up to 100% only in the columns. In Exhibit 6.5, the Row 2 total number of values in the row is 8—only 40% of the total. The Row 3 total number of values is 12—only 60% of the total. On the other hand, the Column 2 and Column 3 numbers each total to 100%.

HINT: A rule of thumb for reading tables is to identify the "100%" columns or rows. If the columns each total to 100%, read across the rows. If the rows each total to 100%, read down the columns. In Exhibit 6.5, each column totals to 100%, so we read across the rows. If each row totaled 100%, we would read down the columns.

Data Reduction and Multivariate Data

A further level of analysis, **multivariate** analysis, is used to study the interaction of three or more variables.

You can see that Exhibit 6.6 has expanded on Exhibit 6.5 by adding the distribution of scores for another variable—knowledge of world affairs (KWA). Our aim is to determine whether there is a relationship between level of Internet use and knowledge of world affairs as well as between gender and these two variables. Accordingly, under each HWI category, we have added the distribution of scores for the KWA variable. We classified the KWA scores as either low (0 to 5) or high (6 to 10). We have taken each category shown in Exhibit 6.5 and for each of the four categories (male and female by HWI 0–40 and HWI 60–100) reported the distribution of scores for KWA, highlighted in the table. We can see, for example, that no males with low HWI values had low KWA scores and that only one female with high HWI values had a low KWA score.

EXHIBIT 6.6   **Summary Table of Knowledge of World Affairs (KWA) by Hours of Internet Use per Week (HWI) by Gender**

	Male	Female
HWI 0–40		
KWA 0–5	–	3
KWA 6–10	3	2
HWI 60–100		
KWA 0–5	5	1
KWA 6–10	2	4
Total	10	10

We could continue this multivariate analysis by adding still further subcategories to our table. For example, we could look at the KWA variable and for each KWA category report the distribution of data for the POLP or PTI variables. It is obvious, though, that increasingly complex tables become increasingly difficult to comprehend and that we must look for more understandable ways to summarize the distributions of data and the relationships among variables.

This is where descriptive statistics, and the inferential statistics described in Chapter 7, come to our aid.

Descriptive statistics help us

- Summarize complex data.
- Show how the data vary, for example whether everyone checked "5" on a 5-point scale or whether "1," "2," "3," and "4" also got votes.
- Show if different groups of people differ in some way.
- Show if there are relationships among variables we are interested in.

Measures of Central Tendency: Mean, Median, and Mode

The three basic statistics used to summarize data are mean, median, and mode. They are called measures of central tendency because they describe the central features of a data set rather than its extreme or outlying values.

- Mean is often called the average value. Calculate it by adding all the individual values and dividing by the number of values. For the variable HWI, the mean is the total of all 20 values (1,097) divided by 20 = 54.85; that is, the respondents averaged 54.85 hours per week on the Internet.
- Mode is the most frequent value. It is commonly, but not necessarily, in the midrange of scores. As shown in Exhibit 6.3, we have more 60s than any other value for HWI, so the mode for this group is 60.
- Median is the midrange value. When all the values are arranged from lowest to highest, we find the value that has an equal number of values on either side of it. When the number of values is even, find the value halfway between the two middle values when the values are ordered from lowest to highest. For the variable HWI, the median value is halfway between the two middle values of 60 and 60. What is halfway between 60 and 60? Answer? 60! Plots such as Exhibit 6.3 can be a quick way to assess basic descriptive statistics for a sample, but obviously counting and calculation are necessary to get precise numbers.

We can also identify the minimum and maximum values (7 and 100) and calculate the range between them (100 − 7 = 93). Range is a measure of dispersion, discussed below.

Generally, we need all three measures of central tendency because any one of them may be misleading.

For example, a group of 10 people that includes one millionaire and nine other people, each with an income of $1,000, has a mean income of $100,900. The mean in this case does not portray the group's individual incomes accurately. The median income is $1,000 because half the incomes are over $1,000 and half are under it. We might decide that the best descriptor in this case is the mode, which by definition states that the most frequent income is $1,000. However, we could also get a mode of $1,000 if only two people each had an income of $1,000 and everyone else had a uniquely different income in the millions. Obviously, none of these measures on its own summarizes the unique characteristics of this group of people well. We need additional measures to do this, and these are discussed below under "Measures of Dispersion."

As summarized in Exhibit 6.7, there appears to be some difference between males and females with respect to measures of central tendency for HWI. Statistical confirmation of this hypothesis will come from such tests as the chi-square and t tests, described in Chapter 7. Note also that for women, the scores of 40, 60, and 80 appear most frequently and with equal frequency. Because there are three modes for females, we refer to their HWI scores as having a tri-modal distribution. Two scores appearing with equal frequency would result in a bi-modal distribution.

EXHIBIT 6.7   **Measures of Central Tendency for Hours of Internet Use per Week (HWI)**

	Measures of Central Tendency for HWI		
	Mean	**Mode**	**Median**
Female	50.7	40, 60, 80	50
Male	59.0	60	60
Female and Male	54.85	60	60

Measures of Dispersion: Minimum, Maximum, Range, Interquartile Range, Variance, and Standard Deviation

Mean, median, and mode summarize the central features of a distribution but do not describe the range of scores. The range and variability of scores are described by **measures of dispersion**. Metaphorically, if measures of central tendency are taking an interest in what most people are wearing, measures of dispersion are taking an interest in the extreme "fashionistas" who are dressing differently from everyone else, and perhaps indicating a new trend or fashion subgroup. Measures of dispersion include the minimum, maximum, range, interquartile range, variance, and standard deviation.

Minimum, Maximum, Range, and Interquartile Range

- **Maximum** = highest value.
- **Minimum** = lowest value.
- **Range** = maximum value minus minimum value.

For our variable HWI, the values range between 100 and 7, so the range is 100 − 7 = 93. If all scores were identical, say 75, the range would be 75 − 75 = 0.

- **Interquartile range** is a way of looking at the "middle ground" of dispersion. This range is calculated simply by ignoring the highest 25% of values and the lowest 25% and then identifying the highest and lowest values and the range for the middle 50% of values. For example, if we look at Exhibit 6.2a and remove the five lowest values and the five highest values (highlighted), we are left with the middle 50% of values, which range from 40 to 80. The interquartile range, then, is 80 − 40 = 40.

Variance and Standard Deviation

Variance and **standard deviation** allow us to compare different measures "on a level playing field."

The range statistic, for example, provides no basis for comparing different sets of values. Suppose a class has test scores ranging between 5 and 48 out of a possible 50. The scores have a range of (48 − 5) = 43, but so do the scores for another class with scores ranging between 53 and 96 on a test scored out of 100. Clearly, we cannot directly compare the two sets of scores and the way in which they vary. Variance, standard deviation, and z scores help us to do this.

Variance, as the term implies, measures the extent to which values in a data set vary. Standard deviation is the square root of variance. The larger the standard deviation of a variable, the wider the range of values on either side of the mean.

Variance: Formula

Computing variance is a four-step process with Steps 1 and 2 repeated for each value of the variable in your sample—as shown in Exhibit 6.8.

1. Subtract the mean value for the group from each individual value.

2. Square each result (to eliminate the problem of dealing with negative numbers).

3. Add the results.

4. Divide the sum of these squares by the number of values minus one to get an average of the squared variations from the mean.

This is expressed in the following formula.

Formula for Calculating Variance	
$$s^2 = \dfrac{\Sigma(X - \overline{X})^2}{(N-1)}$$	s^2 = variance Σ = "the sum of" X = each individual score $\overline{X}$ = the mean score for the group N = the number of scores

Standard Deviation: Formula

Standard deviation (SD) is the square root of the variance. The formula for calculating standard deviation is

$$SD = \sqrt{s^2} = \sqrt{\dfrac{\Sigma(X - \overline{X})^2}{(N-1)}}$$

Variance and Standard Deviation: Example

Let's calculate the variance and standard deviation for the current variable of interest—hours per week on the Internet (HWI). The data for this calculation come from Column 5 of Exhibit 6.1.

As we computed above, the mean for the HWI variable is 54.85. Using the 20 values for this variable, we compute the variance and standard deviation for the group as shown in Exhibit 6.8.

As a quick check, note that the numbers shown in Column 4 of Exhibit 6.8—the differences between each individual score and the group mean—should always add to zero. The sum of the squared differences is 12,978.55, which divided by the number of scores minus one (19) gives us a variance of 683.08.

The standard deviation, the square root of the variance (683.08), is 26.14.

We will revisit this important statistic in Chapter 7. A sneak preview of the importance of standard deviation is that it allows us to make generalizations about the wider population from which we have drawn our sample and to calculate the probability of any particular result occurring.

For example, for the variable HWI "hours per week Internet," our sample of 20 people has a mean of 54.85. We know this is true for the 20 people we sampled, but how likely is it that these numbers represent the population from which the sample was drawn? To get a sense of how likely our calculated mean of 54.85 is true for the bigger population, we use the standard deviation of the sample: 26.14.

Similarly, if we look at the HWI standard deviations for males and females separately as shown in Exhibit 6.9, it is clear that females have more variability in their scores than do males. This is apparent from the ranges (93 versus 70) and variances (949.40 versus 454.44) shown for the sample.

With standard deviation, however, we can move beyond sample statistics and estimate the distribution of values in the sampled population. This estimation of parameters for the sampled population involves some basic assumptions about the distribution of values in the population. These assumptions and the use of standard deviation to estimate the population are discussed more fully in Chapter 7.

EXHIBIT 6.8   Computing Variance and Standard Deviation for Hours of Internet Use per Week (HWI)

ID	HWI	Group Mean	Hours per Week – Group Mean	(Hours per Week – Group Mean)^2
1	07	54.85	−47.85	2,289.62
2	100	54.85	45.15	2,038.52
3	30	54.85	−24.85	617.52
4	40	54.85	−14.85	220.52
5	60	54.85	5.15	26.52
6	60	54.85	5.15	26.52
7	80	54.85	25.15	632.52
8	40	54.85	−14.85	220.52
9	80	54.85	25.15	632.52
10	10	54.85	−44.85	2,011.52
11	20	54.85	−34.85	1,214.52
12	60	54.85	5.15	26.52
13	40	54.85	−14.85	220.52
14	80	54.85	25.15	632.52
15	60	54.85	5.15	26.52
16	40	54.85	−14.85	220.52
17	60	54.85	5.15	26.52
18	90	54.85	−35.15	1,235.52
19	80	54.85	25.15	632.52
20	60	54.85	5.15	26.52
		Sum =	0.00	12,978.55
		Variance (s^2) =		12,978.55/(20 − 1)
		=		683.08
		Standard Deviation (SD) = √Variance =		26.14

EXHIBIT 6.9   Measures of Dispersion for Males and Females on Hours of Internet Use per Week (HWI) Variable

	Measures of Dispersion		
	Range	Variance	Standard Deviation
Female	100 − 7 = 93	949.40	30.81
Male	90 − 20 = 70	454.44	21.32

z Score

Once we have computed a group's standard deviation for a variable, we can compute a **z score** for any individual in the group. A z score is the number of units of standard deviation any one value is above or below the mean. In our data, we have a measure of how many hours per week respondents spend on the Internet. Obviously, there are other ways of asking the same question. For example, we asked them "What percentage of your time do you spend on the Internet?" There is no easy way to compare the two sets of answers even though they address the same question. The two questions use different **metrics** (units of measurement) and are of a different order of magnitude. The first question uses absolute numbers with a maximum possible answer of 7 days × 24 hours = 168. The second question uses percentages with a maximum possible of 100. The two sets of answers cannot be compared unless we standardize them in some way.

A statistic that allows us to compare results from two or more different measures would be desirable, and this is what the z score accomplishes. The z score is the "apples to oranges" statistic. Expressing each individual value in terms of standard deviation allows us to compare data obtained using different metrics. The larger a z score, the further its value from the group's mean; the smaller the z score, the closer it is to the mean. A z score of 0 means that the individual's unstandardized score is equal to the mean—that is, there is zero deviation from the mean. The z score is to an individual's value as standard deviation is to a group's values.

z Score: Formula

Calculate the z score for each individual by subtracting the individual's score from the group mean and dividing that result by the standard deviation for the group. Using the notations shown previously in the formula for calculating variance, the formula for z is

Formula for Calculating a z Score	
$$z = \frac{X - \bar{X}}{SD}$$	z = z score
	X = individual score
	$\bar{X}$ = mean score for the group
	SD = standard deviation

z Score: Example

The calculation below uses the data from Column 5 of Exhibit 6.1. Remember the group mean for HWI is 54.85.

Taking the first two individuals from the group of 20 scores shown in Exhibit 6.1, we can compute their z scores as follows:

$$\text{Helen: } z = \frac{7 - 54.85}{26.14} = -1.83 \qquad \text{Kiri: } z = \frac{100 - 54.85}{26.14} = 1.73$$

We know already that Helen's score is below the group mean and that Kiri's score is above it, but more specifically, we now can say that Helen's HWI value is 1.83 standard deviations below the group mean, and Kiri's HWI value is 1.73 standard deviations above the mean. The z score represents a standard deviation for individuals. As we will see in Chapter 7, we can use an individual's z score to estimate the probability of that response occurring in the total population.

Most z scores are somewhere between −2 and +2—that is, between plus and minus two standard deviations of the mean. Scores greater than 2, whether positive or negative, have a 5% or lower probability of occurring. You might also intuit this from the observations that Helen's and Kiri's HWI scores are at the extreme range of scores for the group and that each score occurs only once, relative to the more frequent midrange scores of 40 and 60.

The Chi-Square Test

What happens when we have variables such as gender or political preference that are essentially labels?

Remember "NOIR" from Chapter 5? Variables such as *religion, liberal,* and *gender* are nominal, that is to say basically labels. We can count them, but we cannot work with them mathematically. They are categories rather than values. We may code *male* as 1 and *female* as 2, but "1" and "2" are simply labels; they do not imply that the two sexes are quantitatively different on some scale that measures gender.

We cannot calculate a mean of male and female, or of liberal and conservative. All we can do is look at the distribution of their values. To assess group differences on such nominal or ordinal variables, we need a test based on the distribution of their values. This is where the chi-square test comes in.

For example, suppose we want to know if there is a relationship between gender and political affiliation. In other words, do males and females differ significantly in political affiliation?

We interview 10 females and 10 males, and ask them for their political affiliation. The results are shown in Exhibit 6.10a.

EXHIBIT 6.10a   **Observed Values (O) of Political Affiliation by Gender**

	Male	Female
Liberal	3	7
Conservative	7	3

EXHIBIT 6.10b   **Expected Values (E), Assuming No Difference Between Groups**

	Male	Female
Liberal	5	5
Conservative	5	5

From Exhibit 6.10a, it appears that males are more likely to be conservative than females. To get a more precise reading, we would want to compare their scores on a conservatism scale with the scores for females on the same scale.

But wait! There are no scores. Exhibit 6.10a shows numbers of people, not the values of a variable. What to do? All we can do is compare the pattern of responses shown in Exhibit 6.10a with the results we would expect if there were no pattern—that is, if each category had the same number of people in it. This is called the expected pattern, and it is shown in Exhibit 6.10b.

The chi-square test is based on computing the difference between the observed result for each cell in a table and the expected result if there was no difference between the groups.

Chi-Square: Formula

The chi-square formula is shown below. χ denotes the Greek letter *chi*, not an *X*.

Formula for Calculating Chi-square	
$$\chi^2 = \Sigma \frac{(O-E)^2}{E}$$	χ^2 = *chi* squared Σ = "the sum of" O = observed value in each cell of table E = expected value in each cell of table

Chi-Square: Example

Exhibits 6.10a and 6.10b show the distribution of observed values (O) along with the expected values (E) if there was no difference between groups. Putting these values in the above formula results in a chi-square value of 3.2 as shown below.

$$\chi^2 = \frac{(3-5)^2}{5} + \frac{(7-5)^2}{5} + \frac{(7-5)^2}{5} + \frac{(3-5)^2}{5}$$

$$= \frac{4}{5} + \frac{4}{5} + \frac{4}{5} + \frac{4}{5}$$

$$= 3.2$$

To interpret the chi-square result, we need to know the **degrees of freedom (df)**. Degrees of freedom is a measure of "room to move." Essentially, it is a question of how many ways our data could be combined and still produce the same value of chi-square. We need to go to a table showing the normal distribution of chi-square values to determine whether the distribution of observed scores can be attributed to chance or not.

For the chi-square test, df is the number of columns multiplied by number of rows, minus one, in this case $(2 \times 2) - 1 = 3$.

EXHIBIT 6.11   **Part of Chi-Square Table**

(df)	Level of Significance			
	.10	**.05**	**.01**	**.001**
2	4.60	5.99	9.21	13.82
3	6.25	7.82	11.34	16.27
4	7.78	9.49	13.28	18.47

We would go to a table of chi-square values, part of which is shown in Exhibit 6.11. Such tables are available in many research texts and on the web. Alternatively, statistical software will calculate the value of chi-square and the probability of it occurring.

Exhibit 6.11 shows that our computed value of chi-square = 3.2 at df (3) is well below the value of 7.82 needed to demonstrate significance at the 95% (.05) **confidence level**. In spite of what appears to be a difference between males and females with respect to political leaning, we conclude that if the study were to be repeated, in 95 cases out of 100 we would find no significant difference in frequencies between gender and political preference.

More formally, we calculated 3.2 as the value of chi-square with 3 degrees of freedom and opted to use the conventional .05 probability level as the criterion for rejecting the null hypothesis that men and women do not differ in political preference. The table of chi-square values tells us that for the above degrees of freedom and probability level, a value of at least 7.82 is needed to reject the null hypothesis of no difference between groups. Because our value of 3.2 is well below 7.82, we accept the null hypotheses that there is no statistically significant difference. That is to say, the results we obtained could have been obtained by chance.

We report our findings as follows: There was no significant difference between men and women with respect to political affiliation; $\chi^2(3) = 3.2, p < .05$.

Ethics Panel: Can Rankings Be Misleading?

The *U.S. News & World Report* annual rankings of colleges and universities have become controversial because some educational institutions have been caught attempting to improve their rankings by manipulating or even falsifying their institutional data (Slotnik, 2012).

Manipulating data with the intent to deceive is obviously an ethical problem and may well be criminal behavior depending on the circumstances. In this case, however, you are invited to consider the ethical implications of ranking, per se. *U.S. News & World Report* lists colleges and universities in several categories—for example, national and regional universities, national and regional liberal arts colleges, best undergraduate business programs, and best undergraduate engineering programs. In each such category, the institutions list out as rankings—number one, number two, number three, and so on.

Such rankings are ordinal. That is, they rank institution A as "better than" institution B but not how much better. "How much better" would be represented by a rating system that uses scores rather than a rank. For example, using a 1–5 scale to rank a campus on its food service might result in hypothetical scores of 4.2 and 4.5 for each of two institutions.

The National Association for College Admission Counseling (NACAC) has drawn attention to this distinction between rankings and ratings. A 2010 survey of its members showed that a majority of college admission counseling professionals held negative opinions of the *U.S. News & World Report* undergraduate rankings (NACAC, 2011).

On a scale of 1 (*strenuously object to rankings*) to 100 (*strongly support the rankings*), high school counselors rated the ranking system a 29, and college admission officers rated the system a 39. A large majority of respondents believed that the rankings offer misleading conclusions about institutional quality.

Some respondents also emphasized that there is little statistical difference between schools and that placing colleges in ordinal rank therefore creates the illusion of differences where there are none.

And, of course, the questions of "best for whom?" and "best for what?" arise. The best college for student A will not be the best college for student B. Nor will the criteria most important to student A be the criteria most important to student B.

Despite the publicity such rankings continue to receive, the NACAC remains critical of the *U.S. News* rankings, critiquing, for example, the ranking's emphasis on ACT and SAT scores, which are a measure of the student, not the college (NACAC, 2014).

In the context of this chapter on basic statistics:

Questions

- How might readers of college rankings be misled by looking only at rankings?

- What attributes of colleges and universities should be measured in order to help a potential student make the most appropriate decisions about his or her education?

- At what level should the attributes you identify be measured—nominal, ordinal, interval, or ratio? Why?

- Would it be helpful or confusing to present readers with every institution's score on every measure so that each reader can develop his or her own "best" ranking? Why?

Websites for *U.S. News & World Report*, NACAC, and the U.S. Department of Education "College Navigator" are listed below under "Recommended Web Resources."

CHAPTER SUMMARY

- The basic aim of data reduction is to make large data sets comprehensible.
- Descriptive statistics describe and summarize the data recorded from a research project.
- Measures of central tendency—mean, median, and mode—describe the "center" of a data distribution.
- Measures of dispersion—range, interquartile range, variance, and standard deviation—describe the range and extreme values of a data distribution.
- The z score is a standardized measure of how far an individual value is from the mean for its group.
- Summary statistics may be presented as tables, graphs, or statistics.

KEY TERMS

anomalous data	IBM SPSS® Statistics
bi-modal distribution	inferential statistics
bi-variate	interquartile range
categorical data	maximum
chi-square	mean
confidence level	measures of central tendency
contingency tables	measures of dispersion
continuous data	median
cross-tabs	metrics
data points	minimum
data reduction	mode
data set	multivariate
degrees of freedom (df)	parameters
descriptive statistics	population
frequencies	proprietary
frequency tables	R

range   tables
sample   tri-modal distribution
standard deviation   univariate analysis
statistical formulae   variance
statistics   *z* score

APPLICATION EXERCISES

Exercise 1: Basic Statistics

For the variables SMCS and KWA in Exhibit 6.1, compute mean, median, mode, range, variance, and standard deviation.

Exercise 2: Brand, Color, and Gender Preferences

Let's hypothesize that men and women differ in their preferences for clothing brands and for color. In a setting such as a classroom, cafeteria, or library, look at the T-shirts and sweatshirts people are wearing. For each person, record your observations of gender, and the color and "brand" (Gap, Nike, a university name, etc.), if any, on each shirt. Produce two contingency tables—gender by color preference and gender by brand.

What conclusions can you come to about how color and brand preferences differ by gender?

Note that this assignment is not quite as simple as it appears because as soon as you start recording color, you will need to make a typical research decision—setting up your own categories. The number of color categories is potentially almost unlimited, so you will want to make that number manageable. How many categories will you set up, and how will you decide what category indeterminate colors ("could be this; could be that") will be assigned to? How will you handle clothing that promotes a cause or a political candidate rather than a brand? For some help with this assignment, you can jump forward to Chapter 12.

Exercise 3: "The Internet of Things"

Find the May 14, 2014, Pew Research Center Internet, Science & Tech Project report on "The Internet of Things" at www.pewinternet.org/2014/05/14/internet-of-things. The Internet of Things, or IoT, is considered the next technology megatrend in which anything from fitness bracelets to jet engines will be connected to the Internet to transmit and share data. In the report and summary, you will find six themes related to the topic of embedded and wearable computing to which experts were invited to respond. For example: "The Internet of Things and wearable computing will progress significantly between now and 2025." Select one of the themes you will find in the above report and write it as a Likert-type question (revisit Chapter 5 for help). Get responses to your question from two different categories of people (for example, two different academic majors or two different class years). Get at least five people in each category. Assign each point in your scale a number so that you can record a score on the question for each respondent. Compute measures of central tendency and of dispersion for each category of respondent and report how these statistics are similar or differ.

Exercise 4: A Social Media Study

Visit LinkedIn.com—the social media site for professionals. Information for some members that is publicly available includes academic qualifications, employment history, group or organizational affiliations, and number of individual connections. Select at least two individuals and look at such information.

Formulate your own research questions about LinkedIn members. For example, are women likely to have more connections than men? Are members with PhDs likely to have more group or organizational affiliations than members with bachelor's degrees?

Note that some of the information displayed can be treated as continuous (the number of academic degrees or jobs) and some as categorical (the type of degree or job). Which type of data should you prefer to best answer your research question(s)? Produce a table of descriptive statistics that will answer your research question(s). What confidence do you have that your results accurately reflect all LinkedIn members of the type you sampled? Revisit Exhibit 6.1 for examples of categorical and continuous data.

Note that this mini-assignment includes almost all the elements of a full communication research study—developing a focus for your study, writing a specific research question, planning your statistical analyses, deciding what type of data to collect and how to collect it, and presenting your results. Note also that deciding what type of statistical analyses and reporting you will do precedes your data collection. If you are interested in continuous data, you will not design a study that collects only categorical data. You need a defensible and demonstrable connection between your initial theory and research question(s), the data you are interested in, and your research method(s).

Note: You can access the information you will need for this project in two ways:

- Search for someone you know or think may be a member of LinkedIn using the "Find a Colleague" window on the home page: www.linkedin.com. This option avoids having to register, but limits you to publicly available information.
- Register with LinkedIn using the "Get Started" window on the home page. This option will give you access to more—members-only—information, as well as enable you to post your own information.

RECOMMENDED READING

Huff, D. (1954). *How to lie with statistics*. New York, NY: Norton.

A statistical "best seller" since 1954. Be guided by the content, not the title!

Paulos, J. A. (1997). *A mathematician reads the newspaper*. New York, NY: Random House.

This book discusses how research results and statistics are reported or misreported in newspapers.

RECOMMENDED WEB RESOURCES

The many statistical resources on the web range from easy interactive tutorials on the basic statistics discussed in this chapter to advanced routines of interest only to a specific discipline. They range from "click and go" to "installation required" and often come with a "no guarantees" warning.

Because statistics is a language that transcends discipline, you will find statistical help at many different academic and commercial sites.

The following list errs on the side of brevity. To see the vast range of statistical websites, do your own search or check out the John Pezzullo web page below.

Easycalculation . . . . www.easycalculation.com

A site for a variety of calculators, including statistics.

GraphPad . . . . http://graphpad.com/quickcalcs/index.cfm

Provides basic statistical calculators online. You will find *t*-test and chi-square calculators here, among others.

John C. Pezzullo's statpages . . . . http://statpages.org

The starting point for statistical websites.

StatSoft . . . . www.statsoft.com/textbook/stathome.html

> An online textbook/tutorial on statistics.

UCLA Statistics Online Computational Resource (SOCR) . . . . http://socr.ucla.edu/Applets.dir/OnlineResources.html

College Rankings

National Association for College Admission
Counseling (NACAC) College Rankings . . . . www.nacacnet.org/studentinfo/CollegeRankings/Pages/CollegeRankings.aspx

U.S. Department of Education "College Navigator" . . . . http://nces.ed.gov/collegenavigator

U.S. News & World Report Education
Rankings Methodologies . . . . www.usnews.com/education/articles/2013/01/14/about-the-us-news-education-rankings-methodologies?int=ad9009&int=ad9009

REFERENCES

National Association for College Admission Counseling. (2011). A view of the *U.S. News & World Report* rankings of undergraduate institutions from the college admission counseling perspective. Survey report from the National Association for College Admission Counseling Ad Hoc Committee on *U.S. News & World Report* Rankings. Retrieved from http://www.nacacnet.org

National Association for College Admission Counseling. (2014). Reaction to revised *U.S. News* rankings methodologies [News release]. Retrieved from http://www.nacacnet.org

Slotnik, D. E. (2012, February 1). Gambling a college's reputation on climbing the rankings. *New York Times.* Retrieved from http://www.nytimes.com

Ⓢ SAGE edge™

Want a better grade?
Get the tools you need to sharpen your study skills. Access practice quizzes, eFlashcards, video, and multimedia at **edge.sagepub.com/treadwell3e**

CHAPTER 7

Generalizing From Research Results
Inferential Statistics

Far better an approximate answer to the right question, which is often vague, than an exact answer to the wrong question, which can always be made precise.

—John Tukey (1915–2000)
Mathematician

❧❧❧

Chapter Overview

Analyzing a sample is done to gain insight on a larger population that the sample is presumed to represent. This means that we want to know whether the results obtained from a sample reflect the results we would get if we studied the entire population. We can, of course, never know this for certain except by researching the entire population, so our next best option is to estimate the probability that our sample represents the entire population. This is what inferential statistics do; they help us make probability-based inferences about the wider population from which we obtained our sample.

More specifically, inferential statistics help with three major tasks—estimating the probability that a sample represents a population, deciding whether there are significant differences between and among groups of people, and deciding whether there are significant relationships between and among variables. In the context of statistics, significance has a special meaning. Significance means that there is a better than random chance that a relationship exists.

Because inferential statistics are based on assumptions about the distribution of data in populations, this chapter begins with a discussion of an important underlying concept—the assumption of a normal distribution of values in a population.

Chapter Objectives

This chapter will help you

- Explain the concept of inferential statistics and how they differ from descriptive statistics.
- Describe the normal curve and its significance to inferential statistics.

(Continued)

(Continued)

- Discuss the concept of statistical significance.
- Describe and compute a *t* test.
- Explain the concept of analysis of variance.
- Compare and contrast the concepts of correlation and regression.
- Define Type I and Type II errors.

Introduction

The **descriptive statistics** described in Chapter 6 go a long way toward helping us to simplify and understand research data and toward identifying patterns and relationships in data. However, researchers looking at the data from a sample of people or of media content have one major question that descriptive statistics cannot answer: "To what extent do my sample data reflect the wider population from which I obtained my sample?"

The question is a very practical one. For example, political communication consultants want to be confident that if 53% of a sample of voters express an intention to vote for candidate X, then 53% of the broader voting population that was sampled will also likely vote for candidate X. If we cannot have confidence in sampling, then the alternative is to survey the entire study population—that is, to conduct a **census**.

A census is likely to be difficult, expensive, and time consuming, so we must find ways to give ourselves as much confidence as possible that data from a sample do reflect the data that would be obtained from a wider population. That means being able to estimate as precisely as possible the probability that our sample findings do reflect the population parameters. This, essentially, is the role of inferential statistics.

To illustrate the calculation and use of inferential statistics, we will revisit some of the data shown in Chapter 6, Exhibit 6.1. First, though, let's visit data distributions and the language of curves.

The Language of Curves

Inferential statistics are based on the assumption of a **normal distribution** of values in a population. This means that when plotted out, the frequency of values in a normal distribution form a symmetrical curve from the lowest to the highest value with the majority of values peaking in the middle.

Not all distributions are normal, however. For example, we discovered in Chapter 6 that our data might plot out with a **bi-modal** profile that approximates two curves, not one. Distributions can also be **tri-modal** (three peaks) or multi-modal, or have no particular pattern.

Data may plot out as an asymmetric curve with most of the values to the left of the plot and a "long tail" of values to the right, in which case we describe the curve as having positive skew or being positively skewed. Conversely, a plot with most of the data points to the right of the plot and few data points to the left is described as having negative skew. **Skew** is where the "tail" of a distribution is. Positive skew means the tail is in the high numbers; negative skew means that the tail is in the low numbers. When a quiz is easy, a high percentage of students will score in the 80 or 90s out of a possible 100, producing a so-called negative skew. If the class has the toughest grader in history, most scores will plot out at the low end, and the skew will be positive.

When data are skewed, mean, median, and mode can differ considerably, and all three become necessary to adequately describe the distribution.

A curve that is flat relative to the normal curve is described as **platykurtic**; a curve that is taller, relatively speaking, is described as **leptokurtic**. (You can remember the difference by thinking platykurtic = flat-ykurtic and leptokurtic as leapt [up]-okurtic.) A platykurtic distribution means that the values are more widely spread; a leptokurtic distribution has most values concentrated within a narrow range.

Generalizing From Data: Inferential Statistics

Inferential statistics help us generalize (make inferences) about a wider population from a smaller sample of it. They are based on two assumptions:

- The population sampled has normally distributed characteristics.
- The sample is randomly selected; that is, every individual in the population has an equal chance of being selected.

The Normal Curve and the Central Limit Theorem

In a statistically perfect world, data conform to a symmetrical, so-called **normal curve** or **bell curve**. Test results, for example, may approach this pattern; one or two people may score 0, one or two will achieve that magic 100, and a large number of people will score around the 50 mark, with fewer numbers scoring in the 80s and in the 30s.

Chapter 6, Exhibit 6.3—our plot of the frequency of values for the variable hours of Internet use per week (HWI)—approximates a normal curve, although positively skewed. If we accept that this distribution of values approximates a normal distribution, we can use the characteristics of the normal distribution to calculate the probability of obtaining any given value in the distribution.

A further assist comes from the **central limit theorem**, which, in summary, states that the distribution of the averages or sums of a large number of samples of a variable will be approximately normal regardless of the shape of the underlying distribution.

By way of example, let's revisit data from Chapter 6, Exhibit 6.1. Look at the knowledge of world affairs (KWA) variable and assume that Exhibit 6.1 shows the data for an entire population. We will attempt to estimate the mean value of KWA for this population of 20 by looking at samples drawn from that population.

We will randomly sample the variable KWA, keeping our sample size constant—three for ease of calculation—and calculate the value of the mean for each sample we take. The individuals in each sample will be randomly selected by using a random numbers generator (discussed further in Chapter 8, "Sampling"). We will take one, two, four, eight, and sixteen samples and record the mean for each sample. The number and size of samples is arbitrary; we could demonstrate the same principles with five, ten, fifteen, and twenty samples, just as we could have selected a sample size of 2, 4, 5, or more.

Exhibit 7.1 shows the distribution of the means calculated for every sample of three as we increase the number of samples from 1 to 16.

The first random sample of three has a mean value of 5.3. It is a problematic value because we have no idea how well this sample represents the mean for the population. Next, we randomly select two samples, compute their means, and get values of 6.3 and 9. This suggests that the mean for the population may lie between 6.3 and 9. With results from four random

Exhibit 7.1 Distribution of Means of Knowledge of World Affairs (KWA) for Samples of Three With Increasing Number of Samples

Number of Samples	Means for Random Samples of Three Scores on KWA																
One								5.3									
Two											6.3						9.0
Four							5.0	5.3	5.7			6.7					
Eight	3.0		3.7	4.0				5.3			6.3			7.3	8.0	8.3	
Sixteen									5.7								
									5.7	6.0		6.7					
		3.3			4.3	4.7	5.0	5.3	5.7	6.0	6.3	6.7	7.0	7.3	8.0		

samples, we might guess that the population mean lies between 5 and 6.7 with the actual value lying somewhere around 5.5. Results from eight samples suggest that the mean lies between 3 and 8.3 and, again, is perhaps around 5.5 as that seems to be the median value for our set of four samples and for our set of eight samples. Results from sixteen samples approximate a normal curve when plotted out and suggest that the population mean lies between 3.3 and 8 with a high probability that the mean is 5.7 as that value occurs most frequently and also approximates the median value.

The results we obtained with sixteen samples approximate what the central limit theorem proposed. The distribution of the means is approaching a normal distribution; that is, most of the means are in the middle of the distribution with greater and lesser values tapering off in number to each side. Looking at the approximately normal distribution of means for our sixteen samples, we can at least feel confident that 5.7 has a greater probability of being the population mean than does an extreme value such as 3.3 or 8.

We can never get the population mean value with 100% certainty, but our level of certainty increases as we increase the number of samples. Our first sample mean of 5.3 leaves us somewhat clueless as to what the population mean might be, but sixteen samples give us much more confidence that it lies somewhere between 3.3 and 8 and is probably around 5.7.

As it happens, our estimate is 100% correct; the mean value for KWA for our small population of 20 is 5.7. However, without population information, we would not normally know that. So our estimate of 5.7 remains just that—an estimate. Unless we have data for the entire population, we will never be 100% confident that we have the true mean.

This is where the z distribution comes to our rescue. Even though we don't have population data, if we assume a normal distribution of values in the population we are sampling, we can calculate the probability that our sample has captured the characteristics of the population.

The Normal Curve, z Scores, and the Return of Standard Deviation

As discussed in Chapter 6, z scores are a way of standardizing values of variables so that they can be compared. A standardized normal curve, based on z scores, is symmetrical with a mean of 0, a standard deviation of 1, and a total area under the curve equal to 1. Conveniently, *z* scores equal standard deviations; a *z* score of 1.5, for example, is 1.5 standard deviations from the mean. The area under the standardized normal curve allows us to calculate the probability of obtaining any given result. For example, the probability of sampling any value under this curve is 100% or 1.0 because you must pull some value if sampling. Any value greater than or less than the mean has a 50% or .5 probability of occurring because half the values lie above the mean and half below it.

A standardized normal curve with two *z* scores plotted from our Chapter 6 data is shown in Exhibit 7.2.

EXHIBIT 7.2   Normal Curve Showing Two *z* Scores

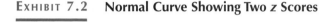

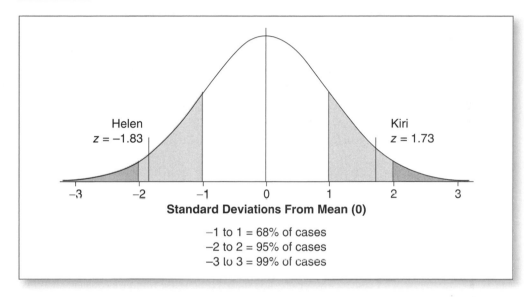

Importantly, under any normal curve,

- 68% of the values occur within ± one standard deviation from the mean—the white area under the curve in Exhibit 7.2. This means that a result greater than one standard deviation, plus or minus, occurs in only 32% (100% − 68%) of the samples or has a .32 probability of occurring.
- 95% of the values occur within ± two standard deviations from the mean—the white plus light blue areas under the curve in Exhibit 7.2. A result greater than two standard deviations, plus or minus, occurs in only 5% (100% − 95%) of the samples or has a .05 probability of occurring.
- 99.7% of the values occur within ± three standard deviations from the mean—the white plus light blue and darker blue areas under the curve in Exhibit 7.2. A result greater than three standard deviations from the mean, plus or minus, occurs in fewer than 0.3% (100%−99.7%) of the samples or has less than a .003 probability of occurring.

Exhibit 7.3 shows a more precise distribution of values under the normal curve.

EXHIBIT 7.3   **Percentage Distribution of Values Under the Normal Curve by Standard Deviation (SD) From the Mean**

	> −3 SDs	−3 SDs	−2 SDs	−1 SD	+1 SD	+2 SDs	+3 SDs	> +3 SDs
By SD From Mean	0.13	2.15	13.59	34.13	34.13	13.59	2.15	0.13
Cumulative SD From Mean	50.0	49.87	47.72	34.13	34.13	47.72	49.87	50.0

The characteristics of the standardized normal curve allow us to calculate a specific level of confidence in our results and help us decide whether any given result should or should not be attributed to mere chance. Let's look at some examples.

Calculating Probabilities Based on the Normal Distribution

Let's revisit the KWA variable, whose mean we calculated to be 5.7. Earlier in this chapter, we estimated its mean to be between 3.3 and 8.0 and more likely to be 5.7 than other greater or lesser values. Following the example of calculating a standard deviation shown in Chapter 6, Exhibit 6.8, we calculate the standard deviation for KWA to be 2.36. We can now estimate specific probabilities of the mean for the KWA population as follows. There is a

- 68% probability that the population mean lies between 3.34 and 8.06; that is, ± one standard deviation (2.36) from 5.7.
- 95% probability that the population mean lies between 0.98 and 10.42; that is, ± two standard deviations (4.72) from 5.7.
- 99% probability that the population mean lies between −1.38 and 12.78; that is, ± three standard deviations (7.08) from 5.7.

Of course, a score of −1.38 makes little sense when we consider that it is capturing knowledge of world affairs. It is difficult to see how anyone could have negative knowledge or score less than zero on a test. We need to remember that we are now looking at a theoretical distribution of values and the statistical probability, not the commonsense probability, of a value occurring.

From Exhibit 7.1, we might guess that the population mean is around 5.7, but we don't know what results other samples would provide. Knowing the standard deviation, having calculated our mean for the sample, and assuming the KWA values are normally distributed, we can, however, now say that if we repeat our sampling, 95 times out of 100 the mean for the sample will lie between 0.98 and 10.42.

Let's now look at how individual z scores can be used to estimate the probability of any given score occurring. Exhibit 7.2 shows the HWI z scores for Helen and Kiri that we calculated in Chapter 6. Helen's z score of −1.83 lies between minus one and minus two standard deviations from the mean and is closer to minus two standard deviations. What is the probability of her score occurring?

Half the scores under the normal curve are negative, so just by knowing that Helen's score is negative, we can say that it has no more than a 50% or .5 probability of occurring. We can get more specific than that, though. Looking at Exhibit 7.3 (bottom line) and the negative scores on the left side of the curve, we can calculate that z scores below −1 have a .1587 probability or less of occurring. (50% − 34.13% = 15.87% = .1587). z scores below −2 have a .0228 probability or less of occurring (50% − 47.72% = 2.28% = .0228). So just by knowing the normal curve, we can say that the probability of a z score of −1.83 occurring is between .0228 and .1587.

EXHIBIT 7.4   Part of a Table of *z* Scores

z	Standard Normal Distribution. Values Represent Area Under the Normal Curve to Left of the *z* Score									
	.00	**.01**	**.02**	**.03**	**.04**	**.05**	**.06**	**.07**	**.08**	**.09**
−1.9	.0287	.0281	.0274	.0268	.0262	.0256	.0250	.0244	.0239	.0233
−1.8	.0359	.0351	.0344	.0336	.0329	.0322	.0314	.0307	.0301	.0294
−1.7	.0446	.0436	.0427	.0418	.0409	.0401	.0392	.0384	.0375	.0367
1.6	.9452	.9463	.9474	.9484	.9495	.9505	.9515	.9525	.9535	.9545
1.7	.9554	.9564	.9573	.9582	.9591	.9599	.9608	.9616	.9625	.9633
1.8	.9641	.9649	.9656	.9664	.9671	.9678	.9686	.9693	.9699	.9706

To get the exact probability, we can go to tables of *z* scores. Part of such a table is shown in Exhibit 7.4. It shows the area under the standardized normal curve to the left of any given *z* score. The probability of a *z* score of −1.83 occurring is located at the intersection of row −1.8 and column .03. The result is .0336—within the range of values we had estimated just by knowing the attributes of the *z* distribution—and closer to .0228 than to .1587, because the *z* score is closer to −2 than −1 as we had noted.

z scores can also help us understand the distribution of values in a population. For example, what percentage of the population is on the Internet between Helen's and Kiri's values of 7 and 100 hours a week? Exhibit 7.4 shows their *z* scores of −1.83 and 1.73 highlighted. The table tells us that .9582 of the HWI values lie to the left of 1.73 and .0336 of the values lie to the left of −1.83. The difference between these two values is (.9582 − .0336) = .9246; that is, over 92% of the scores lie between 7 and 100 hours a week. We can verify this from a quick glance at Exhibit 7.2, which shows that these two *z* scores mark a range of scores ranging from almost two standard deviations below the mean to almost two standard deviations above the mean; that is, almost 95% of the scores fall between them.

(Note that some *z* tables use different conventions for showing the distribution of *z* and need to be read differently; for example, they may show the area between a *z* score and the mean.)

z Scores, Hypotheses, and Decision Making

Conventionally, we use a .05 probability cutoff to decide whether to accept or reject a null hypothesis of "no difference." This means we accept a null hypothesis that all scores lying between plus and minus two standard deviations from the mean—95% of the scores—belong to members of the same population.

There is only a 5% probability of getting values that lie beyond plus or minus two standard deviations from the mean. We assume, therefore, that something other than chance explains these values. That "something" is that these values belong to another population.

Remember that we do not know the real values for the population because we have not conducted a census of the whole population. All we have is a calculated range of possibilities. This range of values is called the **confidence interval**. In our KWA example above, we calculated the confidence interval to be 0.98 to 10.42 at the 95% confidence level.

For a **sampling distribution** (the distribution of the sample results), the standard deviation is called the **standard error**.

When we report results, we report the confidence level and the standard error. For example, public opinion polls often print a statement to the effect that in 19 out of 20 cases the sample results will differ by no more than 3% from the results that would be obtained from a census of the entire population. In other words, they are reporting that at the 95% confidence level (19 out of 20 = 95%) the standard error for their results is plus or minus 3% given their sample size of, typically, 1,200. This means that we can be statistically confident that if the survey were repeated 100 times under the same conditions, we would find that 95 times out of 100 the results would vary by less than 3% (or by more than 3% only 5 times out of 100).

Inferential statistics, random sampling, and the assumption of a normal distribution of data together help us calculate our level of certainty when we project results from a sample to a wider population. Conveniently, inferential statistics also tell us that as long as we are prepared to accept a known level of uncertainty in our projections, we do not need huge sample sizes.

All these calculations of probability are based on the assumption of normal distribution. Statistical procedures based in these assumptions are called **parametric statistics**. When we cannot make the assumption of normal distribution, or have categorical rather than continuous variables, other statistics—**nonparametric**—must be used.

Confidence Level and Sample Size

There is a trade-off among confidence level, standard deviation, and sample size. This is discussed more fully in Chapter 8. For now, let's revisit the formula for standard deviation, shown in Chapter 6 and again below.

Formula for Standard Deviation	
$SD = \sqrt{\dfrac{\Sigma(X - \overline{X})^2}{(N-1)}}$	SD = standard deviation
	$\overline{X}$ = the mean score for the group
	X = each individual score
	N = the number of scores

Revisit the calculation of standard deviation (SD) for the HWI variable, shown in Chapter 6, Exhibit 6.8. Filling in our calculations for the standard deviation and using the sample size, N, rather than N − 1, we have for HWI:

$$SD = \sqrt{\frac{12,978}{N}}$$

Exhibit 7.5 shows how the value of the standard deviation/standard error decreases as the sample size increases.

Exhibit 7.5 **Relationship of Sample Size to Standard Deviation for Hours of Internet Use per Week (HWI) Variable**

Sample Size	Standard Deviation (SD)
20	25.47
40	18.01
80	12.73
160	9.01
320	6.37

The square root in the formula indicates that the sample size needs to be quadrupled to halve the standard error. For example, our sample size of 20 needs to be quadrupled to 80 to halve the standard error to 12.73, needs to be quadrupled again to 320 to further halve the error to 6.37, and would need to be increased to 1,280 to halve the error again. For a national survey of public opinion, a sample of 20 people intuitively seems too small; 1,280 perhaps reasonable; and 5,120, which would halve the standard error yet again, a lot of work! There is obviously a law of diminishing returns here. You could put time and effort into obtaining a sample of 5,000 people (or, in the ultimate, to surveying an entire population), but it is usual to settle for the convenience of a smaller sample and to accept some level of error (which you will be able to calculate) as a trade-off.

Obviously, larger sample sizes become important when a smaller level of error is needed.

Knowing the level of error and the confidence level we can afford allows us to work back to the sample size we need, a discussion we continue in Chapter 8.

Testing for Differences Between and Among Groups

A frequent question in communication research is "Do two groups differ on some variable of interest?" The **chi-square** test introduced in Chapter 6 is used where we have categorical data. With continuous data, one way to answer this question is to compare each group's mean score on our variable of interest using the *t* **test**, described below.

The *t* Test

The *t* test compares the mean scores of two groups on the same variable to determine the probability that the groups are different.

Let's return to Chapter 6, Exhibit 6.1, and look at two groups—the politically conservative and the politically liberal. Let's hypothesize that the groups' knowledge of world affairs (KWA) will differ based on their political preference (POLP).

Column 7 of Exhibit 6.1 lists the scores of the 20 respondents for KWA on a 1-to-10 scale. Column 4 shows POLP for each respondent. We can plot the distribution of scores for the 10 individuals who are politically liberal and the 10 individuals who are politically conservative, as shown in Exhibit 7.6.

EXHIBIT 7.6   **Distribution of Scores on Knowledge of World Affairs (KWA) by Political Preference (POLP)**

Liberal (Mean = 5.0)		4	6		
		4	6		
		4	6		
	2	4	6	8	
Conservative (Mean = 6.4)		4		8	
		4		8	10
	2	4	6	8	10

The distribution of scores suggests something like a normal distribution of scores for the liberal group and a bi-modal distribution of scores for the conservative group, with the conservative group having a greater range of scores and more high scores than the liberal group.

The mean score for KWA for the liberal group is 5.0 (50/10), and for the conservative group it is 6.4 (64/10).

Based only on the means, we might conclude that the conservative group has a greater KWA than does the liberal group, but look at the distribution of the two sets of scores in Exhibit 7.6. The two groups have scores of 2, 4, 6, and 8 in common. The only score unique to any one group is the conservatives' two 10s.

The question then becomes did *all* of the conservatives score higher than *all* of the liberals, suggesting that we have two groups from two different populations? Or, if many of the individual scores are the same in both groups, arc wc basically looking at two groups from the same population? Clearly, the latter appears to be the case in our example.

The question is one of statistical significance, as in "Do the means of the two groups differ significantly?" More precisely, what we are asking is "What is the probability that the mean score for one group falls within one, two, or three standard deviations from the mean score for the second group?"

If we conclude that we are looking at samples from two different populations, we can say that the two groups are significantly different. If we conclude that we are looking at one population with two subgroups in it, we reject the hypothesis that the two groups are significantly different (in this case that the liberal group differs significantly from the conservative group on KWA scores).

The *t*-test calculation results in a value that is then compared against a table showing the probability of the calculated *t* value occurring. Basically, the *t* test shows whether our observed difference in means, corrected for the number of observations and the range of scores, is of low or high probability.

t Test: Formula

Conceptually, the *t* test is based on the differences in means for a variable common to two groups but also takes into account the range of scores for each group and each group's size, as shown below. Tables of *t* values or statistical software show the probability of the calculated *t* value occurring.

$$t = \frac{\text{difference in group means}}{\sqrt{\dfrac{\text{correction for group variance}}{\text{correction for group size}}}}$$

The calculation requires three inputs from each group—the group's mean, the group's size, and the group's sum of the squared differences of each score from the group mean. You will recognize from Chapter 6 that this sum of the squared differences from the mean for each score is the variance.

The formula to calculate the value of *t* where two different groups are compared is called a **t test for independent samples**.

We are looking at data for the KWA variable to see if the KWA scores vary significantly according to the individuals' POLP.

Exhibit 7.7 shows the group means, the size of each group, the calculation of the sum of squared differences of each score from its group mean, and the calculation of the *t* value.

Formula for Calculating t for Independent Samples	
$$t = \frac{\overline{X}_1 - \overline{X}_2}{\sqrt{(\Sigma d_1^2 + \Sigma d_2^2) / [(n_1 + n_2 - 2)/(n_1 + n_2)] * [(n_1 n_2)]}}$$	$\overline{X}_1, \overline{X}_2$ = means for group 1 and group 2 $\Sigma d_1^2, \Sigma d_2^2$ = sum of squared differences of each score from its group mean n_1, n_2 = number of scores in group 1 and group 2

EXHIBIT 7.7   **Calculation of t for the Variable Knowledge of World Affairs (KWA) on Liberal and Conservative Groups**

Data for Liberal Group			Data for Conservative Group		
KWA scores (n_1 = 10)	Difference between score and group mean (5.0)	Squared difference between score and group mean	KWA scores (n_2 = 10)	Difference between score and group mean (6.4)	Squared difference between score and group mean
2	−3	9	2	−4.4	19.36
4	−1	1	4	−2.4	5.76
4	−1	1	4	−2.4	5.76
4	−1	1	4	−2.4	6.76
4	−1	1	6	−0.4	0.16
6	1	1	8	1.6	2.56
6	1	1	8	1.6	2.56
6	1	1	8	1.6	2.56
6	1	1	10	3.6	12.96
8	3	9	10	3.6	12.96

Mean for KWA
  = sum of scores/10
  = 50/10
  = 5.0
		Sum of Squared Differences
		  = Σd_1
		  = 26.0
			Mean for KWA
			  = sum of scores/10
			  = 64/10
			  = 6.4
					Sum of Squared Differences
					  = Σd_2
					  = 71.4

$$t = \frac{5.0 - 6.4}{\sqrt{(26.0 + 71.4) / [(10 + 10 - 2)/(10 + 10)] * [(10 * 10)]}} = \frac{-1.4}{\sqrt{(97.4) / [(18)/(20)] * [(100)]}} = \frac{-1.4}{\sqrt{\frac{97.4}{90}}} = -1.35$$

t Test: Example

The negative value of *t* in this case simply indicates that the mean for the second group is higher than that for the first group. The actual value of 1.35 tells us nothing in itself. It is a measure of the difference between group means, but what we are interested in is the probability of this difference in means occurring. To get this probability, we need to go to a table that shows the normal distribution of *t* values. Part of such a table is shown in Exhibit 7.8. Such tables are readily available in many research and statistical texts and online. Statistical software will, of course, compute both *t* and the probability of the *t* value occurring for you.

Exhibit 7.8   Part of a Table of *t* Values

df		Level of Significance for One- and Two-Tailed Tests			
		.10	.05	.01	.001
17	Two-tailed	1.740	2.110	2.898	3.965
	One-tailed	1.333	1.740	2.567	3.646
18	Two-tailed	1.734	2.101	2.878	3.922
	One-tailed	1.330	1.734	2.552	3.610
19	Two-tailed	1.729	2.093	2.861	3.883
	One-tailed	1.328	1.729	2.539	3.579

To fully understand and interpret a table of *t* values or the output that statistical software will give you, it is necessary to understand two concepts—**degrees of freedom** and **one-tailed** versus **two-tailed** distribution of values.

As noted in Chapter 6, degrees of freedom (df) is a measure of "room to move." Essentially, it is a question of how many ways our data could be combined and still produce the same value of *t*. In this case, it is calculated as the number of scores in group 1 (minus one) plus the number of scores in group 2 (minus one) $= (10 - 1) + (10 - 1) = 18$.

A one-tailed test means we are proposing that the differences between the groups will be in one direction—for example, that the mean score for the conservative group will be higher than for the liberal group. A two-tailed test proposes only that the groups will differ. The part of a *t* table shown in Exhibit 7.8 shows the probability of a *t* value occurring and how it varies according to degrees of freedom and whether the test is two-tailed or one-tailed.

The higher the *t* value, the lower the probability that it will occur. As described above, the result of our calculation for the above groups was $t = 1.35$ for 18 degrees of freedom. You can see from Exhibit 7.8 that for a two-tailed test, the value needed to demonstrate a significant difference is 2.101 or greater at the 95% (.05) probability level. We have a *t* value less than that needed to demonstrate a significant difference between our two groups regardless of whether we are looking at a one- or a two-tailed test. Therefore, we conclude there is a 95% probability that the groups are not different.

Here is how we would think through the above analysis more formally and report it.

At this stage in our research, we have no reason to theorize that the liberal group would have higher scores than the conservative group or vice versa, so we simply propose a null hypothesis of no difference between the groups.

H_0: Scores on knowledge of world affairs will not differ between the politically liberal and politically conservative groups.

We will follow a social science convention and work to the .05 level of significance for hypothesis testing. The level of significance is a decision for you, the researcher. As the *t* table indicates, you could opt to test at the .01 or even at the .001 level of significance.

We calculated 1.35 as the *t* value with 18 degrees of freedom, and we look at the table of *t* values, selecting the two-tailed values because we hypothesized no difference between the two groups. The table tells us that for such a test, a *t* value of 2.101 is needed to reject the hypothesis that there is no difference between groups. Because our value of 1.35 is less than 2.101, we therefore accept the null hypothesis that there is no difference between the two groups. That is to say, the results we obtained could have been obtained by chance.

We report our findings as follows: There was no significant difference between liberal and conservative groups in the scores for knowledge of world affairs; $t(18) = 1.35$, $p < .05$.

Another Type of *t*

The above example is a *t* test for independent samples; that is, the two groups are two separate sets of individuals. Where we have dependent samples—that is, both groups consist of the same individuals—we must use a different *t* test—the *t* **test for dependent samples**.

The classic "pretest–posttest" is an example of dependent samples. For example, advertisers testing a new advertising campaign might run a baseline study of consumer attitudes toward their client's product, expose these consumers to the test messages, and then run the study again. Any difference in attitudes would then be assumed to be a result of the exposure to the test messages. In this case, we are not comparing two groups; we are comparing the same group twice–"pre" and "post"—and the *t* formula gets amended accordingly.

Formula for Calculating *t* for Dependent Samples	
$$t = \dfrac{\overline{X}_1 - \overline{X}_2}{\sqrt{\dfrac{\sum D^2 - \dfrac{(\sum D)^2}{n}}{n(n-1)}}}$$	$\overline{X}_1, \overline{X}_2$ = means for group 1 and group 2
	$\sum D^2$ = sum of the squared differences between pretest and posttest scores
	$(\sum D)^2$ = square of the sum of the differences between pretest and posttest scores
	n = number of pairs of scores

Notice how some of the thinking about the *t* test for dependent groups changes. Because we are comparing "pre" and "post" scores for the same people, we have only one sample, and we calculate *t* using the number of pairs of scores (in most cases the number of individuals). We cannot include the size of the two separate groups being compared because there is only one group. We also treat variance in scores differently in that we not only sum the squared differences between pre and post scores; we also add up the differences between pre and post scores and square that sum.

Analysis of Variance

One problem with the *t* test is that it compares only two groups. What if we wish to compare more than two groups, for example how art, business, communication, and science majors compare on some standardized test?

When it comes to multiple groups, we need multivariate statistics, of which **ANOVA** (ANalysis Of VAriance) is one example.

Calculating ANOVA is conceptually simple. ANOVA is based on variance, which you will recall is a measure of the extent to which the values for a variable differ. To calculate ANOVA is simply to compare the variance within groups with the variance among groups.

Think of three groups of individuals. One is composed of our siblings, a second is composed of our cousins, and a third is composed of our parents and grandparents. Each group is different in some way. Each individual is different in some way—eye color, dress, age, and so on —but each individual also has something in common with other members of his or her own group and also with members of the other two groups.

What defines each group is that its members more closely resemble one another than they do members of the other two groups. The variance within a group—its variety, if you will—is less than it is for the three groups overall.

If the individuals in a group vary more than the three groups considered together, we would assume that we are looking at one large group of individuals and that that there are no distinctive groups. If the individuals in each group show less variety (variance) than the three groups overall, we assume that these individuals have more in common with others in the group than with the three groups overall and that there are therefore three distinct groups of people.

One-way ANOVA is the simplest member of the ANOVA family. It looks at one variable, but unlike the t test, it compares more than two groups. The formula is complicated in that it compares multiple groups, but it is also one of the easiest to comprehend.

Why not just do multiple t tests—comparing groups 1 and 2, 1 and 3, and 2 and 3, for example? Because this would give you three tests rather than one and therefore change the odds of finding a statistically significant result. Repeated testing is analogous to retaking a test that you were not happy with until you get a good grade. The interest in statistical testing is in what our sample is telling us at a given time, not on repeated testing until a desirable result comes up.

The between-groups variance divided by the within-groups variance gives us an **F value.** From a table of F values, we can find the probability of F occurring and therefore whether we have a statistically significant difference among our sample groups.

ANOVA: Formula

The F test for analysis of variance is conceptually simple and computationally complex. The concept is shown below.

$$F = \frac{\textit{variance between groups}}{\textit{variance within groups}}$$

ANOVA: Example

The formula and steps in the calculation of ANOVA are readily available in advanced texts and online. Here, we will work through the concept behind the calculations and interpretation of results. Suppose, for example, we have a question of whether there is a relationship between academic major (art, business, communication, and science) and use of the Internet. We have a group of students from each major, and each student has reported a value for HWI. If the variance for HWI within each group is less than the overall variance, we assume that we have four separate groups. If the variance within each group is greater than that for the groups overall, we assume that there are no separate groups.

The ANOVA calculation results in an F value. We can get the probability of that value occurring from a table of F values or from computer output. If our calculated value of F is greater than the table value for F, we would conclude that our F value is unlikely to have been obtained by chance. We would therefore reject the null hypothesis of no difference between groups and conclude that the difference between the four groups of majors with respect to time on the Internet is statistically significant.

Note that this is the only conclusion we are entitled to. While it is tempting to look at whether specific majors differ in time spent on the Internet, that was not our original question. Our question was whether academic major as a variable interacts with time spent on the Internet, and the answer was that there is a statistically significant interaction. Whether communication majors differ from science majors in use of the Internet is another question, and had we asked that question, we would have selected another test to answer it—most likely a *t* test.

It is important to note again that we have not established any proof of causality. It may be tempting to think that one's academic major predicts time spent on the Internet. We might, for example, speculate that business majors spend less time online because they are too busy negotiating business startups. But the reverse reasoning equally explains our data; time spent online predicts the academic major. Communication majors, for example, may have spent more time online and gravitated to the communication major because they see the job opportunities the Internet and social media offer.

ANOVA tests for relationships among two or more groups, but it is still a simple analysis of variance in that it is exploring the relationship between only two variables. Suppose we want to examine how academic major, political preference, and time spent on the Internet interact in predicting KWA. Now we would need **MANOVA**—multiple analysis of variance.

Testing for Relationships Between and Among Variables

With the *t* test, chi-square test, and ANOVA, we examine differences between or among groups of people.

None of these tests tells us anything about the relationships between or among variables, a question of considerable interest to many researchers. Correlation and regression are two statistical techniques that answer this question.

Correlation

A frequent focus in communication research is the relationship between or among variables. For example, we might want to know whether a higher-than-average use of social media is associated with a lower-than-average level of interpersonal socializing; if there is an association between the amount of time spent online and academic performance; or if there is an association between the level of viewing violent television and the level of antisocial behavior.

Correlation is used to assess such relationships between variables. It provides a measure of the strength of relationships between variables but will not tell us whether the relationship is causal.

One way to visualize correlation is to plot the values for one variable on a horizontal axis against the values for another variable on a vertical axis. If the values plot out close to a straight line horizontally or vertically, we infer that there is little relationship between the two variables because as one changes in value, the other shows little change. On the other hand, a pattern that approximates a 45-degree line indicates a strong relationship between the two variables; for every unit change in one, there is a similar change in the other.

A **correlation coefficient** is a measure of the strength of association between variables. It is usually denoted as r_{xy}, where x and y are the two variables being examined for strength of association. Coefficients express the strength of the relationship between two variables and range between −1.0 and +1.0, indicating a 100% negative and a 100% positive correlation, respectively.

As a rule of thumb, social scientists get excited at correlations of .85 or better, find correlations between .60 and .80 strong or important, and correlations of less than .50 moderate to weak.

Note again that neither a plot nor a correlation coefficient indicates causality. If, for example, we found a strong correlation between time spent online and knowledge of world affairs, we would not know whether time spent online improves one's knowledge of world affairs or whether having a high knowledge of world affairs predicts that individuals are more likely to spend time online. While it might be tempting to assume that the more time we spend on the Internet the more we learn, it is equally plausible that a high level of knowledge predicts that an individual will spend more time on online in order to add to that knowledge. To get an answer to the causality question, we need the experimental methods outlined in Chapter 10.

Regression

Correlation coefficients express the strength of relationships between two variables, but they do not predict what the value of one variable will be given a value of the other. Nor do they express the relationships among three or more variables, a common requirement in communication research. To address such needs, we have the tools of linear **regression**, multiple regression, and part and partial correlation.

Unlike correlation, **linear regression** predicts a specific value for one variable (the **outcome or criterion variable**) given a value for a second **(predictor) variable**.

Because the values of the two variables are typically scattered and do not all plot out precisely on one line, there is almost inevitably an error (which can be calculated) in calculating the value of one variable from another.

Linear regression by definition assumes that the relationship between variables is best captured by a straight line. Some data distributions may be best captured by a curve rather than a line, and, yes, there are regression techniques that assume a **curvilinear** rather than a linear relationship between variables.

If we wish to predict the value of one variable using two or more predictor variables, we use analogous formulae that take several variables into account, at which point we are doing **multiple regression**.

Paths, Partials, and Parts

When the interaction of several variables is being examined, a first cousin of regression, **path analysis**, allows a researcher to map out the likely causal relationships among variables. With techniques such as **partial correlation** and **part correlation** (also known as **semipartial correlation**), esearchers examine the interaction between a predictor variable and an outcome variable while controlling for the effects of other variables. Partial correlation removes the effect of other variables from both the predictor and outcome variables. Part or semipartial correlation removes the effect of other variables from the predictor variables only.

Two Final Decisions

Accept or Reject My Findings?

Statistical testing offers you the probability, not the certainty, of a result occurring in the wider population. You, the researcher, still have to decide whether to accept that probability. Statistically based research errs on the pessimistic side. In a general sense, you are testing your ideas, hoping to be proven wrong. If there is a probability that your results could have occurred by chance, you dismiss your findings as not significant, in a statistical sense, and revisit your initial hypotheses or research questions.

Probability is an important concept. Consider that the trials of new drugs that could have a major impact on human health are based on statistical probability. As a potential consumer, you would want to know the outcomes of such trials at a very high level of probability. But even at the highest level of probability, researchers still have to decide whether to accept or reject their findings. Conceptually, they have a chance of accepting a probability and being wrong or right, or rejecting it and being wrong or right.

In the language of statisticians, they face the possibility of committing either **Type I error** or **Type II error**. As shown in Exhibit 7.9, there are four possible outcomes from deciding to accept or reject a hypothesis.

EXHIBIT 7.9   **Type I and Type II Error**

	Accept Null Hypothesis	**Reject Null Hypothesis**
Null hypothesis is true in the wider population.	**No problem**	**Type I Error** Decided wrongly that there was a significant result.
Null hypothesis is false in the wider population.	**Type II Error** Decided wrongly that there was no significant result.	**No problem**

There are ways to reduce both Type I and Type II errors. Type I error—deciding that you have a significant finding when you do not—is under your control in that you can decide on the level of significance for accepting or rejecting hypotheses. That is why statistical tables typically show distributions of *t* and chi-square at the .10, .05, .01, and .001 levels of probability. Type II error—deciding that there is no significant result when there is—can be decreased by, for example, increasing sample size.

Statistically grounded research is an exercise in minimizing both types of error as far as possible. The standards are a function of the research culture as well as the individual researcher's judgment. Social scientists generally work to the .05 probability level; medical research may work to a .01 or even .001 level of significance given the implications of a false finding for human health. Statistical software provides an exact probability computation (e.g., .047) for any statistical test, but that final "accept/reject" decision remains with you, the researcher.

If It's Significant, Is It Significant?

Generally, research seeks to contribute conceptually significant new insights or to verify existing understandings of human communication. In quantitative research, this is done with the support of statistically significant findings, but statistically significant findings may or may not be significant in a more general or conceptual sense. Suppose we have a finding that proves to be statistically significant at the .10 (90%) level of significance. Conventionally, social science works to a .05 (95%) level of significance, so by convention our result would not be regarded as significant statistically even though outside of that it might well make an intellectually significant contribution to the field.

Further, statistical significance is a function of sample size, as Morin (2014) points out in discussing the controversial Facebook study introduced in Chapter 3. While the Facebook study was controversial and ethically questionable for many people, what the study found, in Morin's words, was "not much—actually." Morin points out that with enormous random samples, such as the Facebook study had, even tiny differences can pass standard tests of significance. The study authors reported changes in Facebook status updates in the order of 0.07% to 0.1%. That translates into between 7 words per 10,000 and one word per thousand.

Significance in a general sense remains a matter of professional judgment. Findings of statistical significance can help us make that judgment but do not necessarily tell us that we have discovered anything important. They contribute to our knowledge, but not necessarily to our wisdom.

Ethics Panel: A Communicative Tension

You might not predict a book titled *Introduction to Statistical Principles* to be a best seller, but *How to Lie With Statistics* by Darrell Huff has been a best-selling statistical text since 1954. What explains this? Could it be the title? *How to Lie With Statistics* does trigger a level of curiosity that the first title does not, and therein lies the dilemma of communicating statistics.

Two forces are at work in reporting statistics and research methods—simplification and selectivity.

Simplification occurs most commonly when journalists writing for lay audiences use their professional skills to report scientific research in a way that their audiences will understand. Most people are not familiar with, and—dare we say—do not care about chi-square, *t* tests, or multiple polynomial regression, so there would be little point writing for most audiences in such terms. News writing, in most cases, has a "get to the point" style, and so journalists understandably focus on a bottom-line "What's in it for the reader?" interpretation of research results.

It is easy to see the nature of this simplification. Just compare a scholarly research paper on media effects with any magazine article on such topics as "Is watching too much TV bad for your kids?"

Selectivity occurs when statistics are used to bolster an argument. For example, a political party may argue that it has reduced income taxes across the board for everyone by an average of 2%. The opposition will point out that because low-income people by definition are paying little tax, the effect of the tax cut on them is minimal in terms of absolute dollars. People in the top income bracket gain much more in terms of tax cuts. Which party is correct? Both. Neither is lying; each is merely selecting the most relevant statistic to make a point.

Questions

- How might simplifying research data mislead readers and thus violate professional standards of behavior for journalists, science writers, and researchers?

- A published research report is ultimately a researcher's personal summary and interpretation of his or her data collection and analyses. What ethical responsibilities, if any, do researchers have to make their nonpublished data and analyses accessible by interested parties? How might you be able to make such nonpublished content accessible?

- You have survey data indicating that 52% of respondents are in favor of a proposed legislative change. Your calculated margin of error is 3%. Which of the following might lead readers of your survey report to misunderstand your findings? Explain why.
  - Not reporting your margin of error
  - Reporting your result as
    - "almost half in favor of"
    - "nearly half in favor of"
    - "over half in favor of"
    - "approximately half in favor of"

CHAPTER SUMMARY

- Inferential statistics help us estimate the probability that our sample data represent the population from which the sample is drawn.
- The two main uses of inferential statistics are assessing relationships among variables and assessing differences among groups.
- *z* scores standardize scores from different measures so that they can be compared.
- The normalized distribution of *z* scores allows us to calculate the probability of a result occurring.
- The *t* test compares two groups based on each group's scores on a continuous variable.
- The chi-square test compares two or more groups based on their distribution of scores on a categorical variable.
- Correlation is a measure of the strength of association between variables.
- Regression allows calculation of the value of one variable, given the value of a second variable.
- ANOVA compares values across multiple groups to help determine the probability that they are statistically different.

KEY TERMS

ANOVA

bell curve

bi-modal

census

central limit theorem

chi-square

confidence interval

correlation

correlation coefficient

curvilinear relationship

degrees of freedom

descriptive statistics

F value

inferential statistics

leptokurtic

linear regression

MANOVA

multiple regression

nonparametric

normal curve

normal distribution

one-tailed test

outcome or criterion variable

parametric statistics

part correlation

partial correlation

path analysis

platykurtic

predictor variable

regression

sampling distribution

semipartial

significance

skew

standard error

t test for dependent samples

t test for independent samples

t test

tri-modal

two-tailed test

Type I error

Type II error

variable

APPLICATION EXERCISES

Statistical analyses typically relate to a group of people, so the following exercises are best done with a group.

Exercise 1: Predicting Group Wealth

Wealth is normally distributed, or is it? Ask one individual in your group to disclose the amount of cash he or she is carrying, then ask group members how confident they are that this amount represents the group average. Ask a second individual, a third, and so on, recording each dollar amount from lowest to highest. As you record each new amount, calculate and record the mean value for the group, as shown in Exhibit 7.1. At what point does your group start to become confident about predicting the group average?

No cash? Try the same exercise with routine expenditures, for example daily expenditures on coffee or lunch, monthly expenditures on entertainment or transport, or annual expenditure on clothing.

Exercise 2: Generalizing From a Sample to a Population

Assume that the group you did Exercise 1 with is randomly selected from a wider student population. Use the formula for standard deviation to calculate the probabilities that the mean value for wealth you calculated from Exercise 1 will be found in that population.

Exercise 3: Gender and Beverage Preferences

Back to the coffee bar. What test would you use to help decide whether beverage preferences are related to gender—that is, whether men and women differ significantly in their drink preferences?

Hint 1: You will be dealing with two categorical variables here—gender and type of beverage.

Hint 2: Before you can develop a table that sets out your data, you will first need to make a decision about how you will categorize beverages. For example, would tea, coffee, soda, and water be an appropriate set of categories, or would cappuccino, latte, espresso, and Americano best capture your group's preferences?

Note also that here we can make a reasonable guess about direction of causality. Coffee drinking has many documented physiological effects, but, to date, demonstrable change in gender is not one of them. If you find a significant difference between men and women in beverage preferences, it would be reasonable to assume that these preferences are predicted by gender rather than vice versa.

Exercise 4: "The Internet of Things" Revisited

Revisit Exercise 3, "The Internet of Things," from Chapter 6. Here, you were capturing responses to statements about the Internet of Things using Likert-type response options. Now you are in a position to compute the standard deviation for the responses you captured to each statement. What is the 95% confidence interval for the mean value of the responses you obtained to each question?

RECOMMENDED WEB RESOURCES

The recommended readings and web resources provided in Chapter 6 are equally relevant for inferential statistics. See also:

Excel tutorials . . . . https://support.office.com/

Support for Windows and Mac versions of Excel.

Getting Started With R Studio https://support.rstudio.com/hc/en-us/articles/201141096-getting-started-with-r

A summary site listing resources for beginners with R statistical software.

GraphPad www.graphpad.com/guides/prism/6/statistics/

Provides basic statistical calculators online.

Online Statistics Education: An Interactive Multimedia Course of Study . . . . http://onlinestatbook.com/index.html

Developed by Rice University, University of Houston Clear Lake, and Tufts University.

Probability and Statistics Ebook . . . . http://wiki.stat.ucla.edu/socr/index.php/Probability_and_statistics_EBook

An open-access statistics book developed by the UCLA Statistics Online Computational Resource (SOCR).

StatSoft . . . . www.statsoft.com/Textbook/

An online textbook/tutorial on statistics.

All of the above are searchable and/or have headings on topics covered in this chapter.

t Distribution . . . . www.medcalc.org/manual/t-distribution.php

A table of t distributions (two-tailed), with examples.

z Distribution . . . . www.medcalc.org/manual/values_of_the_normal_distribution.php

Shows different ways of displaying the distribution of z scores and the area under the normal curve.

z Distribution Values . . . . www.utdallas.edu/dept/abp/zscoretable.pdf

Shows for any z score the area under the normal curve below that score.

REFERENCES

Huff, D. (1954). *How to lie with statistics.* New York, NY: Norton.

Morin, R. (2014, July 2). *Facebook's experiment causes a lot of fuss for little result.* Washington, DC: Pew Research Center Fact Tank. Retrieved from http://www.pewresearch.org/fact-tank/2014/07/02/facebooks-experiment-is-just-the-latest-to-manipulate-you-in-the-name-of-research/

Ⓢ SAGE edge™

Want a better grade?
Get the tools you need to sharpen your study skills. Access practice quizzes, eFlashcards, video, and multimedia at **edge.sagepub.com/treadwell3e**

CHAPTER 8

Sampling

Who, What, and How Many?

Sampling's basic intent
Is selecting to best represent.
Select randomly
Or judgmentally
For people or published content.

———————— ❧ ❧ ❧ ————————

Chapter Overview

We cannot study the entire universe of human communication in one research project, much as we might want to. The universe is too large and the questions too numerous.

What we can do, however, is define populations from that universe and study samples from those populations. The process of selecting the individual units for study is called sampling.

This chapter discusses two types of sampling—probability and nonprobability. Probability sampling strives to obtain samples that statistically represent the overall population. Nonprobability sampling is not statistically representative of the population being sampled but may have greater theoretical relevance and the advantage of convenience.

Sample size—an important issue—depends on the homogeneity of the population and on the level of confidence you want when making generalizations from your data.

Chapter Objectives

This chapter will help you

- Compare and contrast probability and nonprobability sampling.
- Identify and explain major nonprobability sampling methods.
- Identify and explain major probability sampling methods.
- List the factors influencing the size of a sample.
- Describe the concept of a sampling frame.
- Discuss the advantages and disadvantages of the different types of sampling frame.

Introduction

A decision to do research is a decision to sample. As soon as you have a research question, you automatically have questions of who or what and how many you will study in order to answer it. This is true even for qualitative research.

A **population** is defined not by size but by the fact that it contains every one of the units the researcher has elected to study, for example every licensed driver in the U.S, every U.S. edition of a Harry Potter book, or every woman working for a minority-owned public relations agency. Large populations can be difficult to study because their exact size and nature may be unknown. This is one reason we combine sampling and the inferential statistics discussed in Chapter 7. Together, they help us make intelligent estimates from a sample when the population's exact size and nature are unknown or the population is too large to conduct a census. You will recall from Chapter 7 that a **census** is a study of every member of a population. A **sample** is a selected segment of a population presumed to represent that population.

Nonprobability samples are based on a judgment by the researcher; **probability samples** are generated by randomly selecting the sample units. Both approaches have advantages and disadvantages.

In this chapter, we follow the sampling adventures of one student, Elizabeth, as she begins research as the basis for an on-campus campaign aimed at improving campus food offerings.

As a resident student, Elizabeth is well placed to observe students' eating behaviors and the amount and type of foods that the campus dining services provide. After watching her fellow students for several weeks, she arrives at three conclusions. First, even though the director of campus food services might well disagree, she is living on a fast-food campus. Second, her evidence from casual conversations is that some students are not doing well in this environment. She hears complaints about weight gain and how offerings such as all-you-can-eat buffets encourage overeating. Third, she is becoming increasingly aware that many students have special dietary needs for religious, medical, or lifestyle reasons.

All in all, it seems the time is ripe for changes to the campus dietary offerings.

Elizabeth decides to approach the administration about appropriate changes to campus food services but recognizes that her approach will have no effect unless she can back up her proposal with data supporting the demand for change. Those data will consist of students' opinions on food and food services, but from which students exactly, and how many?

Elizabeth is facing the basic questions and issues of sampling, set out below.

Nonprobability Sampling

Nonprobability sampling has the advantages of convenience and providing insight. Statistically, it does not permit generalizations to a wider population, but that does not make it a second-class citizen of the sampling world. There are situations in which it can be the most logical method. For example, a researcher may make a professional judgment that one particular informant or item of text will provide the insights he or she is looking for, or that seeking out volunteers is the only way to build a relevant sample of people. As outlined below, there are several approaches to nonprobability sampling.

Convenience Sampling

As the name implies, **convenience sampling** is based on convenience to the researcher. You may have been part of a convenience sample when an instructor requested your consent to participate in a survey or an experiment; that is, you were part of a group convenient to the instructor. Constraints on time or money may lead researchers to use convenience sampling. It can be useful when pretesting a study or when the results of the research are not intended for scholarly publication. As a matter of convenience, Elizabeth may initially survey her class colleagues about their eating habits and their perceptions of campus food services. She makes no assumption that her survey results would apply to the student body as a whole or that her research will contribute to new theoretical models of human communication. She just wants some basis for her inquiries. After all, she has to start somewhere.

Purposive or Judgmental Sampling

Purposive sampling is based on the idea that a specific person or media content will meet specific criteria the researcher may have. For example, Elizabeth may decide that the director of campus dining services and only the director of campus dining services can provide the insight on the economic, nutritional, and scheduling decisions that lead to the menu options that students see on a day-to-day basis. She will therefore deliberately seek out that individual as part of her research.

She may also seek to interview students who can make a special case or who exemplify a special problem—for example, students who cannot eat at campus facilities for religious reasons or whose health may be at risk because the ingredients in campus food are not clearly documented and displayed. Such students may not represent majority opinion, but the stories they have to tell may be just as enlightening as a "78% of females and 58% of males want more vegetarian offerings" survey finding. In-depth interviews with such students may generate new ideas, insights, and research questions that Elizabeth might not be able to obtain from conventional-diet students. She may even elect to interview such students specifically because they do not represent conventional wisdom.

Quota Sampling

Quota sampling was one of the first attempts to bring a scientific approach to survey research. It attempts to replicate in a sample the features that the researcher thinks are important in the population. Let's suppose that Elizabeth has decided to interview students who live on campus and those who live off campus because she suspects that the attitudes of these two groups will differ with respect to eating and to campus food services.

She decides to interview 10 students. She knows that 80% of students live on campus, so she decides to interview eight resident students, plus two students who live off campus. She has successfully replicated one important feature of the student community in her sample, but the 10 students she interviews are her choice. They have not been randomly sampled, as discussed below under "Probability Sampling." Something other than chance has put them in the sample. That something is the researcher's judgment, which may be biased. For example, she may knowingly or unknowingly sample the students living in a housing unit that—uniquely—has kitchen facilities.

Network or Snowball Sampling

Network or **snowball sampling** is a form of volunteer sampling that occurs when you rely on members of a network to introduce you to other members of the network. Let's suppose that Elizabeth is especially interested in getting the opinions of vegetarians. Despite her best efforts, she can find no campus listing of vegetarians or any links to a local vegetarian group.

She decides that the only way to identify such students is to post on campus bulletin boards or her Facebook page a request that any vegetarians contact her to discuss possible participation in her research.

One such person contacts her, and Elizabeth realizes that the only way to recruit more vegetarians into her study is to ask this person to identify other vegetarians who might be willing to be interviewed. If she is lucky, the size of her sample will grow exponentially as more and more vegetarians introduce her to more and more vegetarians. The quality and size of any such sample depends on the willingness and ability of others to identify other people in their networks to you. One potential problem with snowball sampling is that because friends tend to recommend friends, the snowball sample may consist of individuals with essentially the same opinion and will not capture any diversity of opinion or demographics within the broader student body. Conversely, relative isolates may not be recruited and will be underrepresented as a result.

Volunteer Sampling

Network or snowball samples are obtained by an initial group of volunteers linking to other potential volunteers whom they identify. Volunteers may also be recruited directly by the researcher.

Calling for volunteers may be the only way you can obtain research participants. If, for example, Elizabeth is seeking student members for a focus group to discuss possible changes in campus meal offerings, she has little choice but to use **volunteer sampling**. The focus group method, as we will see in Chapter 11, requires the active participation of people prepared to express opinions.

You may well want volunteers and volunteer enthusiasm if you intend to translate the results of your research into action. For example, the vegetarian volunteers Elizabeth recruits using her snowball sampling may provide her not only with the information she needs but also with the volunteer enthusiasm to help her develop educational materials and with lobbying efforts in support of changes to the campus food offerings.

The bad news is that volunteer samples can be problematic because by definition you are recruiting one type of person—volunteers! Research findings from volunteer samples will be biased because you have not captured what nonvolunteers might have said.

Of course, in a general sense, anyone participating in a research project is a volunteer, as our discussion of ethics and institutional review board (IRB) procedures in Chapter 3 should make clear. Intuitively, though, we can sense a distinction between an individual who has simply agreed to participate in a research project and another who is aggressively determined to see that his or her viewpoint dominates the research findings.

Web-based public opinion polls such as those hosted by local news media can be particularly prone to this problem because they attract people willing, by definition, to visit a website and volunteer a vote—or multiple votes. Other people are not willing to do this, and so these web polls represent only the opinions of a particular personality type. Unless the website has some control over access, the enthusiasts who decide that if one vote is good, two votes would be twice as good may vote repeatedly, further compounding any bias in the results.

Volunteer sampling obviously applies only to human participants. Convenience, judgment, and quota sampling can be used with nonhumans, most typically to select media content for content analysis. In all cases, the researcher would be the one deciding what media content goes into a sample. There will inevitably be some bias behind that decision. For example, Exhibit 8.1 shows the class year and food preferences of a student population that Elizabeth might sample. Exhibit 8.2 shows how a convenience sample (highlighted) could seriously misrepresent the population by leaving out first- and second-year students and three of the four food preference groups.

EXHIBIT 8.1   **Population**

Class Year										Percent of Population
1st		2nd			3rd			4th		
B	B	B	B	B	B	B	B	B	B	
B	B	B	B	B	B	B	B	B	B	40%
B	B	B	B	B	B	B	B	B	B	
B	B	B	B	B	B	B	B	B	B	
P	P	P	P	P	P	P	P	P	P	
P	P	P	P	P	P	P	P	P	P	30%
P	P	P	P	P	P	P	P	P	P	
V	V	V	V	V	V	V	V	V	V	
V	V	V	V	V	V	V	V	V	V	20%
R	R	R	R	R	R	R	R	R	R	10%
20%		30%			30%			20%		100%

The above exhibit shows a population containing 16 subgroups.

Reading down the columns, we see four sets of food preferences:
B = Balanced diet
P = Pizza diet
V = Vegetarian diet
R = Medically restricted diet

Reading across the rows, we see four class levels: first-, second-, third-, and fourth-year.

The right-hand column shows the percentage of each food-preference group in the population. The bottom row shows the percentage of each class year in the population.

This exhibit could equally well represent ethnic or occupational subgroups of a human population or subgroups of a media population (corporate websites, nonprofit websites, talk radio, or lifestyle magazines, for example).

Ideally, we need some mechanism that reduces or eliminates researcher bias so that the sample reflects the population and not the researcher's biases. That mechanism is probability sampling.

Probability Sampling

Basically, probability sampling means turning the selection of sampling units over to a mechanism over which the researcher has no control, so that every unit has an equal chance of being selected.

Probability sampling permits us to make statistical generalizations from our results. A major contribution of sampling theory to communication research is to tell us that we do not necessarily need huge samples as long as we are prepared to live with a level of uncertainty—which can be calculated as discussed in Chapter 7.

EXHIBIT 8.2   **Convenience Sample**

| Class Year | | | | | | | | | | Percent of Population |
1st		2nd			3rd			4th		
B	B	B	B	B	B	B	B	B	B	
B	B	B	B	B	B	B	B	B	B	40%
B	B	B	B	B	B	B	B	B	B	
B	B	B	B	B	B	B	B	B	B	
P	P	P	P	P	P	P	P	P	P	
P	P	P	P	P	P	P	P	P	P	30%
P	P	P	P	P	P	P	P	P	P	
V	V	V	V	V	V	V	V	V	V	
V	V	V	V	V	V	V	V	V	V	20%
R	R	R	R	R	R	R	R	R	R	10%
20%		30%			30%			20%		100%

Exhibit 8.2 represents a convenience sample obtained by arbitrarily selecting 10 individuals from the top right "corner" of the population. The selected units are highlighted.

Convenience sampling may overestimate or underestimate the population. In this case, all Ps, Vs, and Rs have been eliminated from the sample, as have all first- and second-year classes.

The sample is 100% Bs, who make up only 40% of the population.

Of that sample, 30% are third-year students, who make up 30% of the population, and 70% are fourth-year students, who make up 20% of the population.

Researchers, especially in such applied fields as political communication, marketing, broadcasting, and public relations, want to be able to make generalizations to large audiences or markets and therefore put considerable effort into probability sampling.

The master lists from which a probability sample is selected are referred to as **sampling frames**—for example, a list of graduates held by your college or university's alumni office, the membership list of a club, or all registered members of a political party. In practice, and especially in the case of large populations, we sample from sampling frames because we cannot identify every member of the population. **Sampling units** are the units selected for study. Frequently in communication research the unit will be individuals, but the unit could also be couples, corporations, comic strips, athletic teams, *Hobbit* movies, or editorials from the *Chicago Sun-Times*.

There are several approaches to probability sampling.

Random Sampling

Random sampling is the most obvious and perhaps most common example of probability sampling.

Examples of random sampling include throwing dice, drawing names out of a hat, and lotteries. In each case, there is no predicting what specific names or numbers will be sampled. You may control how many names or numbers will be selected, but you cannot control what each specific name or number will be. Random sampling removes the researcher as the agent of selection and replaces him or her with "luck of the draw."

For example, Elizabeth may be able to obtain a list of all students signed up for the campus meal plan (recognizing that students who do not participate in the plan are ignored even though their reasons for doing so should interest Elizabeth). To get a genuinely random sample of students who will represent all participants in the plan, she would assign each student a number beginning at 1 and number each individual systematically. Then she would use a table of randomly generated numbers—or a **random numbers generator**, such as the one available at http://randomizer.org—to generate the list of students who would form her sample. Random number generators allow you to specify how big you want your sample to be and how you want your sample numbers computed and presented. You can have the generator pull numbers randomly, pull every fifth or every tenth number (see "Systematic Sampling" below), and/or begin sampling at a number you define. For example, to randomly generate a series of phone numbers for the 212 area code, you can instruct the generator to randomly produce a series of 10-digit numbers beginning with 212.

A common misconception of random sampling is that it will produce a sample that is diverse. This is not automatically so. For example, married Asian women over the age of 40, living in New Mexico with two children and a household income of between $100,000 and $150,000, would be a very homogeneous population demographically. Random sampling from such a population would produce an equally homogeneous sample; we would not expect the sample to be diverse.

Stratified Random Sampling

Paradoxically, one problem with purely random samples is that they may not reflect the population from which they are drawn. Because "anything can happen" with random sampling, there is always a possibility that an important subgroup could be entirely missed or overrepresented. For example, Elizabeth may have decided that she needs vegetarians in her survey sample, and knows that this group constitutes a small minority of students. But random sampling is blind; a random sample of all students living on campus may not select any vegetarians.

Randomness does not respect the fact that you may need all categories of people in your sample and that random sampling might eliminate some categories from your sample. **Stratified random sampling** is a way to "force" such groups into your sample.

To ensure that all the groups of interest are proportionately represented in a sample, you set aside a number of places in your sample relative to the size of the groups in the population you are drawing from. Then you fill those places by random sampling from those specific subgroups, as shown in Exhibit 8.3.

For example, if Elizabeth needs both resident and nonresident students in her sample, and knows that nonresident students make up 20% of the student population, she needs to ensure that 20% of her sample consists of such students. Suppose she decides on a final sample size of 100 students. She would then randomly select 20 nonresident students from a list of such students, and randomly select 80 from a list of resident students. This is similar to nonprobability quota sampling, the key difference being that the individual units in stratified random sampling are selected by a process of randomization, not by the researcher.

Systematic Sampling

Systematic sampling means sampling every *n*th person on a list—for example, taking every 10th or every 100th person listed in a phone book. The interval that you select (10, 100, etc.) is the **sampling interval**. The method is based on random sampling because typically you use a

EXHIBIT 8.3   **Stratified Random Sample**

Class Year										Percent of Population
1st		**2nd**			**3rd**			**4th**		
B	B	B	B	B	B	B	B	B	B	40%
B	B	B	B	B	B	B	B	B	B	
B	B	B	B	B	B	B	B	B	B	
B	B	B	B	B	B	B	B	B	B	
P	P	P	P	P	P	P	P	P	P	30%
P	P	P	P	P	P	P	P	P	P	
P	P	P	P	P	P	P	P	P	P	
V	V	V	V	V	V	V	V	V	V	20%
V	V	V	V	V	V	V	V	V	V	
R	R	R	R	R	R	R	R	R	R	10%
20%		30%			30%			20%		100%

In this example, the selected units are highlighted.

40% of the sample is *B*s.

30% of the sample is *P*s.

20% of the sample is *V*s.

10% of the sample is *R*s.

These percentages are the percentage of each food preference group in the original population. Within each of these groups, random sampling takes place to select individuals for the overall sample so that the original percentage of each group in the population is protected in the final sample.

Note that this sample overrepresents first-year students (30% of sample; 20% of the population) and second-year students (40% of sample; 30% of the population). The sample underrepresents third-year students (10% of sample; 30% of the population).

random number or numbers to locate a starting point. For example, if you were sampling from a telephone directory, you might generate a random number to decide which page to start sampling at and then another random number to decide which name on that page to start at. Having identified a starting point, you then take every *n*th name until you have the sample size you need. The random starting point means that you have no control over which names get selected, and any researcher bias in who gets selected is therefore avoided.

Systematic sampling is diagrammed in Exhibit 8.4.

One problem with systematic sampling is that if a pattern in the original population matches the sampling interval, you can get an overweighted or underweighted sample. For example, suppose you want to interview residents of a dormitory on their attitudes to safety and security. You use a random numbers generator to select one dorm room as a starting point and then systematically sample every 10th room after that. It so happens that every 10th room selected has an

Exhibit 8.4 **Systematic Sample**

Class Year										Percent of Population
1st		**2nd**			**3rd**			**4th**		
B	B	B	B	B	B	B	B	B	B	
B	B	B	B	B	B	B	B	B	B	
B	B	B	B	B	B	B	B	B	B	40%
B	B	B	B	B	B	B	B	B	B	
P	P	P	P	P	P	P	P	P	P	
P	P	P	P	P	P	P	P	P	P	30%
P	P	P	P	P	P	P	P	P	P	
V	V	V	V	V	V	V	V	V	V	20%
V	V	V	V	V	V	V	V	V	V	
R	R	R	R	R	R	R	R	R	R	10%
20%		30%			30%			20%		100%

Here, a starting point is randomly selected (top row, third unit); then every *n*th individual is selected, in this case every 6th. Using this method, we have 17 individuals in our sample. The selected units are highlighted. If we wanted a larger or smaller sample, we would need to adjust the sampling interval (*n*).

41% of the sample is *B*s (40% of the population).

29% of the sample is *P*s (30% of the population).

18% of the sample is *V*s (20% of the population).

12% of the sample is *R*s (10% of the population).

Based on the sample size of 17,

Second-year students are overrepresented (41% of sample, 30% of population).

Third-year students are underrepresented (18% of sample, 30% of population).

First-year (18%) and fourth-year (24%) student percentages approximate those in the population (20%).

emergency alarm button outside it that residents cannot help but see as they enter and leave their rooms. It is possible, then, that your findings will be biased because every student in your sample will have a greater (or possibly lesser) sense of security than others in the same dorm.

Multistage Cluster Sampling

Suppose you wanted a representative sample of a country's population. In practice, this would mean trying to sample from a list of every resident of that country, assuming in the first place that you could get such a thing. There has to be an easier way, and there is. **Multistage cluster sampling** works by first sampling larger units such as states or provinces. Towns and cities are then sampled from the state, province, or county sample. City blocks are then sampled from the town or city sample, and finally individual addresses are sampled from city blocks.

At campus level, Elizabeth might consider multistage cluster sampling if she were unable to obtain a student directory from which to sample. In that case, she might randomly select housing units, then floors within the selected units, then rooms within the randomly selected floors, and possibly individuals within each room.

The advantage of this method is the relative ease of identifying people, or at least households. It is much easier to go state–city–city block–household than it is to find a comprehensive listing of millions of people. The catch is that at every stage of sampling the potential for bias in the final sample increases. No two states are identical, so any sample of states will have some attributes overrepresented or underrepresented.

Clearly, sampling is more complicated than it may first appear and involves a number of decisions—some theoretical, some practical. Exhibit 8.5 summarizes the advantages and disadvantages of different sampling methods.

EXHIBIT 8.5 **Advantages and Disadvantages of Sampling Methods**

	Advantages	**Disadvantages**
Nonprobability Sampling	Overall: Convenience.	Overall: Sample does not represent the population being sampled.
Convenience	Speed, cost.	Cannot generalize from sample to population.
Purposive/Judgmental	Meets a specific need of the researcher.	Sample may not represent the population.
Quota	Attempts to replicate features of the population in the sample. More readily done than random sampling.	Sample may not represent the population.
Network/Snowball	Identifies research participants the researcher would not otherwise be aware of.	Depends on ability of researcher to network. Sample may over- or underrepresent aspects of the population. Possible loss of diversity in sample.
Volunteer Sampling	Identifies willing participants the researcher might not otherwise be aware of.	Agendas and interests of volunteers may influence the research. Sample may over- or underrepresent characteristics of the population.
Probability Sampling	Overall: Sample represents the population being sampled.	Overall: Time- and resource-consuming.
Random Sampling	Ability to generalize from sample to population.	May eliminate individuals who should be in the sample.
Stratified Random Sampling	Minority groups that should be represented in the sample are forced into it.	Need to identify and sample a sampling frame for each subgroup to be represented in the sample.
Systematic Sampling	Only one or two random number starting points are needed to start sampling.	Sample may over- or underrepresent features of the population.
Multistage Cluster Sampling	Eliminates need for a comprehensive sampling frame of every individual to be sampled.	Sampling frame needed for each stage of sampling. Sample may over- or underrepresent features of the population.

How Big Does My Sample Have to Be?

At a practical level, sample size depends on your resources. Time and money place constraints on research and on sample size. If Elizabeth decides to survey graduating seniors during the spring semester, she needs to complete her survey by the end of that semester. If she has no money, she will be unable to entice people into her focus group with the offer of food and drink or to offer the chance to win a prize for participating. Every research project is a balancing act between striving for the ideal sample and the constraints of resource limitations and deadlines.

A second "it depends" is the nature of your research. Ethical considerations may constrain the size of your sample. For example, if deception is involved, you may decide that you want to minimize the number of participants even if the deception has been approved by an IRB. You might have a sample of any convenient size if you are just **piloting** a survey; that is, you are testing it out to identify any possible problems with questions and question wording before running it "for real." Sample size is also less of an issue if your survey is an informal one aimed at just getting a sense of what people are thinking or has no official or policy implications and is not intended for scholarly publication.

A third "it depends" is the level of confidence—statistical confidence in this case—that you want or need in your research results. If you want absolute 100% confidence in your results, then you will not be sampling at all; you will be conducting a census. Given a small population, you might conduct a census, but as discussed in Chapter 7, a census is often impractical and unnecessary. Most researchers elect to sample and to accept a (calculable) level of error in return.

A fourth factor is the **homogeneity**—the degree of "sameness"—of the population.

Assume, for a moment, that the population is 100% homogeneous; that is, every unit in the population is identical on whatever variables you are researching. In that case, you would need a sample size of only one!

The less homogeneous a population, the more likely you are to need a bigger sample to ensure that its full range of diversity is captured. **Standard error** (the standard deviation of the sample), the homogeneity of the population, and sample size are related. If you know or assume two of these, statistical tables, software, or a relatively simple calculation will tell you the third. Exhibit 8.6 shows how standard error, homogeneity, and sample size relate. The websites listed below under "Sample Size Calculators" will help you calculate a sample size based your needed confidence level and confidence interval.

EXHIBIT 8.6 **Relationships Among Standard Error, Homogeneity, and Sample Size**

	Standard Error	
	1%	5%
Homogeneity	Sample Size	Sample Size
90:10	900	36
50:50	2,500	100

Calculating either a desired sample size or a level of error helps the researcher make the trade-off between level of confidence on one hand and getting the research done expeditiously on the other. That decision is ultimately driven by the purpose of the research. Elizabeth, for example, will most likely be concerned with getting some defensible research results by the end of the semester. Her sample size and the sampling error may be of lesser concern for a report that will be used only internally to stimulate thinking and local action. On the other hand, a research project on student dietary habits that is headed for publication in a refereed scholarly journal will likely have a minimum, required sample size because the journal's publication standards may require reporting results at the 95% confidence level, and that confidence level will then determine the sample size the researcher needs.

Some Issues With Sampling Frames

The basis of almost every good sample is a good sampling frame—the full list of individuals, groups, or media content from which the sample will be drawn. However, for survey research in particular, the nature of the sampling frame may constrain your ability to develop an appropriate sample as discussed below.

Postal Sampling Frames

Postal addresses presuppose a residence, which not everybody has. Sampling postal addresses, then, is likely to eliminate the homeless and the transient from the sample. Furthermore, as people move and zip code demographics change, we may find that we are not reaching the individuals we intended to reach.

Despite these and other problems, interest in postal sampling has returned with the development of **address-based sampling (ABS)**, largely in reaction to decreasing response rates from traditional telephone surveys. ABS uses postal delivery lists made available to qualified private companies by the U.S. Postal Service. For researchers wishing to use such lists, these list vendors may "add value" by appending additional information such as phone numbers, names, geographic coordinates, ages, races, ethnicities, and household incomes (Iannacchione, 2011).

ABS has a relatively slow turnaround and can be problematic in rural areas and in geographically locating households with P.O. boxes rather than street addresses. It may result in overcoverage of households with both street addresses and P.O. box addresses but can be helpful with in-person surveys and multimethod surveys as well as its obvious use in mail surveys.

"Once the exclusive realm of direct mailers, the use of residential mailing addresses now influences the development of sampling frames for surveys regardless of mode" (Iannacchione, 2011, p. 570).

Telephone Sampling Frames

Telephone surveys became attractive to survey organizations and researchers once the majority of U.S. households had a phone. The ease of dialing a number relative to having to knock on doors or mail out surveys and wait for a response was obvious. Autodialing technology made it even easier. But that was then.

Now there are problems, outlined below, with sampling from phone directory listings.

Unlisted phone numbers will not get into a sample taken from directory listings. Survey researchers attempt to overcome this problem with **random digit dialing (RDD)**—that is, dialing computer-generated random numbers in the hopes of reaching unlisted numbers. This technique has its problems because many sequences of numbers are not put into use by phone companies, and because people are increasingly giving up traditional landline phones in favor of mobile phones.

Mobile or wireless phone numbers are also a problem. A 2013 survey found that 41% of U.S. households are wireless-only. For some subgroups, this percentage can be much higher or lower.

For example, 65% of the age group 25–29 lived in wireless-only households versus 13% for those over 65. Hispanic adults are more likely than non-Hispanic Whites or Blacks to be wireless only (Blumberg & Luke, 2014). This means that in traditional landline surveys, the age group 25–29 and Hispanic adults may be significantly underrepresented and the "over 65s" overrepresented.

Traditional landline phone numbers identified the owners' area codes and exchanges and therefore their geographic locations. With mobile numbers, this is not necessarily the case, so information about an owner's location may be lost, or researchers may assume incorrectly that individuals sampled from a specific area code are living in that area code. Between 10% and 12% of people with cell phones live in a different state from that suggested by their phone numbers (Cohn, 2014).

Telephone surveys have low response rates because many people use caller ID and voice mail to filter out marketing and research calls and put their names on "do not call" lists. Even if you reach a working number, people may decline to participate in your survey. The percentage of households in a sample that are successfully interviewed fell to 9% in 2012 from, typically, 36% in 1997 (Pew Research Center Internet, Science & Tech Project, 2012). Even with a successful contact, you have no guarantee that the individual answering the phone is the person you were trying to reach.

Finally, having a telephone account implies the means to pay for it. Sampling phone directories therefore tends to "sample out" lower-income households. Conversely, households with more than one phone number will get those homes disproportionately represented in the sample.

Telephone surveys become even more problematic as phone users abandon both traditional phones and cell phones in favor of Internet services such as Skype and may not have accessible phone numbers at all.

Internet Sampling Frames

Sampling from the Internet offers both advantages and disadvantages. On the plus side is the potential to recruit large numbers of research participants. For example, Bhutta (2012) reported recruiting 2,788 participants for a study within 5 days of releasing a 12-minute survey via Facebook—and close to 4,000 participants within 1 month at an average cost of 1 cent per survey.

Participants can be recruited globally, and social media platforms can be particularly effective for snowball sampling. Recruits can link to large numbers of other potential recruits unknown to the researcher. Related, social media can reach hidden populations such as drug users or the homeless who might not otherwise be accessible (Barratt, Ferris, & Lenton, 2014). In principle, the large samples that the Internet makes possible can help reduce sampling bias and the chance that a few abnormal individuals might bias the results.

Ruths and Pfeffer (2014) identify several problems with sampling social media platforms. For example, a social media platform's publicly available information may not accurately represent its overall data. Spam and "bots" masquerade as humans on the Internet. Online behaviors may be platform specific; for example, the way individuals view a particular social media platform as a space for political discussion will affect how representative its political content will be.

The biggest theoretical problem with Internet sampling is that we cannot develop an Internet sampling frame because we do not know who or what the Internet population consists of. For example, there is no universal list of e-mail addresses to sample; this means that not every e-mail user has an equal chance of being sampled. The relationship between what one assumes to be the population and the actual population is unknown.

By definition, Internet users are different from those in the population who cannot or will not link to the Internet. Even though Internet use is increasingly widespread, any online survey sample is likely to include younger, more educated, and higher-income individuals than are samples from the population at large. The economically disadvantaged; older people; the less educated; and those with limited computer access, interest, or capability will be underrepresented.

Unless your study population is specifically defined as Internet users, it is questionable whether the results from any online sample will be generalizable to the wider population. Even then, it is questionable whether the results from any one social media platform will be generalizable to the wider Internet population. There are demographic differences among the users of different social media platforms, as summarized in Exhibit 8.7.

EXHIBIT 8.7   **Some Distinguishing Characteristics of Social Media Users**

	% of Internet Users Who Use . . .	% of U.S. Population	The platform especially appeals to . . .
Facebook	71	58	Ages 18–29, women.
Twitter	23	19	Under age 50, college-educated.
Instagram	26	21	Ages 18–29, women, Hispanic, African American.
Pinterest	28	22	Ages 18–29, women, White.
LinkedIn	28	23	Ages 30–64, college graduates, higher-income, employed.

Adapted from Duggan, Ellison, Lampe, Lenhart, & Madden (2015).

The practical problem with Internet sampling, then, is how to combine its advantages (notably speed, reach, and economy) with some level of assurance that your sample has in fact captured the attributes of the population you are really trying to sample. Fortunately, there are some solutions to the problem, as follows.

Couper and Miller (2008) propose two basic approaches to the problem. The "design-based" approach attempts to build probability samples using traditional means such as RDD and then providing Internet access to the sampled households that do not have it. Basically, you add to your online sample by recruiting from outside the Internet.

The "model-based" approach uses volunteer or opt-in panels of Internet users and then corrects such panels for any representational bias. With estimates of how the Internet population differs from your research population, you can estimate what the research results would have been had your actual research population been sampled. Suppose, for example, that you used traditional mail or phone techniques to sample a population of interest and found that 60% of those sampled were over the age of 65; then you sampled online and discovered that only 30% of those sampled were over the age of 65. You can then weight the results from your online sample by calculating what your results would have been if 60% of that sample had been over the age of 65.

It may be possible to check your findings against the results from analogous surveys that used probability sampling. For example, Bhutto's (2012) Facebook sample was nonrepresentative, but she was able to show that many of the statistical relationships she found among variables were also found in similar surveys that used traditional probability sampling. Similarly, Best, Krueger, Hubbard, and Smith (2001) ran two versions of a survey on political attitudes—one using an Internet sample, the other using a probabilistic telephone sample. Comparing results from the two surveys, they concluded that they would have reached the same conclusions about political attitudes from a diverse convenience sample of Internet users as they would have from a more expensive, time-consuming, probabilistic telephone sample.

Barratt and colleagues (2014) suggest that generalizability may be improved by using population sampling as a complement to purposive sampling. Also, ethnographic, qualitative studies of research participants can yield a better understanding of online sites and networks and allow researchers to better interpret survey findings. (See Chapter 11 for further discussion of ethnographic research.)

Best and colleagues (2001) suggest that Internet sampling should be limited to circumstances where there is clear evidence that the hypotheses being tested are uniformly applicable across the entire population; that is, participants' Internet usage should not alter the hypothesized relationships among variables.

For example, Bhutto (2012) argues that Facebook has some specific advantages over other social media platforms as a sampling frame. If, however, your study involves social media use as a variable, then sampling only from Facebook will bias your results because the characteristics of users vary from platform to platform.

Much depends upon your need to generalize. Researchers are often content to explore the relationship among variables without necessarily being interested in the distribution of those relationships in a wider population. If you have no reason to generalize from your research results to a larger population or if you are just pretesting a survey, then concerns about the representativeness of Internet samples can take a backseat relative to your theoretical interests.

Special Population Sampling

Sampling or even accessing special populations such as military families, immigrant communities, prisoners, or people with a particular medical condition can be tricky. Listings of special populations, such as people with a specific medical condition, exist, but typically and with good reason, organizations will not release members' names and contact information. On the other hand, organizations that see a potential benefit to your research and that it is legitimate may be happy to cooperate once they have approved your research design and been assured of protections such as confidentiality that you have in place for the participants.

As noted, Internet-based snowball sampling can be an effective way of reaching special populations. For traditional mail surveys, the list rental industry can provide specifically targeted mailing lists, often developed from information about subscribers to special interest publications.

The Future of Survey Sampling

Where do the above considerations leave us with respect to survey sampling? Brick (2011) suggests that due to costs, the era of traditional probability sampling may be over. That said, there appears to be no generally accepted method of sampling from the Internet. Brick argues that a well-conducted probability sample with a low response rate is likely to be of higher quality than a sample of volunteers; others argue that a probability sample with a low response rate is itself a volunteer sample and therefore has no advantages over a nonprobability sample.

In the meantime, new approaches such as sample matching are evolving. In sample matching, a "target" sample from a known sampling frame such as the U.S. Census is selected and then compared to different web panels—that is, groups of online participants. The closest-matching web panel is then selected for research.

Ethics Panel: Checking the Ethics of Survey Research

Just as statistics can be used to misrepresent as well as to represent, so too abuses of sampling or shoddy sampling can contribute to misrepresentation.

First, there is the issue of convenience. Under pressure of time, researchers may sample a student class, friends, or local media. Such sampling may be defensible, but generalizations from such samples probably are not.

Second, there is the pressure to get results. In applied fields such as audience research, marketing, and political communication, research companies can come under client pressure to get the "right answer." This can lead to sample selections that give clients the results they want to hear. If the research results get further summarized by news media and their "get to the point" writing style, the research data can become further simplified and overgeneralized.

Questions

Check local and national newspapers for reports of public opinion polls.

- What populations can you detect were sampled?

- How were the samples obtained?

- What sampling procedures, if any, raise ethical questions with respect to representing or perhaps misrepresenting the original population? Why?

- Could this poll be reported in a scholarly journal? Why or why not?

CHAPTER SUMMARY

- A census is a study of an entire population.
- A sample is a part of a wider population selected for study.
- The two major categories of sampling are probability and nonprobability.
- Probability sampling includes random, stratified random, systematic, and multistage cluster sampling.
- Nonprobability sampling includes convenience, purposive or judgmental, quota, network or snowball, and volunteer sampling.
- Probability sampling is required in order to make generalizations to a population from a sample.
- Larger sample sizes reduce sampling error, but the extent to which they do so depends on the homogeneity of the sample.
- Statistical formulae allow us to calculate an ideal sample size for a given margin of error, or vice versa, and to make generalizations from a sample to a larger population (assuming the sample has been randomly drawn from a population whose attributes have a normal distribution).
- Internet samples may be obtained rapidly and inexpensively but may not reflect characteristics of the wider population.

KEY TERMS

address-based sampling (ABS)

census

convenience sampling

homogeneity

multistage cluster sampling

network or snowball sampling

nonprobability sample

piloting

population

probability

purposive sampling

quota sampling

random digit dialing (RDD)

random numbers generator

random sampling

sample

sampling frames

sampling interval

sampling units

standard error

stratified

systematic sampling

volunteer sampling

APPLICATION EXERCISES

Exercise 1. Systematic Sampling

Using Exhibit 8.1 as your population, change the starting point and sampling interval, and create a systematic sample. How does the resulting sample reflect the original population?

Exercise 2. How Does Sampling for One Variable Affect Another Variable?

Using Exhibit 8.1 as your population and a random numbers generator such as that found at http://randomizer.org, draw a stratified random sample that reflects the proportion of dietary preferences in the population. Calculate the proportion of each class year in your sample and decide whether the sample reflects the population with respect to class year.

Exercise 3. Multistage Cluster Sampling

You decide to survey communication majors across the country with respect to their views on required courses in communication research. Design a multistage sampling procedure that identifies the stages you will sample and how you will sample at each stage.

Exercise 4. Pew Research Center Internet Knowledge Survey

The 2014 Pew Research Center Internet, Science & Tech Project survey "What Internet Users Know About Technology and the Web" asked a sample of Internet users such questions as what the letters URL stand for, the name of the first university on Facebook, and the name of the first popular graphical web browser. You can take the survey and see the results and a discussion of the sampling procedures at www.pewinternet.org/2014/11/25/web-iq.
 For each question,
 - How might you expect the results from your own web-based convenience sample of college students to differ from the results reported here, and why?
 - How might you expect the results from a traditional landline telephone survey of Internet users to differ from the results reported here, and why?
 - How might you expect the survey results to vary as the age of the sample varies, for example, sampling those over the age of 65 or under 18? Why?

RECOMMENDED READING

Crespi, I. (1998). Ethical considerations when establishing survey standards. *International Journal of Public Opinion Research, 10*(1), 75–83.

Discusses the tension between ethical and practical considerations in survey design.

Sudman, S., & Blair, E. (1999). Sampling in the twenty-first century. *Journal of the Academy of Marketing Science, 27*(2), 269–277.

An overview of issues and problems in sampling.

RECOMMENDED WEB RESOURCES

Pew Research Center Internet, Science & Tech Project . . . . www.pewinternet.org

Click on "Datasets" at the above site to get current statistics on Internet use and on the characteristics of Internet and other technology users.

Pew Research Center U.S. Politics and Policy . . . . www.people-press.org

Click on "Methodology" for discussions of survey sampling.

Research Randomizer . . . . http://randomizer.org

One online site for generating random numbers.

Sample Size Calculators

The following three websites will help you calculate a sample size given your inputs such as standard error, confidence interval, and homogeneity of the sample. Commercial survey sites such as SurveyMonkey can also help with sample size calculations.

National Statistical Service (Australia) . . . . www.nss.gov.au/nss/home.nsf/pages/Sample+size+calculator

Calculator.net . . . . www.calculator.net/sample-size-calculator.html

Research Basics by Del Siegle . . . . www.gifted.uconn.edu/siegle/research/samples/samplecalculator.htm

StatPac . . . . www.statpac.com/surveys/sampling.htm

A commercial survey software site with tutorials on sampling and other survey procedures.

Survey Sampling International . . . . www.surveysampling.com

A commercial site providing sampling services internationally

WebSM . . . . www.websm.org

A European site on web survey methods and sampling.

World Association for Public Opinion Research (WAPOR) . . . . http://wapor.org

Provides a code of professional ethics and practices at http://wapor.org/wapor-code-of-ethics/.

Council of American Survey Research Organizations (CASRO) . . . . www.casro.org

Provides basic information on surveys and survey sampling.

REFERENCES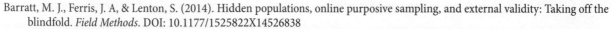

Barratt, M. J., Ferris, J. A, & Lenton, S. (2014). Hidden populations, online purposive sampling, and external validity: Taking off the blindfold. *Field Methods*. DOI: 10.1177/1525822X14526838

Best, S. J., Krueger, B., Hubbard, C., & Smith, A. (2001). An assessment of the generalizability of Internet surveys. *Social Science Computer Review, 19*(2), 131–145. DOI: 10.1177/089443930101900201

Bhutta, C. B. (2012). Not by the book: Facebook as a sampling frame. *Sociological Methods & Research, 41*(1), 57–88. DOI: 10.1177/0049124112440795

Blumberg, S. J., & & Luke, J. V. (2014). Wireless substitution: Early release of estimates from the national health interview survey, July–December 2013. National Center for Health Statistics. Retrieved from http://www.cdc.gov/nchs/data/nhis/earlyrelease/wireless201407.pdf

Brick, J. M. (2011). The future of survey sampling. *Public Opinion Quarterly, 75*(5), 872–888.

Cohn, N. (2014, October 30). Why polls tend to undercount Democrats. *New York Times*, October 13, 2014.

Couper, M. P., & Miller, P. V. (2008). Web survey methods introduction. *Public Opinion Quarterly, 72*(5), 831–835. DOI: 10.1093/poq/nfn066

Duggan, M., Ellison, N. B., Lampe, C., Lenhart, A., & Madden, M. (2015). Social media update 2014. Retrieved from http://www.pewinternet.org/2015/01/09/social-media-update-2014/

Iannacchione, V. G. (2011). Research synthesis. The changing role of address-based sampling in survey research. *Public Opinion Quarterly, 75*(3), 556–575.

Pew Research Center Internet, Science & Tech Project. (2012, May 15). Assessing the representativeness of public opinion surveys. Retrieved from http://www.pewinternet.org/search/Assessing+the+representativeness+of+public+opinion+surveys/

Ruths, D., & Pfeffer, J. (2014). Social media for large studies of behavior. *Science, 346*(6213), 1063–1064. DOI: 10.1126/science.346.6213.1063

$SAGE edge™

Want a better grade?

Get the tools you need to sharpen your study skills. Access practice quizzes, eFlashcards, video, and multimedia at **edge.sagepub.com/treadwell3e**

CHAPTER 9

Surveys
Putting Numbers on Opinions

A public opinion poll is no substitute for thought.

—Warren Buffett

❧❧❧

Chapter Overview

Surveys are frequently used in communication research for reasons of speed, coverage, and cost-effectiveness.

A **survey** is a series of formatted questions delivered to a defined sample of people with the expectation that their responses will be returned somewhere between immediately and within a few days. The survey process starts with theoretically or pragmatically driven research questions or hypotheses and continues through question wording, formatting, and ordering; getting questions to respondents; collecting answers; and analyzing and reporting answers. A **questionnaire** is the specific set of questions that respondents answer.

This chapter discusses the advantages and disadvantages of surveys; different types of surveys; methods for delivering surveys, especially online methods; and the important topic of wording survey questions.

Chapter Objectives

This chapter will help you

- Explain the advantages and disadvantages of surveys as a research method.
- Describe the main types of surveys, including their advantages and disadvantages.
- Demonstrate with examples major ways of formatting survey questions.
- Describe with examples common problems in survey wording and how to correct them.
- Identify ways to improve survey response rates.
- Discuss the advantages and disadvantages of using other people's survey data.

Introduction: Advantages and Disadvantages of Surveys

One advantage of surveys is that respondents can answer large numbers of questions rapidly. Typically, this is because surveys rely on formatted questions such as yes/no, multiple-choice, and the Likert and semantic differential formats discussed in Chapter 5.

A second advantage is that large numbers of people can be surveyed rapidly. Phone- and Internet-based surveys with real-time processing of data permit national surveys of thousands of respondents to be run, analyzed, and reported within hours of the questions being finalized.

A third advantage is that with appropriate sampling and the assumption of normally distributed attributes in the sampled population, you can make generalizations with a known level of confidence from your sample to a much larger population.

A major problem with surveys stems from the question formats. Questions with limited response options such as yes/no or selecting a point on a scale will give you numbers but little understanding of the "why" behind those numbers. For example, you may discover from a survey that 78% of voters would vote for candidate X, but you would not necessarily learn why the voters prefer candidate X. Even if you provide a series of possible answers such as "position on the environment" or "economic policy," you will have captured responses only to concepts that you have defined as important. You cannot be sure that you have captured all the reasons that your respondents think are important, or in fact that your respondents' understanding of "environment" or "economic policy" is the same as yours.

A second problem is that most survey designs do not allow us to assess causal relationships. For example, survey data indicating that overweight individuals are more likely to watch television does not permit us to conclude either that watching television causes obesity or the reverse. Correlation is not causality, as you will hear repeatedly in communication research. To make with confidence the statement that A causes B requires the experimental designs discussed in Chapter 10.

A third problem with surveys is the increasing unwillingness of consumers to participate in them. Because marketing communications via phone, mail, and the Internet are often disguised as consumer research, consumers have grown increasingly resistant to anything resembling a survey. They use voice mail and caller ID to filter out phone surveys, and may trash mail and e-mail surveys, unopened, as "junk."

A fourth problem, though not unique to surveys, is having to decide whether or not the responses you received are valid; that is, do respondents' answers really match their behavior? People may report eating nutritionally balanced meals but may not do so, or they may provide researchers with answers they think the researcher is looking for. Especially for questions targeting personal behaviors and beliefs, researchers may well discover a gap between what they are told and what is happening in practice.

In this chapter, we will follow another student—Caroline—who finds herself in the middle of a campus controversy. Her university's administration is proposing to demolish the historic "Hunter" building in order to expand parking space on campus. The Hunter building has no special historic-site protections. Nonetheless, generations of students have strong and sentimental attachments to its "24/7" snack bar, idiosyncratic architecture, and sweeping campus views from the bell tower, site of many a first date. The Hunter building has been part of Caroline's campus life, and she is a committed member of the "Save the Hunter" movement. She recognizes that the administration will likely decide the fate of Hunter based on the opinions of both the proponents and the opponents of the proposed demolition. A logical first step for her, then, is to run some campus surveys to find out what exactly those opinions are so she can develop arguments in favor of preserving the building and countering any opposing views. The types of surveys she might run are outlined below.

Types Of Surveys

Cross-Sectional

Cross-sectional surveys are typically "a slice of life" or cross section in that they capture what is going on at one point in time. A public opinion poll capturing attitudes to a consumer product one day may produce remarkably different results the next day if in between there is a product recall, the launch of a better product, or adverse publicity about the product. Of course, there are occasions when a cross-sectional survey at a specific time would be expected to produce results unique to the time—after a major disaster, for example. Often, though, in opting for a cross-sectional survey, we are assuming that the opinions captured on Tuesday will not differ greatly from the opinions captured by the same questions put to the same people using the same method on the following Thursday or Sunday. Caroline is likely to run her public opinion surveys on this basis because there is no reason to expect dramatic day-to-day fluctuations in campus opinion, even from the uncommitted and "don't knows."

If a "snapshot" from one point in time appears to be problematic, an alternative is to use **longitudinal studies**, which track people's changes in knowledge, attitude, or behavior over time. Some types of longitudinal study are outlined below.

Trend

Trend studies measure the same items over time but draw different samples from the population each time. The questions remain the same, but different individuals are sampled each time to answer the questions. The advantages of trend studies are that a researcher can maintain sample size as people move or drop out of the study, and obviously track shifts in public opinion toward issues such as gun control or recycling. A disadvantage is that there is no assurance that new people in the sample will not differ in some way from the people they replaced.

Panel

In **panel** studies, a group of individuals is sampled and recruited, and the same individuals are retained to answer questions over time. The advantage of a panel is that there is no variation in the composition of the sample over time. The disadvantage is that because people die, move, or decide not to participate, panels can have a high attrition rate. Predictably, the number of individuals in a panel will decline over time. For example, Caroline may have success surveying a panel of resident students during their time on campus, only to find that maintaining the panel becomes impossible once its members graduate and in some cases become untraceable.

Cohort

Cohorts are groups of people defined, most typically, by having an event in common. Thus all female corporate executives born in 1995 would be a cohort, as would the graduating class of 2016. Researchers study cohorts to see how, for example, career paths develop, how the health status of a particular age group changes over time, or how the political views of "Gen-Xers" or "Millennials" change over the decades. Generally, cohort studies are long term and aimed at assessing broad shifts in the nature of a population. Individuals in each sample of a cohort will vary because sampling of the cohort takes place each time the cohort is surveyed.

If the demolition of the Hunter building was scheduled to take place in 10 years with a final decision point in 8 years' time, Caroline might decide to select as a cohort students who were first-year students at the time the demolition was proposed. She might then survey members of that class annually to see how their knowledge of the project and their levels of affection for the Hunter building change over time as the students move into their alumni years.

Cross-Lagged

Cross-lagged surveys measure a dependent variable and an independent variable at two points in time and thus allow us to draw conclusions about the causality. It is the only survey design that permits us to assess causality. More typically, we would use the experimental designs discussed in Chapter 10 for this.

One example would be surveying a cohort of children about their television viewing habits and then surveying them as young adults with respect to their predispositions to violence. The researcher could then make some assessment of the relationship between television viewing and violence, and of causality, knowing that the measured television viewing preceded any measured predisposition to violence.

Caroline might decide on a medium-term study that surveys students' residence status, as well as attitudes toward their majors, the university, and the Hunter building, and then follow up later with a survey that explores whether these individuals had donated money or time in support of preserving the building. This would then give her some assessment of the type of student most likely to support a campaign to save the building, and whether attitudes toward one's major or the university more generally translate into a willingness to donate time or money to its preservation. As opposed to a "one-shot" survey that captures intentions toward the Hunter building, such a cross-lagged survey might demonstrate a link between, say, major, residence status, or attitude and behavior with respect to the proposed demolition.

Writing and Formatting Questions

Developing a successful survey—by which we mean one that captures the information you want to capture from the highest possible percentage of respondents—requires more than just typing questions. Question format, question wording, and question order can all influence respondents' answers and survey results, so time developing and pretesting questions is time well spent.

Most surveys seek to find out four things about respondents: demographic data such as age, gender, religion, income, and marital status; knowledge of an issue; attitudes toward the issue; and behaviors, if any, toward the issue.

In the case of our campus controversy, advocacy groups on both sides would be interested to know student and alumni demographics such as class year, major, and residence status; whether respondents are aware of the issue; how they feel about the issue; and what actions they might be prepared to take to defeat or support the proposal.

The function of question formats is to clarify both the question and the response options as far as possible for respondents while giving researchers relevant categories of answers that will help them analyze results.

Some questions are easier than others for respondents and researchers alike. At one extreme, questions can be completely open ended so that respondents can reply as they see fit. At the other extreme, a question can be written to restrict respondents to one of only two available answers—for example, yes or no. The following section discusses some typical question formats and the advantages and disadvantages of each. Some of these formats will be familiar from Chapter 5.

Open-Ended Questions

Open-ended research questions allow respondents to answer in their own words but in practice may limit the number of words in the case of online surveys, or space in the case of printed survey forms.

Examples:

- In what building do you attend most of your classes?

- How do you feel about the proposed demolition of the Hunter building?

The advantage of this format is that you may get insights that you could not get with the highly structured questions shown below. Open-ended questions are generally avoided in survey research because they are time-consuming to code and analyze relative to multiple-choice and scaled questions. Where the answers exist in digital format, they can be scanned to find the most frequent word occurrences or searched for specific words or word combinations the researcher is interested in. Essentially, this becomes an exercise in content analysis (discussed in Chapter 13). For survey research, the "In what building do you attend most of your classes?" question may be appropriate because it will generate relatively simple, brief responses. The second question—feelings about the proposed demolition—however, may elicit responses ranging from "OK" to a fulsome five-page essay and is more appropriately used as a focus group or interview question rather than a survey question.

Dichotomous Questions

Dichotomous questions force respondents to select one of two possible answers.

Examples:

- What is your residence status?

  _____ Commuter
  _____ Resident

- Have you read the statistics chapters in this text?

  _____ Yes
  _____ No

This format has the advantage of simplifying data coding and analysis. The problem with such questions is that life is rarely yes/no simple. For example, the above residence status question can be answered easily, but the following question as formatted (reading the statistics chapter) is problematic. For a student who has read only part of the statistics chapters, neither "yes" nor "no" is an accurate answer.

Surveys typically provide some dichotomous response options such as "resident/commuter," "graduate/undergraduate," or yes/no," but these questions are appropriate only when they provide a clear "either/or" option and respondents will not be looking for a third option that the researcher did not think to provide.

If there will be more than two possible responses to a question, other formats such as the multiple-choice questions and scaled questions discussed below become appropriate.

Multiple-Choice Questions

Multiple-choice questions provide respondents with several possible answers and, depending on the precise question format, ask them to select one or more answers or to rank order them.

Example:

If you are willing to help the "Save the Hunter" campaign, which of the following would you be most willing to do?

_____ Picket the building

_____ Contribute money

_____ Work on a publicity campaign

_____ Phone alumni

_____ Other (please identify)

This basic format may be used with a variety of different instructions, such as "Please check one option," "Please check as many answers as apply," or "Please rank order your choices by writing '1' after your first choice, '2' after your second choice, and so on."

The difference between "Select one" and "Select as many as apply" is the level of information the researcher needs. "Select one" questions force respondents to a single choice. This question format may be appropriate in political polling where a voter can vote only for one candidate and that one candidate may be all the researcher is interested in knowing about. On the other hand, the researcher may be interested in looking for patterns of responses. Allowing multiple responses to the above "help save the building" question, for example, may tell the researcher whether or not the students who are willing to donate money are also willing to be campus activists and join a picket line.

Note that the above question begins with an "*If* you are willing . . ." If you word it simply as "Which of the following are you willing to do?" you create a problem for those respondents who are not willing to help the campaign. They would be unable to answer the question or might feel forced into checking an answer that does not reflect their true feelings. As discussed under "Filter Questions and Instructions" below, another way around this problem is to provide instructions in the questionnaire that route respondents around the questions that will not apply to them.

Rank order questions get around the problem of respondents checking every possible answer. If respondents do check every possible answer, the researcher will have no understanding of which items are most important to respondents. With a rank order format, respondents are asked to assign each answer a score. The researcher adds the scores respondents assign to each answer to get the overall ranking of each answer.

Likert Scale

Recall from Chapter 5 that Likert scales are statements with which respondents are asked to locate their level of agreement somewhere between "strongly agree" and "strongly disagree."

Example:

Please rank your level of agreement with each of the following statements by marking one point between "strongly agree" and "strongly disagree."

	Strongly Agree	Agree	Neutral	Disagree	Strongly Disagree
1. I know the rules of plagiarism.	_____	_____	_____	_____	_____
2. I have never plagiarized.	_____	_____	_____	_____	_____
3. I would never copy others' work without their permission.	_____	_____	_____	_____	_____

Likert scales are always presented as statements. The response options usually run between "strongly agree" and "strongly disagree" on a 5-point scale, although 7-point and, infrequently, 3-point scales may be used.

Note that the three plagiarism-related statements above appear similar and perhaps redundant. Here is why we might run all three of them. Comparing the answers to Statements 1 and 2 lets us see if there is a difference between knowing and doing. Comparing the answers to Statements 2 and 3 lets us understand whether respondents have understood the term *plagiarism*. If we get wildly different responses to Statements 2 and 3, we can assume that the term *plagiarism* is not being understood in the same way as "copying others' work without their permission."

Semantic Differential Scale

Semantic differential scales present a topic, object, or concept followed by scales anchored at each end by words or phrases that have opposite meanings. Respondents express their opinions of that topic by marking their positions between these word pairs.

Example:

The Hunter Building

Friendly	_____	_____	_____	_____	_____	Unfriendly
Warm	_____	_____	_____	_____	_____	Cold
Ugly	_____	_____	_____	_____	_____	Beautiful

A semantic differential scale is always anchored by bipolar adjectives or terms, such as *strong* and *weak*. As in the example above, Caroline might use semantic differential scales to assess how campus members see the Hunter building in terms of its "personality."

While these scales appear superficially easy to construct, considerable work can be involved in ensuring that the words do capture the concepts that you want to capture (i.e., that the scales have high validity). Related, it is also important to ensure that the word pairs chosen do represent true opposites. For example, which best captures the opposite of "works hard": "plays hard" or "lazy"?

Survey Wording:
"If It Can Be Misinterpreted, It Will Be"

Misinterpretation occurs primarily because a question has been poorly worded and/or has not been pretested to see what misinterpretations are possible. Consider how even a simple question such as the following could be misinterpreted.

"What is your age?" _____

A respondent counting down the days to his 21st birthday could write in "as of today I am 20 years, 11 months, and 18 days old." Another respondent one day short of her 23rd birthday might conscientiously reply "22" when "23" would be more accurate. And because there's always someone out there with a sense of humor, you might get "Three—in dog years."

We can clarify the age question by rewording it to "What is your age as of your last birthday?" We could also reformat the question. Generally, we don't need to know people's ages to the nearest year (although specific age as it relates to driving, drinking, smoking, or voting might be exceptions). In most cases, categories of age will suffice, so we can ask respondents to check the age group within which they fall, as follows:

_____ 15–19

_____ 20–24

_____ 25–29

In this option, respondents don't have to think about how exactly to define their age, and for those who are reluctant to give a specific age, providing them with an age range may help them feel more comfortable answering the question.

Common Problems With Wording

Leading Questions

Leading questions force the respondent into an assumption that may not be true; they "lead" the respondent to a particular answer rather than letting respondents respond in their own terms. Examples:

- Why do you think the campus administration is unethical?
- When did you first start plagiarizing your research papers?
- When should the Hunter building be demolished?

The above examples force respondents to assume that the campus administration is unethical, that the respondent is plagiarizing, and that the Hunter building will be demolished. None of these is necessarily true, but by answering the questions, regardless of their answers, respondents acknowledge that they are.

Check for leading questions and avoid them. For example, the above questions can be reworked in several ways as follows:

- Describe the ethical standards of the campus administration.

- The campus administration is ethical.

Strongly Agree	Agree	Neutral	Disagree	Strongly Disagree
_____	_____	_____	_____	_____

- What position on the following scale best describes your view of the campus administration?

Completely ethical   ___   ___   ___   ___   ___   Completely unethical

Double-Barreled Questions

Double-barreled questions ask two questions simultaneously but allow for only one answer. Examples:

- Do you think the Hunter building is an asset to the campus, or should it be demolished?
- Will you vote against the Hunter building demolition, or are you not going to vote?

There is no way anyone can answer these questions logically because they are not either/or situations. Deal with them by splitting each question into two. In the case of the above two questions, make four questions, as in

- Do you think the Hunter building is an asset to the campus?
- Do you think the Hunter building should be demolished?
- Will you vote against the Hunter building demolition?
- Are you planning to vote?

Each of the above questions can be formatted as either a "yes/no" question or a Likert statement.

Framing Questions

Wittingly or unwittingly, researchers can influence respondents' answers to questions by framing questions in a particular way, or by question order. For example, people are much less likely to favor cuts to U.S. foreign aid spending if first told that it makes up just 1% of the federal budget. The average voter believes it's more like 25% (Oremus, 2012).

Negative Wording

Whenever possible, avoid phrasing survey questions or statements as negatives. **Negative wording** may be simple and clear but still misunderstood by people reading in a hurry or misheard over the phone. For example, a simple question or statement such as "A course in statistics should not be required as part of the communication major" may be misread or misheard as "should be required." The solution is to phrase the question in the positive "should be required."

The Double Negative

A combination of negative wording and a double-barreled question results in the **double negative**. As Rosenthal (2006) reported, a classic "double negative" question in a 1992 Roper poll asked "Does it seem possible or does it seem impossible to you that the Nazi extermination of the Jews never happened?" What does this mean? What would you answer?

In a follow-up survey, Roper asked a clearer question, and the percentage of respondents expressing doubt that the Holocaust happened (which was the crux of the question) dropped from the original 22% to 1%.

Language

In a global world, languages and dialects are inevitably a consideration in question design. Whether it is a local social services agency researching the health care status of immigrant communities or a multinational company researching consumer opinion in Lithuania, language use can make the difference between a successful survey and an unsuccessful one. For example, a question about a "program" will be met with puzzlement in countries that have "programmes." You would be well advised to seek a local consultant to ensure that subtle shades of meaning are translated successfully—for example, that the word *family* means the nuclear family living under one roof and not the extended family.

To minimize the possibilities for misinterpretation, check your questions at draft stage and then pretest them with a sample of the people you will be surveying.

Guiding Respondents Through Surveys

Generally, you have a choice of either a "**funnel**" or an "**inverted funnel**" format for overall questionnaire design. The funnel design starts with broad questions that a respondent will be comfortable with and then progresses to specific questions. The inverted funnel takes the reverse approach by starting with specific questions and then moving to broader ones. For example, a funnel format may be used to first establish where respondents are on a broad liberal-conservative scale before moving to very specific questions that ask about the relationship of their political views to broadcast regulation or abortion. An inverted funnel format might start, for example, by asking respondents very specifically how many times a week they dine out; this would then be followed by broader questions focusing on why respondents dine out and their attitudes to online coupons and advertising for restaurants.

With mail surveys, respondents can answer questions in any order, but with phone and face-to-face surveys the question order is determined by the researcher. This suggests that mail surveys need to begin with relevant questions that will hold the reader's attention. Phone surveys, on the other hand, may be best begun with relatively easy questions, such as "How many laptop computers are in your household?" This gives respondents a comfort level that may predispose them to answer more difficult questions.

Generally, questions related to the same theme should be grouped together, but sometimes a question may be "sandwiched" between unrelated questions as a check that all questions on the same topic are being answered consistently. Sensitive questions related to alcohol or drug use, sexual activity, or criminal background, for example, may be placed among questions with which respondents have a comfort level so that they are more comfortable answering them.

Filter Questions and Instructions

You may have some questions that some respondents cannot or should not answer because they are irrelevant to those respondents. For example, you may be studying how families get their news of the world. One obvious source of news is the Internet, but not all households have Internet access, so you will need to route the respondents from such households past your Internet questions and on to the next set of questions related to radio, television, or newspapers.

This can be done with a simple instruction, such as

- If this home has an Internet connection, please continue with Question 6. If it has no Internet connection, please go to Question 18.

Alternatively, you might use a **filter question** followed by an instruction, as in

- Does this home have an Internet connection?

  _____ Yes

  _____ No

If you answered "yes," please continue with Question 6. If you answered "no," please go to Question 18.

Such questions are called filter questions because they filter out respondents who do not need to answer specific questions.

Online Surveys

As Couper and Miller (2008) point out, the term *web survey* provides little information about how a survey was done, relative to terminology such as **random digit dialing (RDD)** that immediately tells us how the survey sample was selected and identifies the technology (telephone) used to reach respondents.

A web survey could include hosting a survey on your own website, using commercial web-based surveys such as Zoomerang and SurveyMonkey, using social media to recruit selected respondents or for snowball sampling, e-mailing a survey form to respondents with the request that they complete the form and e-mail it back to you, and adapting surveys for use on tablet computers and smartphones.

The advantages of online surveys are most notably speed, low cost, geographic coverage, and the potential to present multimedia content. Their low cost means they can be run with equal facility—though not necessarily professionalism—by amateurs and experts alike. Another advantage is the ability to rapidly experiment with survey designs in order to optimize response quality and response rate. The two major disadvantages of online surveys are discussed below.

Online Survey Design

Response quality implies responses that are credible, valid, and reliable. Sampling and wording aside, response quality will be largely a function of survey design. In the case of online surveys in particular, design issues such as the size and placement of answer boxes, and the presence and placement of instructions and audio or video components can influence response quality. For example, Smyth, Dillman, Christian, and Mcbride (2009) found that adding an explanation that respondents' answers were not limited by the answer box size significantly increased response quality for both early and late respondents.

In addition to the traditional considerations of sampling and survey content, the following issues, derived from Couper (2011), need to be considered when designing online surveys.

Involvement

The level of involvement with respondents can range from zero as with a web survey that respondents complete (we hope) in their own time and at their own pace through 100% involvement in which the interviewer interacts with a respondent via phone or video.

Control

Self-administered phone or online surveys where the respondent is in full control may be inexpensive, but some respondents may be more likely to drop out of a self-administered survey, which may bias the results. With an interview, researcher and respondent share control in that either party can slow down or speed up the interview. Web-based surveys may indirectly control the time spent on open-ended questions by limiting the length of the answers that can be typed. Control of video presentation may be required to prevent respondents from exiting a video before they have seen it all (Shapiro-Luft & Cappella, 2013).

Privacy

Group interviews and online focus groups offer respondents no privacy. There can be advantages to this in that group interviews can generate information and ideas that might not have come from any one individual. On the other hand, a high degree of privacy is likely to be required if respondents are to answer sensitive questions related to personal behaviors or religious or political beliefs. One-on-one interviews offer respondents an intermediate level; mail and web surveys can offer a high degree of privacy.

Technology

"High-tech" surveys have the advantages of speed, coverage, and low cost, but may misrepresent a targeted survey population because the technology chosen "filters out" individuals who, for example, do not have smartphones or Internet access. Web surveys have the advantage of being able to offer visual content as well as audio, but may lose those respondents attempting to view video via slow-speed Internet connections. Automated phone surveys are inexpensive to run but have low response rates. With some exceptions, it appears that web surveys generally get lower responses than mail surveys (Couper, 2011).

Mobile Surveys

It is becoming increasingly important to design surveys that are compatible with mobile technologies and with the psychology and demographics of mobile respondents. Mobile technologies mean that survey interfaces must be designed for small-screen legibility and to minimize the physical dexterity required to enter responses.

Cell phone users may be more likely to be multitasking, prone to distraction, and in the presence of others when completing a survey. Conversely, given that cell phones can be used anywhere and can give their users more privacy, users may feel less pressured to respond with socially desirable answers.

Lynn and Kaminska (2012) suggest that for a successful mobile survey, respondents must have the ability to hear audio content, pay sufficient attention, make sufficient effort to complete the survey, and be willing to reveal answers. This means that researchers using mobile technologies first must be able to reach respondents successfully and then present surveys that motivate respondents to begin and to continue until all questions have been answered honestly.

Not all smartphones have the ability to display surveys, and not all users have the dexterity to complete smartphone surveys. Smartphone users have been found to take longer to complete surveys and to have a higher rate of suspending their responses and then returning to the surveys than do PC, laptop, or tablet respondents. Smartphone surveys have a "**break-off rate**" of 2–3 times that of PC surveys (Cook, 2014).

To minimize break-off and maintain respondents' attention, mobile researchers need to consider layout, formatting, the number of response options per question, and how or if graphics and video will be used in smartphone surveys.

Relative to traditional phone and mail surveys, online surveys require many more decisions about the design and presentation of survey content. More detailed reporting of your research methods is therefore required so that readers know exactly how you obtained the results you are reporting.

Improving Survey Response Rates

All survey methods share the problem of an ever-increasing number of surveys targeting an ever-decreasing number of individuals willing to participate in them. Your own exposure to phone, mail, and online solicitations to participate in surveys will give you a sense of how and how many individuals respond to such solicitations.

Intuitively, we can identify some of the tactics that might increase our willingness to participate in surveys. For example, we probably need to be reminded more than once, but not to the point of annoyance, to do the survey. We are also more likely to respond to a request from a credible source than to a marketing pitch disguised as research. It should come as no surprise that the perceived sponsor of a survey can affect respondents' attitudes toward the survey. For example, Groves (2006) reports that central government surveys are likely to get a better response than academic surveys, which in turn are likely to get better returns than commercial surveys.

We will likely prefer to complete a survey in our own time and at our convenience. We will also want some assurance that any sensitive information we provide will be kept confidential and that dropping out of a survey or refusing to do one will not penalize us in some way. We might also be interested in seeing the results of the research when completed. A small "thank you" would probably make us feel better about the time we contributed when we could have been doing something else. Perhaps a small reward offered in advance would make the difference between electing to do the survey or not.

The main problem with mail surveys is that potential respondents may see them as "junk mail" and trash them, or just not get around to responding. To improve response rates, use a preliminary postcard, letter, or phone call to tell respondents about the survey and ask for their participation. Include a phone number that respondents can call to verify the legitimacy of the survey and ask any questions they may have. Follow-up reminder postcards and phone calls can also increase the response rate. Reply-paid envelopes are a must if you want mail questionnaires returned.

Similarly, phone survey response rates may be increased by using a letter or postcard to let respondents know that a research phone call will be made to them at a certain date and time and to offer a 1-800 number they can call for further information. Restaurants and other consumer outlets that use phone surveys to assess consumer satisfaction may provide customers with a receipt that includes the number to dial and a code number good for a discount on a subsequent purchase. Such surveys are typically short, "push-button" surveys and will be described to customers as "brief" or "easy."

The Internet does not consist of an infinite number of people all willing to answer your survey questions. As noted above, it appears that web surveys generally get lower responses than mail surveys, so the traditional methods of response optimization apply here as well. People cannot go to a website they do not know about, so phone calls, postal solicitations, and e-mail may all be needed to drive individuals to the website hosting your survey.

Millar and Dillman (2011) found that offering a simultaneous choice of response modes (for example, web or mail) does not improve response rates. However, offering the web option first with a mail follow-up for the final contact improves web response rates and is overall equivalent to using mail only. They also found that a combination of postal and e-mail contacts, and delivering a token cash incentive in advance, can both improve web response rates. They conclude that the most effective strategy is the combined use of multiple response-inducing techniques.

Olson, Smyth, and Wood (2012) found that web-only and phone-only modes got significantly higher response rates from those respondents who preferred the web or phone mode, respectively. They also found some evidence that using a respondent's preferred mode may lead to slightly faster responses.

Respondents' willingness to participate in a survey, online or not, will be a function of the topic and its relevance; their level of interest in the topic; the perceived cost/benefit to doing the survey; the survey sponsor; interviewer characteristics such as appearance, voice, and language if the interviewer has a visual and/or audio presence; any incentives for doing the survey; and respondents' ability to do the survey. The ability to do a survey includes lifestyle issues that permit the time to participate, educational and cultural characteristics that may help or hinder comprehension of questions and instructions, and, for technology-based surveys, web literacy and the ability to access and use the relevant technology.

As de Leeuw and Hox (2004) discovered, if there is one "magic bullet" to improve the level of consumer participation, it may be your opening words—"I'm not selling anything."

Chapter 8 introduced some of the advantages and disadvantages of different sampling frames with respect to survey methods. Exhibit 9.1 summarizes some of the considerations with respect to designing and running surveys. Time, budget, and the size of the survey in terms of both number of questions and number of respondents will influence your method decision. Ultimately, there is no substitute for pretesting all aspects of the survey to ensure that it does not present a problem for respondents.

Exhibit 9.1   Advantages and Disadvantages of Specific Survey Methods

Method	Advantages	Disadvantages
Phone	• Can survey large samples in a short time. • Most households have phones. • Potential to assist interviewees if necessary.	• Typically limited to a few short questions. • Consumer resistance. • "Barriers" of voice mail, caller ID, and "do not call" lists. • "Cell-only" users differ demographically from traditional landline users. • Respondents' competing activities/ multitasking.
Mail	• Gives respondents time to consider questions and the ability to answer questions in any order. • Good for delivering questions on complex issues that require thought. • Suited to asking personal lifestyle questions, especially if respondents are guaranteed confidentiality and the questions are seen to come from a reputable source. • May remain in front of respondents as a reminder. • May be seen as more legitimate than phone or e-mail surveys.	• Low response rate. • No way of knowing who completed the survey. • Can target only respondents who are literate. • May not know who completed the survey.
Websites, e-mail, and social media	• Can be administered quickly, flexibly, and inexpensively. • Asynchronous (can be done in respondents' own time). • Can target special interest groups. • Can present audio, video, or graphics. • Can engage respondents in real-time "chat" or videoconferencing. • May elicit sensitive information that respondents would not provide face-to-face to an interviewer. • Results can be analyzed in real time as data come in. • Surveys can be e-mailed to respondents or posted to a website.	• Results may not represent the opinions of Internet users in general, or of the public as a whole. • Cannot control the survey presentation because different browsers may display the survey differently. • May need mail, e-mail, or phone to drive respondents to your survey website. • May not know who completed the survey. • E-mail invitations can be overlooked or deleted as spam. • Requires more effort than responding to a phone call. • Respondents' competing activities/ multitasking. • Problematic sampling frames.

	• Can detect respondent patterns in answering the survey (e.g., response time per question and question order). • Survey software makes survey design and data collection easy. • Web facilitates survey pretesting and experimenting with survey designs. • Wide geographic and demographic coverage. • High speed. • Useful for recruiting participants and snowball sampling	• Low response rates. • Difficult for surveys to stand out from others. • Decreased willingness of individuals to participate. • Social media platforms differ in the type of user. • Problem knowing who answered online questions.
Face-to-face	• Respondents may be less likely to refuse a face-to-face request. • Potential to assist interviewees if necessary. • Opportunity to assess respondent's nonverbal responses. • No technology required (unless interview is by video link). • Some control over timing and pacing of interview.	• Time consuming. • Expensive. • Need for repeat visits for home-based surveys if respondents are not at home. • Respondents may not feel that interviews are confidential. • Some geographic areas may be hazardous for interviewers. • Interviewers may need additional training in interpersonal skills and cross-cultural communication.

Capturing and Processing Survey Data

The next step after you have obtained survey data from respondents is data analysis. While you might use a calculator to analyze data from a small survey, it is more common to enter survey data into proprietary data-processing software such as IBM SPSS® Statistics, open-source software such as R, or a spreadsheet such as Excel.

Web-based surveys mean that respondents essentially do the data entry themselves by keying in answers to questions on web survey pages. There is no intermediate process such as scanning forms or entering data by hand. Web-survey software such as SurveyMonkey and Zoomerang can host the survey plus analyze the survey data and display summary results at the push of a button.

With some phone surveys, people are invited by mail or other print media to take a survey by dialing a special phone number. The survey uses voice mail technology to capture respondents' answers as they move from question to question. Although the technology allows for capturing spoken comments, it typically captures answers of the "push 1 if you agree; push 2 if you disagree" type. In this case, the respondents are doing the data entry, direct into a computer for subsequent data analysis.

Using Other People's Surveys

Before launching your own research, it is wise to check whether or not the answer to your question already exists. For scholarly research, this is, of course, one of the functions of a literature review. If you are seeking public opinion data, for example, a simple web search may reveal that the information you need is publicly available and reported by national media or available from any number of public opinion pollsters. There are three potential problems with such data. First, they may be proprietary, and you may not be able to access or use them without permission. Second, they may be from a source that has an agenda in conducting the research. This means that you will need to carefully evaluate the questions and how they were worded, together with the sample and how it was obtained. Third, you may not be able to process the data to meet your own needs. For example, you may find data reported by gender but not by ethnicity.

For example, the Pew Research Center Internet, Science & Tech Project, which has been the subject of many questions and exercises in this book, makes its raw survey data available so that you can do your own further analysis of the data. To protect the privacy of respondents, telephone numbers, counties of residence, and zip codes are removed from all public data files.

An intermediate step between using such publicly available information and designing and running your own surveys is to hire a professional survey firm to do the work for you. Such firms will work with you to develop and test the questions and will analyze the results for you and help you interpret them. The cost may be less than that of doing the entire project on your own, especially if your questions can be "piggybacked" onto other surveys targeted at the sample that interests you.

Ethics Panel: Clients and Methods as Ethical Decisions

I. Crespi (1998) distinguishes between professional standards and ethical standards in survey research. Professional standards are the standards of competence that govern sampling, survey design, and implementation. Ethical standards are the standards of responsibility to all parties affected by your research—clients, participants, those who will read your research reports, and society more generally. The two sets of standards are not necessarily related. For example, a professionally perfect survey may be ethically suspect. Or an ethically defensible survey may be professionally unsound as in the case where a judgment is made to conduct a needed low-budget survey rather than no survey at all.

Professional researchers have ethical and professional responsibilities to their clients and ethical obligations to respondents, their profession, and society.

Questions

Thinking of a survey you might design for a commercial client such as a software company or a restaurant:

- What are the ethical implications of using the survey results to publicize your own research firm?

- Why might you want to control how your clients publicize the survey results you obtained for them?

- Your client cannot afford a survey using sophisticated random sampling but may be able to afford a less expensive survey that uses the (probably) cheaper convenience sampling. What is your advice to your client?

II. Surveys must not be morally objectionable, says Crespi. He finds it morally unacceptable to do surveys for a tobacco company, a right-wing–racist political party, or a military dictatorship.

- Is Crespi's position defensible? Why or why not? Or are researchers, be they academic or commercial, obligated to do the most professional research they can, regardless of client or topic? Why or why not?

- Why might you personally decline a potential client or research topic?

Refresh your ethics thinking with a visit to Chapter 3. The following two websites will give you some more specific help with two areas of applied communication—public opinion research and direct marketing:

American Association for Public Opinion Research
Code of Professional Ethics and Practices. . . . . www.aapor.org/AAPORKentico/Standards-Ethics/AAPOR-Code-of-Ethics.aspx

Direct Marketing Association Corporate
Responsibility Resource Center . . . . www.dmaresponsibility.org

CHAPTER SUMMARY

- Surveys are a "mainstream" method for capturing public opinion at a point in time.
- Surveys commonly use formatted questions such as multiple-choice checklists and scaled questions.
- Survey questions may be delivered to respondents by phone, mail, e-mail, websites, mobile technologies, or personal interview.
- Survey questions must be carefully written and pretested to ensure that they are not misunderstood.
- With proper sampling procedures, survey results can be generalized to a wider population with a known level of statistical confidence.
- Surveys can be fast and cost-effective.
- Most survey designs cannot assess causal relationships between variables.
- Survey results are "true" only as of the time the survey was done; there is no guarantee that the results will be true tomorrow.
- Online surveys can be fast and inexpensive but may misrepresent the population being sampled by excluding respondents who cannot or will not access online technologies.

KEY TERMS

break-off rate

cohorts

cross-lagged surveys

cross-sectional surveys

dichotomous questions

double negative

double-barreled questions

filter question

funnel

inverted funnel

leading questions

longitudinal studies

multiple-choice questions

negative wording

open-ended research questions

panel

questionnaire

random digit dialing (RDD)

rank order questions

survey

trend studies

APPLICATION EXERCISES

Exercise 1. Survey Wording

Are you in favor of _____? Yes / No

   Fill in the blank in the above question with a topical or campus issue. Now take this basic question and rewrite it in multiple-choice, semantic differential, and Likert-type formats so that you are capturing more subtle responses to the questions. Check your wording carefully for any leading or double-barreled questions. Having written the questions, what questions can you identify that are unnecessary or that duplicate each other? What questions, if any, would you now eliminate, and why? Remember that there may be good reasons for keeping questions that appear to duplicate each other. What additional questions will you need to write in order to capture information about your respondents as well as their knowledge of the issue and their possible actions toward it?

Exercise 2. Survey Method

There are many ways of surveying campus communities, ranging from "pencil-and-paper" survey forms to Internet-based surveys. List as many possible survey methods as you can think of. Many are outlined in this chapter, and under the discussion of sampling frames in Chapter 8. Which method or combination of methods would you recommend for running the survey you designed in Exercise 1 above? For your recommended method(s), identify the campus groups that are most and least likely to respond to your survey, based (a) on its delivery method and (b) on its content.

Exercise 3. Mobile Technologies

This chapter suggested that successful use of mobile technologies for surveys means that researchers must first successfully contact respondents and then present survey questions that will motivate respondents to begin the survey and continue with it until all questions have been answered honestly by all respondents. Assume that you need to survey your campus community on a contentious issue. How would you contact respondents in the mobile community? What incentives, if any, might entice them to begin—and complete—your survey? To minimize the break-off rate for cell phone, smartphone, and tablet users, how many questions do you think could be asked? What format(s) should they have?

Exercise 4. Survey Mode

 A Pew Research Center 2013 report on civic engagement in the digital age examined the extent to which Americans engage in political activity such as participating in a civic group or activity, contacting a government official, or engaging in social or political activity on a social networking site.

   Survey data were obtained from telephone interviews conducted in English and Spanish by landline (1,353 respondents) and cell phone (900 respondents, including 469 without a landline phone). You can find the survey details, including many of the responses reported by age, education level, race/ethnicity, and household income, by searching the Pew website—www.pewinternet.org—for the report "Civic Engagement in the Digital Age."

   The survey found that, overall, 48% of adults directly take part in a civic group or activity. This figure is 36% for Hispanic respondents, 48% for non-Hispanic Blacks, and 50% for non-Hispanic Whites. This chapter has suggested that response mode (phone, mail, face-to-face, or online) can shape survey results because different types of respondents are associated with each mode. With this in mind, how might the above figures have changed if no cell phone respondents and only landline telephone respondents had been surveyed? To answer this question, you might want to review Cook (2014), cited below.

RECOMMENDED READING

Cobanoglu, C., Warde, B., & Morco, P. J. (2001). A comparison of mail, fax and web-based survey methods. *International Journal of Market Research, 434*(4), 441–452. doi: 10.1177/0193841X09340214

Compares three survey methods for response rate, response time, and cost.

Rosenthal, J. (2006, August 27). Precisely false vs. approximately right: A reader's guide to polls. *New York Times*, The Public Editor. Retrieved from http://www.nytimes.com

Discusses the problem of bad polls, reporting and misreporting bad polls, and how bad polls can undermine confidence in good polls.

RECOMMENDED WEB RESOURCES

Council of American Survey Research Organizations (CASRO) . . . . www.casro.org

This site has links to industry groups, colleges, and universities doing research and research databases, and a code of ethics. See also CASRO's list of survey research databases at www.casro.org/surveyresdata.cfm.

Gallup . . . . www.gallup.com/home.aspx

A research company known for studies of attitudes and behaviors of employees, customers, students, and the public. Check Gallup's Methodology Center for information on the variety of methods used to track public opinion.

Harris Interactive . . . . www.harrisinteractive.com

Provides information on Harris Interactive's research specializations and methodologies. The Harris "Vault" provides survey results as far back as the 1960s at www.harrisinteractive.com/Insights/HarrisVault.aspx.

The Harris Poll Online provides a sign-up opportunity for students who wish to participate in polls, at http://www.harrispollonline.com.

National Centre for Research Methods, University of Southampton . . . . www.restore.ac.uk

A training unit on online research methods for the social sciences.

National Opinion Research Center at the University of Chicago . . . . www.norc.org

Known for its national surveys of public opinion. See also the online booklet explaining surveys produced by the National Opinion Research Center at www.whatisasurvey.info.

Pew Internet, Science & Tech Project . . . . www.pewinternet.org/datasets

Visit the above web address for information on downloading Pew raw survey data for your own analysis. Also view the methodology section of any of the survey reports for details on sampling, survey methods and weighting of samples.

Roper Center for Public Opinion Research . . . . www.ropercenter.uconn.edu

The Roper Center for Public Opinion Research is a leading archive of social science and public opinion data. The data range from the 1930s to the present. Most of the data are from the United States, but over 50 nations are represented.

Survey Research Laboratory (SRL) of the University of Illinois at Chicago . . . . www.srl.uic.edu

. . . . www.srl.uic.edu/Srllink/srllink.htm

The above SRL links page provides links to research organizations, research ethics codes, sampling, and data analysis.

Web Survey Methodology . . . . www.websm.org

> A European university resource on web survey methodology.

World Association for Public Opinion Research . . . . http://wapor.org

> See especially the WAPOR code of ethics at http://wapor.org/wapor-code-of-ethics.

Cool Surveys . . . . www.coolsurveys.com

QuestionPro . . . . www.questionpro.com

Zoomerang . . . . www.zoomerang.com

> The above three sites give you the ability to create surveys, collect data, and analyze data.

REFERENCES

Cook, W. A. (2014, June). Is mobile a reliable platform for survey taking? Defining quality in online surveys from mobile respondents. *Journal of Advertising Research, 54*(2), 141–148. DOI: 10.2501/JAR-54-2-141–148

Couper, M. P. (2011). The future of modes of data collection. *Public Opinion Quarterly, 75*(5), 889–908. DOI: 10.1093/poq/nfr046

Couper, M. P., & Miller, P. V. (2008). Web survey methods. *Public Opinion Quarterly, 72*(5), 831–835. DOI: 10.1093/poq/nfn066

Crespi, I. (1998). Ethical considerations when establishing survey standards. *International Journal of Public Opinion Research, 10*(1), 75–82. DOI: 10.1093/ijpor/10.1.75

De Leeuw, E. D., & Hox, J. J. (2004). I am not selling anything: 29 experiments in telephone introductions. *International Journal of Public Opinion Research, 16*(4), 464–473. DOI: 10.1093/ijpor/edh040

Groves, R. M. (2006). Nonresponse rates and nonresponse bias in household surveys. *Public Opinion Quarterly, 70*(5), 646–675. DOI: 10.1093/poq/nfl033

Lynn, P., & Kaminska, O. (2012). The impact of mobile phones on survey measurement error. *Public Opinion Quarterly, 77*(2), 586–605. DOI: 10.1093/poq/nfs046

Millar, M. M., & Dillman, D. A. (2011). Improving response to web and mixed-mode surveys. *Public Opinion Quarterly, 75*(2), 249–269. DOI: 10.1093/poq/nfr003

Olson, K., Smyth, J. D., & Wood, H. M. (2012). Does giving people their preferred survey mode actually increase survey participation rates? *Public Opinion Quarterly, 76*(4), 611–635. DOI: 10.1093/poq/nfs024

Oremus, W. (2012, May 17). Minority opinions. *Slate*. Retrieved from http://www.slate.com/articles/news_and_politics/politics/2012/05/survey_bias_how_can_we_trust_opinion_polls_when_so_few_people_respond_.html

Rosenthal, J. (2006, August 27). Precisely false vs. approximately right: A reader's guide to polls. *New York Times*, The Public Editor. Retrieved from http://www.nytimes.com

Shapiro-Luft, D., & Cappella, J. N. (2013). Video content in web surveys: Effects on selection bias and validity. *Public Opinion Quarterly, 77*(4), 936–961. DOI: 10.1093/poq/nft043

Smith, A. (2013, April 25). Civic engagement in the digital age. Pew Research Center Internet, Science & Tech Project. Retrieved from http://www.pewinternet.org/2013/04/25/civic-engagement-in-the-digital-age/

Smyth, J. D., Dillman, D. A., Christian, L. M., & Mcbride, M. (2009). Open-ended questions in web surveys: Can increasing the size of answer boxes and providing extra verbal instructions improve response quality? *Public Opinion Quarterly, 73*(2), 325–337. DOI: 10.1093/poq/nfp029

⑤SAGE edge™

Want a better grade?
Get the tools you need to sharpen your study skills. Access practice quizzes, eFlashcards, video, and multimedia at **edge.sagepub.com/treadwell3e**

CHAPTER 10

Experiments

Researching Cause and Effect

Nothing is so good as an experiment which, whilst it sets an error right, gives us (as a reward for our humility in being reproved) an absolute advancement in knowledge.

—Michael Faraday (1791–1867)
Natural Philosopher

Chapter Overview

If the guiding thought for surveys is "let's ask people and see what they think," the guiding thought for experimental methods is "let's do something and see what happens."

This chapter introduces the principles of experimental method. All experimental designs have one thing in common; they focus on manipulating one variable to see what will happen to another variable as a result. In practice, **experiments** range from simple field observations that lack rigor to sophisticated designs in which all variables are rigorously controlled and measurable.

The major contribution of experimental method to communication research is its potential to identify variables that have a significant effect on other variables and to determine whether variables have causal relationships.

Chapter Objectives

This chapter will help you

- Identify the advantages and disadvantages of experiments as research methods.
- Describe the basic experimental design.
- Explain the concept of control in experimental design.
- Discuss the concept of random assignment in experimental design and why it is important.
- Compare and contrast time series analysis with basic experimental design.
- Explain the concept of factorial design in experiments.
- Compare and contrast between-subjects and within-subjects experimental design.
- Explain the concept of validity in experimental design and identify the threats to validity.

Introduction: Advantages and Disadvantages of Experiments

Stereotypical images of white-coated scientists manipulating "high-tech" gadgetry notwithstanding, experimentation means nothing more than manipulating one variable to see if another variable thought to be related to it changes as a result. In the context of communication research, this might mean exposing consumers to different versions of an advertisement to see which version is the most persuasive, asking web users to use different websites to determine which site is the most navigable, or asking groups to solve problems under different conditions of group size or leadership style to see which type of group performs most effectively.

In all such cases, the experimenters are doing something to see what happens rather than just asking people questions. The basic rationale for experimental design is summarized by Gilbert, Light, and Mosteller (1975): "We will not know how things will work in practice until we try them *in practice*" (p. 46).

One important purpose of experimental design is to determine which variables have an authentically **causal relationship**.

Causality can be the focus of intense political, regulatory, industry, and academic interest. Parents and politicians want to know whether exposure to video games or violent or explicit sexual content causes some undesirable effect in children or adolescents. Educators want to know if a particular teaching method will improve student performance. Marketers want to know if a particular marketing strategy will cause an increase in sales. The answers to such questions feed into often-contentious debates about media regulation, investments in educational technology, or where advertising dollars should best be spent.

From a communication perspective, we might be interested in knowing whether heavy use of the Internet causes a change in the nature or frequency of interpersonal communication. We might want to know if exposure to alcohol advertising causes adolescents to drink more or to start drinking at a younger age than they might otherwise, or if a redesign of menus will result in more profitable items being ordered.

Generically, all such questions ask the generic question "Does A cause B?"

To be satisfied that A (the **independent variable**) does cause B (the **dependent variable**) to change, we need to be assured of three things:

- A must precede B in time.
- A and B must vary together (**covariance**).
- B must demonstrably be caused by A and not by something else.

A must precede B if we are to argue that A causes B. We cannot argue that a new monthly newsletter for employees improved their morale if the only observed jump in morale occurred before the newsletter was launched. To measure change in the variables we are interested in, we must measure them at "time 1" and then later at "time 2." This is a major weakness of surveys, which typically measure variables only once, at "time 1."

Also, A and B must vary together if we are to demonstrate causality. If we introduce our new employee newsletter into an organization and employee morale remains unchanged, we cannot argue that the newsletter had any effect on morale. We must be able to demonstrate that as the nature or frequency of communication with employees changed, so too did their level of morale.

However, knowing that A and B vary together is not in itself evidence of causality. We also need to eliminate the possibility that other variables might explain the effect(s) we see. For example, a human resources manager might observe that employee morale is indeed rising after the launch of a new newsletter and therefore conclude that the newsletter caused the increase in morale.

Suppose, however, the newsletter had been launched as part of a package of employee benefits that included additional benefits, salary increases, and profit sharing. In this case, there is indeed an apparent relationship between the introduction of the newsletter and the increase in morale, but it may not be the causal relationship. If we investigated further, we might find that the improvement in morale is explained by the salary increases and not at all by the newsletter. The particular strength of experimental method is its potential to identify variables that have significant causal relationships, to assess the direction of causality, and to identify variables that have no significant effect on other variables.

The main disadvantage with experimental methods is the artificiality of the experimental conditions. Typically, participants in an experiment are invited into a lab or room to watch videos or a demonstration of a new product, to react to a message of some kind, or to work together solving a problem. The researcher may be trying to study how people watch sporting events, shop for products, or solve problems in groups, but experimental designs rarely capture the natural environments in which people watch sports, shop, or solve problems with colleagues. This problem is referred to as a lack of **ecological isomorphism**. The experimental condition is not the same as the outside world it seeks to replicate and therefore may have a questionable validity.

As we shall see, a further problem with experiments is that more sophisticated designs may require large numbers of people who are willing to become experimental participants perhaps for extended periods of time.

In this chapter, we will follow Professor Michaels, who hypothesizes that peer interaction among students may influence their academic performance. We will see Professor Michaels move from basic to more and more sophisticated experimental designs as his thinking about this relationship develops.

Field Experiments and Ex Post Facto Designs

As often happens, Professor Michaels's interest in the relationship between group interaction and academic performance is sparked by a casual observation. One of his classes takes a quiz after a widespread power outage, and he notices that unlike the normal distribution of test scores he usually sees, scores on this quiz appear to fall into two groups. (Remember bi-modal distributions?) He sees a group of students with scores somewhat below the average and a second group with scores somewhat above the average. From what he knows of his students, it appears that the group with the higher scores consists mostly of resident students; commuter students mostly have lower scores. Why might this be? He does the obvious thing and asks them. Their answer is that as a result of the power outage and loss of such distractions as television and Internet access, many of the resident students in his class got together and studied for the test. The commuter students did not.

Professor Michaels is getting the benefit of what we might call a natural experiment or **ex post facto** design. He did not design an experiment but merely took the opportunity to observe "after the fact" that a temporary change in study conditions seemed to have affected quiz results.

This natural experiment can be diagrammed as follows:

Unique or unusual event → *observation*

Intrigued, he decides to run a simple experiment to test his initial observation. Prior to the next quiz, he asks some student volunteers to form a study group and to study together. This basic design is a **field experiment** or simple observation. Here, he is manipulating a variable (study conditions) and observing the results (quiz scores) for the study group versus the rest of the class.

This level of experimental design can be diagrammed as follows:

Study condition 1 (group study) → *observation (test scores)*

Study condition 2 (no group study) → *observation (test scores)*

Suppose Professor Michaels finds once again that the group study students scored higher than the nongroup students. It might be tempting for him to recommend that students study together if they want to improve their quiz scores. Unfortunately, ex post facto designs and field experiments do not let him make that recommendation with any confidence. There are two reasons for this. The first is that he has no baseline measurement of student performance. The resident and commuter groups differ in quiz performance, but they may well have differed anyway; in other words, the difference in scores may not be due to the study conditions at all. He therefore needs to compare the groups' performances before they studied under the two different conditions, as well as compare their performances after they did this.

The second—and a major—problem is that he has no idea how the two groups differ in composition outside of their apparent commuter versus resident difference. It may well be that some attribute other than residence status best explains the difference in quiz scores.

For example, you should already be thinking that the high-scoring group consisted of students who volunteered to study together whereas the low-scoring group does not. Could it be that something other than residence status—personality type, gender, or class year, for example—explains the difference in scores?

Nor can we be confident about the direction of causality. Professor Michaels has observed an apparent relationship between study conditions and quiz performance, but in which direction does the causality run? Did the group study experience lead to an increase in quiz scores, or is it that students who score highly on quizzes anyway prefer to study together?

At this point in the research process, Professor Michaels is refining both his research question and his experimental design. Basically, he has started with a broad research question (RQ) such as

RQ: Is there a relationship between how students study for tests and their test performance?

His simple field experiment suggested that this might be the case, and it is now time to review the relevant scholarly literature and arrive, if possible, at a more specific hypothesis.

His review of the literature suggests that studying as a member of a group can mean getting instant answers to questions, group support, shared resources, help from knowledgeable colleagues, and perhaps peer pressure to succeed. On the other hand, he suspects that any study group also may have the potential to degenerate into uncontrolled socializing and that studying alone offers unique advantages such as no interruptions and the potential to study at any time and for as long as the individual needs to. He decides that the evidence is inconclusive; obviously, much depends on the nature of the study group and the individual student.

He decides that he now has enough evidence to propose a two-tailed hypothesis:

H_1: There is a relationship between studying in groups and test performance.

(Recall from Chapter 2 that a two-tailed hypothesis proposes that a difference between two groups could be in any direction, whereas a one-tailed hypothesis proposes a specific direction, for example that there is positive relationship between studying in groups and test performance.)

What experimental design should Professor Michaels use to establish that there is such a relationship? There are several possibilities.

Basic Experimental Design

The different levels of experimental design are expressed as follows:

X = manipulation of a variable; what is done to the experimental group or groups. In the case of our example, it is Professor Michaels's manipulation of study conditions.

R = random assignment of individuals to groups, a key concept in experimental design.

O_1, O_2, etc. = observation 1, observation 2, etc.

One-Group Pretest–Posttest Design

A basic experimental design consists of a baseline observation (O_1), followed by exposure to an experimental condition (X), followed by postexperimental observation (O_2) to see if any change has occurred in the experimental group. It is diagrammed as

$$O_1 \qquad X \qquad O_2$$

With this design, we can see any changes that might occur as a result of the experimental condition. In the case of our example, Professor Michaels would get a baseline measure (O_1) of quiz performance of a group of students, place them in a group study session (X), and then measure their quiz performance again (O_2).

If he found a difference between the "before" and "after" measures (O_1 and O_2), he might propose that the group study sessions are what caused it, but this design is not rigorous enough to answer the causality question.

To be certain that he has found a causal relationship, he needs to rule out two possibilities: first that any observed change in test scores might have occurred anyway for some reason and second that some influence other than the study conditions caused the change.

The problem with the one-group pretest–posttest design is that many other variables not in the experimental design—such as location of the group meeting, or students' major or class year—might also be playing a part. Furthermore, the experiment itself is likely to have some effect on student test scores. The one-group pretest–posttest design has a baseline quiz (O_1) followed by a second quiz (O_2) taken after the students study for that under experimental conditions. If they have remembered anything from the first quiz, this in itself will almost inevitably have some effect on the second set of quiz scores.

We need to be sure that we have ruled out all other possible explanations before deciding that study conditions, *and only study conditions*, explain the difference in test scores. This means designing a level of control into experiments.

Designing for Control

In a general sense, **control** means to remove all other possible variables from the experimental design so that we can be sure that our treatment variable and only our treatment variable is causing any changes we see. **Control groups** are groups not exposed to any experimental variable. As shown in the following example, they are used as baselines against which to measure any changes in groups that are exposed to experimental variables.

Two-Group Pretest–Posttest Design

One way to be more certain that group study sessions do have an effect on quiz scores is to use two groups of students and to place only one of them into group study sessions. If the students in the group study sessions show a measurable change in quiz scores and the second group (the control group) does not, we can be more confident that the group study sessions did have an effect.

This design is diagrammed as

$$O_1 \qquad X \qquad O_2$$
$$O_1 \qquad\qquad O_2$$

Here, both groups' quiz scores are measured before and after one group took part in a group study session (X). Because the second group (the control group) has no exposure to this session, we would expect to find improved quiz performance only for the group study group. If we find a change in the control group, we have to accept that something other than the group study sessions is causing the observed changes in quiz scores.

The contribution of the O_1 observations is that even if the control group shows a change in scores, we can compare that change in scores with that of the experimental group. This lets us determine whether we are seeing a change in the experimental group scores that is significantly greater than the changes in scores for the control group.

If Professor Michaels determines that the study group had demonstrably higher test scores, he might now conclude that studying together does explain the improved test scores. Unfortunately, he could still be wrong because he has not accounted for other possible differences between the groups that might also explain his results. A yet more sophisticated experimental design is needed if he is to have full confidence in his results.

Designing for Random Assignment

If we have more of one characteristic in a group than in another group, it may be that characteristic and not the experimental variable that is explaining the results. For example, in addition to residence status, variables that might differentially influence test scores could include a student's age, number of years at college, work commitments, presence or absence of a first-year orientation to campus, level of Internet access, attitudes toward education, and so on. Professor Michaels has considered none of these in his experimental design. We cannot fault him for this because he cannot possibly know in advance what all the relevant variables might be. Nor can he control all of them experimentally even if he is able to identify them.

This is where **random assignment** comes in. Your reading of Chapter 8 should have you thinking about the merits of randomly assigning students into groups. In experimental design, random assignment of individuals into groups becomes especially important. With random assignment, we can assume that the probability of some peculiarity occurring in one group is no greater or less than the probability of it occurring in another group. Any difference we observe between groups should then be due to the variable we are manipulating and not something unique to one group.

For example, random assignment would mean that individuals with a particularly high IQ would be randomly assigned across both groups. Any effect of IQ is then equalized across both groups, and IQ can be eliminated as an explanation because in principle it affects both groups equally.

Two-Group Random Assignment Pretest–Posttest Design

The following design is essentially the same as a two-group pretest–posttest design but with the very important distinction that individuals are now randomly assigned to groups, as shown below. *R* denotes random assignment to groups.

$$R \quad O_1 \quad X \quad O_2$$
$$R \quad O_1 \quad\quad O_2$$

At this point, Professor Michaels is no longer asking students to volunteer to study in a group; rather, he is using **random numbers** (see Chapter 8) to assign students to a group. It is always possible that as a result of random assignment he may end up, unknowingly, with Republicans or rugby players overrepresented in one group and Democrats or disk jockeys in another. But random assignment allows him to argue that all such attributes have the same probability of occurring in each group. If his experimental group shows changes, he can reasonably argue that the change is due to the experimental variable.

With random assignment, a control group, and a pretest–posttest design, Professor Michaels is well on the way to answering the causality question, but now this design has in itself created a problem. As noted above, it seems likely that taking a quiz on any topic must affect one's performance on a second quiz on the same topic. More generally, what is the possibility that the pretest or baseline measurement itself had some effect on participants?

To eliminate this possibility, Professor Michaels needs yet another group that has not been exposed to the pretest. These students will participate in group study sessions prior to the posttest (O_2), but to eliminate any possible influence of the pretest, there is no O_1.

The experimental design for this group would look like this.

$$R \quad X \quad O_2$$

Finally, to ensure that the experimental variable and only the experimental variable explains his results, he adds one further group to the design. It is a group of randomly assigned individuals to whom absolutely nothing happens except the final posttest. In the unlikely event that this group's posttest results are the same as for other groups, he would be forced to conclude that something other than the experimental variable is at work. This group's design is as follows:

$$R \quad O_2$$

The Solomon Four-Group Design

Adding the above two groups to the experimental design results in an overall design known as the **Solomon Four-Group Design**, as shown in Exhibit 10.1.

With this design, we can compare pretest with posttest results, compare control groups with experimental groups, and take a look at a group to which nothing has happened except for a final test. Now we can be assured that the experimental variable preceded the posttest and that no other variable explains the changes we have observed.

We have now met two of the conditions needed to establish causality: **temporal ordering** (the causal variable must precede in time any effect) and the elimination of any other variables that might have caused the observed effect. If we can demonstrate that the independent variable and the dependent variable vary together (covariation), we will have met the third condition for demonstrating a causal relationship between them.

EXHBIT 10.1   Solomon Four-Group Design

Diagram	Explanation
R O_1 X O_2	Random assignment, pre- and posttesting, subject to experimental variable. This is the "test group."
R O_1 O_2	Random assignment, pre- and posttesting, *not* subject to experimental variable. This control group shows what would have happened without the experimental variable.
R X O_2	Random assignment, posttesting only, subject to experimental variable. This control group checks that the pretest is not influencing the results.
R O_2	Random assignment, posttesting only, *not* subject to experimental variable. This control group checks that nothing other than the pretest and the experimental condition is influencing the experiment.

Covariation is usually expressed in the form of a correlation coefficient. Revisit Chapter 7 for a further discussion of correlation.

Time Series Analysis

Even though experiments run over a period of time, that time typically is short, and we cannot know if the results obtained at the end of the experiment will still be true at some point in the future. We can address that problem with a procedure called **time series analysis**.

As the name implies, time series analysis is a series of observations made over time. Instead of the classic experimental O_1, O_2 observations, time series analyses require a repeated series of observations at times O_1, O_2, O_3, O_4, and so on. Done before an experimental manipulation, these observations can check for the stability of the preexperimental condition. Done after an experimental manipulation, they can check whether an experimental result is stable over time.

Time series analyses can be diagrammed as

$$O_1, O_2, O_3, O_4 \ldots X, O_5, O_6, O_7 \ldots$$

Factorial Designs

The experimental designs described so far in this chapter assess the relationship between two variables—study conditions and quiz scores. Analyses that examine the relationship among three or more variables are referred to as **multivariate analyses**, and experimental designs that manipulate two or more variables are referred to as **factorial designs**.

Professor Michaels gets interested in a multivariate design as the next step in his research because intuition, observation, and his literature review all tell him that the relationship between studying in groups and test performance must be influenced by other factors—gender, for example. Is it possible that men and women differ in their study preferences? His review of the literature suggests that men and women may differ in their communication styles and preferences, so could it be that study groups have a greater effect on test scores for one gender than for another?

He formulates another hypothesis (two-tailed because he has no evidence to suggest that males will show a greater effect than females or vice versa) as follows:

H_2: The effect of study condition on test scores will differ between men and women.

His experimental design to test this hypothesis now requires four groups of participants, as shown in Exhibit 10.2, along with some hypothetical experimental results.

Because there are two categories of gender (male and female) and two types of study style (group and individual), the design is referred to as a 2 × 2 design. If there were three types of study style such as group, individual, and online, the design would be a 2 × 3.

Suppose the initial (bi-variate) study showed that the average test scores for group study students were not statistically significant from the scores for other students. Professor Michaels might conclude that group study sessions do not improve test scores, but suppose he runs the experiment as a 2 × 2 design and gets the results shown in Exhibit 10.2.

EXHIBIT 10.2   **2 × 2 Factorial Design, Test Results by Gender by Study Condition, Showing Hypothetical Results**

	Average Score on 10-Point Test	
	Male	**Female**
Individual Study	10	5
Group Study	5	10

The pattern here suggests that male students score better under individual study conditions and that female students do better under group study conditions. In other words, there is an interaction between gender and study condition that influences test scores. The scores shown in Exhibit 10.2 mean that the average scores for the individual study and group study groups would be the same. It is only when the study is run as a 2 × 2 design, with gender as an additional variable, that we can see that study condition does have an effect but that it varies according to gender.

We can add more variables to the experiment at a cost of increasingly complex experimental design. Suppose Professor Michaels's review of the literature leads him to hypothesize that residence status may also have an effect on test scores. (Intuitively, commuter students may be less able than resident students to socialize with peers and to access library and academic support services.) He proposes two hypotheses and from his reading and experimental work to date is now prepared to make them one-tailed, directional as follows:

H_3: On-campus residence status will be associated with improved test scores for both male and female students.

H_4: On-campus residence status will be associated with improved test scores for both group study and individual study students.

How can he examine the interaction among residence status, gender, and study conditions as they relate to test scores? Basically by expanding the number of cells in the experimental design. Let's assume that Exhibit 10.2 represents the results for resident students. The same experimental design is repeated with male and female groups consisting of commuter students. Overall, this is now a 2 × 2 × 2 design; two levels of residence status by two types of study condition by two categories of gender.

The design now has eight experimental groups (2 × 2 × 2 = 8). Hypothetical results from this design are shown in Exhibit 10.3.

EXHIBIT 10.3   **2 × 2 × 2 Factorial Design, Test Results by Gender by Residence Status by Study Condition, Showing Hypothetical Results**

	Average Score on 10-Point Test	
	Male	**Female**
Resident Students		
Individual Study	10	5
Group Study	5	10
Commuter Students		
Individual Study	1	6
Group Study	6	1

Looking for the effect of residence, we can see that the average test score for resident males studying individually (10) is much higher than that for their commuter counterparts (1), and resident females in a study group score much higher (10) than their commuter counterparts (1). On the other hand, male commuters in a study group score somewhat better (6) than their resident counterparts (5), and female commuter students studying individually score somewhat better (6) than their resident counterparts (5).

It appears that the above hypotheses are only partially supported. On-campus residence status is clearly associated with improved test scores only for male students studying individually and for female students studying as a group. So while Professor Michaels can conclude that residence status does have an effect on test scores, the effect is mediated by gender and conditions of study.

Between-Subjects and Within-Subjects Design

One problem with experimental design is the number of people that may be needed to participate in an experiment. The 2 × 2 × 2 experimental design discussed above could require in the order of 100 people if each person is exposed to only one experimental condition. Where each person participates under only one set of conditions, such as "female–group study–resident," the design is called a **between-subjects design**. One way to reduce the number of participants required is to in effect use them twice, that is expose them to more than one experimental condition, for example to both group and individual study conditions. This is called a **within-subjects design**.

One obvious problem with within-subjects design is that one experimental condition may have an effect on another condition. Participants already exposed to a group study condition, for example, may have a different reaction to an individual condition than they would have if they had not been exposed to a group study condition. A second problem is that for some conditions, a within-subjects design is simply not possible. In our example, we cannot ask males to be females for the duration of the experiment or resident students to suddenly become commuters.

Validity and Experimental Design

Validity raises the question of whether the experiment has captured the concepts the researcher set out to capture or whether something else has been captured. There are two types of validity to consider in experimental research—internal and external.

Internal Validity

Internal validity relates to questions of experimental design. In effect, it asks the "What could go wrong?" question. Unfortunately, many things can go wrong.

These include **spurious relationships**, where a relationship between variables has been found but it is not the relationship the researcher is looking for. For example, Professor Michaels may assign students to groups based on their class years (freshman, sophomore, etc.). However there is not a 100% relationship among class year, age, and number of credits. Two students, both in their third year, may differ significantly in number of credits if one of them is a full-time student and the other is part-time. Two seniors, both with the same number of credits, may differ significantly in age if one of them is beginning a degree program after a career in the workplace. Thus a finding of significant difference between class years may actually be a finding of difference in age or between full-time and part-time status.

Selection bias occurs when the experimental groups are not comparable. For example, let's assume that one of Professor Michaels's experimental conditions—studying in a group—can take place only at night because of student schedules. This, arguably, requires more effort than the other experimental condition of studying alone. Professor Michaels must depend on volunteers for his study. If a number of his volunteers cannot study at night, his experimental groups have to some extent become self-selecting. The evening group perhaps has a higher level of volunteer enthusiasm, and so we now have a threat to internal validity because the two experimental groups are not the same and the research results are capturing a difference between willingness to volunteer, not a difference between the two study conditions.

Attrition occurs when people drop out of a study. In the case of our example, this may be due to boredom, a student suddenly realizing that he or she is not getting paid for the study, a change in the pace of academic life due to examinations, or a clash of personalities. Suppose in this case the attrition is due to the pressure of examinations. Even if Professor Michaels started his experiment with random assignment of individuals to pretest groups, he can no longer assume that his posttest groups are the same as the pretest groups. Any difference he finds between groups may be due to differences in ability to deal with stress while studying, not to differences between his two study conditions.

Repeated testing, almost by definition, can be a threat to internal validity. As group participants become more and more familiar with a test or its close relatives, the better they can be expected to do at it. The threat to internal validity in our example is that differences in group scores may reflect increasing levels of competence and/or confidence in test taking and not differences in the experimental study conditions.

Somewhat related, the concept of **maturation** simply means that people change over time. If Professor Michaels runs his experiment over the course of a semester, his participants will be one semester older, one semester more experienced, and perhaps one semester more fatigued than they were at the beginning of the experiment. Again, there is a threat to internal validity because any difference in "pre" and "post" scores may be capturing maturation and not the level of exposure to studying in a group or alone.

Diffusion refers to a treatment effect spreading from group to group. Paradoxically, a problem for Professor Michaels as a communication researcher is that people communicate! Male students talk to female students, sophomores talk to seniors, pretest groups talk to posttest groups, and so on. In this case, an especially important problem may be that students who study alone do talk to students who study in groups. The experimental treatment (study condition) in effect gets "spread" across all groups. This threatens internal validity because the results of the study may be to suggest no difference between experimental groups when in fact there is one.

Another related problem could be rivalry between groups. At the point where both experimental groups decide that they are in a contest to see which group can do best on test scores, rivalry sets in. Individuals study extra hard to maximize their scores, and group members crank up the peer pressure in order to have the group "win." Again there is a threat to internal validity because differences among experimental groups may reflect differing levels of motivation, zeal, or disillusionment rather than differences in experimental conditions.

Some threats to internal validity may not be obvious to the researcher, for example the fact that the experimental groups are spending a lot of time talking to each other and swapping stories about their experiences. The researcher may be fully aware of other threats to internal validity but have no control over them. For example, you will recall from Chapter 3 that institutional review board (IRB) guidelines allow a research participant to drop out of a study at any time without penalty.

What researchers can be attuned to, however, is **experimenter bias**, their own threat to internal validity. Professor Michaels is in a problematic situation with respect to experimenter bias for a number of reasons. As he very likely recruited participants from his own classes, his student participants know that he has specific views about student behavior, including study habits. Unwittingly, he may have primed his research participants to behave in a particular way. If he has offered extra credit for participating in his experiments, he will have biased his sample in favor of those students who are keen to get extra credit. Depending on when and where his study groups and students studying individually are working, he may see more of one kind of student than another. This may be read as implicitly favoring one type of student over another.

You might think that sophisticated designs such as the Solomon Four-Group Design would rule out any problems with validity, but even the most sophisticated design is not immune to threats to internal validity.

External Validity

External validity relates to whether the experiment has in fact captured the external world that the researcher is investigating.

The ultimate test of external validity is that the findings of an experiment generalize to the wider population from which the experiment's participants are sampled. Professor Michaels would likely tell us that there are two important reasons he is running the experiments outlined in this chapter. The first is the driving force behind most scholarly research—an intellectual curiosity about the relationships among phenomena of interest. The second is the hope that he will gain ideas about effective study habits that will apply successfully to other students on campus and in the wider academic community. If the findings do not apply, his study will have a serious lack of external validity. Ideally, his research findings will be valid not only across "space" (as in from sample to population) but also across "time" (as in generalizable from now into the future).

Probably the most serious threat to external validity is the issue of ecological isomorphism introduced earlier in this chapter. The students briefed to study alone may find themselves in a realistic study scenario. However, if Professor Michaels directed a group of students on where to study, when to study, and how long to study, it is unlikely that they would regard their study experience as typical. In other words, the **experimental situation** or setting may be a threat to external validity because it does not reflect external reality. The second obvious threat is the participant sample(s). By definition, all the students in this study are volunteers, which is not true for the wider population of students. To the extent that the sample does not fully capture the population's characteristics, there is a threat to external validity.

Another threat to external validity is the so-called **Hawthorne effect**, named after productivity studies conducted at the Hawthorne Works, a Western Electric plant, in the 1920s. These studies were designed to see what changes in working conditions might improve worker productivity. An unanticipated conclusion from the studies was that observed increases in productivity seemed to be explained by the fact that the workers apparently interpreted the research as management and the research team as taking an interest in them. Professor Michaels will undoubtedly have a Hawthorne effect on those students who are impressed by a professor taking a special interest in them (and who may then work hard to give the professor the research results they think he is looking for).

A further question arises with the operationalization of constructs. As you will recall from Chapter 5, validity implies developing measures that do in fact capture the concepts that the researcher intends to capture.

In the study example in this chapter, there are four variables of interest—gender, residence status, quiz scores, and study conditions. Of these, residence status can be operationalized simply by asking students to identify themselves as resident or commuter. Gender can be operationalized as male or female although some research participants may find this an inappropriate oversimplification.

Study conditions and test scores are more tricky. At one level, the study condition is simple; either students are in a study group, or they are not. However, student behavior within a study group can vary widely in terms both of attendance and of participation. Conversely, students categorized as studying individually may well be studying as members of a group by virtue of their participation in online discussions. Defining them as not being in the experiment's group study group does not mean they are not in an informal study group. The biggest question may be quiz scores. We would like to be able to make some general statements about academic performance, or perhaps even more generally "intellectual ability" as a result of our experiments, but Professor Michaels operationalized academic performance as "quiz scores," which may or may not capture academic performance at a more general level outside of the classes he is studying.

A further issue is that the experimental design requires a sufficient number of participants assigned randomly to each of the cells in the experiment's design. Typically, we would be thinking of 10 to 15 participants per cell, with no fewer than 5 per cell. The design shown in Exhibit 10.3 has eight cells. At 5 to 15 participants per cell, this design would require 40 to 120 participants.

Manipulation Checks

Manipulation checks are a check on whether the research participants interpreted the experimental conditions as the researcher intended. The interest here is not so much in the relationship between independent and dependent variables but in looking for possible reasons that no effect was observed. For example, in a study of responses to online advertising for fast food, we might want to check that participants are responding to nutritional information in the advertisements (if that is the focus of the research) and not to production values such as animation or sound effects. A manipulation check is usually done by asking the question or presenting the same information in two different ways. If participants respond differently in each case, we have reason to suspect that a question or experimental stimulus is being misinterpreted.

The Likert-type questions shown in Chapter 9 are an example of a manipulation check. A researcher looking at different answers to "I know the rules of plagiarism" and "I would never copy others' work without their permission" would assume that the concept of plagiarism has not been understood. Suppose an experiment was testing for a relationship between peer pressure and willingness to plagiarize and that no relationship was found. A manipulation check would allow a researcher to suggest that the relationship may exist but was not found because the question(s) were not understood as they were intended to be understood.

Professor Michaels pours himself a coffee, reviews his research, and decides that he has made a good start untangling the relationship among some of the variables that might influence his students' academic performance. He feels that he has a level of insight beyond anything a survey would have provided but wonders if his experimental designs really captured all the influences on students' study behavior. He realizes, for example, that his experimental designs have completely ignored students' off-campus commitments. All other things being equal, students who have job commitments have less time to study than those who do not and therefore could be expected to do less well on quizzes. Then there are innate capabilities such as memory. All things being equal, we might expect that students with a greater ability to memorize relevant content would do better on quizzes.

As he contemplates the logistics of finding 40 or more students who can be randomly assigned to experimental groups on the basis of gender, residence status, and study conditions—let alone the other attributes he is now identifying—he considers other approaches to answering his basic research question. He wonders if perhaps good, in-depth interviews with one or two students might not give him just as much understanding, or perhaps a different understanding, of the variables that influence academic performance.

We will discuss such qualitative techniques as interviews and focus groups in Chapter 11.

Ethics Panel: Two Famous and Controversial Experiments

Chapter 3 discusses codes of ethical behavior for human communication research. The many codes discussed converge on some important ideas about the treatment of research participants. These include:

- Participants must be given the opportunity to choose what shall or shall not happen to them.

- Subjects must be fully informed, comprehend the study, and volunteer to be in the study.

- Participants should not be harmed.

- The research should maximize possible benefits and minimize possible harm.

- The researcher should systematically assess the risks and benefits from the study.

- The selection of research subjects should be fair and equitable; subjects ought not to be recruited simply on the basis of accessibility or manipulability.

Stanley Milgram's Experiments on Authority

In the 1960s, Yale University researcher Stanley Milgram found that most of his subjects were willing to give apparently harmful electric shocks to another person simply because a scientific "authority" told them to do so. Even though the other person was apparently in pain, many, though not all, participants continued to increase the level of shock at the command of the researcher. The overall objective of these experiments was to explain the conditions of obedience to authority. The "victim" was, in fact, an actor, and the "pain" was simulated, and this information was revealed to participants at the end of the experiment.

Philip Zimbardo's Stanford Prison Experiment

In 1971, Professor Philip Zimbardo randomly assigned 23 male student volunteers to two experimental groups. One group was to act as prisoners, the other group as guards, in a simulated prison environment that was to run for two weeks. Over the next few days, the "guards" became increasingly sadistic to the point that on day five Zimbardo felt obliged to discontinue the experiment. Zimbardo argues that such behaviors were born of boredom and that under such conditions good people are capable of turning bad.

See the "Recommended Reading" section of this chapter for more information about both of these studies.

Questions

Based on the principles summarized above,

- What criteria would you use to assess the ethical standards of these two controversial experiments?
- Where on a "completely ethical" to "completely unethical" continuum would you place each of these experiments, and why?

CHAPTER SUMMARY

- Experimental methods range from simple observation to sophisticated factorial designs.
- Experimental methods involve exposing participants to controlled conditions such as different versions of a persuasive message or different instructions for a group project.
- Experimental methods can determine whether there is a causal relationship between variables.
- Experimental methods can isolate the effect of different variables on a variable of interest.
- Good experimental design requires random assignment of participants to experimental and to control groups.
- To determine the specific influence of a variable, sophisticated experimental designs such as the Solomon Four-Group Design may be required.
- Factorial designs examine the interaction among three or more variables.
- The basic weakness of experimental design is that experimental conditions rarely resemble real-life situations.

KEY TERMS

attrition

between-subjects design

causal relationship

control

control groups

covariance

dependent variable

diffusion

ecological isomorphism

ex post facto

experimental situation

experimenter bias

experiments

external validity

factorial designs

field experiment

hawthorne effect

independent variable

internal validity

manipulation checks

maturation

multivariate analyses

random assignment

random numbers

repeated testing

selection bias

solomon Four-Group Design

spurious relationships

temporal ordering

time series analysis

within-subjects design

APPLICATION EXERCISES

Exercise 1. Further Adventures With Study Conditions

Revisit Professor Michaels's efforts to research the link, if any, between study conditions and academic performance. His experiments used two study conditions—group and individual. Study conditions involve a lot more than whether a student is studying alone or with others, though. What other factors might be part of a study condition? Availability of coffee and snacks? Internet access? Identify at least five factors that you would see as part of study conditions and design an experiment or experiments that show how you would test for the influence of at least one of these factors on academic performance.

Exercise 2. An Experiment in Persuasion

Assume that campus surveys over time show a steady decline in the willingness of students to engage in volunteer community service work. Your campus administration and student government are both concerned about this trend and have asked you to research student responses to volunteerism with a view to reversing the trend. As part of a broader research strategy, you decide to focus on the messages that students get about volunteer service. Your working hypothesis is that the appeals used in public service announcements and the like to motivate students to volunteer are not persuasive with the current generation of students. Design an experiment that will test different persuasive appeals about volunteerism with students in order to identify the most effective appeal(s).

Exercise 3. Hybrid or Regular?

In this case, the topic is online education, not vehicles. As online education has developed, three modes of instruction have emerged—100% online with no physical contact among students and instructor ("click"); traditional classroom instruction ("brick"); and hybrid classes in which regular classroom instruction is supplemented with online resources, quizzes, electronic submission of assignments, and discussion sites ("brick and click").

Research indicating that one of these modes should be preferred over the other two obviously could trigger important policy changes such as budget allocations, technology acquisition, and faculty teaching loads. The issue is complex enough that a series of studies will likely be needed in order to arrive at any definitive findings. Draw up an outline of the experiments that will be needed as the basis for any changes in online education policy at your institution. The Althaus (1997) article referenced below will give you some ideas about experimental design on this topic.

Exercise 4. Assessing the Effect of an Instructional Program

A Pew Research Center Internet, Science & Tech Project study (Smith, 2014) found that while a majority of Americans were able to correctly answer many questions about the Internet, relatively few were able to correctly answer questions about some basic concepts. For example, only 44% were aware that when a company posts a privacy statement, it does not necessarily mean that the company is keeping the information it collects on users confidential. Just 23% were aware that the Internet and the World Wide Web do not refer to the same thing.

Assume that in response to such data your college has introduced new programs to ensure that all students graduate with a basic knowledge of the Internet. Subsequent surveys of graduating seniors indicate that they have an acceptable level of Internet knowledge, but as we know, surveys do not address causality. In other words, how do we know that the college's new programs caused the satisfactory outcomes it is seeing? Is it possible that many students would have this level of knowledge without the instructional programs? (College students as a group overall did relatively well on the Pew survey.)

What experiment(s) might you design to help assess whether the seniors' level of knowledge of the Internet is a function of the college's instructional program and not of other relevant experiences such as using social media, gaming, or buying and selling on the Internet?

Assume that your dependent variable is knowledge of the Internet, as operationalized by the above Pew survey.

Identify the independent variables that might influence a student's knowledge of the Internet and design an experiment to help the college decide whether its programs are in fact making a contribution to students' awareness of the Internet.

RECOMMENDED READING

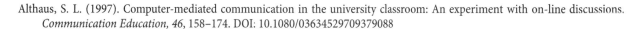

Althaus, S. L. (1997). Computer-mediated communication in the university classroom: An experiment with on-line discussions. *Communication Education, 46*, 158–174. DOI: 10.1080/03634529709379088

Blass, T. (2004). *The man who shocked the world: The life and legacy of Stanley Milgram.* New York, NY: Basic Books.

Dreifus, C. (2007, April 3). A conversation with Philip G. Zimbardo: Finding hope in knowing the universal capacity for evil. *New York Times.* Retrieved from http://www.nytimes.com

An interview with Professor Zimbardo, in which he discusses both his Stanford Prison Experiment and Stanley Milgram's experiments. See also:

Field, A., & Hole, G. J. (2003). *How to design and report experiments.* Thousand Oaks, CA: Sage.

This book takes you through the entire research process including getting ideas about research, refining your research question(s), designing the experiment, statistical analysis, and writing up results.

Haney, C., Banks, W. C., & Zimbardo, P. G. (1973). Interpersonal dynamics in a simulated prison. *International Journal of Criminology and Penology, 1,* 69–97.
Milgram, S. (2004). *Obedience to authority: An experimental view.* New York: HarperCollins.

This 2004 edition of Milgram's 1974 book explains Milgram's obedience experiments and his findings.

Slater, M., Antley, A., Davison, A., Swapp, D., Guger, C., Barker, C., . . . Sanchez-Vives, M. V. (2006). A virtual reprise of the Stanley Milgram obedience experiments. *PLoS ONE, 1*(1), e39. DOI: 10.1371/journal.pone.0000039

A paper on replicating Milgram's experiments but using "virtual humans" as recipients of supposed electric shocks.

RECOMMENDED WEB RESOURCES

Web Center for Social Research Methods . . . . www.socialresearchmethods.net

This site provides an overview of social research methods, including experimental design.

Dr. Philip Zimbardo's Stanford Prison Experiment . . . . www.prisonexp.org

Contains a slide show presentation on the Stanford Prison Experiment and a link to Dr. Zimbardo's website.

Many websites discuss the Stanley Milgram "obedience to authority" experiments. One starting point would be YouTube for videos of the experiments and their many replications.

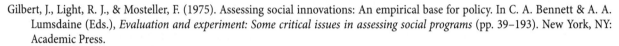

REFERENCES

Gilbert, J., Light, R. J., & Mosteller, F. (1975). Assessing social innovations: An empirical base for policy. In C. A. Bennett & A. A. Lumsdaine (Eds.), *Evaluation and experiment: Some critical issues in assessing social programs* (pp. 39–193). New York, NY: Academic Press.

Smith, A. (2014). What Internet users know about technology and the web. Pew Research Center Internet, Science & Tech Project. Retrieved from http://www.pewinternet.org/2014/11/25/web-iq/

$SAGE edge™

Want a better grade?
Get the tools you need to sharpen your study skills. Access practice quizzes, eFlashcards, video, and multimedia at
edge.sagepub.com/treadwell3e

CHAPTER 11

Watching and Listening

Qualitative Research
for In-Depth Understanding

Not everything that can be counted counts, and not everything that counts can be counted.

—Albert Einstein (1879–1955)

·❦·❦·❦·

Chapter Overview

Not all human communication can be summarized satisfactorily as a "6" on a 7-point scale. As the above quote from Albert Einstein suggests, qualitative approaches to human communication may provide more insights and different insights than quantitative approaches. Intuitively, watching people and talking with them often seem preferable to measurement as research approaches, just as comprehension and understanding often seem preferable to simply being informed as research goals.

The methods discussed in this chapter—interviews, focus groups, ethnography, and observational methods—are all essentially qualitative methods, and all may be used online as well as offline. More importantly, they share a common goal of trying to understand and interpret human behavior. Excellent listening, interviewing, and observational skills are needed to obtain valid understandings of human communication, and excellent reporting skills are needed to capture and convey to readers your research methods and what you have learned from your research participants.

Chapter Objectives

This chapter will help you

- List the advantages and disadvantages of qualitative research methods.
- Compare and contrast qualitative methods with quantitative methods.
- Explain, with examples, how to conduct the major methods of qualitative research.
- Compare and contrast online qualitative methods with traditional qualitative methods.
- Explain, with examples, the basics of coding qualitative data.
- Identify and discuss potential ethical issues with interviews, focus groups, ethnography, and unobtrusive measures.

Introduction: Advantages and Disadvantages of Watching and Listening Methods

This chapter covers some basic qualitative approaches to communication research—**interviews, focus groups, ethnography, observational studies,** and **unobtrusive measures**.

Overall, these methods offer the opportunity to explore the thinking and communication behavior of individuals in depth. Interviews and focus groups are particularly well suited to capturing people's opinions in their own words. Ethnographic methods can capture behavior and language, as well as people's explanations of language and behavior, and can provide a check on the relationship between people's expressed views and their behaviors. Qualitative research can use naturally occurring data—that is, direct contact with human communication. In contrast, surveys and experimental methods are obliged to view communication through the lenses of questionnaires or experimental manipulation, respectively.

Researchers who research human communication in "full listening mode" are likely to be rewarded with insights, language, and unique logics and reasonings that surveys and experiments may not uncover. Such researchers are more likely to discover minority and dissident voices and to emerge with new understandings and insights in contrast to the mere confirmation or disconfirmation of an idea that surveys and experiments largely provide.

Because many observational methods emphasize working with research participants in real-life settings, their findings are likely to have a much higher validity compared with the results of experimental research, which typically takes place in artificial settings.

At a practical level, interviews and focus groups can be set up quickly relative to experiments, which may take some time to organize. Interviews especially can be set up immediately, sometimes as the fortuitous outcomes of fleeting opportunities. However, observational methods are not automatically more convenient than quantitative methods. For example, the fieldwork for a sound observational study may take months, if not years, whereas a survey—a predominantly quantitative method—can be completed in days if not hours.

Disadvantages of qualitative methods include the fact that the variability of human behavior over time puts a question mark over the reliability of findings. Because the participants in an interview or discussion are typically selected on the basis of judgment by the researcher rather than by random assignment, there can be questions about the validity of the selection and the extent to which participants represent a broader population.

The nature and level of interaction between the researcher and research participants affect what is observed and reported, and so how to account for the researcher's own influence on the outcome of an interview or observation becomes an issue.

In summary, qualitative methods offer insight, understanding, and validity but not necessarily reliability or the ability to generalize with a high level of confidence.

Qualitative and Quantitative: Similarities and Differences

At first glance, the difference between the approaches discussed in this chapter and the surveys and experiments discussed in previous chapters is the difference between qualitative and quantitative. It is important to realize, though, that the "qualitative or quantitative" question is neither the first nor the most important difference. Rather, as noted in Chapter 2, it is a secondary question that comes after the researcher has made basic assumptions about people and the basic purposes of his or her research.

As Curt (1994) points out, "all research is participant observational whether people recognize it or not" (p. 121). Anyone who researches human communication does so by directly or indirectly observing it.

Qualitative and quantitative researchers differ not so much on the use of words versus numbers as on the purpose of the research, its generalizability, and their assumptions about human nature. **Quantitative** researchers look for relationships among phenomena; **qualitative** researchers look to understand phenomena as seen through the eyes of their research participants.

As cultural anthropologist Clifford Geertz (1973) phrased it, the difference is between an experimental science in search of law and an **interpretive** one in search of meaning.

Let's take an example. Every now and then I purchase a lottery ticket. Why? There are many reasons. Retiring as a millionaire would give me a feeling of security in my old age and would fund a first-class trip around the world. If I won a million dollars, I could be really generous to friends and relatives. Donating a million dollars to my graduate school might get a lecture theater named after me. Maybe a million donated to medical research would help advance cancer research or the fight against malnutrition. With respect to a state lottery, I might even decide that spending money on lottery tickets will hold off an increase in my taxes because the greater the state lottery revenues are, the less likely an increase in taxes will occur. Behind all this, though, is my basic belief that I have a 50-50, flip-of-the-coin chance of hitting that magic winning number. Heads I win; tails I don't. For a couple of dollars, that seems to be a gamble worth taking. Right?

"Wrong!" thunder the statisticians. You have a better chance of being struck by lightning than ever winning a lottery. Go to the website for any lottery, and you will discover that odds of hitting a winning number are in the order of one in several million. (As I write this, the multistate "Powerball" lottery has posted the odds of winning its jackpot prize as one in 175,223,510.)

Looking at these two different perspectives, we can understand the basic difference in assumptions between survey and experimental methods and the watching and listening methods described in this chapter. Both points of view with respect to winning a lottery are valid. It's just that one is valid from the external viewpoint of a statistician looking at probabilities and the other is valid from the internal, subjective viewpoint of a research participant.

The important difference is that it is the individual's subjective viewpoint that explains the purchase of lottery tickets more than any external logic of statistical probability. We can argue, then, that perhaps the best explanations of human communication behavior will come from understanding individual subjectivities, and that these subjectivities by definition can be expected to vary from individual to individual. Researchers will not be able to capture those subjectivities unless they observe participants closely and/or provide participants with opportunities in the form of interviews or focus groups to express them. Ultimately, this is the basic rationale for qualitative methods.

Researcher–Participant Relationships

A basic research decision is the level at which we engage with the people whose communication behavior we seek to understand. In principle, the closer we get to naturally occurring behaviors, the greater our understanding of them is likely to be. It is this basic assumption that leads researchers to observe or participate in communication in natural settings such as assembly lines, schools, hospitals, bars, or college campuses.

There is an interaction between the act of observation and what we observe and report. We can strive for distance and an impartial relationship with our informants and perhaps miss important insights, or we can decide that close personal involvement will produce more detailed accounts of our informants' lives, framed though the accounts may be by our own subjectivity. This basic decision about one's relationship with research participants is common to all of the research approaches outlined in this chapter.

Gold (1958) described four possible relationships a researcher might have with research participants:

- The complete observer has no interaction with informants; they are not aware that they are being observed.
- The observer-as-participant role happens in one-visit scenarios, according to Gold. Because the level of involvement is low, possibly working with a lot of people in a short time, researchers in this role may inadequately understand or misunderstand their informants.
- The participant-as-observer role occurs typically in studies of communities, where the researcher may spend some time. Over time, mutual trust may develop between researcher and research participants, but within this trust lie potential problems. For example, as the relationship approaches friendship, one or both parties may be reluctant to ask or to answer questions in a way that will hurt the friendship.
- In the complete-participant role, the researcher participates so closely in informants' lives that his or her research role may be unknown to them. A potential problem with this role is that researchers may become so involved in their participant role that they cannot function well as observers.

The precise balance between participant and observer is a function of how best to study the communication phenomena you are interested in, how each of the above roles might shape the nature of the data you gather and your reporting, and the ethical standards influencing your relationship(s) with research participants.

Watching and Listening Methods

In this chapter, we will follow a hypothetical research project focusing on students' use of social media. We will follow Bonnie—the observant director of a campus career services office—as she uses qualitative research methods to get some insight on a campus trend affecting her work. Her office has two major responsibilities. The first is preparing students for the world of employment by offering, for example, workshops in the art of the employment interview, networking, and résumé preparation. The second is alerting students to new employment opportunities.

Bonnie describes the effects that students' ever-increasing use of social media seems to be having on the services her office provides. For example, she is seeing a dramatic decline in the number of students using career center job search resources because, she thinks, they are bypassing the career services office and directly accessing the many online search services. Similarly, workshops on networking and résumé preparation are poorly attended. She speculates that this is because students are actively networking via social media and see no need for workshops on how to do that. As for résumé workshops, one student has told her, "We don't need them. Every job application is online now. You just go online and answer the questions."

Bonnie tries to summarize the pluses and minuses of social media with respect to her getting students successfully employed.

She hypothesizes that students who are active in the social media world will be more likely than less active students to be informed of the job market and to have good job search competencies. However, a second hypothesis is that they are more likely to lack such interpersonal skills as maintaining a face-to-face conversation, interviewing, problem solving with a team, cross-cultural communication, and superior-subordinate communication. In either case, there are practical implications for the career center, which may have to shift the type of services and training it offers. Of course, Bonnie may find no evidence to support her hypotheses. It may well be that students who are active social media users are highly competent in interpersonal skills, teamwork, and problem solving; it is just that they do it online rather than face-to-face.

A logical start to getting some answers would be to interview students.

Interviews

Essentially, an interview is a conversation between a researcher and one or more **interviewees**. Interviewees, the individuals interviewed, may be **informants**—individuals selected because they can talk about others as well as themselves—or **respondents**, who are basically defined as speaking only for themselves.

At the heart of the conversation is a series of questions the interviewer wants answered. At one extreme are very specific questions requiring nothing more than a simple "yes/no" response. At the other extreme are questions based on the researcher's assumption that she does not necessarily know what is going on and therefore must take an open-minded, exploratory approach. This case calls for generic, **open-ended questions**, starting perhaps with something like "I'm new to this; can you explain to me what's going on here?"

Interview Structure

As Bonnie is at the beginning of her research project and has hypotheses that are tentative for now, it is most likely that she will start with unstructured interviews.

Unstructured interviews come from the researcher's decision that she needs to understand communication phenomena in her informants' own terms. In this situation, interviews will at least begin with very broad, open-ended "tell me about . . ." questions. There is no predetermined set of questions although as the interview progresses the questions are likely to become more focused and tuned to the researcher's basic interests.

Unstructured interviews allow the interviewer to establish a relationship with the interviewee and to deal with any questions or anxieties the interviewee may have. They give the interviewer a sense of any agenda the interviewee may have and insight into the interviewee's language and vocabulary. Understanding interviewees' vocabulary is essential if the interview is going to be used to develop specific survey questions that need to be fully understood and unambiguous. They are also the starting point for an in-depth exploration of interviewees' meaning and logic (for example, do students categorize online classes as social media?). They are also an opportunity to begin "snowball sampling" if the researcher needs to recruit additional participants to the study.

Semistructured interviews dictate the broad questions to be asked, but the interviewer has discretion in how the questions will be asked. The interviewer may even drop some questions to allow respondents to respond fully to more important (to the researcher) questions. The interviewer might also ask additional questions with the aim of eliciting full and responsive answers. For a semistructured interview, Bonnie may decide that she has two broad questions: What sources of information do students use to find jobs, and where do they get advice on interview skills? The questions are important and guide the interview, but they are general because "sources of information" may also include people, movies, and newspapers, not necessarily just social media. Because there are only two questions, she has time for follow-up questions and for interviewees to volunteer information they think is important. Semistructured interviews keep the interview focused but allow both the interviewer and the interviewee room to move.

Fully structured interviews mean that the interviewer becomes not much more than a recording device. In this type of interview, the researcher has determined what questions are important, their format, and the order in which they will be asked. In our example, Bonnie would have a specific list of questions related to use of specific social media, the role of friends in a job search, attitudes toward the career center, and the like. She could ask the questions by phone, mail, or web or have someone else ask the questions because she has no plans to digress from these questions. The questions may even be formatted as Likert-type, semantic differential, or multiple-choice questions.

The interview **structure** we choose will be determined largely by our theoretical starting point. If our research objective is to obtain new insights, then we will prefer unstructured interviews that maximize the opportunity for interviewees to talk. We are open to the possibility that an interview related to social media and finding employment may have interviewees free-associating about texting, online movies, or why they "tweet" their friends but not their parents.

By contrast, we might have developed specific hypotheses based on our reading of, for example, **uses and gratifications theory**. Uses and gratifications theory proposes that media audiences are not passive media consumers but are active in selecting the media content to which they expose themselves, and that they do so for a variety of reasons. These reasons include, for example, surveillance of the world for events and issues that might affect them, diversion or escape from routine and problems, or substituting the media for companionship and personal relationships. Research to determine how frequently these reasons are mentioned by interviewees may generate very structured interviews with very specific questions, perhaps even scaled or ranking questions.

Effective interviews require practice, preparation, and attention to each of the following aspects.

Interview Persona

It is important to develop trust and a rapport with interviewees. What kind of person might best accomplish this? Another person just like them; a high-powered scholarly PhD researcher; a newcomer hoping to learn from them; a compassionate, engaged, empathetic listener; or a dispassionate, neutral, nonjudgmental listener? We are all predisposed to respond differently to questions depending on who asks them. Consider, for example, how you might respond differently to personal questions from a physician, a police officer, a psychologist, or a work colleague.

While you will not have this range of roles available to you, you certainly will have choices as to how you present yourself to interviewees, and, as the saying goes, you have only one opportunity to present a first impression. In terms of introducing yourself successfully, honesty is probably the best policy for reasons of ethics, credibility, and maintaining a consistent persona, but note from the Ethics Panel in this chapter that positioning yourself as a different person may be necessary and that necessary deceptions may be approved by institutional review boards (IRBs).

Interview Setting

Just as an experimental setting may influence the results of experimental research, so too can the interview setting affect the nature of the interview. For example, Bonnie may have student interviewees come to her office; meet them in a dining area; or, moving into ethnographic mode, sit with them in campus apartments while she observes their use of social media and the Internet. Each setting has advantages and disadvantages. In Bonnie's case, students may feel more relaxed about meeting on neutral space such as a dining area rather than in an administrator's office or in what they may regard as the private space of their apartments. Interviews in her office may free interviewees from feelings of peer pressure but then have them feeling a need to provide answers that they think she is looking for.

Workplace interviews will require the permission of management, and workplace settings may constrain what employees feel they can tell you.

Interview Sensitivities

Consider religious, cultural, and technology sensitivities when arranging interviews. For cross-cultural interviews in particular, dress, body language, vocabulary, status, and gender relations all need to be considered. For example, first-name relationships may be inappropriate. Intermediaries may be needed to set up interviews or to conduct them on your behalf. For example, Xerri (2005) reports how he used his sisters to set up interviews with women who for cultural reasons would have otherwise been reluctant to be interviewed by a male.

Interview Recording

Audio- or video-recording interviews can save you from taking notes and allow you to focus on the interview. However, people may "clam up" in front of a camera, may be nervous about what will happen to the recorded interview, or may decide to talk "for the record." In other words, what they say "on the record" may differ from what they might have told you "off the record." You have an ethical obligation to disclose that the interview will be recorded, if that is your plan, and may have to negotiate whether recording will happen or not.

Interview Sequence

Sequence refers to the order in which questions occur. You will recall from Chapter 9 that often a "**funnel**" metaphor is used to describe question order. In a funnel format, questions move from broad and general to narrow and specific. An "**inverted funnel**" sequence means that the interview starts with specific questions and moves to broader questions.

For example, a funnel sequence of questions on social media and the job search might begin with "Generally, how do you feel about social media?" The "how do you feel . . . ?" question opens up the opportunity to ask more specific follow-up questions, and the interviewee's answers provide the interviewer with a launchpad for further questions exploring social media use. An inverted funnel sequence might begin with the specific "How many times this semester have you applied for a job online?" In this case, interviewees are presented with a specific question that should be easy to answer and that gives them a level of confidence about answering more general questions that ask them to elaborate on and explain the first answer.

Most interviews begin with questions such as class year or job title that most informants can easily handle. Note, though, that seemingly harmless questions such as age and religion or even names may be intensely personal and emotional to interviewees and not a good starting point for an interview. If you sense that these questions might affect substantive aspects of the interview, it would be wise to consider whether they are necessary.

Interview Question Types

You need different types of questions to fully elicit, probe, and interpret informants' understandings of the phenomena you are interested in. Anthropology professor James Spradley (1979) developed several question categories that can be summarized as follows:

- **Descriptive questions** ask informants to describe the phenomena. "Mini-tour" questions are one type of descriptive question that ask for an overview of everyday occurrences. For example, "In a typical semester, how do you use your social networking sites?"
- **Structural questions** explore the relationships among the terms informants use. For example, "Would you describe an online job search as part of your social networking?"

- **Contrast questions** help the researcher understand differences between and the relative importance of informants' concepts. For example, "You talk about 'job search' and 'career search.' Could you explain the difference between these two?" Another type of contrast question is a rating or **ranking question**. For example, "With respect to job searches, you talked about search engines, social media, and texting. Which of these two are most similar? Which one would you say differs most from the other two? Why?"

If you use all of the above question types, you can have some confidence that you have thoroughly explored your interviewees' views of their worlds and that you have an in-depth understanding of them.

Interview Question Prompts

No type of question guarantees an answer. Interviewees may be nonresponsive for many reasons. They may be naturally reticent, protective of sensitive information, puzzled about which one of several possible answers they should provide, or intimidated by the perceived status of the interviewer, or they may simply have misunderstood the question.

What to do? Use **prompts**. Prompts are simply the follow-up questions that elicit more information and keep the interview progressing. Classic prompts include "tell me more" and the "5Ws + H" of journalism—for example, *Who* (else feels the same way that you do?), *What* (are the steps involved in ___?), *When* (do most people ___?), *Where* (did you first ___?), *Why* (do you say that?), and *How* (does ___ differ from ___?).

Reflecting interviewees' words back to them may get a further response. For example, "I heard you say that a job is not the same as a career; can you explain that?"

And then there is strategic silence. If you have ever noticed that someone in a discussion will ultimately fill a silence, you have noticed one basic interview technique. Keep silent in the hope that your interviewee will fill the silence.

Interviews need not be 100% talk. As part of an interview, respondents could be asked to demonstrate how they do something (for example, their Internet job search strategies), to describe what they see happening in a video, or to rank order photographs of different products or a series of statements describing their ideal political candidate.

Focus Groups

A disadvantage of the one-on-one interview is that no matter how well informed and representative of others the interviewee may be, the interviewer is getting the views of only one person and no sense of how others might agree or disagree with those views.

A common method to elicit and test ideas that one single interviewee might not have had is to bring a small group of people together in a focus group. Traditional "in-person" focus groups typically consist of 6 to 12 people in a discussion setting led by a **moderator** or **facilitator** to discuss a topic of interest. Focus groups can be used to explore such pragmatic issues as how people interpret and respond to political campaign messages or to help researchers operationalize theoretical constructs and hypotheses. They are often used before surveys to pretest survey questions and may be used after surveys to help researchers understand the survey results.

Focus groups are based on the assumption that the ideas that emerge from several people discussing a topic can provide greater quality, diversity, and insight than the ideas generated by the same people interviewed separately as individuals. They should provide new insights, concepts, and vocabulary; a sense of why members think the way they do; and the ideas that members agree and disagree on. We hope for a "2 + 2 = 5" effect, noting, however, that a poorly selected group has the potential to provide a "2 + 2 = 3" effect, especially with an inept moderator.

Because focus group members most commonly are sampled judgmentally or on the basis of convenience, the method's major weaknesses are reliability and the ability to generalize to a wider population. Often the reliability question can be addressed by running a second focus group and comparing the results with those from the first group.

Generally focus group participants are selected by the researcher to represent a defined demographic group such as college seniors looking for jobs. Within such groups, the researcher hopes to find a diversity of opinions on the topic by recruiting, for example, social media "geeks" and students who have yet to join a social networking site.

A focus group on students' use of social media would give Bonnie insight on new "buzz words" and terminology that she needs to understand, and, importantly, the meanings that students associate with these words. Ideally, the group should generate new ideas she has not thought of, and also show her areas where students agree and disagree.

Focus group moderators need the skills to encourage reticent members to speak and to control the more verbose members. They need to take a middle ground between allowing group members free expression and keeping the discussion focused on the topic at hand. To keep the discussion on track and to maintain order, it is a good idea to prepare in advance a discussion guide that lists key questions and the question order. The same prompts that help an interview along can be used to prompt a reticent focus group, but the ideal focus group has a level of interaction among its members such that prompting should be unnecessary.

Typically, the group's discussion will be audio- or video-recorded to provide transcripts for subsequent analysis. Professionally run focus groups often take place in a room with one-way mirrors so that observers can follow the discussion without their presence disrupting it. Group members may be offered drinks and snacks and may receive a small payment or a donation to a charity of their choice.

Online Focus Groups

Increasingly, focus groups are run online, especially in applied communication research areas such as marketing. Online groups offer the advantages of low cost, time saving, and the ability to link people internationally. Focus group software can record the discussion; offer anonymity to participants; and allow the moderator to contact participants individually and, if necessary, privately. Online groups can run for days or weeks as necessary and offer members the convenience of participating from their homes or offices.

The disadvantages of online focus groups include anonymity, the absence of nonverbal communication, and Internet technology itself. The same anonymity that can encourage free and frank discussion can also present a focus group moderator with the problem of knowing who exactly is participating in a group. Online groups that depend on typed responses do not provide moderators with nonverbal cues as to what participants are thinking and how they are interacting. There is a related problem of how to interpret text; for example, online communities often regard USING CAPITAL LETTERS as the equivalent of impolitely shouting at others. Should a moderator regard capitals as someone trying to dominate the discussion, an attempt at emphasis, or perhaps just an inadvertently locked caps key? The technology itself can have a negative impact in that group members with poor Internet connections will be less able to participate. Even with high-speed reliable connections, members with limited keyboard skills will be less able to participate and to express themselves spontaneously.

Online groups may be **asynchronous,** with members contributing in their own time, or **synchronous,** with members interacting in "real time." The asynchronous mode allows for a greater number of participants and may reduce feelings of pressure to respond to an idea. It may also reduce anxieties about answering sensitive questions and encourage in-depth responses because members can reply to questions in their own time. The synchronous mode is likely to be more efficient and to stimulate more interaction, but participants may be more likely to tire of the discussion than in asynchronous mode.

A new world for online focus group research is the virtual world of avatars. Houliez and Gamble (2012) explored conducting focus groups with **avatars** in the virtual world of Second Life. They found difficulties ranging from poor audio quality to problems with distributing and getting back consent forms as well as the limitations of navigation and communication by keyboard. On the other hand, virtual groups offer members the advantages of anonymity and the opportunity to express opinions they might not express in the "real world."

A theoretically and practically important question for moderators of virtual groups is the status of the avatar. Is the research interest in the avatar or the person behind the avatar? The question is further complicated by the fact that one "real" person may be the force behind several different avatars.

You can make your own good assessment of the relative advantages and disadvantages of online, offline, and perhaps virtual focus groups by thinking about your own experience with online and regular in-class discussions and identifying the factors that hindered and facilitated discussion in each case.

Any successful focus group has clear objectives, a membership appropriate to the research questions(s), carefully prepared questions and facilities (offline and/or online), and a moderator who facilitates an active, creative discussion that involves all members and remains focused on the topic.

Ethnographic Methods

Many varieties of watching and listening research take place under the umbrella of ethnography. Ethnography is basically the study of human social behavior or cultures. The term *ethnography* (from the Greek *ethnos* = people; *graphein* = writing) suggests that we are observing, describing, and interpreting people's behavior.

Some principles of ethnographic research (adapted from Kirsch, 2001) are

- Conduct research primarily in natural settings.
- Combine direct observation with interviews.
- Focus on local, subjective, knowledge, and categories.
- Engage directly with the community's members.

A number of important decisions must precede ethnographic research. These include defining research question(s), which may or may not be specific; identifying potential gatekeepers and informants; deciding whether to interview people individually or in groups; choosing between structured and unstructured interviews; and deciding what to observe and how to record, analyze, and present ethnographic data.

Whether the culture of interest is a village, a virtual world, a surgical team, a film studio, or a local pub, ethnographers seek to immerse themselves in the culture and its natural setting. They seek to accurately describe the culture and the behaviors that define it and that differentiate it from other cultures. They seek to understand the culture's shared meanings that explain its behaviors and norms. While the generic research question is simple—"How and why do things get done in this culture?" or even more simply "What's going on here?"—getting answers and credible explanations of those answers may take months or years. Because the time available for research may be limited, some communication studies may be "ethnographically informed" rather than being the full ethnographies that may require a researcher's full immersion for a year or more. For example, it may be possible to study a group of students for only one semester, but not for the four years of their college careers.

In practice, ethnographies of all types begin with the formal and informal **gatekeepers** who make access to a community or culture possible. Formal gatekeepers are those individuals whose permission makes the access officially possible. Access to a work team, for example, will typically require a formal approval from management in return for which the researcher may have to provide written assurances that the organization and the individuals in it will not be identified, that no competing organization is involved in the study, and that no proprietary information will be published. Management approval can be a mixed blessing; you get access to employees but then may have to address employee suspicions about a management-approved survey.

Formal approvals do not necessarily ease the way into the community to be studied. For a successful entry into the community, **key informants** are required. These are the individuals who are part of the study community and who for their own reasons have agreed to introduce the researcher to their community and legitimize the researcher's work as nonthreatening.

Some research requires that researchers work in disguise, for example as "fake" hospital patients or students (see the Ethics Panel in this chapter). It is more likely that researchers will identify themselves as they are—researchers with a genuine interest in how and why the community or culture functions. This reduces the potential for ethically suspect relationships and potential complications such as being exposed as a phony when the members of a work team discover that their fellow employee is not actually an employee.

All ethnographies involve detailed observation and recording, typically in the form of voluminous written notes but increasingly with audio and video recording. Regardless of the recording media, the researcher typically will aim to record a rich diversity of data—behaviors; dress; decor; rites and rituals; language and the meanings associated with specific words and phrases; greetings and salutations; respect for authority; relationships between men and women, old and young, and superiors and subordinates; use of time; work versus social behaviors; and so on.

Generally, ethnographers record at least three different kinds of notes. **Descriptive notes** are the primary records that detail the raw data of human interactions and the settings that are the focus of the ethnography. **Method notes** record the specific methods used to gather data on any given day—for example, direct observation, group interviews, video recording, screen capture, or reading social media content. Method notes are necessary because of the interaction between method and data. For example, individuals are likely to behave and speak differently in one-on-one interviews than they are in a group setting.

Analytic notes are the notes the ethnographer writes in order to interpret the raw data. They are reflexive in that the ethnographer will visit and revisit the notes repeatedly, and her theories and explanations will change as the study progresses and as more data are gathered. For example, she might initially see a power relationship between two individuals as best explained by an age difference or a respect for authority and then, as she gathers more data, come to understand the relationship as best explained by a difference in technical expertise. This interpretation would then trigger further observations and interviews. Such "looping back" through data, method notes, and analytic notes continues until the ethnographer is comfortable that there is no new information to be had and that she has considered all possible explanations and arrived at her best possible understanding of the culture she is studying.

At this point, the task becomes writing the best possible narrative that will explain to interested readers how life is lived as a member of the culture. One feature that distinguishes an ethnographic report is the use of the participants' own language. The availability of audiovisual media and hypermedia presents new challenges and opportunities for recording and reporting, as we shall see in Chapter 14.

Ethnographic Starting Points

"What specifically should I focus on?" can be a difficult question to answer for ethnographic studies because there are so many possible starting points. Sociolinguist Dell Hymes (1974) developed a system for examining communication as a cultural practice and proposed six basic units a researcher might focus on. They are:

- **Speech community**—a group of people who share common signs, a language that differentiates them from other groups, and rules governing their speech. Example: a group of communication majors.
- **Speech situation**—the occasions within a speech community when people talk. Example: An introductory class on research methods or an annual awards dinner.
- **Speech event**—the specific speech activity that takes place. Example: a student presentation or an awards speech.
- **Communicative act**—the smaller units of speech within a speech event. Example: asking a question or telling a joke.
- **Communicative style**—the speech style that is characteristic of someone. Example: being habitually ironic or using "geek" jargon.
- **Ways of speaking**—the styles of speech that may be used in specific situations and events or that are characteristic of a culture. Example: at the beginning of a class, the instructor speaks before students do.

After choosing one of the above units to study, you would then analyze it by asking a set of questions that Hymes developed. These questions are summarized in the acronym SPEAKING, and each item helps a researcher document the language and meanings in a speech community. The SPEAKING items are

- **Situation**—the setting where the activities take place and the overall scene of which they are a part. Example: a college classroom.
- **Participants**—the people present and their roles and relationships within the speech situation. Example: students and faculty.
- **Ends**—the ends or goals of the communication being studied. Example: mastering the language of communication research.
- **Acts**—the language and behaviors that convey meaning to the participants. Example: instructors demonstrating a specific research method.
- **Key**—the tone of speech. How the speech sounds. Example: formal or friendly.
- **Instrumentality**—the channels or methods used to communicate. Example: an online discussion group.
- **Norms**—the rules governing speech and its interpretation. Example: students cannot ask questions until after the instructor has spoken.
- **Genres**—the traditional types of speech found in most cultures. Examples: commencement speeches, election "stump" speeches, lectures, and funeral orations.

By working through Hymes's units of analysis, we can describe how people communicate, their patterns of communication, and how language is used and understood. This approach is far from being the only entry point into ethnography, but the emphasis on communication and the specific questions to be asked will help you with potential starting points for an ethnographic study.

Online Ethnography

The approaches and issues outlined in this chapter are all applicable to online ethnography, but online ethnography has some unique characteristics to be considered. For example, the online world provides no direct observation of human behavior, and the researcher is faced with data unique to the web such as **emoticons**, avatars, web pages, blogs, wikis, and hyperlinks.

Typically, online text, audio, graphics and video can be easily recorded using screen-save software so the effort of recording raw data is much reduced relative to traditional ethnographies. Online ethnographers then face serious decisions about how to analyze and report such data, given that most scholarly research is still reported and published as text.

Kozinets (2013) sees the differences between online and traditional ethnographies such that a new term—**netnography**—becomes necessary for online ethnographies. He defines netnography as "a specialized form of ethnography adapted to the unique computer-mediated contingencies of today's social worlds" (p. 1). He describes it as an applied, interdisciplinary approach involving anthropology, sociology, and cultural studies. Whereas ethnography is entirely face-to-face, netnography is entirely online.

Kozinets's distinction notwithstanding, there is not necessarily a choice between offline and online ethnography because a research question may well imply both. For example, an exploration of how graduating seniors communicate with each other about employment would be seriously shortchanged if it were restricted to web-only communication or to interpersonal communication only.

Ethnography at first sight may seem unstructured and unfocused, especially coming off a chapter on experimental method in which very specific research designs are proposed to test very specific hypotheses about human communication. It may conjure up the image of earnest explorers in pith helmets living with strange tribes in remote places. The image has some validity as a metaphor for serious, committed, and engaged inquiry into the communication behaviors of others, but ethnographers' interests are as modern as today, as witness their interests in cyber-ethnography and the seemingly accepted neologism of "netnography."

Observational Studies

Observational studies typically record and interpret individual and group behaviors in their natural settings. Ethnography depends upon observation, but not every observational study is an ethnography. You could, for example, observe the behavior of music fans at a rock concert without doing any of the in-depth interviews or long-term observations that ethnography typically requires.

Many qualitative studies are observational without being ethnographies, for example observations of student-teacher interaction in the classroom or of small groups engaged in problem solving. In these two examples, observational methods will not necessarily provide an understanding of what it means to be a teacher, a student, or a member of a group, but they may well provide valid findings about communication and perhaps even reliable findings that will allow us to predict whether a particular teaching style will be effective with reticent students or what specific behaviors most facilitate or hinder a group's problem solving.

Observational studies use many of the methods described above and possibly even quasi-experimental methods where, for example, a group may be put together specifically to solve a problem assigned by the researcher under conditions defined by the researcher.

At the other extreme, a researcher may have no contact with the individuals being researched at all. This means using unobtrusive measures, as described below.

Unobtrusive Measures

Unobtrusive measures document people's behavior without them being aware of it. This can be important where we suspect that there may be a gap between words and action. For example, suppose our research participants assure us in interviews or surveys that they would never text while driving and that they always wear their seat belts. True? Take a look at campus traffic to observe directly the extent of texting and seat belt usage. Interested in whether your informants' accounts of healthy eating match reality? You can unobtrusively observe campus dining behavior to get a sense of the cheeseburger-to-fruit ratio on cafeteria trays, or you can ask the dining services manager for data on what items are best sellers. Want a check on student alcohol consumption? Check out dormitory or apartment garbage, or campus police records. For a check on campus political sentiments, check out campaign stickers on employee and student vehicles, or graffiti. How might a car dealer decide which radio stations to advertise on? Have service staff record what station each car radio is tuned to when the vehicle comes in for service.

Most unobtrusive measures do not provide a direct check on any one individual's self-report, but they can provide a general sense of whether the self-reports you get of people's behaviors are credible.

Conversation Analysis

Many research methods are based on observation and listening. For example, **conversation analysis** is a method for analyzing how people negotiate understanding and the rules for understanding. For example, if a question is posed during a conversation or discussion, what are the rules that determine whether it gets an answer or not? If the question does not get an answer from somebody, how does the conversation then change? As the method is in practice an analysis of transcripts of recorded conversations, we discuss conversation analysis further in Chapter 13.

Making Sense of Qualitative Data

When you gather data on people's behavior by watching and listening, you record words and actions rather than numbers. The question then becomes how to establish a sense of order and interpret what may be hours of audio or video recordings or page after page and box after box of notes, transcripts, or observations.

The basis of many qualitative analyses is **categorization**—that is, identifying each piece of data as belonging to a particular category predetermined by the researcher or generated from the data itself. By analyzing these categories and the relationships among categories, researchers are able to see patterns of behavior or thinking that shed light on their research interests.

Fundamentally, there are three ways of categorizing qualitative information. The first is to assign items to specific nonchanging, preassigned categories (fixed coding). The second is to start with theoretically informed categories that may change as new data come in (flexible coding). The third is to start with no preconceived categories and to allow categories and theories to emerge as data analysis progresses (grounded-in-data coding).

Fixed Coding

Coding typically means assigning units of information to preassigned categories and then counting the frequency with which these different units occur. Suppose, for example, we are questioning students in an attempt to understand their use of social media. With **fixed coding** we might, for example, hypothesize from a review of the uses and gratifications literature that four important factors will explain students' use of social media—convenience, relaxation, escape, and the opportunity for social interaction with friends. We would then develop a simple record sheet that records the number of times we find each of these mentioned in our data. Such a coding sheet would look like Exhibit 11.1.

EXHIBIT 11.1   Sample Analysis Sheet for Qualitative Data: Predetermined Categories

Understanding Student Use of Social Media		
Categories Derived From Theory	Number of Mentions	Reasons Item Is Considered Important
Convenience		
Relaxation		
Escape		
Social Viewing		

Flexible Coding

A problem with fixed coding is that it provides no room for the inevitable "other" categories that will emerge as we read through our interview or focus group transcripts. Furthermore, one of the reasons we listen to people in the first place is to gain new insights. **Flexible coding** allows for new categories to emerge rather than forcing every piece of information into preconceived categories or perhaps one additional and less-than-useful "other" category.

For example, as we read though people's answers about social media, it appears that there are two broad reasons for using them—convenience and the opportunity to socialize. As we examine the explanations we have been given about convenience, we see that several different notions of "convenience" emerge—geographic (*I can stay home and socialize*), scheduling (*I can socialize anytime*), portability (*I can socialize on my smartphone*), and cost (*I don't need money to go to the movies or a restaurant*). All of these ideas seem to fit under the umbrella of "convenience," so we decide to set up four subcategories, as shown in Exhibit 11.2.

Similarly, "socializing," turns out to have three components. Two are perhaps predictable—"relaxation" and "social interaction." Also, it appears that online socializing is a social learning opportunity in the sense that students learn from other students and recently graduated friends about the social behaviors associated with careers and different types of employment. If students' definition of social media includes movie sites such as YouTube, they may even be learning about career behaviors specific to criminal justice, health care, business, and entertainment. They may even change courses or majors on the basis of what they learn from such sites. This is clearly a new concept, and it might be reasonable to set up a new "social learning" category called "career skills." For the moment, use of movie sites appears to be seen as part of socializing, but as our analysis progresses, we may decide that this is a major new concept related to career development and that we will be able to rationalize setting it up as a third major category, alongside "convenience" and "socializing."

Many qualitative analyses are grounded in an approach developed by Glaser and Strauss (1967) that considers theory as "grounded in data." That is to say rather than using data to test a theory or hypothesis, the theory itself emerges as the data analysis proceeds.

A basic of the **grounded theory** approach is the "constant comparative method." In this technique, we would look at statements and ideas that emerge from our observations and assign each statement to a category. The constant comparative method consists of testing each new statement or idea against the categories we have developed and reworking categories as necessary as our data analysis proceeds. We in effect did this in previous paragraphs when we analyzed the data students provided on their use of social media and developed the summary table shown as Exhibit 11.2.

Exhibit 11.2   Sample Analysis Sheet for Qualitative Data: Categories Emerge From Data

Understanding Student Use of Social Media			
Categories Emerge From Data			Working Notes
Convenience	geographic		1. *Which of these are most used as reasons to use social media?*
	scheduling		2. *Is there a difference between weeknight relaxation and weekend relaxation?*
	portability of medium		3. *Am I hearing different words for the same concept?*
	cost	money	4. *Are residents and commuters telling me the same thing?*
		time	5. *Note: Need to be able to write an account that student would recognize as authentic.*
Socializing	relaxation	gaming	
		social planning	
	social interaction	keeping current	
		academic work	
		networking	
	social learning	careers	
		work behaviors	

The above examples of coding might be regarded as an analytic approach, in which the number and relationship of categories of data help build a theory about human communication. Another approach is interpretive, in which the researcher probes for the values and motivations that seem to be behind the observed data. The researcher tries to understand what it is that individuals are trying to achieve with, for example, their social media postings or what values define a community for its members and make it different from other communities.

Moving between analysis and interpretation, between data and hypotheses, and between different samples of data can help establish the relative importance of different observations and the relationships among them. Your hypotheses should change and evolve as a result. You can test your hypotheses by looking for data that contradict them. They should become less and less tentative to the point where you can have confidence in proposing a general theory about human communication in a particular setting.

There is no compelling reason to analyze all your data at once. Starting with a small judgmental sample of data may allow you to categorize and interpret it more readily. You can test your initial reading of your data by checking it against a further sample.

Drowning in Data? CAQDAS to the Rescue

Just as there are statistical programs to handle numeric data, computer-assisted qualitative data analysis software (CAQDAS) handles qualitative data, including text, audio, graphics, video, and social media chat.

Basically, such programs allow the user to enter text such as interviews and then to search for words and phrases and pull together items that are flagged as belonging to a particular category. New coding categories can be created as new ideas emerge from examining the data. Typically, you will be able to search for terms, examine terms in context, display the frequencies of key terms, and produce graphic displays of the relationships among terms. Most programs offer tutorials, webinars, free trials, and user forums. Websites for some such programs are listed at the end of this chapter.

Ethics Panel: In Which a Professor Becomes a Student

Nathan, R. (2005). *My freshman year: What a professor learned by becoming a student.* Ithaca, NY: Cornell University Press.

"Rebekah Nathan," a "50-something" professor of anthropology, decided that she needed to better understand her students and their lives. She took a sabbatical leave and, on the basis of her high school transcript, enrolled as a freshman student at her own university for a semester. She moved into a dorm, took on a full course load, ate in the student cafeteria, joined student clubs, played volleyball and tag football, and, of course, attended class and completed (most) assignments.

To understand student life, she drew on interviews and conversations with classmates, and observations and interactions with professors and university staff. The issues she explored included friendships, race relations and social life, classroom participation, eating and sleeping in class, plagiarism, scheduling conflicts, dropping readings and assignments, holding down a job, not holding down food, and relations with faculty.

Nathan did not volunteer that she was a professor but also did not lie if anyone specifically asked her. In day-to-day interactions, she allowed students to assume she was one of them. When conducting formal interviews, she identified herself as a researcher, explained her study, and obtained written permission to publish informants' words. She did reveal her identity to some students with whom she developed a close relationship.

Nathan has been on one hand criticized for enhancing her own academic career at the expense of students and on the other hand commended for following approved procedures such as obtaining informed consent and clearing her study through her university's IRB.

Academic opinion on the need for such "undercover" studies is mixed.

Review Chapter 3, "Ethics: What Are My Responsibilities as a Researcher?" and answer the following.

Questions

- Why would "Ms. Nathan" not want to be open about her status, occupation, and reason for being on campus?

- Do you feel that students involved in this study were exploited in any way?

- Do any aspects of this study strike you as ethically suspect? If so, why or why not?

- Nathan's research was approved by the campus IRB. Do you agree or disagree with the board's decision? Why?

Resources

American Psychological Association Ethical Principles
of Psychologists and Code of Conduct . . . . www.apa.org/ethics

National Communication Association Code of Professional
Ethics for the Communication Scholar/Teacher . . . . www.natcom.org/Tertiary.aspx?id=2120&terms=
code%20of%20professional

CHAPTER SUMMARY

- Qualitative methods are generally based on the assumption that people are idiosyncratic and have unique and subjective views of their world. The inability to generalize to a larger population is not therefore regarded as a problem.
- Qualitative researchers may begin with theoretically derived hypotheses or develop theories from research data as it is analyzed.
- Qualitative methods are generally preferred over surveys and experiments for their ability to elicit people's views in their own words.
- Qualitative research may be structured and ask questions predetermined by the researcher or be open ended and elicit ideas that informants volunteer.
- Participant or unobtrusive observation provides a check on whether people's words match their behavior.
- Qualitative studies of online communication must deal with entities unique to the web such as avatars and emoticons and can be limited because much online social behavior is text-based.

KEY TERMS

acts
analytic notes
asynchronous
avatars
categorization
communicative act
communicative style
contrast questions
conversation analysis
descriptive notes
descriptive questions
emoticons
ends
ethnography
facilitator
fixed coding
flexible coding
focus groups
fully structured interviews
funnel
gatekeepers
genres
grounded theory
informants

instrumentality
interpretive
interviewees
interviews
inverted funnel
key
key informants
method notes
moderator
netnography
norms
observational studies
open-ended questions
participants
prompts
qualitative
quantitative
ranking question
respondents
semistructured interviews
sequence
situation
speech community
speech event

speech situation

structural questions

structure

synchronous

unobtrusive measures

unstructured interviews

uses and gratifications theory

ways of speaking

APPLICATION EXERCISES

Exercise 1: An Ethnographic Study

Review in this chapter the broad research question of how students use the Internet to find out about employment and apply for jobs. You decide that the best insights on student job hunting on the Internet will come from an in-depth ethnographic study of students as they do this. Using the Dell Hymes questions outlined in this chapter, set out your plans for such a study. It should include key informants, an outline of the observations you would make, the questions you would ask your research participants, media content that you might want to read, and any permissions that you might need to obtain before your study begins.

Exercise 2: An Interview

You are interested in how exactly a student might go about using the Internet to locate jobs and apply for them. Assuming that a structured interview with specific questions is the best way to get this information, write out the specific questions you would want to ask a student you know to be highly experienced in the art of the online job search.

Exercise 3. Understanding Social Media Stress

A Pew Research Center Internet, Science & Tech Project study (Hampton, Rainie, Lu, Shin, & Purcell, 2015) looked at the relationship between social media use and stress. Overall, the researchers found that frequent Internet and social media users do not have higher levels of stress, but there are circumstances under which the use of social media increases awareness of stressful events in the lives of others. Especially for women, this greater awareness is tied to higher levels of stress.

The study used an established scale called the Perceived Stress Scale (PSS) that is based on people's answers to 10 questions.

Suppose you wish to explore the relationship between social media use and stress. Which of the approaches discussed in this chapter would you prefer, and why? What advantages might they offer relative to surveys or experiments?

RECOMMENDED READING

Daymon, C., & Holloway, I. (2010). *Qualitative methods in public relations and marketing communications* (2nd ed.). New York, NY: Routledge.

A guide to planning, implementing, and writing research in the applied fields of public relations and marketing.

Denzin, N. K., & Lincoln, Y. S. (Eds.). (2011). *Handbook of qualitative research* (4th ed.). Thousand Oaks, CA: Sage.

A summary volume on qualitative research.

Garcia, A. C., Standlee, A. I., Bechkoff, J., & Cui, Y. (2009). Ethnographic approaches to the Internet and computer-mediated communication. *Journal of Contemporary Ethnography, 38*(1), 52–84. DOI: 10.1177/0891241607310839

A summary and discussion of many aspects of online ethnography.

Krueger, R. A., & Casey, M. A. (2014). *Focus groups: A practical guide for applied research* (5th ed.). Thousand Oaks, CA: Sage.

> Covers the practicalities of planning and running focus groups and analyzing and reporting results.

Lindlof, T. R., & Taylor, B. C. (2010). *Qualitative communication research methods* (3rd ed.). Thousand Oaks, CA: Sage.

> Shows with examples how qualitative studies are designed, conducted, and written.

Paunksniene, Z., & Banyte, J. (2013). Methodological issues in online qualitative consumer behavior research. *Socialines Technologijos, 3*(2), 261–277. Retrieved from http://archive.ism.lt/handle/1/529

> Discusses methodological issues related to online qualitative consumer behavior research.

Spradley, J. P. (1979). *The ethnographic interview.* New York, NY: Holt, Rinehart & Winston.

> Describes 12 steps for developing an ethnographic study. For a sense of how "readable" such studies can be, see also Spradley's *You Owe Yourself a Drunk: Adaptive Strategies of Urban Nomads* (1970) and *The Cocktail Waitress: Woman's Work in a Man's World* (1975). In addition, see Spradley's *Participant Observation* (1980).

RECOMMENDED WEB RESOURCES

Atlas.ti . . . . www.atlasti.com/product.html

> A qualitative data analysis software package.

Ethnography of Communication . . . . www.cios.org/encyclopedia/ethnography/index.htm

> An overview of Dell Hymes's Ethnography of Communication in the Communication Institute for Online Scholarship's Electronic Encyclopedia of Communication.

Forum: Qualitative Social Research . . . . www.qualitative-research.net

> An open-access online academic journal of qualitative social research.

HyperRESEARCH . . . . www.researchware.com/products/hyperresearch.html

> A qualitative data analysis software package.

NVivo . . . . www.qsrinternational.com/products_nvivo.aspx

> A qualitative data analysis software package.

Qualitative Research Consultants Association . . . . www.qrca.org

> Links to qualitative research practitioners.

Transana . . . . www.transana.org

> Open-source qualitative data analysis software.

University of Surrey, social research update . . . . http://sru.soc.surrey.ac.uk/

> A resource for interviewing, focus groups, study design and analysis, and more.

REFERENCES

Blumler, J. G., & Katz, E. (1974). *The uses of mass communications: Current perspectives on gratifications research.* Beverly Hills, CA: Sage.

Curt, B. C. (1994). *Textuality and tectonics: Troubling social and psychological science.* Buckingham, UK: Open University Press.

Geertz, C. (1973). *The interpretation of cultures.* New York, NY: Basic Books.

Glaser, B. G., & Strauss, A. L. (1967). *The discovery of grounded theory: Strategies for qualitative research.* Chicago, IL: Aldine.

Gold, R. L. (1958). Roles in sociological field observations. *Social Forces, 36*(3), 217–223. DOI: 10.2307/2573808

Hampton, K., Rainie, L., Lu, W., Shin, I., & Purcell, K. (2015). Social media and the cost of caring. Pew Research Center Internet, Science & Tech Project. Retrieved from http://www.pewinternet.org/2015/01/15/social-media-and-stress/

Houliez, C., & Gamble, E. (2012). Augmented focus groups: On leveraging the peculiarities of online virtual worlds when conducting in-world focus groups. *Journal of Theoretical and Applied Electronic Commerce Research, 7*(2), 31–51. DOI: 10.4067/S0718-18762012000200005

Hymes, D. (1974). *Foundations in sociolinguistics: An ethnographic approach.* Philadelphia: University of Pennsylvania Press.

Kirsch, S. (2001). Ethnographic methods: Concepts and field techniques. In R. A. Krueger, M. A. Casey, J. Donner, S. Kirsch, & J. N. Maack (Eds.), *Social analysis: Selected tools and techniques* [Social Development Paper #36]. Washington, DC: World Bank. Retrieved from www.worldbank.org/reference

Kozinets, R. V. (2013). *Netnography: Doing ethnographic research online.* London: Sage.

Spradley, J. P. (1979). *The ethnographic interview.* New York, NY: Holt, Rinehart & Winston.

Xerri, R. C. (2005). *Gozitan crossings: The impact of migration and return migration on an island community.* Qala, Malta: A&M Printing.

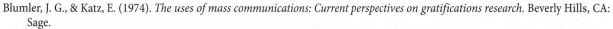

$SAGE edge™

Want a better grade?
Get the tools you need to sharpen your study skills. Access practice quizzes, eFlashcards, video, and multimedia at **edge.sagepub.com/treadwell3e**

CHAPTER 12

Content Analysis

Understanding Communication Content in Numbers

Content analysis means
Counting what can be seen.
Use counting and categories
For basic analyses
And insights on speech, text, or screen.

❧ ❧ ❧

Chapter Overview

Media for content analysis can include any recorded communication from papyrus to podcast, published or unpublished. Approaches to studying media content are almost as diverse as the approaches to studying human communication behavior. In a general sense, any study of media content is a content analysis, but in communication research, the term often implies a quantitative approach and a series of specific steps aimed at ensuring systematic sampling, coding, and counting of units of media content. This chapter provides an overview of content analysis as a quantitative procedure. Other approaches to understanding content, primarily qualitative, are discussed in Chapter 13.

Chapter Objectives

This chapter will help you

- Explain the advantages and disadvantages of quantitative content analysis.

- Describe, with examples, the steps of a basic content analysis.

- Identify and explain the units that might be used in content analysis.

- Discuss, with examples, the use of content analysis in understanding human interaction.

- Explain the circumstances under which content analysis may have ethical implications.

Introduction: Advantages and Disadvantages of Content Analysis

In the context of communication research, **content analysis** is often regarded as a quantitative, systematic, and objective technique for describing the manifest content of communications (Berelson, 1952).

- Quantitative means we must count occurrences of whatever we are interested in.
- Systematic means that we must count all relevant aspects of the sample. We cannot arbitrarily pick what aspects get analyzed.
- Objective means that we select units for analysis and categorize them using clearly defined criteria.
- **Manifest** means tangible and observable. For example, we cannot count patriotism in consumer advertising because patriotism is ultimately an abstract or **latent** (hidden) notion. What we can count is the frequency with which the word *patriotism* occurs, the frequency with which a patriotic image such as a national flag appears, or perhaps the number of minutes that music defined as patriotic is played.

In this chapter, we discuss the systematic sampling, coding, and counting of content that is characteristic of quantitative content analysis.

Such analysis can be used with almost any form of content. It is possible to content-analyze almost any recorded medium—press, radio, web, billboards, T-shirts, license plates, lawn signs, photographs, love letters, maps, and tweets. Usually, the raw material of content analysis is readily accessible, be it presidential speeches, advertisements for liquid soap or lingerie, BBC foreign news coverage, comic strips, or *New York Times* editorials.

Content analysis has been used to examine environmental themes in newspaper advertising (Özkoçak & Tuna, 2011); antisocial behavior in a reality TV show (Wilson, Robinson, & Callister, 2012); portrayals of obesity on YouTube (Yoo & Kim, 2012); risk taking in action movies (Beullens, Roe, & Van den Bulck, 2011); global reporting of nanotechnology (Fisk, Fitzgerald, & Cokley, 2014); and, more generally, media representations of health, parenthood, food, religion, social groups, politicians, and occupations.

On the plus side, content analysis is an unobtrusive approach. Human participants are not involved. Human research approvals are typically not required though permission to access content and to publish content analysis studies may well be required where the content is unpublished or personal—for example, diaries, psychiatric records, or e-mail—or proprietary—for example, corporate records.

A strength of content analysis is its emphasis on systematic sampling, clear definitions of units, and counting. The procedures should be explicit, precise, and replicable so that other researchers can verify the results of the research. Content analysis can have 100% **reliability** if using computers because content analysis software will automatically code all occurrences of a unit of text the same way. Ultimately, though, computers do nothing but recognize strings of characters; they are not reading texts for meaning.

Human coders can read for meaning, but because this involves judgments about content, the challenge is to have them code with 100% reliability. In principle, this can be accomplished with detailed coding manuals and training. By having each coder code the same unit, we can compute a level of intercoder reliability. If the level is unsatisfactory, we may need to (re)train coders until their level of agreement reaches an acceptable level or revisit our coding scheme.

A limitation of content analysis is that it addresses only questions of content. For example, "Have representations of the military on television changed since 9/11?" is an appropriate question for content analysis. "Are media representations of the military causing more people to enlist?" is not a question content analysis can answer (though it may contribute to an answer).

Another limitation is that the method really only has application if used for comparisons. A "one-shot" survey indicating that 72% of voters would vote for candidate X if the election were held tomorrow produces a finding that is useful to a campaign manager. However, a content analysis indicating that candidate X used the term *patriotism* 17 times in the course of a campaign is not inherently useful information unless it has some point of reference. What we are interested in as content analysts are questions such as "How does the frequency of *patriotism* in candidate X's speeches compare with that of candidate Y's?" or "How do candidates' use of the term *patriotism* compare with their use of the term *environment*?" or "Has the frequency of use of the term *patriotism* increased or decreased over the course of the campaign?"

A further issue is **validity**. Validity in content analysis can be problematic in terms of relating its findings to the external world. Detecting that the frequency with which the word *patriotism* appears in a politician's speeches has increased over time does not entitle us to assume that the politician has become more patriotic over time; it tells us only that his use of the term has become more frequent. An impassioned speech against patriotism may reveal the same frequency of the word as an equally impassioned speech in favor of it.

In this case, the word *patriotism* needs to be examined in context. One way to do this is to define our units of analysis as sentences or paragraphs rather than words and then code each sentence or paragraph as positive, negative, or neutral with respect to patriotism.

A Basic Content Analysis

Traditional content analysis can be summarized in one sentence. Simply, it is assigning units of content to predetermined categories and then counting the number of units in each category.

Accomplishing this requires successful completion of several specific steps, as follows:

- Develop a hypothesis or research question about communication content.
- Define the content to be analyzed.
- Sample the content.
- Select **units** for coding.
- Develop a **coding scheme**.
- Assign each occurrence of a unit in the sample to a code in the coding scheme.
- Count occurrences of the coded units.
- Report results, patterns of data, and inferences from data.

In this example, we follow a student—Rafael—who develops an interest in political biases on campus. He is aware of news media coverage of research suggesting that, overall, higher education faculty are more likely to be liberal than conservative (see, for example, Gravois, 2007, and Gross, 2012). If true, a concern stemming from this finding would be that if there is a manifest faculty political bias, students might be subject to subtle—or perhaps not-so-subtle—unbalanced political influence in the classroom.

Rafael decides that this topic has both theoretical and practical significance. However, he reasons that interviewing faculty on this topic may not be productive as many will not want to be interviewed or to go public with their political views if they are interviewed. He decides that he can get an unobtrusive measure of faculty's political views and of their willingness to express them by using content analysis.

He reasons that faculty vehicles often carry stickers supporting political candidates. A basic count of these stickers would be an indirect measure of faculty political bias, where the stickers can be linked to a political party, and also a measure of faculty members' willingness to express their views in public. Based on his reasoning and the above content analysis steps, his study might take the following form.

Research Questions

Research questions or hypotheses are needed to guide or frame the analysis. Especially given the vast amount of content on the web, an implicit research question is needed at least—if only to define the context of the research and limit the content that will be analyzed. In Rafael's case, two possible research questions might be

RQ_1. Do faculty demonstrate a willingness to publicize their political views?

RQ_2. Do faculty vehicle stickers overall demonstrate a political bias?

Define the Content to Be Analyzed

The analyst needs to define the content of interest, both as a theoretical interest and as a practical matter of limiting the content to be studied.

Rafael limits the content he is interested in to vehicle stickers that specifically support political candidates. These stickers may not identify a specific political party, but most of them will promote candidates whose affiliations Rafael will be able to identify if necessary from the records of electoral commissions.

Sample the Content

Rafael decides to sample faculty vehicles; these are defined as vehicles with faculty parking permits on them. He decides to sample faculty vehicles in employee parking lots late morning through early afternoon, midweek. He reasons that this timing will maximize the number of faculty on campus. He decides on systematic probability sampling. That is, he will use a random number to identify his starting vehicle and will then select every nth vehicle until he has completed his sample of all faculty parking lots. A variety of sampling methods are possible, as discussed in Chapter 8.

Select Units for Coding

Vehicles with faculty parking permits are the sampling units, but they are not the primary focus of interest. What Rafael will record—his recording or coding units—will be campaign stickers and more specifically the candidate names on these stickers. He decides to treat multiple names appearing on a sticker, for example a presidential and a vice presidential candidate, as one name because the ultimate objective is to code each sticker by party affiliation, not by candidate names.

Develop a Coding Scheme

Developing a coding scheme means developing a classification system or categories into which each sampled unit can be placed. Content analysis requires that all sampled units be placed in a category. Vehicles, for example, can all be categorized by manufacturer, color, or state of registration. Rafael's study is such that he cannot develop a coding scheme in advance of his study because he cannot predict all the candidate names that he is going to find. This means that he will start recording candidate names at the beginning of his study and may well be adding new names to his list at the end of his study. Ultimately, his coding scheme will be the list of candidate names he builds from his sampling of faculty vehicle campaign stickers.

Assign Each Occurrence of a Unit in the Sample to a Code in the Coding Scheme

The number of times each candidate sticker occurs will be counted. To simplify recording, Rafael decides on a simple numbered list. The first name he records will be coded 1, the second name 2, and so on. The numbering will stop at the point where there are no new names to be added. Each repeat name that he finds will get coded with the number assigned to the first occurrence of that name. In this way, every candidate sticker will be coded.

Count Occurrences of the Coded Units

Rafael will end up with a raw data sheet similar to that shown in Exhibit 12.1. For this study, he will have a further step to make, and that is to recode each candidate name, where necessary, into a party affiliation. He has two options as to how to do this. As he is interested in overall political affiliations, he may set up a simple three-part coding scheme in advance—"Democrat," "Republican," and "Other"—and assign each candidate name to one of these categories.

EXHIBIT 12.1 **Data Coding Sheet for Content Analysis of Political Campaign Stickers**

	Candidate Name(s)	Tally	Count	Political Affiliation
1	Williamson	/ / / / / /	6	Other
2	Chee	/ / /	3	Other
3	Rowden	/ / / / / / / / /	9	Other
4	McLeod	/ / / / / / / / / / / / / / / / / /	18	Republican
5	Szydlo	/ / / / / / / / / /	10	Democrat
6	Organ	/ / / / / / / /	8	Democrat
etc.	etc.			
None		/ / / / / /	6	–

If he is planning to look at patterns of affiliation in more detail, another option is to develop categories of political parties that will emerge as he translates candidate names into party affiliation. This means he will end up with a coding scheme such as Democrat, Republican, Green, Communist, Libertarian, and so on, depending on the candidate affiliations he finds in his sample. Because this coding scheme will cover every party he identifies in his sample, the "Other" category will not be necessary here.

In both cases, however, an additional category is necessary—"None"—because Rafael is also interested in the percentage of faculty vehicles with no candidate stickers. In other words, as his systematic sampling takes him across the faculty parking lots, he is also recording the sampled vehicles that have no candidate stickers and coding those vehicles as "None."

The need for this "None" category relates directly to his research questions. Rafael's first research question asked whether faculty were willing to express their political views and operationalized this willingness as the presence or absence of campaign stickers. Therefore, he is obliged to include in his sample vehicles with and without stickers in order to get a measure of what percentage of these do have campaign stickers. If he was looking for an answer only to his second research question about political affiliation, he could select only those vehicles with campaign stickers.

Report Results, Patterns of Data, and Inferences From Data

Data reduction is necessary to detect any patterns in the raw data and to make any such patterns comprehensible to readers of the final research report.

Exhibit 12.2 shows the summary data Rafael is now in a position to interpret with respect to his research questions. Ninety percent of the vehicles he samples have a candidate sticker on them. The answer to his first research question, then, is that the majority of faculty on campus do appear to be willing to publicly express a political preference—at least on their vehicles. The second research question was whether there was an overall faculty affiliation with one political party more than others. His data for the 90% of vehicles with political stickers show an even split across all three categories—Republican, Democrat, and Other. Rafael could reasonably conclude that his analysis of candidate stickers indicates no predominant political affiliation by faculty. His discussion of his findings would then center on the observation that while a majority of faculty appear willing to go public with their political affiliations, it is unlikely that they have an overall political mind-set that campus critics should be concerned about.

EXHIBIT 12.2   **Summary Data From Exhibit 12.1**

Percentage of Vehicles With Campaign Stickers	54/60 = 90%
Campaign Stickers by Party Affiliation	
Democrat	18/54 = 33%
Republican	18/54 = 33%
Other	18/54 = 33%

Rafael's data reduction is a simple tabulation of party affiliation by frequency, but an analyst might well aim for more sophisticated analyses. For example, if he had recorded vehicle details as part of his observations, he might be able to determine whether Republican and Democrat vehicle preferences differ by age, make, or type of vehicle. If he could identify the owners of the vehicles and the disciplines they teach in—for example, business, science, or humanities—he might discover that one discipline is more likely than others to have a political bias and/or to express it in public.

His study has a number of assumptions and problems, some of which are raised in the Application Exercises at the end of this chapter. The most obvious is whether willingness to go public with a candidate sticker on one's vehicle translates in any way to a willingness to go public in the classroom. Indeed, a reverse argument might be made that because faculty feel obligated to restrain their political views in the classroom, they are more likely to express their opinions outside of the classroom in the form of vehicle stickers.

The results of an analysis are important, but more important are the inferences drawn from the results. Rafael's study, for example, provides no evidence one way or the other that faculty might be prone to expressing political bias in the classroom, or even that they vote. Making either connection will require much more than content analysis data. This is where prior steps such as the literature review, theoretical grounding, development of research questions, sampling procedure, and the like all become important. They should all help support the inferences the analyst is trying to draw about the relationship between observed content and its relationship to human behavior.

An Expanded Content Analysis

In the following example of an expanded content analysis, we work through the thinking behind a project that involves many more decisions because it involves more categories, units that do not always fit into an obvious category, the question of how to deal with that problem, and the problems and possibilities of working with both text and visual content. For our example, we will take a look at pharmaceutical advertising.

Many questions can be asked about the promotion of pharmaceuticals in advertisements, news, and entertainment media. For example, to what extent do newspaper medical columns report the failures as well as the successes of new pharmaceuticals? What pharmaceutical products feature most prominently in daytime television advertising? Which prescription pharmaceuticals appear most frequently in the news coverage of major metropolitan newspapers?

Let's go down a relatively untraveled road—the representations of pharmaceuticals and their use in contemporary comic strips. Our rationale for this study is that comic strips may promote an image of pharmaceutical use to comic strip readers, just as much as pharmaceutical advertising promotes this product category to consumers.

From a critical perspective, we might theorize that the presentation of pharmaceuticals in the everyday life of cartoon characters legitimizes their use to vulnerable readers not attuned to comics as a subtle form of advertising. From a public health or criminal justice perspective, we might want to know whether the appearance of a new substance in popular media reflects what is already happening "on the street" or is indicating the presence of a new drug culture. Educators may be interested in the potential of comic strips to educate young people about drugs. Of course, not all of these interests are ones that content analysis can address on its own, but let's assume that a basic starting point is to determine the extent to which pharmaceuticals are a part of the comic strip world.

An overview of pharmaceutical use in the comic strip world would reasonably include examining the nature of the users and the conditions of use. For this study, we will assume a theoretical interest in whether users are male or female, and code accordingly, noting that we could equally well have categorized them by age or occupation. Again somewhat arbitrarily we will categorize the conditions of use as either home or work, recognizing that other such categories are possible (campus, "the street," vehicles, and vacation settings, for example).

As noted, content analysis data are most useful when they are used as a basis for comparison rather than standing on their own. The above design already has the potential for some interesting analyses—for example, the most- and least-frequently occurring pharmaceuticals, how males and females differ in their portrayed use of pharmaceuticals, and whether pharmaceutical use is shown as primarily at home or at work.

To get comic strip characters' use of pharmaceutical substances in context, another comparison seems appropriate, and that is a look at how pharmaceutical use compares with use of other substances such as alcohol and tobacco. We will expand the study to include alcohol and tobacco because our overall interest is in how comic strips portray substance use and because we need a point of reference against which to assess our findings about pharmaceuticals. We start, then, with a research question about the portrayal of all these substances in comic strips and a hypothesis that—because tobacco and alcohol may be more readily available—pharmaceuticals will differ in frequency of occurrence from tobacco and alcohol.

RQ_1. What is the relative frequency of use of tobacco, alcohol, and pharmaceuticals as depicted in comic strips?

H_1. Alcohol and tobacco products will differ from pharmaceuticals in frequency of occurrence in comic strips.

Note that this is a two-tailed hypothesis because we have no evidence that one type of substance is more likely to appear than another.

Define the Content to Be Analyzed

The content to be analyzed is comic strips. We decide that our interest is in current content, and so we opt for the most recent comic strips. We also opt to capture a full year of seasons and events because we suspect that drinking, smoking, and pharmaceutical consumption may have seasonal patterns. Spring break behaviors, for example, may not be representative of student behaviors during the rest of the year. Commencement may see a peak in consumption of champagne and cigars, and Super Bowl weekend may see a peak in beer consumption in some zip code areas. If comic strips are in fact capturing the ups and downs of life and the associated use of chemical substances, a random sample of just one week of content may under- or overrepresent patterns of behavior overall.

We could sample all comics sold over the counter in book form; we could go to a site such as www.gocomics.com, which has over 200 comic strips; or we could look at newspaper editorial cartoons. We decide on syndicated comic strip pages from the Sunday edition of our major local newspaper because the Sunday comics reach a large national audience and are therefore important because of their potential impact on a wide variety of readers. Because so many of the strips in this paper are nationally syndicated, we make the assumption that our major local Sunday paper will represent most other major papers nationally in terms of comic strip content. This assumption could, of course, easily be tested by comparing the comic strips printed in a random selection of Sunday newspapers from across the country.

We narrow the content to be sampled by deciding that we will sample only comic strips that regularly show human characters, recognizing that cartoon animals may well smoke, drink, and pop pills and that there is an argument that they should be in our sample. That gets our universe down to, say, 20 weekly strips or a total of 1,040 over the course of a year.

Sample the Content

We now have a **sampling frame**—the list from which specific samples will be drawn—of 1,040 comic strips.

We decide to systematically sample the first Sunday of every month. If we randomly sampled the year, we might sample out some important seasons, and we have decided that all seasons need to be included. We want to capture all the seasons, so systematic monthly sampling is appropriate. That gives us a manageable sample of $12 \times 20 = 240$ comic strips. Note that sampling at the level of months may eliminate some week-specific comic strip activity that might be relevant to our research, for example keg parties around Super Bowl weekend or *Guinness*-drinking leprechauns (who themselves represent another sampling decision) around St. Patrick's Day. For a preliminary study, though, we opt for monthly sampling, recognizing that weekly samples may be needed to provide a more precise picture.

Select Units for Coding

Having developed a sampling frame, we are now faced with the question of what units we will sample. Rafael's content analysis of campaign stickers, above, was based on the reasonable assumption that words—in the form of candidate names—would be appropriate units to sample. There are, however, several other types. Krippendorff (2013), for example, identifies five possible types of unit:

- **Physical units** occupy an observable space, length, or size in print media or time in audio-visual media—for example, one-minute sequences of recorded interactions or, in our case, an entire comic strip or the individual panels within each strip.
- **Syntactical units** are units of language, such as words, sentences, books, or chapters—for example, the names of political candidates in Rafael's study of vehicle campaign stickers.
- **Categorial units** are defined by having something in common or belonging to a researcher-defined category—for example, teachers, a specific type of cartoon character, or an event such as drinking coffee.
- **Propositional units** are entities such as stories, dramas, and basic claims or assertions—for example, a cartoon character rejecting an offer of alcohol.
- **Thematic units** are broad topics within a structure, such as relationships with the boss or with peers. Identify them by repeated ideas or actions—for example, the continuing efforts of a son to have his father stop smoking, or a character repeatedly accepting the offer of a drink, shown again and again over a series of comic strips.

As we progress from physical units to thematic units, we can face increasing difficulty making decisions about them. Physical units such as photographs are apparent; either they are there, or they are not. Themes such as "environment" or concepts such as "physical fitness" may appear only in the eye of the researcher or differently to two different coders. Typically, themes would be validated by a group of judges looking at the content being analyzed.

In this example, we are looking at substance use in the broad setting of people's lives, so we decide to examine entire comic strips rather than each frame within a strip for instances of substance use. For example, a comic strip with five frames, each of which shows the same character smoking a cigarette, will be coded as one occurrence of smoking, rather than five. We could equally well rationalize coding each frame rather than strips on the grounds that this captures every occurrence of drug use and therefore provides a more accurate representation.

We have a further decision to make. Should we look at visual content only, words only, or both? Each has its advantages and disadvantages. For example, words may show specific brand names and the specific strength of an individual's relationship to a product ("I like product X" versus "I love product X," for example). On the other hand, the visual content is likely to better show the conditions of use—for example, whether an individual drinks alone or in company.

We decide that portrayal of substance use implies visual portrayal and that therefore we will analyze the visual content as a priority. A strip's emphasis on, for example, smoking may well occur in text form, and the presence of text in the strips gives us an opportunity to see if text gives us the same results as images. We will therefore also analyze the strips' text as a way of validating, or not, the results we get from our analysis of visual content.

For text, our units of analysis will be syntactical; that is, we will be looking to count the number of times specific substances are mentioned. For visual content, our units will be categorial; that is, we will count the number of times a substance is depicted.

Develop a Coding Scheme

Because our interest focuses on the frequency with which substances are referenced in comic strips, we develop a coding scheme with categories as shown in the "Substance" column of Exhibit 12.3. The coding sheet will record the number of times we find a mention or depiction of the substances we are interested in.

A simple study might compare the relative frequency of appearance of different drug categories (the "Overall" column). A more detailed study might look at the relative frequency by, for example, setting ("Work" or "Home") or type of person ("Male" or "Female") using the substance.

Note that it is possible to break down every category into more specific categories. For example, "Tobacco" could have subcategories of "Cigarettes," "Cigars," "Pipe," "Smokeless," and perhaps "e-Cigarettes." The "Alcohol" category could have subcategories of "Beer," "Wine," and "Spirits." Conversely, it would be possible to coalesce the categories of "Prescription Drugs," "Over-the-Counter Drugs," and "Illegal Drugs" into one category called "Drugs" and to code every appearance of a substance as either "Tobacco," "Alcohol," or "Drugs." The level of categorization depends on the research question being addressed. A preliminary study might require little more than "Tobacco," "Alcohol," and "Drugs" categories. On the other hand, if comic strips are argued to influence social trends, then the "Cigarettes," "Cigars," "Pipe," and "Smokeless" categories for tobacco would be needed to track whether, for example, smokeless tobacco was becoming more popular at the expense of cigarettes or cigars.

Similar decisions arise with respect to drug categories. The thousands of names used by pharmaceutical manufacturers for their products provide far more categories than any content analyst would ever use. (A possible exception would be a content analysis of medical or pharmaceutical journals.) So the question arises of how to develop a few workable categories. Consider how pharmaceuticals might be categorized. You could categorize them by proprietary name, active ingredient, common names used by consumers, purpose (for example, antacid or antibiotic), or method of administration (for example, oral, injection, ointment, or inhalant).

With comic strips, it is most likely that what we would find in use would be a combination of lay terminology and purpose of the product—for example, *sunscreen*, *contraceptive*, *antibiotic*, or *pain medicine*.

The possibility of categorizing pharmaceuticals by "Tablet," "Liquid," "Injection," "Ointment," and "Inhalant" flags one of the differences between content-analyzing text and visuals. In our study of comic strips, it is likely that we will see whether characters are popping pills and drinking liquids, but we probably would not get that information from an analysis of the text only. On the other hand, text may be more likely than the cartoon illustrations to provide the names of specific products.

None of the above generalizations can be made with 100% accuracy. For example, the name of a specific substance may come from a graphic of a large pill bottle with the word *aspirin* emblazoned on it.

Ground rules for content analysis are that categories must not overlap and that no unit can be coded twice. "Substance X," if shown, or the word *aspirin*, if found, must fit one and only one category. Anticipating that some characters in the cartoons may be doing illegal drugs, we need a coding scheme that allows for that possibility. Another issue arises. How do we handle occurrences of "umbrella" words such as *drug(s)*, *pharmaceutical(s)*, or *medicine(s)*? We can't ignore such a reference to a substance, so we need to add another category—"General Reference to Drugs"—to our coding scheme.

This discussion of coding indicates the type and level of decisions that are required in setting up a content analysis study. Two things will help you establish a defensible coding scheme. The first is a clear theoretical background and research question. For example, if your theoretical interest is prescription drugs, you can eliminate nonprescription drugs from your coding scheme.

EXHIBIT 12.3   Sample Coding Sheet for Content Analysis of Comic Strips

| Substance | Frequencies of Appearance | | | | |
| | User | | | Setting | |
	Overall	Male	Female	Work	Home
Tobacco					
Visuals					
Words					
Alcohol					
Visuals					
Words					
Prescription Drugs					
Visuals					
Words					
Over-the-Counter Drugs					
Visuals					
Words					
Illegal Drugs					
Visuals					
Words					
General Reference to Drugs					
Visuals					
Words					

The second, and essential, item is a test run or pilot study that pretests your categories and sampling before you run your analysis. Almost inevitably you will identify categories that can be eliminated and categories that need to be added. You may also detect changes that need to be made to your sampling. In the above example, we may find that monthly sampling is inadequate and that we need to sample comic strips weekly.

Assign Each Occurrence of a Unit in the Sample to a Code in the Coding Scheme

With coding categories set up, we now proceed to code the units of analysis we find in our comic strips.

Identifying word references should be easy; we are looking for specific words such as *beer*, *cigar*, or *aspirin* that clearly identify a substance. With visual occurrences, we may have more of a judgment call. What *is* that character ingesting? Where more than one interpretation is possible, it is usual to form a panel of judges who will vote on how to code an item. This is likely to be necessary in our study.

For any analysis involving multiple coders, it is usual to ask each of them to code the same units as a trial run. Formulas are available to help calculate the degree to which the coders are in agreement. If they are in agreement, we can have some confidence that our criteria for coding are clear; if not, it is time to revisit our criteria and redefine them so they are clear.

Count Occurrences of the Coded Units

The results of a study like this would be reported as the frequency of occurrences for each of our substance categories.

Report Results, Patterns of Data, and Inferences From Data

We would report and discuss the relative frequency of the substances shown in our coding sheet. This gives us the basic comparison that quantitative content analysis does well and helps us decide whether our initial hypotheses are supported or not.

Our study thus far has done little more than help us decide the relative occurrence of substances by category even though we have data for both text and visual content.

It would be much more informative if we could assess the conditions under which these substances appear and perhaps the types of people using them. A further level of analysis, then, would be to categorize substance use according to type of user—for example, male or female, blue collar or white collar—or conditions of use—for example, home or work. Our coding sheet would then include the columns shown in the right-hand columns of Exhibit 12.3.

As with Rafael's study of vehicle stickers, the final report will require theoretical argument and discussion of the reliability and validity of the content observations to make the large inferential jump from cartoon characters to human beings. Two possible connections can be made from this study to other data. First, because data on human use of pharmaceuticals is available from industry and survey data, it may be possible to answer the question of whether the behavior of cartoon characters reflects those of humans. Second, because human use of pharmaceuticals is documented by year and cartoon strips are dated, it should be possible to determine whether the cartoon behaviors precede or follow human behaviors. This would help answer the question of whether cartoons track public behavior or influence it.

Content Analysis of Human Interaction

The principal use of content analysis is in analyzing media content such as news, entertainment, or advertising (in part because of the ready availability of media content), but it can also be applied in such areas as organizational communication and interpersonal communication. Transcripts of interactions among people constitute texts and are open to content analysis just as much as television advertising, newspaper editorials, or State of the Union addresses.

For example, **interaction analysis**, pioneered by group dynamics scholar Robert Bales (1950), seeks to capture and understand interactions among members of a group and the different roles that group members play. Three broad categories of group behavior are task-oriented, group-oriented, and self-centered. Task-oriented individuals focus on the group's work—for example, asking if the group has all the information it needs or assigning specific tasks to members of the group. Group-oriented individuals work to ensure that the group remains cohesive—for example, by making jokes to relieve tension or by showing supportiveness for other members' ideas. Self-centered individuals may refuse to participate or, at the other extreme, may dominate discussions.

Suppose we are looking at the transcripts or a video of a corporate team trying to develop a marketing strategy for a new product. The ebb and flow of discussion over the weeks leading up to the group's final decision can be coded using Bales's categories or subcategories as shown in Exhibit 12.4. Here the group is the unit of analysis, and we are coding observed behaviors for three different meetings at Time 1, Time 2, and Time 3.

Exhibit 12.4　Sample Coding Sheet for Group Behaviors Over Time

Behavior	Frequencies of Appearance		
	Time 1	Time 2	Time 3
Task-Oriented			
Reminds group members of deadlines			
Proposes solutions to problems			
Group-Oriented			
Makes statements supporting a group idea			
Makes statements approving of group's progress			
Self-Centered			
Refuses assignments			
Makes antagonistic statements			

We could use the results of such an analysis to test a hypothesis that group behaviors change over time—for example, that group-oriented behaviors occur more frequently in the preliminary stages as group members clarify their roles and relationships before moving on to task-oriented behaviors. We could compare the results of such analyses for two different groups, one known to produce excellent decisions, the other known to produce mediocre decisions. This might then allow us to identify the characteristics of high-performing groups and provide a basis for training low-performing groups to do better. We could also use exactly the same criteria to analyze individual behaviors. For example, if we were to replace "Time 1," "Time 2," and "Time 3" in the chart with "Person 1," "Person 2," and "Person 3," we could record, analyze, and compare the behaviors of those individuals.

We could also combine both approaches and record individual behavior over time. Note that if we did record the behavior of each individual at different times, we would have a within-subjects design (Chapter 10). Such data are not statistically independent, and we would need a more sophisticated statistical test to assess any changes over time. By contrast, the data from the study of bumper stickers are statistically independent, and a simple chi-square test may serve to assess whether the distribution of bumper stickers shows significant variation.

Purposes and methods for analyzing media content often overlap. For example, content analysis may be used to obtain a critical reading of texts.

The boundaries of content analysis are shifting. For example, Krippendorff's (2013, p. 24) definition of content analysis as "a research technique for making replicable and valid inferences from texts (or other meaningful matter) to the contexts of their use" contains none of the defining words listed at the beginning of this chapter—*quantitative, systematic, objective, manifest*. Krippendorff points out that quantification is not an end in itself; that using numbers is a convenience, not a requirement; and that qualitative analyses follow many of the steps of quantitative analyses, though perhaps less explicitly so. "Ultimately, all reading of texts is qualitative, even when certain characteristics of a text are later converted into numbers" (p. 22).

We will discuss qualitative approaches to understanding content in Chapter 13.

Content Analysis Software

Content analysis of language can be automated and expedited with content analysis software. This software can process and classify massive amounts of raw data and display results graphically, often interactively. For example, Professor Benjamin Schmidt used data from 14 million student reviews on the Rate My Professors website to build an interactive display showing how evaluations of teachers vary by gender of the teacher. You can search for this at benschmidt.org.

All such software needs "training." Training can be a complex and finicky operation. Without training, software will be unable to distinguish whether the word *right* is being used in the sense of "not wrong," "not left," or the verb form "to correct." Without training with respect to hyphenation, compound words, capitalization, and foreign word equivalents, a computer will not know whether to regard *United States* and *united states* as four different terms, two terms, or the same term. Similarly, *nighttime, grasshopper, sunglasses,* and *low-profile* can each be read as one term or as two. *Neighbor* and *neighbour* can be read as two different words or as the same depending on the software's programming.

Two ways to simplify computer analyses are **stemming** and **lemmatization**. Stemming means changing all variations of a word to its basic stem. For example, *fish, fishing, fished, fisherman,* and *fisher* can all be stemmed to *fish*. This means instead of identifying five separate words, the software will count the occurrence of the basic term *fish* five times. Lemmatization works similarly by grouping words together based on their basic dictionary definition so that they can be analyzed as a single item—for example, *car* and *automobile* have no common stem, but both can be described by term *vehicle*. Similarly, *trout, cod, shark,* and *marlin* cannot be stemmed, but all of them can be lemmatized under the basic dictionary definition of *fish*.

The power of software to process large amounts of data does not mean the researcher can go on "autopilot" and avoid the need to develop a defensible coding scheme, data analysis procedures, and careful programming of the software. For current listings of such software, see the Text Analysis Overview and Content-analyis.de websites under "Recommended Web Resources" at the end of this chapter.

If word frequency is your only interest, and your documents are short, you have a crude content analysis device in the form of your word processing software. Simply use the software's "search" function to find how many occurrences of a word a document has. This will also show you how key words are used in context—**KWIC** in content-analysis shorthand. You might, for example, search this chapter for sentences containing *content analysis* to find out how many sentences refer to content as qualitative versus quantitative, whether the sentences describe content analysis or evaluate it, and whether the evaluative sentences are positive or negative. You can also request readability statistics, which will give you no insight on content as such but will give you measures of average word and sentence length and a readability score for documents.

Ethics Panel: Could Analyzing Media Content Result in Harm?

A literature search using the terms *content analysis* and *ethics* will show you many studies focused on the content analysis of codes of ethics. This panel addresses a different issue—the ethical implications of content analysis, and textual analyses more generally. Such analyses focus on text and do not involve human participants directly. Why, therefore, would any of these methods have any impact on individuals that would give rise to ethical concerns?

Consider the applications, overt or covert, of content analysis in the world of electronic communication. "Pop-up" advertisements on your web browser are based on an analysis of the websites you visit.

Many software packages offer e-mail administrators a way of monitoring incoming e-mail for "spam," viruses, and attempts at "phishing." Such software can also monitor outgoing e-mail for compliance with company policy. The software administrators can set up e-mail monitoring to analyze content and prevent sensitive content leaving an organization or to identify potential policy violations and thus protect intellectual property, company reputation, and business relationships. Content analysis of employee e-mail is routine in many corporations for all the reasons noted above.

While we can all be thankful for e-mail spam filters that themselves are based on analysis of incoming e-mail message content, we might see such software as an invasion of privacy if applied to our own e-mail.

Questions

- In what ways could the knowledge that one's business or personal communications are being monitored and analyzed cause psychological distress?

- Should the institutional review boards (IRBs) responsible for human subjects safety be required to review content analysis studies even if no human participants are studied directly? Why or why not? Revisit Chapter 3 for more detail on IRBs.

- With respect to obtaining permissions, should content analysts treat personal or business e-mails, Internet discussion content, and correspondence differently from television commercials or newspaper pages? Why or why not?

CHAPTER SUMMARY

- Content analysis is a process of systematically sampling, coding, and analyzing media content.
- Content analysis techniques can be applied to both text and visual content.
- The steps in a basic content analysis are define content to be analyzed; sample content; select units for coding; develop a coding scheme; code each occurrence of a unit; count occurrences of the coded units; and report results, patterns of data, and inferences from data.
- Interaction analysis examines the behaviors of individuals in groups.
- Content analysis software can analyze large quantities of data but requires careful programming.

KEY TERMS

categorial units

coding scheme

content analysis

interaction analysis

KWIC

latent

lemmatization

manifest

physical units

propositional units

reliability

sampling frame

stemming

syntactical units

thematic units

units

validity

APPLICATION EXERCISES

Exercise 1. Sampling

Review the content analysis study of vehicle campaign stickers outlined at the beginning of this chapter. List the factors that might influence the composition of the sample. What problems can you identify with the sampling decisions made here?

Exercise 2. News Media Bias

Both ends of the political spectrum complain about biased reporting by the news media. Set out the basic elements of a content analysis project that would answer the question of whether a particular news medium is biased toward or against a political figure, government policy, or program. Identify the content you would sample from, the units of analysis, and the coding scheme you would use.

   HINT: Visit the George Mason University Center for Media and Public Affairs website at www.cmpa.com.

Exercise 3. Stereotyping in Entertainment Media and Advertising

A criticism of advertising and entertainment media such as movies and television is the stereotyping of people by, for example, gender, ethnicity, occupation, or age. Pick one of these types—for example, occupational stereotyping—and outline a content analysis study that would test for the presence or absence of stereotyping. Define the content you would sample from, the units of analysis, and the coding scheme you would use. Note that for this exercise you will need some operational definition of stereotyping so that you can identify it and code it when you see it.

Exercise 4. Analyzing Online Harassment: Quantitatively

A Pew Research Center Internet, Science & Tech Project (2014) study of online harassment asked respondents about six different forms of online harassment. The study also provides selected quotes about harassment from several of those surveyed at www.pewinternet.org/2014/10/22/online-harassment-experiences-in-their-own-words.

   Using the steps described and discussed in this chapter, do a quantitative analysis of selected quotes from the above website and report your conclusions. In Chapter 13, you will be invited to think about analyzing the same data qualitatively.

   The full report, questionnaire, and respondent comments are available at www.pewinternet.org/2014/10/22/online-harassment (Duggan, 2014).

RECOMMENDED READING

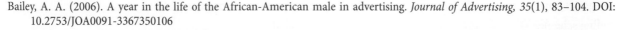

Bailey, A. A. (2006). A year in the life of the African-American male in advertising. *Journal of Advertising, 35*(1), 83–104. DOI: 10.2753/JOA0091-3367350106

An example of content analysis of advertising.

Hirokawa, A. Y. (1988). Group communication research: Considerations for the use of interaction analysis. In C. H. Tardy (Ed.), *A handbook for the study of human communication: Methods and instruments for observing, measuring, and assessing communication processes* (pp. 229–246). Norwood, NJ: Ablex.

Shows ways of coding behaviors in groups.

Krippendorff, K. H. (2013). *Content analysis: An introduction to its methodology* (3rd ed.). Thousand Oaks, CA: Sage.

The concepts and practice of content analysis. An updated edition that covers electronic texts, social media, and Internet sampling.

Neuendorf, K. A. (2002). *The content analysis guidebook*. Thousand Oaks, CA: Sage.

Has step-by-step instructions and examples.

RECOMMENDED WEB RESOURCES

Annenberg Robert Wood Johnson Media Health Coding Project . . . . .www.youthmediarisk.org

An ongoing project analyzing media content for health-related behaviors. Look at the codebook and sampling procedures in particular.

George Mason University Center for Media and Public Affairs . . . . .www.cmpa.com

Provides an explanation of content analysis in practice, with links to a variety of content analysis studies.

Content-analysis.de . . . . .www.content-analysis.de

Software and other resources related to content analysis.

National Centre for Research Methods . . . . .www.restore.ac.uk/lboro

A site on new methods for content analysis, including a comparison of software packages for qualitative data analysis.

Pew Research Center Content Analysis . . . . www.pewresearch.org/methodology/about-content-analysis

An overview of Pew Research Center's content analysis.

Text Analysis Overview . . . . www.textanalysis.info

Links and news on text analysis software.

REFERENCES

Bales, R. (1950). *Interaction process analysis: A method for the study of small groups*. Reading, MA: Addison-Wesley.

Berelson, B. (1952). *Content analysis in communication research*. New York, NY: Hafner.

Beullens, K., Roe, K., & Van den Bulck, J. (2011). The portrayal of risk-taking in traffic: A content analysis of popular action movies. *Journal of Communications Research, 2*(1), 21–27.

Duggan, M. (2014, October 22). Online harassment: Summary of findings. Pew Research Center Internet, Science & Tech Project. Retrieved from http://www.pewinternet.org/2014/10/22/online-harassment/

Fisk, K., Fitzgerald, R., & Cokley, J. (2014). Controversial new sciences in the media: Content analysis of global reporting of nano-technology during the last decade. *Media International Australia, 150*, 156–166.

Gravois, J. (2007). The battle over studies of faculty bias. *The Chronicle of Higher Education, 53*(21), A8.

Gross, N. (2012, March 3). The indoctrination myth. *The New York Times.* Retrieved from http://www.nytimes.com

Krippendorff, K. (2013). *Content analysis: An introduction to its methodology* (3rd ed.). Thousand Oaks, CA: Sage.

Özkoçak, L., & Tuna, Y. (2011). A content analysis: Environment themes and tools in newspapers advertisements. *Online Journal of Communication & Media Technologies, 1*(3), 1–13.

Pew Research Center Internet, Science & Tech Project. (2014, October 22). Victims of online harassment describe their experiences. Retrieved from http://www.pewinternet.org/2014/10/22/online-harassment-experiences-in-their-own-words/

Wilson, C., Robinson, T., & Callister, M. (2012). Surviving *Survivor*: A content analysis of antisocial behavior and its context in a popular reality television show. *Mass Communication & Society, 15*(2), 261–283. DOI: 10.1080/15205436.2011.567346

Yoo, J. H., & Kim, J. (2012). Obesity in the new media: A content analysis of obesity videos on YouTube. *Health Communication, 27*(1), 86–97. DOI: 10.1080/10410236.2011.569003

Ⓢ SAGE edge™

Want a better grade?

Get the tools you need to sharpen your study skills. Access practice quizzes, eFlashcards, video, and multimedia at **edge.sagepub.com/treadwell3e**

CHAPTER 13

Rhetorical and Critical Analyses, and More

Understanding Communication Content in Words

A likely impossibility is always preferable to an unconvincing possibility.

—Aristotle (384 BCE–322 BCE)

⁂⁂⁂

Chapter Overview

This chapter provides an overview of some primarily qualitative approaches to understanding and explicating content. These include:

- Rhetorical and dramatistic analyses—the study of argumentation and persuasion.
- Narrative, discourse, and conversation analyses—the study of stories and talking.
- Semiotics—the study of signs, interpretation, and meaning.
- Critical analyses—the study of the forces behind the content

These approaches share a common interest in using words rather than numbers to understand, interpret, and report content, but the approaches can differ considerably in perspective. For example, conversation analysts look closely, second by second, at transcripts of conversations to understand human interaction whereas rhetoricians are more likely to step back and analyze the strategic use of language in order to assess the persuasive power of a speech or advertisement. This chapter in particular captures the concept behind the book's subtitle, "Paths of Inquiry." As you follow the examples in this chapter, you should see that qualitative analyses of text offer you many different paths to understanding and explaining media content.

Chapter Objectives

This chapter will help you

- Describe the advantages and disadvantages of qualitative analyses of content.

- Explain, with examples,
  - the main types of rhetorical analysis;
  - narrative, metaphor, and discourse analyses;
  - semiotic analysis; and
  - critical analysis and the assumptions underlying it.
- Describe the basic concepts and coding used in conversation analysis.

Introduction: Advantages and Disadvantages of Qualitative Analyses of Content

One advantage to the methods discussed in this chapter is the multiplicity of approaches to understanding text and image. Any text, image, or documented human interaction is potentially capable of being analyzed from multiple perspectives.

The analytic approaches outlined in this chapter are diverse but share a common interest in interpretation—that is, in understanding what content analysts might refer to as the latent content of communication. As you will recall from Chapter 12, the primary interest of traditional content analysis is in categorizing and counting manifest or observable content. The approaches in this chapter go beyond developing a taxonomy of content; they also seek to understand and interpret content. Suppose, for example, that a quantitative analysis of comedy television demonstrates that certain occupations are played predominantly by minority characters. The approaches in this chapter would seek to analyze the same content but with a view to describing, understanding, and explaining how these minority characters interact with other characters; who the heroes and villains are and how we know which is which; how viewers' perceptions of minorities are shaped by language and image; what aspects of the characters' speech make them credible or not; and what interests are served by portraying minorities and occupations in a particular way.

The possibility of multiple interpretations for any given content can frustrate the interested reader seeking a definitive interpretation, but scholars using the approaches in this chapter are generally interested in interpretive possibilities. They accept that there can be more than one way of understanding content and that different interpretations may be equally valid, and they may well take the view that one definitive interpretation is impossible. To revisit the metaphor introduced in Chapter 1, researchers simply opt to use different modes of transport to get to their destinations.

If qualitative methods can be accused of being somehow less than precise, they can also be credited with providing close readings and multiple perspectives that enhance our understanding. These readings and perspectives result in a rich, ongoing discussion of how human communication should be understood and in insights that numbers alone cannot provide.

Rhetorical Analyses

We begin this discussion with one of the oldest approaches to understanding human communication—rhetoric—and with a founding figure of communication theory—Aristotle.

Aristotelian Analysis

The Greek philosopher Aristotle (384–322 BCE) defined **rhetoric** as the study of the available means of persuasion in any given situation. In this context, **rhetorical analysis** (or **Aristotelian analysis**) means examining communication content to identify and assess its persuasive strategies. While the focus at the time was on how an advocate or politician might successfully argue for a cause, rhetorical analyses today can be used to assess the persuasiveness of advertising, editorial columns and blogs, and the persuasive strategies of the corporations, nonprofits, government agencies, and individuals behind such content.

Aristotle proposed that the purpose of argumentation was not to discover verifiable absolute truths but rather to influence belief—what people thought was true. Argumentation, therefore, was based on probability. It meant appealing to audiences in such a way that they were left with the highest level of certainty that the argument was valid.

It is unfair to distill the breadth and richness of Aristotle's writings down to just a few concepts, but his identification of **logos**, **pathos**, and **ethos** as keys to successful persuasion remain an enduring contribution to communication research in the 21st century.

- Logos addresses the use of fact and logic. The assumption is that audiences engage in rational decision making and so the speaker can lead audiences through such thought processes as induction and deduction (Chapter 2) to arrive at a conclusion.
- Pathos addresses the use of emotion. For better or worse, humans are not cold-blooded logic machines. Aristotle recognized that the variety of human emotions might also lead individuals to prefer one argument to another. He wrote about common human emotions, recognizing that an orator could draw on emotion to be persuasive.
- Ethos addresses the nature or character of the speaker. For Aristotle, ethos was the most important of these three modes of persuasion. Rational argument and appeal to emotions would have little or no effect unless the audience saw the speaker as credible and of good character.

Credibility and good character are of course in the mind of the beholder. A fourth and important consideration in Aristotelian rhetoric therefore was the audience and its characteristics. Audience was what drove the nature of the speech. Related, Aristotle identified sources or topics of argument that might help an orator develop a persuasive argument. He identified special topics for use in legal settings, ceremonial settings, and deliberative or political settings. A speech appropriate to one setting would not be appropriate to another. We can see Aristotle's ideas at work in the 21st century. Politicians, for example, tailor their speeches to specific audiences and invest a great deal of effort in convincing voters of their good character.

Analyzing persuasive content such as speeches, advertising, and editorials using an Aristotelian framework gives us insight on whether the content might or might not be effective. In analyzing an advertisement, for example, we might examine for its persuasive effect the nature and character of the spokesperson(s), the use of fact and logic, and the use of emotion. While this can be done purely from the researcher's perspective, in principle the assessment is done with respect to the effect of the content on the target audience.

Dramatistic Analysis

Kenneth Burke, a 20th-century literary theorist, devised a **dramatistic** approach to communication behavior. He regarded communication essentially as performance, as actors acting out a drama against a particular background or scenario.

Burke's **dramatistic pentad** (five-part) analysis asks the following questions:

- **Act**—what act is taking place?
- **Agent**—who is taking this action?
- **Agency**—how or by what means did the act take place?
- **Scene**—where and when did the act take place?
- **Purpose**—why was the act done?

Burke believed that by examining the first four components of the pentad, one could obtain an answer to the question posed by the fifth—what was the purpose or motivation of the act?

For example, our Chapter 12 hypothetical study of substance use in comic strips could be analyzed using Burke's pentad. If we identify an act (smoking), agent (employee), agency (offer of a cigarette from the boss), and scene (work), we might infer a purpose or motivation, which is not always overt or explicit, of the boss trying to socialize with the employee.

Burke proposed that information about the dynamics and motivations of communication could be obtained by "ratio analysis." **Ratio analysis** means examining the relative significance of each pentad unit in any given situation, for example act-scene, act-agent, act-agency, act-purpose, agent-agency, agent-scene, and so on. By examining all of these ratios, we can gain insight into the motives behind the communication, uncover a dominant motivation, or reveal inconsistencies between elements.

For example, if we examine a series of comic strips and find that the scene (workplace) was a dominant element every time the employee was offered a cigarette, we might infer that the boss was attempting to socialize the employee into part of an organizational culture and demonstrating a workplace norm (smoking) more than just cultivating an interpersonal relationship with the employee.

Fantasy Theme Analysis

Fantasy theme analysis, pioneered by professor Ernest Bormann (1972), is a method of rhetorical analysis that provides a way of understanding group consciousness and the development of shared values. Fantasy themes are sagas, stories, or ideas shared by members of a group. These themes give members of the group a common perspective, motivate them, and provide a shared understanding of the group's accomplishments. As with Burke's dramatistic analysis, fantasies involve characters in a setting acting out a theme or plotline. Fantasies typically emerge out of uncertainty as to what the group is all about or how it should handle a new, problematic situation. Over time, competing stories emerge of how the group in its situation should be understood. Eventually, one **master narrative** gains credence with members to the point of **symbolic convergence** or an agreed-upon understanding of what unites group members, differentiates the group from other groups, and explains their successes or failures.

The role of the researcher using fantasy theme analysis is to identify the characters involved in the fantasy, the scene, the plotline, the rationale, or logic behind the fantasy and the **master analog** or deeper structure within the vision. Basically, the analyst seeks to uncover the collective vision that sustains the organization or group. The raw material for fantasy theme analysis can include interviews with group members, organizational histories, mission statements, and the like, and even seemingly minor items like bumper stickers that capture and remind members of the fantasy in three or four words.

A strength of the method is its ability to explain what at first sight might be illogical behaviors. For example, tax resisters or small start-up companies competing against giants in the marketplace might logically recognize that they are fighting against a superior force and will ultimately lose based on their relative lack of resources. A logical decision would be to quit while it is still possible to do so—and before arrest or bankruptcy happens.

It seems illogical to fight a losing battle, but from a careful analysis of documents, speeches, and policy statements, the fantasy theme analyst might discover that group members have adopted a David and Goliath—one individual "in the right" can beat a larger foe—fantasy that motivates them and explains an otherwise illogical behavior. For some such groups, a powerful vision is the fantasy of martyrdom—the vision that there can be no higher calling than to give up one's life for a worthy cause. In that context, a public defeat of the cause is not to be avoided but to be welcomed because of the reward of a blessed future that martyrdom will bring.

Fantasy theme analysis as the study of sagas and stories and visions has a close relationship to narrative analysis.

Narrative Analysis

Narrative analysis is the analysis of the formal properties of stories that people tell and the social role that stories play. It generally attempts to identify a plot, setting, characters, and order of events in people's accounts of their lives.

Narratives take on a special meaning depending on the social context and provide meaning to members of that social context. Very likely you will recall narratives told when you first moved into a dormitory, started work, or joined a sports team or social group. Typically, these narratives are important because they provide examples of the values of an organization and of the unofficial but important rules that govern its behavior. For example, a simple narrative from the workplace might describe how a new employee started work showing an impressive display of tattoos, was sent home by a supervisor to cover up, and returned to work wearing clothing that hid the tattoos (or possibly did not return to work). Such a narrative demonstrates expected standards of behaviors to new group members and shows who has the power to enforce them.

Similar narratives are told in informal settings such as families and transmit to family members the values and the attributes that make the family unique. The narratives make sense only in the social group within which they are told. The story of Uncle Harry riding his bicycle in the snow has a meaning for Uncle Harry's family that it would not have for other families and helps define how his family differs from others.

Narrative analysis pays specific attention to how stories play out over time and how events are sequenced from beginning to end. Analysts may be interested in how narratives are used to mark out the identities of a group and differentiate the group from others. They may focus on the formal properties of stories—that is, the plot, setting, characters, and order of events. They may analyze how stories are reproduced, change over time, change as a result of the settings in which they are told, or are used politically to influence attitudes and behaviors. Analysts may also be interested in identifying key events or "triggers" that flag a vital learning experience or the point at which an organization changed its vision or culture.

The raw material of narrative analysis includes organizational documents, such as mission statements and histories, and may also include interviews with organizational members who may be asked specifically to tell stories they have heard, describe key events, or perhaps even talk about the weirdest thing or the funniest thing that happened to them in their organization.

For example, Martin, Feldman, Hatch, and Sitkin (1983) describe a story from IBM involving the chairman of the board and a young employee in charge of entry to an IBM manufacturing plant. With some considerable trepidation, the employee denied the chairman entry because he was not wearing the correct security badge. Events could have gone in a number of directions at this point, but the outcome was that the chairman got the appropriate badge before entering the plant. Martin et al. argue that the story was repeated throughout the company and reinforced a collective understanding that everybody, regardless of their status in the organization, should follow the rules.

Metaphor Analysis

The vocabulary of any group includes the analogies and metaphors used by members to explain and interpret their group and to help simplify the complexities and ambiguities that are part of any organization. One such summary device is metaphor—a simple term used to categorize or summarize a more complex entity or concept. You hear metaphors on a daily basis—for example, "This class is hell," "That music was heaven," or "On this campus, we are all family." None of these statements is literally true, but they capture in a brief, compelling way what the experience or organization behind it is all about, and in the case of "family"-type metaphors, they simplify the complexities of a large organization so that its members can easily comprehend it. Metaphors include direction—he was "up" or "down"; color—she was "feeling blue" or "in the pink"; and activities—war, parenting, cooking, rocket science, or even herding cats.

Metaphor analysis includes a search for the basic or root metaphors that shape the way organizational members think. The raw materials of such research are once again documents and careful interviews with organizational members, along with specific questions that probe for analogies and metaphors in use. For example, Smith and Eisenberg (1987) interviewed employees at Disneyland and discovered words in use such as *script, cast, show, costume*, and *role*. They concluded that underlying such terminology was a **root metaphor** of "drama." Similarly, they identified another root metaphor—"family"—that had become increasingly adopted over time. Smith and Eisenberg interpreted the conflict described in their paper as the outcome of hard business decisions being made by management conflicting with employees' views of their organization as "family."

The search for governing or root metaphors is inductive; it is built from specific observations of language in use on up to a conclusion about metaphors. The root metaphor itself may not be apparent or in common use as a word or phrase. Researchers entering an organization and asking each member "Excuse me, are you a tree?" are likely to be met with looks of befuddlement or even propositions about the researcher's sanity. On the other hand, careful interviewing may reveal the fact that words such as *roots, branches, growth, decay*, and *change* are more commonly used than words such as *kill, defend, attack*, and *territory*. A reasonable conclusion from this observation is that the organization or group is best explained by a root metaphor of a living organism growing, changing, adapting, and perhaps being pacifist, at least relative to the root metaphor of war suggested by the second set of terms.

Discourse Analysis

From a research perspective, Curt (1994) refers to **discourse** as the interest in the constructive, productive, or pragmatic uses of language. This interest in how language is used emerges from the recognition that "language can never neutrally describe the world, because language itself is an active part of the world" (Curt, 1994, p. 234). **Discourse analysis** focuses on how language shapes meaning and understanding of events and how particular labels or concepts are developed and made powerful by the use of language.

Discourse analysis has several roots—sociology of knowledge, cultural analysis, rhetoric, the psychology of human interaction, and conversation analysis (introduced below). Predictably, then, there are a variety of approaches to discourse analysis, but most analysts would agree that they share a common interest in language as a social practice more than in the characteristics of the language itself. They are interested in the frameworks within which ideas are formulated and how ideas and concepts give meaning to physical and social realities.

For example, an analyst might ask what configurations of advertising, news coverage, consumer reviews, web content, and perhaps the writings and speeches of Steve Jobs and Bill Gates led to the perception of two "computer cultures"—Mac and PC. The raw data for discourse analysis often can be found in politics and contentious public issues. For example, an analyst might study how the language of "right to life" versus that of the "reproductive rights" movements shapes public views of abortion, or how the language of the "defense hawks" versus fiscal conservatives shape views—and decisions—on defense spending. Maeseele (2015), for example, used critical discourse analysis to analyze how two newspapers differently (re-)defined and interpreted events in the debate on genetically modified crops and food.

Discourse analysis is best understood as a field of research or an interest area rather than as a specific method. It has no specific, agreed-upon procedure, but typically discourse analysis involves starting with a research question and then selecting samples of news, videos, interview transcripts, social media, and such. Then comes coding, which unlike conventional content analysis is qualitative, and analysis. Coding and analysis are basically a search for patterns and variations in content. They vary according to the researcher's perspective on the research and may change as both the research and the analyst's thinking progress. Most analyses, though, are based on how the discourse appears to be shaping our views of the world rather than on categories of language or frequencies of occurrence, as with content analysis.

Conversation Analysis

Imagine a world with no rules, guidelines, or accepted ways of doing things. Imagine, for example, no traffic rules about what side of the road to drive on, stopping for red lights, and especially no "right-of-way" rules. Now imagine an analogous scenario with respect to human interaction. The prospect of anyone being able to speak at any time to anybody on any topic may be an ideal of democracy, but it predicts conversational chaos.

One way around this problem is to produce formalized rules such as parliamentary procedure or formal judicial proceedings to control interaction and allow every participant a voice, but these formal rules apply only where organized groups of individuals agree to adopt them. That leaves most people living without any such rules. What, then, governs our daily interactions with other people? That is what conversation analysts seek to discover and to document. Steensen (2014), for example, used conversation analysis to study power relations between journalists and audiences in interactive journalism. Conversation analysis has also been used to study physician-patient interaction, pilot-to-flight control interaction, business meetings, family discussions, and political debate.

Document is an appropriate word here because the raw material of conversation analysis is the transcripts of conversations. Researchers begin with a close reading of such transcripts, marking them up as shown in Exhibit 13.1 to show pauses in a conversation, the time lag between responses, words that get emphasized, where speakers overlap, and so on. From this they are able to document, describe, and classify the unspoken agreements that govern conversations—for example, the mechanisms that govern **turn taking** or who speaks next in a conversation and the mechanisms that indicate possible types of responses to a question. These mechanisms are not formal rules with penalties attached to them for noncompliance; rather, they are the procedures that individuals follow in order to allow a conversation to take place.

If rhetorical and discourse analysts look for the broad sweep of ideas and how they are made persuasive, conversation analysts study the fine detail of human interaction on a second-by-second basis in order to identify the specific rules that allow a conversation to continue as a coordinated sequence of events rather than degenerating into chaos.

Analysts are interested in the mechanisms of a conversation rather than its content. Their focus is specifically on a detailed analysis of the transcripts of conversations and what they reveal rather than the context (work or home, for example) in which the conversation takes place. If a variable such as the gender of a participant explains the nature of a conversation, that conclusion will be drawn from references to gender in the transcript, not from the analyst's prior knowledge of a participant's gender. There is, therefore, no need to work directly with individuals involved in the conversation.

A fundamental concept in conversation analysis is that discrete units of a conversation can be recognized and categorized in order to understand the mechanisms that sustain the conversation. A major difference between content analysis and conversation analysis is that the analyst adds to the conversation's transcript a standardized series of codes that mark particular aspects of the conversation, such as the time between a speaker's utterances or the volume of an utterance.

Exhibit 13.1 shows an example of a transcript marked up with some of the basic conversation analysis annotations, which are explained in the right-hand column. The following section sets out some of the basic concepts in conversation analysis.

Utterances

Utterances are units of speech preceded by silence and followed either by silence or by another speaker. They are not necessarily linguistic or grammatical units such as sentences or phrases.

Adjacency Pairs

Adjacency pairs are units of speech that occur together. They are one of the basic units of conversation analysis. Once the first utterance is heard, a second is required in response. Many adjacency pairs have been identified, such as the following:

Adjacency Pair	Utterance	Response
Question—Answer	What's the time?	Time for a coffee break.
Offer—Rejection	Do you need help with that homework?	Nope! Finished it already.
Compliment—Acceptance	You did a great job on that report.	Thanks. I used Ted's new software for the cover.
Greeting—Greeting	G'day, mate.	Well, hello there.

Affiliative responses to a question, compliment, offer, or command maintain a link with the speaker; **disaffiliative responses** break the link with the speaker.

Turn Taking

Speaking out of turn is disruptive. If conversations are not to turn into chaos, individuals need to coordinate who speaks when. Nonverbal cues such as body language do not explain this coordination as telephone conversations are accomplished with more precise timing than face-to-face conversations (Levinson, 1983, as cited in Seedhouse, 2004).

Obviously, there must be some agreed-upon management system for turn taking, which conversation analysts conceptualize as having two parts—a **transitional relevance place** (TRP) and a **turn constructional unit** (TCU). A transitional relevance place is the point in the conversation at which turn taking may take place, and the norms of turn taking govern the conversation. For example, if the current speaker designates a second speaker to talk, the current speaker must then stop. If the current speaker does not select a second speaker, then any member of the group may self-select as the next speaker. A turn constructional unit is a sentence, word, or exclamation that signals a TRP—a point at which turn taking can occur.

Repair Mechanisms

There are four types of **repair mechanism** that might occur when a conversation is running into trouble. These are self-initiated–self-repair; self-initiated–other-repair; other-initiated–self-repair; and other-initiated–other-repair.

Self-initiated–self-repair means that the speaker identifies and corrects his own mistake. This is the preferred mechanism in that, being self-initiated, it gets the conversation back on track efficiently without other participants having to detour from the focus of the conversation to make sense of the mistake and correct it. At the other extreme, other-initiated–other-repair requires the work of other participants, which may lead to further conversational difficulties, to get back on track.

Conversation analysis is distinguished by its attention to the micro-detail of human interaction. You can see from Exhibit 13.1 that transcribing one minute of conversation requires considerably more than one minute of work. Transcription also requires a keen ear and a respect for what was actually said. Conversation analysts do not correct for errors in speech or grammar in the course of transcribing. Their mission is to accurately record and annotate what they heard. Transcriptions of real conversations are far more complex than the simple examples shown in Exhibit 13.1. Visit the websites at the end of this chapter for further discussion of conversation analysis and examples of the detail involved.

Semiotics

A rose by any other name would smell as sweet, according to Shakespeare. On the basis of such thinking is the study of semiotics founded. At heart, semiotics is concerned with the relationship between language, and especially signs, and meaning.

Signs and language are arbitrarily connected to meaning and are culturally specific. You could call a book a "kkjtckl," and it would still be a book, as Shakespeare probably would not have said. *Book* can in fact be an action verb or an object that varies considerably in size, design, cost, and content. Stop signs have a commonly accepted meaning of "Stop—and then proceed when safe to do so." Taken literally, a stop sign says "Stop!" It does not say "and then proceed when safe to do," so where did the "and then proceed" meaning come from, and why do most of us agree to accept that meaning?

Semiotic analysis means exploring the relationships between signs and their meanings. It helps us understand how messages might be interpreted and misinterpreted. Note the plurals. If the relationships between signs and meanings are arbitrary, then multiple interpretations of the relationships are always possible. There are drivers who, at least by their behavior, appear to interpret a stop sign as "Slow down a bit . . . if you feel like it and you do not see a patrol car."

Semiotic Thinking: The Tobacco King, Restrooms, and Sleeping Policemen

Edward Bernays, a pioneer of U.S. public relations in the 1920s, recalled that in his meetings with a major client, the president of American Tobacco, the president was always seated and

EXHIBIT 13.1   **Example of Conversation Analysis Transcript**

Annotated Transcript	Explanation of Annotations
13. Brian: What's the [time?]	*13, 14, 15, etc., indicate line numbers in transcript.*
	] (right bracket) indicates Brian has stopped talking while Tshinta continues.
14. Tshinta: [Almost time to get to our next class.	*[(left bracket) indicates where Tshinta's response overlaps with Brian's question.*
(0.3)	*(0.3) denotes timed length in seconds of a pause between speakers.*
15. Caroline: Yeah.	
16. Mike: What day's that guest speaker?	
(.)	*(.) denotes a just noticeable pause.*
17. Caroline: Tuesday.	*Line 17 shows an affiliative response to the question in line 16; no explanation is required.*
18. Mike: And. (.) Can you clear my campus mailbox tomorrow?	
19. Caroline: NOPE. No can do.	*Line 19 shows a disaffiliative response to the question in line 18. NOPE in capital letters indicates a much higher speaking volume.*
(0.5)	
20. Caroline: Sorry—uh—gotta go to my—uh—research site and—uh—do—ah—interviews.	*An explanation as in line 20 is required if the conversation is to continue.*
21. Mike: So when are we working on this project again?	*Line 21: Mike asks a question relevant to each individual in the group. Line 21 requires an answer, but Mike does not call on anyone to provide one.*
22. Elizabeth: How about Tuesday night? Tshinta?	*Line 22: Elizabeth self-nominates as the next speaker, then nominates Tshinta as speaker.*
23. Tshinta: Nope. We have that guest speaker, remember?	*Line 23: Tshinta speaks but does not designate the next speaker.*
(.)	
24. Caroline: How about Tuesday?	*Line 24: After a brief pause, Caroline self-designates as speaker and then engages in self-initiated self-repair of her error in line 24.*
25. >Oops. Sorry. Wasn't listening. Sorry.<	*Line 25: Inward arrows > and < indicate faster speech.*

always wore his hat in the office. To Bernays, a Freudian by background, this symbolized royalty seated on a throne and wearing a crown. The company president might well have been happy to have that hierarchical interpretation shared among the lesser beings he employed. **Semioticians**, however, would query the power of such monarchical symbolism in corporate America, post-1776, and indeed whether the hat should be interpreted as monarchical at all. They would want to further question Bernays's interpretation. For example, could the hat be read as a Lincolnian/ presidential top hat generating respect for an American institution—American Tobacco—and its president?

Signs denoting restrooms often use simplified male and female silhouettes on the doors, presumably to bypass any language problems. At one time, such doors in theaters had somewhat elaborate silhouettes of gentlemen in top hats and long-tailed coats or coiffured ladies in long evening gowns. A semiotic interpretation might be that theaters at one point tried to reflect, or establish, an image of "up market" entertainment attended by "ladies and gentlemen of class." Perhaps as the demand for mass entertainment grew, theaters responded via the symbolism on their restroom doors that they were open to all, regardless of class. Thus, the "ladies" and "gentlemen" doors lost their ball gowns and top hats and became class-free and modernistic.

Speed bumps in some countries are referred to as "sleeping policemen." This seems like a major putdown of the local constabulary—asleep in the middle of the road and driven over at frequent intervals by the motoring public. So what might be another interpretation? A more favorable meaning, at least from the point of view of the police, might be that there is a constant police presence on the roads, ready to "wake up" at any time. Drivers sensitive to the latter meaning would obviously drive with caution, a decision reinforced by the very real consequences of speeding over a tangible "sleeping policeman."

Much applied semiotic research centers on consumer products and the meanings that attach to them (Mick, Burroughs, Hetzel, & Brannen, 2004). In an applied setting, researchers may combine semiotic analyses of new products and product designs with other approaches such as surveys and focus groups to determine what meanings consumers assign to products and why they choose to affiliate with a particular brand. Semiotic researchers have studied the relationship between self-image and the shape of the perfume bottle a woman is likely to buy, the images conveyed by corporate logos such as IBM and Apple, and how the shapes of vehicles affect the memorability of vehicle brands.

The value of semiotic analysis is that the researcher explores the multiple possibilities for (mis) interpretation and so becomes alert to all the nuances and possibilities of interpretation associated with a product.

The following section demonstrates one of many approaches to semiotic analysis and how it might be applied in practice.

Roman Jakobson Visits Sam's Car Lot

A classic telecommunications-based model of human communication, introduced in Chapter 1, has four major components—source, message, channel, and receiver.

Linguist and communication theorist Roman Jakobson expanded the model and assigned a **semiotic function** to each component. Jakobson's six semiotic functions identify how language functions for specific purposes.

Exhibit 13.2 shows how Jakobson's semiotic functions might be used to analyze and understand the advertising run by a hypothetical car dealer—Sam. For example, a statement such as "I have to be mad . . ." is an **expressive** statement establishing Sam's condition. "Come on down . . ." is a **conative** statement establishing Sam's expectations of his advertising audiences. "Our deals are steals on wheels" is a **poetic** usage; we can take pleasure in the alliteration even if we disagree

EXHIBIT 13.2   **Jakobson's Semiotic Functions**

Communication Component	Semiotic Function	Example
Sender	Expressive. Describes or establishes the speaker's condition or emotional state.	"I have to be mad to sell at these prices."
Receiver	Conative. Establishes the sender's expectations of the receiver or what the receiver is expected to do as a result of receiving the message.	"Come on down—now!"
Message	Poetic. Uses language for its own pleasure, as in jokes or alliteration because they are pleasurable in their own right.	"Our deals are steals on wheels."
Context	Referential. Establishes the communication context, dominant message, or agenda.	"We have the nation's best deals in used cars."
Channel	Phatic. Keeps communication participants "on track" and in contact by establishing how communication will take place.	"Visit, phone, e-mail; let's hear from you."
Code	Metalingual. Establishes agreed-upon meaning for a word—for example, by establishing that *Rose* refers to the name of a girl, not a flower.	Sam's cars are *the* cars."

with Sam's message. We might infer that Sam assumes that the poetic quality of his phrasing will make his advertising memorable. "We have the nation's best deals" has the **referential** function of establishing overall what the dominant message of Sam's advertising is. "Visit, phone, or e-mail" has a **phatic** function; it establishes how communication should take place between Sam and his potential customers. "Sam's cars are *the* cars" is a **metalingual** statement establishing the preferred meaning, or at least Sam's preferred meaning, of the term *Sam's cars*.

Jakobson's six functions can be used for semiotic analysis in a number of ways. For example, Jakobson argued that one of the six functions is always dominant in a text. Determining which function is dominant would help you understand the motivation behind the message, as with Burke's ratio analysis. Or you could examine each function systematically to see how emotions, relationship messages, and "play with words" overall help Sam establish an image of his dealership with his advertising audience.

Semiotic analysis is an exercise in the possibilities of interpretation. For an overview of other semiotic theories and their applications, see the resources listed at the end of this chapter.

Critical Analyses

Critical analyses explore the way in which communication establishes, reinforces, and maintains power structures in society. As you might anticipate, there are a number of approaches to critical analyses. The ranks of critical theorists are drawn from a variety of disciplines, there are no widely agreed-upon theoretical assumptions or methods, and as Curt (1994) points out, "Writing produced from a critical theory perspective is often pretty impenetrable to the uninitiated" (p. 13). Nonetheless, critical scholars share a basic interest in identifying the power structures behind communication content and actions.

One way to understand this interest is to appreciate that all communication is based on having the resources with which to communicate. Any public communication—be it print media, broadcast media, websites, billboards, transit advertising, course syllabi, or sponsored Little League uniforms—requires resources in the form of time, money, and influence to produce. So do events such as halftime shows, religious rituals, initiation ceremonies, funeral services, and graduation ceremonies. We might argue, then, that much of the communication content to which we are exposed is a product of individuals and organizations with the power and resources (however defined) to communicate.

While the Internet and social media may have democratized global communication to a degree, it remains true that your ability to "tweet" or maintain a web presence is based on the fact that you have the resources to do so. Your presence on the Internet reflects a communicative power that those on the other side of the "digital divide" do not have.

Critical perspectives question the idea of objectivity and address social problems or inequalities in such a way as to provide more equitable access to society's collective resources. Critical scholars analyze communication with a view to determining whose voices are dominant in any given communication, the power structures behind the observed communication, and how communication is used by those in power to maintain the status quo.

In this section, we will revisit from a critical perspective some of the research approaches outlined in this chapter.

From a critical perspective, the analysis of rhetoric seeks to establish how communication is used to maintain power relationships. The three rhetorical settings identified by Aristotle are formal settings for debate in any society—legal/judicial proceedings, ceremonial proceedings such as graduation, and deliberative proceedings such as political or policy debates. Rhetorical analysis can be understood from a critical perspective as an analysis of the argumentation to win the assent of the powerful or how the powerful use argumentation to maintain their status. Similarly, Kenneth Burke's dramatistic analysis and narrative analysis can be understood as ways of understanding dramas and stories that tell of power relationships and the clash of values.

From a critical perspective, metaphor analysis can reveal how language maintains and promotes organizational power structures. For example, suppose you are reading interview transcripts and documentation with a view to understanding why an organization is successful. As you read, it occurs to you that certain words and phrases appear repeatedly—*team*, *team player*, *plays*, *leader*, *goals*, *scored*, *captain*, *time out*, *rules*, and *coach*. It occurs to you that even though individual informants have not used the term *game* or *contest*, it appears that they are collectively viewing their organizational life as a game or contest. They would probably agree that there is a "captain" coordinating players, each of whom has specific responsibilities, an agreed-upon set of rules, and an overall objective to beat other teams playing the same game. In other words, there is a root "team" metaphor framing their thinking and perhaps shaping their behavior.

At one level, this metaphor implies a group of people working in harmony and coordinating their efforts toward a common goal. However, a critical analyst will point out that the team metaphor is capable of an alternative interpretation—that teams are hierarchical, with a captain and/ or coach in charge and making the strategic decisions. Team members are expected to implement these decisions at a tactical level and to put their individuality aside for the good of the team. Members who persist in being individualistic at the expense of the team risk being thrown off the team for not being team players. From a critical viewpoint, then, the team metaphor promotes a message of obedience to authority, doing as one is directed, and maintaining the team's hierarchy. From a critical perspective, this is obedience not just to any authority but to authority rooted in historically identifiable forms of social, economic, or cultural power, which restrict participation by groups such as the disenfranchised.

Similarly, a critical interpretation may be made of the "family" metaphor, common to many institutions. Family may suggest a caring group of individuals with close personal relationships, but families regardless of size, structure, or level of democracy most often have a head or heads (parents) making decisions that others (children) are expected to abide by. In a critical view, the family metaphor, as with team, subtly promotes the notion of hierarchy, respect for authority, and not behaving in any way that would disappoint "the family."

With respect to organizational communication, the critical interpretation of such metaphors gains some additional validity in that such metaphors are typically found in new-employee materials, employee newsletters, recognition events, and the like. Who controls the content of such employee communications? Management!

In the case of narrative analyses, let's revisit the IBM story outlined above under "Narrative Analysis" and its interpretation. While the story emphasizes that all members of the organization are subject to its rules, Mumby (1987) interprets the story as having a political function. A surface reading omits the fact that the rules are made by management, not by employees. Furthermore, the story has the rule being enforced by a low-level employee, from the "bottom up," not the "top down." From a critical perspective, this story serves to remind employees that they are the ones responsible for enforcing the rules that management has decided on—a story that is made all the more powerful because it is painlessly propagated in the organization as a story, not as a directive from management.

The above analyses are informed by a **Marxist perspective**, which begins from a critique of capitalism and its attendant social relationships and values. From this perspective, critics examine communication content for the (often hidden) messages that reinforce the **ideology** or vision that guides those in power. A critical organizational scholar might, for example, analyze employee newsletters to determine the extent to which a management ideology dominates the content.

Criticism from a feminist perspective generally seeks to critique patriarchal hierarchies and ideologies and, in the context of communication research, the communication content and practices that reproduce and perpetuate such hierarchies and ideologies. **Feminist criticism** focuses on gender, and more specifically gender inequities and their portrayal, lived experiences, and replication. Critical approaches may range from determining the relative dominance of male versus female "voices" in media content to identifying sexism in language to analyzing such perceived masculine concepts as hierarchy. Media researchers, for example, would take an interest in how the relationships between men and women are portrayed in entertainment media, advertising or employee communications, and more specifically the power relationships between male and female characters; how male and female roles are defined; and how behaviors and roles perpetuate patriarchal behaviors and hierarchies in organizations and interpersonal relationships.

Critical discourse analysis aims to explore the relationships between language and power. As you will have gathered from this section, one assumption we can make about society is that societal elites and the powerful have the ability to interpret and describe the world in a way that favors them, and that implicitly or explicitly marginalizes minority voices. The basic aim of critical discourse analysis, then, is to uncover the ideological assumptions behind public discourse and to link communication content with underlying power structures. The interest of the critical analyst is in injustice and inequality. In examining discourse in this light, the researcher may look for taken-for-granted assumptions, use of evidence, style, use of rhetoric, media used, the ways in which text and graphics interact, and omissions—what is not said as much as what is. Because the discourse of the powerful may be countered by minority discourse, the critical discourse analyst may study both in order to see how one influences the other.

Unlike the content analyst who takes a primary interest in the frequency with which words occur, the critical analyst will take an interest in the words and phrases thought to be significant in promoting a viewpoint, not in their frequency.

The purposes and methods for analyzing media content often overlap. For example, content analysis may be used to obtain a critical reading of advertising, and critical methods may be used to assess the effectiveness of advertising. Different methodologies may also be combined. See, for example, Holsanova, Holmquist, and Rahm (2006), in which a semiotic analysis of newspapers was combined with eye-movement scans of newspaper readers.

Ethics Panel: Research as Manipulative Practice

This chapter has discussed approaches to research that focus on persuasion, argumentation, and the maintenance and shaping of relationships through communication. From a critical perspective, we can see that any and all of these approaches can reveal communication in the service of power and of power relationships.

The idea that communication research is manipulative has both theoretical and practical support. For example, Parker (1972) posits that most human relationships are manipulative and that rhetoric and argumentation fall under the "umbrella" of manipulation, along with political power, authority relationships, physical force, and rewards and punishments. Parker uses the term *manipulation* in an "ethically neutral sense" (p. 73). Nonetheless, from a critical perspective, one can argue that research participants are often manipulated into becoming participants and that research has a power component in that researchers use their research activities if not for social change, then certainly for personal advancement.

This critical view of research is evidenced by what we know of some research in practice. For example, Lindlof and Taylor (2002) suggest that behind the myths of "researchers practicing universal informed consent, consistent empathy, honest disclosure, accurate reporting and unobtrusive observation . . . are the harsh realities of improvised consent, mutual dislike, strategic deception, creative reconstruction and intentional shaping of events" (p. 140).

Where the stakes are high, for example with respect to funding or being first to publish, research can be seen as a "winner-take-all game with perverse incentives that lead scientists to cut corners, and, in some cases, commit acts of misconduct" (Zimmer, 2012).

What has all this to do with the approaches outlined in this chapter to understanding communication content? From a critical perspective, documents that seek institutional review board (IRB) approvals or funding; propose projects; solicit research participants; and report research findings, conclusions, and recommendations can all be regarded as manipulative. Research writing is not neutral, as we shall further discover in Chapter 14.

Thinking of communication as persuasion and the exercise of power, answer the following questions.

Questions

Consider the following three research questions.

- What are the effects of fast-food advertising on children's food preferences?

- What is the relationship between social media use and the academic performance of college students?

- What communication behaviors facilitate the integration of new immigrant groups into society?

For each of these research topics,

- What persuasive appeals might a researcher use to obtain research funding?
- How might the appeals to government agencies, private foundations, and citizen activist groups differ in their emphases, and why?
- What persuasive appeals might a researcher use in letters to individuals soliciting their participation in the research?

CHAPTER SUMMARY

- Rhetorical analyses examine content to understand the nature of persuasion and argumentation.
- Narrative and discourse analyses focus on stories and their uses.
- Conversation analyses examine the details of human interaction to determine how conversations are coordinated among participants.
- Semiotic analyses focus on the meanings and interpretations of texts and signs.
- Critical analyses focus on the use of language as it promotes and maintains power in organizations and societies.

KEY TERMS

act

adjacency pairs

affiliative responses

agency

agent

Aristotelian analysis

conative

critical analyses

critical discourse analysis

disaffiliative responses

discourse

discourse analysis

dramatistic

dramatistic pentad

ethos

expressive

feminist criticism

ideology

logos

Marxist perspective

master analog

master narrative

metalingual

metaphor analysis

pathos

phatic

poetic

purpose

ratio analysis

referential

repair mechanism

rhetoric

rhetorical analysis

rhetoricians

root metaphor

scene

semiotic function

semioticians

symbolic convergence

turn constructional unit

transitional relevance place (TRP)

turn taking

utterances

APPLICATION EXERCISES

Exercise 1. Discourse Analysis

You will find competing discourses frequently in local and national news media. Often, the issue will be an environmental one as conservationists and historians compete with developers and investors over the proposed use of a historic or environmentally important site. Generically, the two competing discourses are likely to be jobs and economic growth versus nurturing and maintaining the local environment and its history. Another contested discourse especially at election time is the place of government in society—for example, the discourse of freedom and individual enterprise versus the discourse of care and fair treatment for all citizens.

Identify one such current discourse conflict and outline the media you would study; list specific techniques you might use to differentiate the competing discourses; and decide which is the most powerful.

Discourse analysis is frequently done with dominant and minority discourses already identified. How might you predict from discourse analysis which of two competing discourses is likely to become the dominant one?

Exercise 2. Matching Method With Interest

Which of the methods outlined in this chapter would you prefer for researching the following interest areas? Why?

- Identifying the political agenda, if any, of a newspaper or television network.
- Identifying the agenda of management in internal organizational media.
- Explaining how a group makes its decisions.
- Explaining how two people make a decision.

Exercise 3. Analyzing Organizational Stories

Stories about organizations are frequently told informally to new members of organizations. Whatever the motivation behind the storytelling, the stories often have the effects of explaining how to survive in the organization and of identifying the informal rules that members need to follow if they are to adjust successfully.

Identify stories that you and others heard during the first year of study at your institution. How do these stories differ from one another? What topics do they cover that are not addressed by the official student handbook or institutional policies? Which of the approaches identified in this chapter do you find the most useful for understanding these stories as a way of orienting newcomers to the institution?

Exercise 4. Analyzing Online Harassment: Qualitatively

Revisit the Pew Research Center Internet, Science & Tech Project (2014) survey of online harassment outlined in the Chapter 12 end-of-chapter exercises. The study also provides several hundred selected quotes about harassment from those surveyed at www.pewinternet.org/2014/10/22/online-harassment-experiences-in-their-own-words.

Looking at these quotes collectively, what qualitative approach(es) might provide the best understanding of harassment? For example, collectively, do they add up to a summary narrative that can be further analyzed? Looking at these statements, how valid do the six specific types of harassment identified by Pew for its survey appear? If you had these statements before running a survey, how might your survey questions differ from the Pew questions?

The full report, questionnaire, and respondent comments are available at www.pewinternet.org/2014/10/22/online-harassment (Duggan, 2014).

RECOMMENDED READING

Aristotle

Dean, D. (2005). Fear, negative campaigning and loathing: The case of the UK election campaign. *Journal of Marketing Management, 21*, 1067–1078. DOI: 10.1362/026725705775194111

A paper that uses Aristotle's concept of rhetoric as a basis for understanding how messages are conveyed to the electorate.

Shanahan, F., & Seele, P. (2015). Shorting ethos: Exploring the relationship between Aristotle's ethos and reputation management. *Corporate Reputation Review, 18*(1), 37–49. DOI: 10.1057/crr.2014.19

Explores the role of Aristotle's notion of ethos in corporate reputation and repairing reputational damage.

Bormann

Adams, A. S. (2013). Needs met through role-playing games: A fantasy theme analysis of Dungeons & Dragons. *Kaleidoscope: A Graduate Journal of Qualitative Communication Research, 12*, 69–86

Using fantasy theme analysis, this study identifies four themes within D&D player talk on Facebook: democratic ideologies, friendship maintenance, extraordinary experiences, and good versus evil.

Bormann, E. G. (1972). Fantasy and rhetorical vision: The rhetorical criticism of social reality. *Quarterly Journal of Speech, 58*, 396–407.

An overview of fantasy theme analysis.

Burke

Foss, S. K. (2004). Pentadic criticism. In *Rhetorical criticism: Exploration and practice* (4th ed., pp. 355–386). Long Grove, IL: Waveland Press.

A discussion of Burke's pentad and examples of its use in rhetorical analysis.

Milford, M. (2015). Kenneth Burke's punitive priests and the redeeming prophets: The NCAA, the college sports media, and the University of Miami scandal. *Communication Studies, 66*(1), 45–62. DOI: 10.1080/10510974.2013.856806

A Burkean analysis of organizational adaptation to new circumstances.

Conversation Analysis

Clifton, J. (2006). A conversation analytical approach to business communication: The case of leadership. *Journal of Business Communication, 43*(3), 202–219. DOI: 10.1177/0021943606288190

A study of the normally unnoticed machinery of talk by which leadership in a group is enacted.

Richards, K., & Seedhouse, P. (2005). *Applying conversation analysis.* New York, NY: Palgrave Macmillan.

See in particular the chapter on conversation analysis as a research methodology.

Discourse Analysis

Bingham, A. (2010, Winter). Discourse of the Dammed: A study of the impacts of sustainable development discourse on indigenous peoples in the Brazilian Amazon in the context of the proposed Belo Monte hydroelectric dam. *POLIS Journal, 4,* 1– 47.

A discourse analysis study of a dominant discourse of sustainable development based on science, technology, and management versus a secondary discourse of decentralization and full participation and the impact of the former on indigenous peoples.

Gee, J. P. (2014). *An introduction to discourse analysis: Theory and method* (4th ed.). New York, NY: Routledge.

An introductory text that discusses a variety of approaches to discourse analysis.

Metaphor

Lakoff, G., & Johnson, M. (1980). *Metaphors we live by.* Chicago, IL: University of Chicago Press.

Discusses metaphor and its role in our lives. Why is "up" good and "down" bad, for example?

Narrative Analysis

Nettleton, P. H. (2011). Domestic violence in men's and women's magazines: Women are guilty of choosing the wrong men, men are not guilty of hitting women. *Women's Studies in Communication, 34*(2), 139–160. DOI: 10.1080/07491409.2011.618240

Using narrative analysis, this study found that men's magazines show ongoing tolerance for domestic violence and that women's magazines hold women responsible for male violence.

Semiotics

Chandler, D. (2002). *Semiotics: The basics.* London, UK: Routledge.

An overview of semiotics. Shows how language and signs cannot be regarded as neutral carriers of meaning.

Floch, J. (2001). *Semiotics, marketing and communication: Beneath the signs, the strategies.* London, UK: Palgrave.

An overview of semiotic theory and its application using specific examples from advertising and marketing.

Harrison, C. (2003). Visual social semiotics: Understanding how still images make meaning. *Technical Communication, 50*(1), 46–60.

A paper, illustrated with examples, on analyzing imagery in documents and websites. Discusses the relationship of words and text and how to choose images to enhance text.

Pagel, S., & Westerfelhaus, R. (2005). Charting managerial reading references in relation to popular management theory books. A semiotic analysis. *Journal of Business Communication, 42*(4), 420–448. DOI: 10.1177/0021943605276803

Uses semiotic analysis to find out how business people actually read popular business theory books.

Zhao, S., Djonov, E., & van Leeuwen, T. (2014). Semiotic technology and practice: A multimodal social semiotic approach to PowerPoint. *Text & Talk, 34*(3), 349–375. DOI: 10.1515/text-2014-0005

Considers PowerPoint as a semiotic practice with three dimensions—the software's design, the multimodal composition of slide shows, and their presentation.

RECOMMENDED WEB RESOURCES

Daniel Chandler, University of Wales, Semiotics for Beginners http://visual-memory.co.uk/daniel/Documents/S4B/semiotic.html

Professor Charles Antaki's conversation analysis tutorial www-staff.lboro.ac.uk/ssca1/sitemenu.htm

Qualitative Data Analysis on the Web . . . . http://onlineqda.hud.ac.uk/

Department of Behavioural Sciences, University of Huddersfield. Qualitative data analysis methods, resources and a glossary.

Signo . . . . www.signosemio.com

Check out this site for more information on theoreticians such as Jakobson.

TalkBank . . . . www.talkbank.org

At TalkBank, you can find downloadable conversation analysis transcripts linked to audio or video recordings, and other resources.

Umberto Eco . . . . www.umbertoeco.com

Eco is a semiotician, literary critic, and novelist, popularly known for his novel *The Name of the Rose*, among others. Check out his website on semiotics.

REFERENCES

Bormann, E. G. (1972). Fantasy and rhetorical vision: The rhetorical criticism of social reality. *Quarterly Journal of Speech, 58,* 396–407. DOI: 10.1080/00335637209383138

Curt, B. C. (1994). *Textuality and tectonics: Troubling social and psychological science.* Buckingham, UK: Open University Press.

Duggan, M. (2014, October 22). Online harassment: Summary of findings. Pew Research Center Internet, Science & Tech Project. Retrieved from http://www.pewinternet.org/2014/10/22/online-harassment/

Hajer, M. A. (1995): *The politics of environmental discourse: Ecological modernization and the policy process.* Oxford, UK: Clarendon Press.

Holsanova, J., Holmquist, K., & Rahm, H. (2006). Entry points and reading paths on newspaper spreads: Comparing a semiotic analysis with eye-tracking measurements. *Visual Communication, 5*(1), 65–93.

Levinson, S. (1983). *Pragmatics.* Cambridge, UK: Cambridge University Press.

Lindlof, T. R., & Taylor, B. C. (2002). *Qualitative communication research methods* (2nd ed.). Thousand Oaks, CA: Sage.

Maeseele, P. (2015). Risk conflicts, critical discourse analysis and media discourses on GM crops and food. *Journalism, 16*(2), 278–297. DOI: 10.1177/1464884913511568

Martin, J., Feldman, M., Hatch, M. J., & Sitkin, S. B. (1983). The uniqueness paradox in organizational stories. *Administrative Science Quarterly, 28,* 438–453.

Mick, D. G., Burroughs, J. E., Hetzel, P., & Brannen, M. Y. (2004). Pursuing the meaning of meaning in the commercial world: An international review of marketing and consumer research founded on semiotics. *Semiotica, 52*(1–4), 1–74. DOI: 10.1515/semi.2004.2004.152-1-4.1

Mumby, D. K. (1987). The political function of narrative in organizations. *Communication Monographs, 54*(2), 113–127. DOI: 10.1080/03637758709390221

Parker, D. H. (1972). Rhetoric, ethics and manipulation. *Philosophy & Rhetoric, 5*(2), 69–87.

Pew Research Center Internet, Science & Tech Project. (2014, October 22). Victims of online harassment describe their experiences. Retrieved from http://www.pewinternet.org/2014/10/22/online-harassment-experiences-in-their-own-words/

Seedhouse, P. (2004). Conversation analysis methodology. *Language Learning, 54*(S1), 1–54. DOI: 10.1111/j.1467-9922.2004.00268.x

Smith, R. C., & Eisenberg, E. M. (1987). Conflict at Disneyland: A root-metaphor analysis. *Communication Monographs, 54*(4), 367–380. DOI: 10.1080/03637758709390239

Steensen, S. (2014). Conversing the audience: A methodological exploration of how conversation analysis can contribute to the analysis of interactive journalism. *New Media & Society, 16*(8), 1197–1213. DOI: 10.1177/1461444813504263

Zimmer, C. (2012, April 16). A sharp rise in retractions prompts calls for reform. *The New Times.* Retrieved from http://www.nytimes.com

$SAGE edge™

Want a better grade?

Get the tools you need to sharpen your study skills. Access practice quizzes, eFlashcards, video, and multimedia at **edge.sagepub.com/treadwell3e**

CHAPTER 14

Writing and Presenting Research

Language is not simply a reporting device for experience but a defining framework for it.

—Benjamin Whorf (1897–1941)

༺ ༻ ༺ ༻

Chapter Overview

It would be inappropriate to conclude a book on communication research without discussing how research findings are communicated. Research cannot contribute to our wider knowledge unless people know about it. In this chapter, we look at scholarly writing and presentation, reaching interest groups and the news media to whom your research may be relevant, and the implications of multimedia and hypermedia for presenting research results.

Chapter Objectives

This chapter will help you

- Identify the major publics for research writing and explain why each of them is important.

- Describe the format and style of a conventional scholarly research report.

- Explain why the format and style of scholarly reports are necessary when writing for a scholarly audience.

- Compare and contrast writing for interest groups with writing for news media.

- Discuss the advantages and disadvantages of the web as a publication medium for research.

- List the steps in bringing raw research data into scholarly publication format.

- Explain, with examples, how reporting research findings can have ethical implications.

Introduction

You have read all the relevant literature, reasoned through to hypotheses or research questions, identified an appropriate research strategy, and implemented it. Now comes your reward! You should have a keen sense of anticipation as your project data start to come in. Your data analyses will confirm or refute your hypotheses, lead you down new paths, or perhaps produce ambivalent results that lead you to a "definite maybe" conclusion and the beginnings of another round of research.

It would be nice if you could stop and relax at the point where you have new data, and a satisfactory analysis and interpretation of those data, but the model of research introduced in Chapter 1 tells us that there is one more step to take. After problem posing and problem solving, we have the important final step of peer persuasion. And, as we will discover in this chapter, we have audiences in addition to our peers to be persuaded—in particular, interest groups and the news media.

This book began with a basic notion that the purpose of research is to contribute to knowledge. There can be no contribution unless your research is presented so that others come to know about it and understand it.

This is understood increasingly in the scholarly community. For example, the American Association for the Advancement of Science (AAAS) argues that responsible conduct of research includes engagement and multidirectional communication with public audiences, including citizens, journalists, policy makers, and skeptics (Graveline, 2011). In a recent survey, 87% of American scientists agreed that scientists should take an active role in public policy debates about issues related to science and technology. Over 70% believed the public has either some or a lot of interest in their specialty areas (Rainie, Funk, & Anderson, 2015).

Conventionally, scholarly writing has been regarded as writing for fellow scholars in a formal style used by the scholarly publications introduced in Chapter 4. We need to loosen the boundaries of that definition for three reasons. First is the need to communicate with other important audiences such as the news media and interest groups. "People" research and media research are often relevant and interesting to news media audiences and interest groups, and increasingly there are expectations that researchers should be willing and able to present their work outside of formal scholarly channels. Second, and related, is the need to adapt scholarly writing to popular publication formats and styles and to master a variety of presentation skills.

The third reason is the web and its attributes that should have us rethinking how we report research. The web can host and make searchable large amounts of raw data; it can also host **multimedia** and **hypermedia** content. These attributes mean that branched, multimedia presentations of research now challenge the traditional linear, written accounts.

A mastery of writing basics remains essential if you are to help readers navigate your research successfully, but this chapter will be free of micro-level advice about subject-verb agreement, sentence fragments, parallel structure, and comma splices. Rather, it will invite you to think strategically about the many potential audiences for your research and how you will need to adapt your scholarly reporting to the needs of each audience.

Writing for Scholarly Publics: Voices in the Conversation

Here we consider writing for scholarly publication and the voices of scholarship, authors, and research participants.

Publication is the way scholars engage in formal conversation with one another. The best way to find out whether your research findings hold up is to publish them and in doing so invite others to examine your research, critique it, and perhaps replicate it to see if they get the same results.

The typical scholarly journal in communication is published quarterly. Preceding publication, there are review and editorial processes outlined later in this chapter. These editorial processes plus a quarterly publication schedule mean that scholarly articles may not see the light of day until months after their authors first submit their work for publication.

This rather glacial speed makes the publication-as-conversation metaphor less than compelling; nevertheless, scholarly journals are the arena for evidence-based and theoretically based arguments by members of the scholarly community. Every piece of new research is based on previously reported research and will be subject to critical evaluation and form the basis of further research.

The Voice of Scholarly Publication

Content aside, the overall "**voice**" of a scholarly publication comes from its combination of vocabulary, structure, use of quotes, use of passive or active style, and other details that all add up to knowing that you are reading *Journal A* and not *Journal B*. Two important components of a scholarly publication's voice are format and style.

One way to facilitate the understanding and discussion of published research papers is to **format** them in a way that allows for easy comparison. "Format" here refers to the standardized headings that most journal editors require for any paper they accept. The scholarly community basically expects that any research paper will have an informative title; an abstract that summarizes the paper; a literature review that provides a background to the study; a research question or questions; a method section; results, discussion, and conclusions; and a list of references. You will recall from Chapter 4 that it is this combination of features that distinguishes scholarly papers from popular and trade publications.

The precise nature and number of sections may vary, but overall this basic structure helps other scholars rapidly understand what a paper has to say and how it relates to other papers. Researchers working in the same area of interest and familiar with the relevant literature and the methods in use can skip directly to the results section to see how these published results compare with others. Researchers new to the field may want to spend more time reading the literature review and method sections to get ideas that will spark their own research.

One way to ensure that all relevant aspects of your research are appropriately reported is to follow the appropriate **style guide** such as APA (American Psychological Association), Chicago (University of Chicago Press), or MLA (Modern Language Association), introduced in Chapter 4. Such guides provide specific instructions for formatting scholarly papers, thereby ensuring before publication that all aspects of a scholarly paper are present.

In addition to specific citation guidelines, style guides provide guidelines on layout, typography, heading levels, and page formatting. For the beginning researcher, the specifics of a massive style guide can be daunting in their detail, but one way to appreciate their necessity is to imagine reading a scholarly paper that has no style. Imagine an author who is referenced by his last name on page 5, initials plus last name on page 7, and first name and last name on page 9. Imagine some citations placed arbitrarily at the bottom of pages and others at the end of a paper, plus headings in a variety of formats and fonts, and you can see why stylistic "rules of the road" are both necessary and useful. Style guides provide an essential checklist for planning your research before you do it, a check that you have reported everything a scholarly audience will want to read once you have completed your research and written it up, and a consistent style that will help readers.

Style guides are not necessarily the final word. For example, Chicago style allows for two style options depending on the type of work being published; some scholarly journals have their own **house styles**, which are variations on a basic style such as APA.

Help with the specifics of any style is also available in the form of journal editors and a variety of online sources. The specific style used by any given publication will typically be found in the publication and/or on the publication's website.

Exhibit 14.1 shows a generic outline of a scholarly report.

EXHIBIT 14.1 Scholarly and Professional Report Formats

Scholarly Report	Professional Report
Title Page	Title Page
	Table of Contents (if necessary)
Abstract	Executive Summary
Introduction	Introduction
Goals and Significance of Research	Body of Report
Literature Review	
Research Questions and/or Hypotheses	
Method	*The headings used in a professional report depend on the length, purpose, and intended audience of the report.*
Participants or Media Sampling	
Procedures Used	
Measures Used (if quantitative study)	*A professional report may or may not contain the sections expected for a scholarly report (left column).*
Results	
Discussion	
Significance of Results	
Limitations and Flaws of Study	
Conclusions	
Recommendations for Future Research	Recommendations
References	
Appendices	Appendices

Citations (see Chapter 4) must be accurate because scholarly readers, and especially newcomers to the field, will want to be able to access the same material you did. Accurate citations help other scholars locate material you have found useful. In addition, you give the authors whose work has helped you the courtesy of public recognition, and you avoid potential issues of plagiarism.

Review the resources listed at the end of this chapter for an overview of APA, Chicago, and MLA styles and how they differ. For example, Chicago and MLA citation styles use the authors' full first names; APA style uses initials only. Chicago and other styles also permit the use of footnotes, in which a number in the body of the paper refers to the publication details of a book or journal article placed at the bottom of the same page.

The Voice of the Author

Layered within the journal's voice and also shaping reader understandings is the voice of the author.

Scholarly writing inescapably has its own tactics aimed at convincing readers that the author has made a significant contribution to our knowledge of human communication. One such tactic is to distance the author as far as possible from the research by using a passive, abstract style. You will be familiar with this dispassionate "Three participants were interviewed" style from reading many scholarly reports.

While this style may be regarded as a laudable attempt to remove the author's personal influence from the research and to allow the research data and results to speak for themselves, the question arises of whose voice is being heard. The answer is "basically nobody's." The author is identified at the beginning of the article but then disappears and becomes an abstract entity for the remainder of the paper. The researcher is not actually recorded as doing anything. We have what Alcoff (2008) calls an "erasure of responsibility" (p. 486).

For some publications, a way to acknowledge the authors' presence and give them a voice is simply to shift to a first-person, active style of writing. So the "Three participants were interviewed" style becomes "I interviewed three participants." The paper becomes more interesting as a result because we now have a character—the author—on a quest to answer a question about human communication. The author's presence is now explicit; he or she has a voice and is taking responsibility for the research reported. There is a story to engage the reader. If the notion of the author as a character reporting on a research journey has you thinking that research writing itself can be analyzed using rhetorical, narrative, discourse, and dramatistic analyses and critical approaches, you are correct.

The Voices of Research Participants

For research of the ethnographic and participant observation variety, the voices of the research participants need to be heard. Research papers coming out of the researcher's interaction with participants raise a further problem of voice.

Clearly, the author as the coordinating force behind the paper must be heard, but so also should the participants. APA style suggests that our writing should capture the idea of our research participants as active in their own right. This means, for example, preferring the active "Three participants completed the survey" to the passive "The survey was administered to three participants."

The extent to which participant voices can be fully heard is limited by the conventional size of research papers, but it is also a function of the researcher's assumptions about the nature of research. If the researcher is using, say, a focus group to identify opinions about a consumer product, there will be a need to capture those opinions but not so much the people behind the opinions. Another researcher concerned with how a particular group of individuals uses language to define themselves and what they do will want to report examples of the language in the participants' own words, however incoherent, ungrammatical, and offensive those words may appear to others. A third researcher, doing **action research** aimed at improving the lives of the research participants, may publish the voices of an otherwise voiceless minority but elect to do so in professional language in a professional publication in order to communicate effectively with policy makers and those with influence in society.

The question of participant voices arises particularly with "people-intensive" research, such as ethnography, and "people-first" research, such as action research, and is a complex one (Alcoff, 2008). By electing to speak for others, "others" being typically a minority group in the case of action and some critical research, the researcher becomes a gatekeeper deciding what specific language—and whose—will or will not be heard as a result of publication. Thus the research itself can exemplify the very problem the research may have been intended to address—control of minority voices. One solution to the problem of enabling research participants to be heard is to facilitate their expression in their own nonscholarly media.

As communication research tells us, the source of a message can have a significant effect on how the message is understood. The audience for scholarly studies is likely to perceive the source of information about research participants as the scholar-author, rather than the participants who provided the research data. Consider, for example, politicians, policy experts, and news consumers reading stories told by members of a street community about their experiences. Now consider the same audiences reading about the same experiences but as told, interpreted, and backed up by data, by a scholarly researcher with full academic credentials. While the first set of stories may be seen as authentic by all groups, policy makers especially will more likely see the second set as more credible and relevant.

Voice becomes an important practical issue when considering how and to whom scholarly research results should be disseminated and how best to have the voices of research participants heard. It is a research topic in itself as critical theorists and other scholars turn their attention to scholarly and scientific writing.

In terms of communicating research results effectively, the problem of voice can be addressed by first considering potential audiences rather than the voices to be heard. In other words, identifying the potential audiences for your research and their needs and interests will tell you how best to present the voices of research participants and researchers.

Qualitative and Quantitative Writing

Research reports reflect the basic nature of the research—qualitative or quantitative—as well as the formal publication guidelines the author is following and the author's personal style. One advantage of quantitative studies is that the language of quantitative methods provides a convenient, commonly understood shorthand for authors and readers. Generally, the assumption is that one's peers doing research in the same field will know, for example, what regression, correlation, mode, and level of significance are and that these terms will not need explanation. The same is true with statistics and statistical tests. Reporting a chi-square value, with level of significance and degrees of freedom, can summarize an analysis and its results in about two lines.

Paradoxically, this is one reason that style guides for quantitative studies are so specific. By identifying precisely what needs to be reported and how, a great deal of detail can be eliminated. On the assumption that readers share a basic grounding in research methods and statistics, our friends from Chapters 6 and 7—t, chi-square, correlation coefficients, and the like—will need little or no explanation because the author's peers "speak the same language."

By contrast, reports of qualitative studies such as ethnography and participant observation need a greater level of explanation.

A quantitative researcher running a survey may report that her sample consisted of a randomly selected sample of 120 people of a particular type and then describe the survey questions, the statistical analyses, and the results. This will give readers with an understanding of survey research methods a clear idea of the research.

On the other hand, a researcher reporting an observational study will need to clarify his relationship to the participants and explain his selection of participants because the selection will have been based on judgment. In addition, he will need to describe and explain the type(s) of data collected, the methods of collection, and the analyses used to make sense of the data.

This means that qualitative research reports will differ from quantitative reports not only in the obvious way of being nonstatistical but also in requiring relatively greater explanation of sampling, methods, and analyses. Qualitative reports may also be more flexible with respect to their headings. Quantitative papers usually have explicit research questions or hypotheses that are answered or tested by statistical analyses of survey or experimental data. Qualitative papers written on the assumption that a new theory or insight will emerge out of the research as it progresses may report just a general line of inquiry rather than specific research questions or hypotheses.

Writing for Interest Groups and News Media: Answering the "So What?" Question

Relatively speaking, the readerships of *Text and Performance Quarterly, Communication Monographs, Feminist Media Studies, Discourse and Communication*, and the many other scholarly communication journals are small and specialized. Most people do not read such publications, and nonscholarly readers approaching such journals may well be intimidated by their level of detail and by terminology ranging from *multiple polynomial regression* to *phallocentric interpretive stances*.

This does not mean that nonscholarly audiences might not be interested in your research. To the contrary, interest groups and news media are two audiences that may be very interested, but only if your writing and presentations answer the "So what?" or "Why should we care?" questions. Research writing must therefore be made relevant to such audiences, and in order to be made relevant it must also be made comprehensible. This means making a break with scholarly style in favor of using language and formats that meet the needs of nonscholarly audiences.

Most nonscholarly audiences will not be aware of scholarly research unless made aware of it, so there may well be the additional task of disseminating the results of your research as appropriate.

That first "So what?" question that almost all audiences will have means that they will want to see research presented not in a scholarly style but in a "results first–why should I care?–details (maybe)" style. Every audience has its more specific needs with respect to type and level of vocabulary and channels of communication. The needs of interest groups and the news media are discussed more specifically below.

Interest Groups

Communication research findings have relevance to corporations, nonprofit organizations, and government agencies generally and to sectors such as advertising, technology, education, and health care specifically. For example, a study giving new insights on how advertising can influence the food preferences of children may interest parents, nutrition advocates, the food industry, the advertising industry, and regulatory agencies.

Such entities will be interested in research from a policy perspective; that is, they may want to promote, oppose, or change organizational policy or legislation based on research findings. They will therefore be interested in getting research details, but only those details that are relevant. Typically, their primary interest will be in research results and their implications—perhaps in some detail—but not in, for example, detailed descriptions of research method(s).

We will refer to the reports written for such interest groups as **professional reports** because typically they are written for professionals working in a particular sector. You may need to write research you have done or summarize the research of others in the form of a professional report for a client or an employer.

Professional reports at their most basic level have a structure of introduction–body–conclusion. The introduction summarizes the research and its relevance. The body summarizes the research method(s) and results. The conclusion summarizes the relevance of the results and proposes any action that might be required, based on the research findings. Typically, there will be no literature review and no list of scholarly references. The focus of the report is on helping readers understand the results and their relevance and the practical implications rather than the theoretical implications.

Because interest group members have a vested interest in the research topic as well as some knowledge of it, the language of a professional report is likely to be somewhere between formal, scholarly language and the lay language of most news media—discussed below.

Interest groups will not automatically be aware of relevant research projects, so there may be an additional responsibility of ensuring that relevant reports are distributed to them, as appropriate. Where the research has been conducted specifically for an interest group, that group will of course receive an appropriate report. Otherwise, it is typical for research institutions to develop mailing lists of groups that are likely to be interested in their reports, and of course to post their research reports in full and summary forms to their websites.

An example you will be familiar with by now is the Pew Research Center Internet, Science & Tech project at www.pewinternet.org. You will see at this site that Pew makes available raw data, reports, presentations, interactive graphics, information on its researchers, and the opportunity to subscribe to newsletters and new report alerts.

Exhibit 14.1 shows the basic outline of a professional report. Because many of the components of a scholarly report are not required or expected in a professional report, the author has a much greater level of flexibility in what does and does not get reported.

News Media

News media editors look for stories that are relevant to their readers, viewers, or listeners. A research story must clearly answer the "So what?" question if a news editor is to be interested in it. In terms of communication research, relevant stories might range from cross-cultural communication to technology impact. For example, the results of a study in cross-cultural communication might translate into a story on how to date someone from another culture, or the results of a study on families watching television might translate into a story on how to organize a family TV-viewing night.

As news veterans tell it, media audiences tune into only one station—WIIFM ("What's In It For Me?")—a question that basically asks "So what?" Relevance is one of several **news determinants** or aspects of a story that make it newsworthy, and is one of the most important determinants. Other determinants include timeliness—the research findings are newsworthy just by virtue of being new or topical; proximity—the research or the researcher is local and known to local readers and viewers; and human interest—somewhere in all those data there is a story about "real people" to be told.

Adapting scholarly research reports to the needs of news media implies two strategic tasks—answering the WIIFM question and writing to news media style, be it news or feature, for print, broadcast, or web media.

In essence, news writing is characterized by a "get-to-the-point" style. Feature writing is characterized by rich description that maintains reader interest. Broadcast writing has a spoken, conversational style. As discussed below, web writing uses **hyperlinks** and a layout that makes it clear how website visitors can easily navigate a site. The hyperlinks embedded in each page allow visitors to jump to more detail on a topic if they need it.

Because of the diversity of news media, researchers face the prospect of translating scholarly reports into print, radio, television, websites, and podcast formats, for example, as well as adapting the content for each medium to meet the interests and reading levels of each news audience. This challenge can be met in a variety of ways. For example, science, technology, or psychology writers for magazines with a highly educated readership may prefer to get the original scholarly report and to interview the author(s) so that they can do their own "translation" to meet their readers' needs. At the other extreme, a busy news editor may prefer a simple, brief, newsworthy news release that can be published without further rewriting.

Generally, you can facilitate the work of news editors by

- Providing content that meets their standards for news and relevance to their audiences.
- Providing content in the language of their news audience(s) and in format(s) that minimize the time and effort required to edit scholarly content into news content.
- Proactively ensuring that the research news reaches them.

Writing for the news media and the web is, of course, the subject of many books and many courses in their own right.

In summary, writing for interest groups, news media, and other nonscholarly audiences means

- Writing to make research comprehensible.
- Writing to make research relevant.
- Disseminating research results to relevant audiences.

Editorial Processes

As a research writer, you become a gatekeeper, deciding what aspects of your research will appear or not appear in the final draft of your research report. Getting your report published requires that you meet the standards of other gatekeepers who are responsible for deciding whether or not to publish your content. These gatekeepers are the editors of scholarly journals and of the news media.

For scholarly journals, the **editorial process** begins with you submitting your final research report to a journal's editor. Prior to this, you have, of course, identified the journals most likely to be interested in publishing your research.

These journals will be those that have the same content interest (for example, political communication) plus the same methodological interest (for example, critical, quantitative, or applied) that you do. In all likelihood, they will be the journals that provided the most relevant articles when you were writing your literature review. Each journal will have guidelines for submission on its website or in each issue. These guidelines will cover content, specific style issues, and, often, length. If you decide that your research and the journal's interests match, you submit the final draft of your research report to the journal's editor. The journal's editorial staff has a basic responsibility to assess whether your report meets scholarly standards and adds to our understanding of human communication. If it does not, it is unlikely to be published. Most major journals have a high rejection rate; submissions are more likely to be rejected than accepted.

Rejection or acceptance is not, however, an arbitrary decision by the editor. The final decision is based on **peer review**. Peer review means that the journal's editor solicits the opinions of other scholars working in the same field to ensure that each submitted article meets scholarly standards and makes a contribution to its field. That established, the editor then ensures that the article is written to the journal's style, schedules the article for publication, and oversees production of the journal.

You can expect peer review to be rigorous. Reviewers will want to see that your research is exploring areas not previously explored, or that it is revisiting previously published research from a new perspective. They will want to see that there is a match between your theories, the data you collect, and the method(s) used to collect and analyze your data.

Reviewers may disagree, at which point the journal editor will make some final decisions. Even if the decision is to accept your paper for publication, there will inevitably be some rewriting and/or reworking of data to meet the requirements of reviewers. The research project itself plus the editorial process explain the length of time to bring any research to publication. Many journals will tell you how long the publication process took for each article; they print key dates such as first submission, revision, second revision, and so on, for the articles they publish.

Another type of gatekeeper with control over getting your research results to a wider audience is the news media editors who will basically assess your research on its relevance to their reading, listening, or viewing audiences rather than on its scholarly merits. Acceptance here depends not on a panel of reviewers but on an editor's determination that your research meets the criteria for news as the editor sees it. Fundamental to getting news coverage is a clear answer to the WIIFM question. As noted above, news editors are always looking for content that has clear news determinants such as timeliness and relevance and, ideally, formatting and style that meets the needs of the print medium, be it broadcast, print, or web.

The Interplay of Style and Accuracy

Even when rigorously following the dictates of a style manual, every author decides what information will be reported, or not, and what specific words will describe a method, sample, result, or conclusion.

In an often-cited example of rhetorical analysis of science writing, Gusfield (1976) points out that language for the scientist is supposed to be a "windowpane"—a panel of clear glass through which the external world can be seen clearly and without distortion.

Scholarly writers strive for this goal in two very different ways.

At one extreme, authors may remove themselves from the narrative by writing passively in the third person and avoiding personal commentary as far as possible so that the research methods and data speak for themselves.

At the other extreme, researchers may use what Van Maanen (1988) calls "impressionist writing," which uses a literary style to attract and engage the reader, and may well sacrifice objectivity in the interests of reader understanding. One such example is "A Small-Town Cop," in which organizational scholar and consultant Michael Pacanowsky (1983) experiments with fiction style to describe a police officer's response to his partner being shot.

Between these two approaches is a style in which the researcher documents her own biases, impressions, and opinions, thus permitting readers to identify the author's presence and allow for it in making their own interpretations of the reported research.

No approach can be regarded as totally neutral, however. And given that research reporting is always an act of interpretation, it is questionable whether Gusfield's clear glass windowpane can ever exist. Regardless of overall style, writers wittingly or unwittingly shape readers' interpretations of research simply by choice of words. For example, we discussed in Chapter 11 how terms such as *informant, participant,* or *subject* may shape both the researcher's and readers' attitudes toward participants in the research.

Herbers (2006), a biologist who studies "slavemaking ants," discusses how she became uneasy with slavery as a metaphor for insect behavior and whether appropriating the terminology of slavery might not have the effect of perpetuating racism. She concluded that the term *slavery* was damaging and not especially accurate, and found a more accurate metaphor (*pirate*) for the ant behaviors she was studying. She warns against delusions of objectivity in science writing and argues that scientists have a responsibility for the rhetorical impact of their writing.

APA guidelines for reducing bias in research reporting include mentioning people's differences only when this relevant to the research; for example, there is no need to identify peoples' marital status, sexual orientation, disabilities, race, or ethnicity unless any of these are relevant to the study. A second guideline is being sensitive to labels and calling research participants what they prefer to be called—recognizing that this may change over time. A third is writing in a way that presents research participants as active rather than passive individuals (APA, 2015).

A problem with disseminating the results of scholarly research is that summary reports, news media stories, and even detailed professional reports lose the detail and terminology that may have a specific meaning for scholars. In other words, as scholarly research findings become increasingly comprehensible to a lay public, they also become increasingly generalized to the point of losing what may be important detail to a scholar.

The question arises of whether, as conscientious writers, we can achieve the goal of giving all our potential readers an unbiased, comprehensible reporting of our research. Happily there are some answers to this question.

First, systematic reporting of research questions, literature review, method, and sampling decisions will help scholarly readers decide whether our results and conclusions are unbiased and defensible.

Second, the peer review process helps ensure that published papers meet scholarly standards and do not make unsubstantiated claims.

Third, we can aim not for the impossible goal of eliminating all our biases but for the achievable goal of making any biases explicit so that readers will have as full an understanding of our research as possible.

Fourth, by working with news editors, journalists, and other professional writers we can maximize the chances that nonscholarly versions of our research will be written and presented both comprehensibly and accurately.

Presenting for Scholarly Publics: Conferences and Panels

Published research reports are not the only forum where researchers engage in conversation. A second major forum is academic conferences. National associations such as the National Communication Association (www.natcom.org), Canadian Communication Association (www.acc-cca.ca), and International Communication Association (www.icahdq.org) and many regional associations hold annual conferences.

Research presentations at such conferences typically take two forms— **panel presentations** and **poster papers**.

A panel consists of six or so scholars with shared interests presenting the results of their research. Typically, each panelist presents for 10 or 15 minutes, and there is additional time for discussion among panelists and with audience members at the end of the presentations. The papers presented are often "works in progress." The feedback that presenters receive on their papers gives them ideas for improving their research or revising their papers before submitting them for publication.

Conference organizers may request a full scholarly paper for review and acceptance (or rejection) before the conference, but the presentation time of 15 minutes or so for accepted papers means that the authors will present only the key points of their research. In most cases the full paper will be available for interested readers—often via a conference website—so the value of a panel is in the direct discussion with the author.

The strategy needed for both panel and solo presentations is to coordinate each component of the presentation so that the speaker and any discussions, handouts, or slides complement one another rather than distract. For example, providing the audience with a handout during your presentation means that you should give them time to read it, which means pausing your presentation and not projecting slides while they do so. Conversely if the handout can be read after your presentation, provide it at the end of your presentation so your audience's attention does not shift from you to your handout.

In poster sessions, presenters are provided with a display panel upon which to post a summary of their research. There is no formal presentation, but anyone interested in a topic can meet researchers alongside their poster papers and discuss the research informally. This gives a greater opportunity for discussion with the authors and gives the authors more feedback from a self-selected group of people who are specifically interested in their research. Poster papers need summary points only because the author can provide the details personally and/or provide a full research paper.

An FYI on PPT

The uncritical acceptance of PowerPoint as a presentation device was probably marked by its arrival as a verb, as in "I'll PowerPoint it." PowerPoint, or more generically **slideware**—that ubiquitous presentation software in classrooms, meetings, and academic conferences—is certainly one of the methods you may choose to present your research findings, but proceed with care.

PowerPoint has been criticized for its false simplicity, its rigid "bullet point" hierarchy, and the line-by-line logic it imposes on an audience (Tufte, 2006). Contemplate for a moment the power of metaphor and whether a "bullet" metaphor really captures the relationship you want to have with your audience. For a sense of how slideware can destroy an otherwise eloquent and moving presentation, check out the PowerPoint Gettysburg Address cited below under "Recommended Web Resources."

You can easily identify what constitutes a good slide presentation by thinking of all the bad ones you have endured. How about slides presented so fast you couldn't read them? Each slide packed with illegible text? Slides that required so much attention that you couldn't follow what the speaker was saying? How about handouts given out in the middle of a presentation so that you did not know whether to listen to the speaker, read the handout, or look at the presentation?

Slides clearly can have a place in helping your audience understand the basics of your presentation. The most productive mental shift with respect to such presentations is to stop thinking "slide presentation" and start thinking "slide-supported presentation." First, consider what presentation methods will most effectively help your audience understand your message—a full copy of your paper, a one-page summary of your paper, audio or video clips, a slide presentation, hard copies of your slide presentation, or posting to a website individuals can visit in their own time? Then, knowing your audience demographics, interests, and size; the venue; and available time, you can decide which combination of methods will most effectively maintain your audience members' interest and leave them with the information they need.

Design every slide to be rapidly understood by the audience. Generally, use a plain background with light type on a dark background or dark type on a light background. "Think Six": about six words per line, six lines per slide. Use large type, simple graphics, and simplify, simplify, simplify. Slides should appear in a logical sequence with appropriate timing. Slides have a role in your presentation; they are not the presentation.

Obviously, the above guidelines can be bent depending on audience, venue, and topic, but the one rule that should never be broken is to rehearse your presentation. Go to the back of the room and make sure that each slide is legible. Run through your presentation with a friend to get feedback and a check on timing before the real event.

Writing and Presenting With the Web

Traditional print media limit the type and the amount of research information we can present and influence how our research is understood. Consider the student discussions documented at the beginning of Chapter 1. You have a less-than-full understanding of these discussions simply by virtue of a decision to record them as print-media transcripts. There are no audio or video files—either or both of which would have further helped your understanding of these conversations.

The web, by contrast, allows the publication and archiving of original visual and audio content that cannot be presented via traditional print media. It has the capacity to host large amounts of raw data, multimedia content, and hyperlinks that link documents to other documents. It also has search capabilities that make it easy to search any such content.

Because the web is accessible to most scholars, it increases the possibilities for collaborative research and data analysis. Researchers can post original video, interviews, or numeric data on the web with the implicit or explicit invitation to other researchers to conduct their own analyses of the same data.

The potential to present "everything" does not mean that you should do so, which raises the questions of what specifically to present and how. Traditional print formats such as journal articles in effect force researchers into a somewhat standardized, print-oriented presentation format, with perhaps some multimedia presentations being an option for conferences and seminars. Traditional research papers are linear; they move logically from an initial research question to a method description and then to results and conclusions. This structure exists because print media impose a linear structure and because scholarly conventions are to write and to read beginning with a research question followed by a method description and then results—whether or not this captures what actually happened in the research process.

The web, on the other hand, offers almost unlimited potential for customizing research presentations and, importantly, the opportunity for nonlinear, branched reporting. One can visualize, for example, a standard scholarly research report linking on one hand to the original raw data and on the other to a one-paragraph news summary.

Hyperlinks allow the reader to branch to raw data such as a video interview or to numeric data that can be opened up in public domain statistical software. However, because hyperlinks connect to other hyperlinks beyond the control of the researcher, the researcher can lose the ability to define the boundaries of a study. The question then becomes how to define the nature of hyperlinks for the reader—now the reader/viewer. Hyperlinks, as such, provide no information about what reader/viewer experience they will provide. Should a link be understood, for example, "Visit this link for additional information that is not essential but is available if you want it"? or "Here is essential information that is too detailed to fit into a standard report format"? or even "Not that relevant to the research, but thought you might find this amusing"?

The question is part of a bigger question of how best to guide the reader/viewer through your research to the results and conclusions you arrived at and to establish your version of events as an authoritative one. This becomes an increasingly important question on the web, where your readers/viewers have the ability to build their own versions of your research through cut-and-paste, annotation, highlighting, linking your research to other related research, and the like. What, then, is the status of your research report and the author (you) behind it?

We can detect perhaps three different author roles in the 21st century. First is the traditional "absent author." "Absent author" reports are written in the passive, third-person voice. The author apparently did nothing and the logic of the research is presumed to speak for itself. Second is the "involved author," where the writing is active and first-person and the author is an active participant in the research. The web and in particular hypermedia suggest a third type of research author, and that is the "expert tour-guide author." The expert tour-guide author web-publishes raw data we might want to explore in our own ways, but also chooses to emphasize particular aspects of it and ways of looking at it by providing a conventional research report plus web-based ancillary resources and links.

By analogy, tour guides showing visitors a city, historic site, or wildlife park that is foreign to them will point out the overall characteristics but then select a few highlights and take the visitors to specific locations that are best for viewing each highlight. Visitors might also be given a few hours to explore the site on their own and at their own pace. They recognize the many ways a location might be understood, but defer to the guide's expertise in guiding and translating for them.

Metaphorically, the tour-guide author can readily arrange tours for many different parties, such as scholars, interest groups, and the news media. However, tour-guide authorship can make research writing and presentation even more daunting because the web and hyperlinks allow many different interpretations of the raw data. Researchers therefore must use compelling evidence, analyses, and logic to establish their "tours" and interpretations as authoritative.

EXHIBIT 14.2 **Summary Guidelines for Scholarly, News, and Web Formats**

Scholarly Paper	Abstract, literature review with references, rationale, research questions and/or hypotheses, description of method(s), sampling, measures used, results, conclusions, discussion, list of references—accurately cited. Follow a specific scholarly or journal style.
Panel Presentation	Brief notes on an index card or one page if necessary. Key points only.
Poster Paper	Title, summary of research questions/hypotheses, method(s), and results. Summary graphic(s) as necessary. Large type on poster-size paper so people can read the poster at a distance.
Slides	Plain background. Light type on dark background or dark type on light background. "Think Six": no more than six words per line; six lines per slide. Large type. Simple graphics. Simplify. Simplify. Simplify. Key points only. Use a handout for detail.
Professional Report	Executive summary; introduction/background; sections and headings in body of report, determined by purpose of report and audience; conclusions; recommendations; supplementary material.
Talking Points for News Interview or News Media Handout	One page summary sheet. Key points include objective of research, method (brief), results, conclusions/so what?
News Stories	Answer *who, what, when, where,* and *how* questions.
	Base the story on news determinants such as relevance, proximity, and timeliness.
	"Get-to-the-point" writing for hard news.
	Human interest emphasis for feature.
	Conversational/speech style for broadcast.
	Language appropriate to the news audience.
"Tweet it!"	In 140 characters or less, what have I discovered, and why is it important?
Web Presentation	Needs underlying logical structure and periodic review to ensure hyperlinks are active and linked to current sites. Need to archive content if sites or documents for a specific date are to be retained and made available. Ensure navigational aids direct visitors forward, back, and to home page easily. Include author contact information and date of postings.

Some Communication Guidelines

In Chapters 8 through 13, we outlined a variety of approaches to researching human communication. The researchers behind such approaches differ on their assumptions about human communication and how best to understand it but would agree on the need to disseminate the results of their research as widely as possible and have the research understood as clearly as possible.

They would recognize at the very least the need to write a paper for publication in a scholarly journal and to present their results at an academic conference. They should also anticipate questions from academic colleagues, funding agencies, and the news media. On their campuses, the offices of student affairs and academic affairs might be interested to know if some research has implications for the way student study sessions are organized or how classes are taught or scheduled. The campus public relations office will want a summary of the research in order to write news releases, and the alumni office may be interested in doing feature stories relevant to alumni.

Some of our researchers are no doubt recalling the communication disasters they have experienced—the colleague whose presentation consisted of reading a 20-page paper for 35 minutes. "Why," they wondered, "could he not have just given us copies of the paper?" Then there is the 30-slide presentation, each slide packed with text, that sent half the audience to sleep. As people think about this, they are getting a renewed sense of how students feel at times. Some might wonder why their most recent interview with a local television reporter did not get on air and conclude that their explanation of "variance attributable to exogenous variables" should have been much shorter, jargon-free, and to the point.

Collectively, they would agree that guidelines such as shown in Exhibit 14.2 would be a good idea. The guidelines summarize some of the formats you might consider in addition to scholarly papers, and some of their basic requirements. You can use the guidelines as a basic checklist for your own writing and presentations, always referring to specific style guides such as APA, Chicago, and MLA for the details of scholarly writing.

Ethics Panel: Balancing Between Scholarly and Popular Writing

Accounts of communication research become less specific and more general as they "move" from the original scholarly journals to popular media. They may also get embellished with metaphors, analogies, and commentaries as journalists try to interpret and explain the original research to lay audiences.

Questions

Based on your reading of this chapter

- To what extent could publishing a scholarly research paper limit the extent to which all potentially interested publics will know about the research?

- To what extent is writing a news release or professional report on a research project an ethical decision about disseminating the results of your research?

- What responsibility do journalists have to cite the original research papers they are reporting on so that interested readers and viewers can find them?

- What responsibility do researchers have for what journalists write when they interpret and report on scholarly research papers?

CHAPTER SUMMARY

- Scholarly research papers present the theory behind the research, the research method(s), sampling, results, and conclusions.
- Style guides such as APA, Chicago, and MLA give guidance on how to report scholarly research.
- The exact style and format of your research paper will be determined by the scholarly association or journal you are writing for.
- Interest groups and news media will be interested in your research only if it is timely and relevant.
- You can make your research relevant to news media and their audiences by writing in the appropriate news format and style.
- Research reports written for interest groups emphasize results, conclusions, and relevance to the reader.
- Web-based research presentations may be branched rather than linear and demand design and web-navigation skills in addition to writing skills.

KEY TERMS

action research

editorial process

format

house styles

hyperlinks

hypermedia

multimedia

news determinants

panel presentations

peer review

poster papers

professional reports

style guide

voice

APPLICATION EXERCISES

Exercise 1. Readability

Your word processing software should have an option to check the readability of your writing. Typically, this check will provide a number of indirect measures of readability such as the average number of sentences per paragraph, words per sentence, characters per word, and percentage of passive sentences. You may also be able to get specific measures of readability such as the Flesch Reading Ease score and the Flesch–Kincaid Grade Level score.

Type or import sample paragraphs from a scholarly journal such as *Communication Monographs* into your word processing software and obtain readability statistics, especially the Flesch–Kincaid Grade Level score. This latter statistic gives you the grade level of readers capable of reading the content. Repeat this exercise for an extract of science writing from *The New York Times* and from your local newspaper.

As a point of reference, 2014 U.S. Census data indicate that approximately 12% of U.S. citizens over the age of 25 have an advanced academic degree; 32% have a bachelor's degree; and 88% are high school graduates (U.S. Census Bureau, 2015). Based on the readability scores you obtained, what percentage of the population is likely to be able to successfully read each of the articles you sampled?

What information is lost as you compare a scholarly article with a local newspaper account of scholarly research?

Exercise 2. Slideware Presentation

Select two articles from a scholarly journal—one qualitative, one quantitative. Using slideware such as Microsoft PowerPoint or Apple Keynote, design no more than six summary presentation slides for each article. Which type of article can be most easily summarized using slideware? Why?

Exercise 3. Writing Styles

Compare the report of a conventional survey or experimental study from a scholarly journal with a narrative report such as Pacanowsky's "A Small-Town Cop" (1983). What differences do you find between the two reports with respect to

- Your ability to relate to the individuals in each study?
- The level of insight each study provides you?
- The ease with which policy makers could make policy decisions based on each study?

Exercise 4. Assessing Researchers' Community Engagement

A 2015 survey of members of the AAAS (Rainie et al., 2015) found that about 40% of them often or occasionally do at least two of four activities—talk with nonexperts, talk with the media, use social media, or blog. Nearly half engage in one of these four activities either often or occasionally. These activities suggest that that researchers need to move—and are moving—beyond traditional scholarly publishing if they are to engage with the community at large.

You can use these four activities as a crude measure of community engagement by scholarly authors.

Use your online research skills to identify communication scholars in your area(s) of interest and research their professional communication activities as far as possible. Assign each a score between 0 (*you find no evidence of the above four activities*) and 4 (*you find evidence for all four of the activities*). How do you rate these scholars for community engagement? What other measures of community engagement can you think of?

RECOMMENDED READING

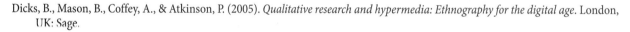

Dicks, B., Mason, B., Coffey, A., & Atkinson, P. (2005). *Qualitative research and hypermedia: Ethnography for the digital age.* London, UK: Sage.

Gusfield, J. (1976). The literary rhetoric of science: Comedy and pathos in drinking driver research. *American Sociological Review, 41*(1), 16–34.

A classic analysis of scientific writing as a persuasive literary form.

Lipson, C. (2011). *Cite right: A quick guide to citation styles—MLA, APA, Chicago, the sciences, professions, and more* (2nd ed.) Chicago, IL: University of Chicago Press.

Important citation styles, all in one book.

RECOMMENDED WEB RESOURCES

APA's Online APA Style Tutorial . . . . www.apastyle.org/learn

The home page for APA style.

Chicago-Style Citation Quick Guide . . . . www.chicagomanualofstyle.org/tools_citationguide.html

The home page for Chicago style.

Citation Machine* . . . . http://citationmachine.net

Easybib* . . . . www.easybib.com

EndNote* . . . . www.endnote.com

MLA Handbook Site . . . . www.mlahandbook.org/fragment/public_index

The home page for MLA style.

Peter Norvig's Gettysburg PowerPoint Presentation . . . . http://norvig.com/Gettysburg

An example of what not to do with a slide presentation.

Refworks* . . . . www.refworks.com

Helps manage, store, and share information, as well as generate citations and bibliographies.

Web Journal of Mass Communication Research . . . . www.scripps.ohiou.edu/wjmcr/policy.htm

This is a web-published "e-journal," not a traditional print journal. Read the brief home page to see the procedures for manuscript submission and review. Note the "footnotes" style. This journal does not use the more conventional APA style.

*The above sites provide online help or software for formatting scholarly citations. They are listed without criticism or endorsement, and no criticism of similar websites not listed is intended or implied.

REFERENCES

Alcoff, L. (2008). The problem of speaking for others. In A. M. Jaggar (Ed.), *Just methods: An interdisciplinary feminist reader* (pp. 484–494). Boulder, CO: Paradigm Publishers.

American Psychological Association. (2015). The basics of APA style. Retrieved from http://www.apastyle.org/learn/tutorials/basics-tutorial.aspx

Evered, R., & Reis, M. (1981). Alternative perspectives in the organizational sciences: "Inquiry from the inside" and "Inquiry from the outside." *Academy of Management Review, 6*(3), 385–396. DOI: 10.5465/AMR.1981.4285776

Graveline, D. (2011). Making public communication part of research responsibility: What scientists can and should do. *Professional Ethics Report, 24*(2), 1–3. Washington, DC: American Association for the Advancement of Science.

Gusfield, J. (1976). The literary rhetoric of science: Comedy and pathos in drinking driver research. *American Sociological Review, 41*(1), 16–34.

Herbers, J. M. (2006, March 24). The loaded language of science. The Chronicle Review, *The Chronicle of Higher Education*, p. B5.

Pacanowsky, M. (1983). A small-town cop: Communication in, out, and about a crisis. In L. Putnam & M. Pacanowsky (Eds.), *Communication and organizations: An interpretive approach* (pp. 261–282). Beverly Hills, CA: Sage.

Rainie, L., Funk, C., & Anderson, M. (2015, February 15). How scientists engage the public. Pew Research Center Internet, Science & Tech Project. Retrieved from http://www.pewinternet.org/2015/02/15/how-scientists-engage-public/

Tufte, E, R, (2006). *The cognitive style of PowerPoint: Pitching out corrupts within* (2nd ed.). Cheshire, CA: Graphics Press.

U.S. Census Bureau. (2010). *Educational attainment by selected characteristic: 2010*. Retrieved from http://www.census.gov/compendia/statab/cats/education.html

U.S. Census Bureau. (2015, January 20). *Educational attainment in the United States: 2014*. Retrieved from www.census.gov

Van Maanen, J. (1988). *Tales of the field: On writing ethnography*. Chicago, IL: University of Chicago Press.

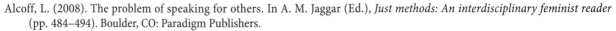

Want a better grade?
Get the tools you need to sharpen your study skills. Access practice quizzes, eFlashcards, video, and multimedia at **edge.sagepub.com/treadwell3e**

Glossary

A

Abduction. Reasoning from an observed effect to possible causes.

Act. In Burke's **dramatistic analysis**, the behavior that is taking place.

Action research. Research engaging with groups or communities specifically to solve problems.

Acts. In Hymes's ethnography of communication, the language and behaviors that convey meaning to the participants—for example, an instructor demonstrating a specific research method.

Address-based sampling (ABS). Survey sampling using address data provided by the U.S. Postal Service.

Adjacency pairs. In conversation analysis, units of speech that occur together and one of the basic units of conversation analysis—for example, question/answer.

Affiliative responses. In conversation analysis, responses to a question or statement that maintain a social link with the speaker. See also **disaffiliative responses**.

Agency. In Burke's **dramatistic analysis**, the means by which an act takes place.

Agent. In Burke's **dramatistic analysis**, the individual(s) taking the action.

Analytic notes. Notes an ethnographer writes as a way to make sense of or interpret the raw data or **descriptive notes**.

Anomalous data. Data that appear suspicious or not anticipated by a researcher.

Anonymity. A way of protecting research participants in that the data collected from them does not identify them in any way. Typically, anonymity is ensured by instructing **respondents** not to put their names on any information they provide.

ANOVA. Analysis of variance. A comparison of the variance within groups with the variance among groups. See also **MANOVA**.

APA. American Psychological Association. APA is the standard style for many communication scholars when they reference other people's work. APA style uses an "author (date)" style in the body of the paper and places the full citation, alphabetized by author, at the end of the paper. APA is also relevant in terms of the American Psychological Association Ethical Principles of Psychologists and Code of Conduct.

Appeals. The bases of persuasion—for example, sex appeal and fear appeal in advertising.

Aristotelian analysis. Analysis of communication content for its persuasive effects, using Aristotle's concepts of rhetoric.

Asynchronous. Occurring at different times or uncoordinated—for example, members of a social media site contributing individually to it, in their own time. See also **synchronous**.

Attrition. The loss of participants from a study.

Authority. A way of knowing based on knowledge from a credible or respected source of information.

Autonomy. A **Belmont Report** principle that research participants should be treated with respect.

Avatar. A graphical representation of a computer user, such as an icon or a three-dimensional character.

B

Bell curve. See **normal curve**.

Belmont Report. A report by the National Commission for the Protection of Human Subjects of Biomedical and Behavioral Research. It outlines three basic ethical principles of **autonomy**, **beneficence**, and **justice** covering research with human subjects.

Beneficence. A **Belmont Report** principle that human subjects research should maximize possible benefits and minimize possible harm to participants.

Between-subjects design. An experimental design in which subjects are exposed to only one experimental condition. See also **within-subjects design.**

Bibliographic. Pertaining to books and journals.

Bi-modal distribution. Distribution of data that shows two values occurring with equal frequency.

Bi-variate. Pertaining to two variables, as in **bi-variate analysis** or **bi-variate statistics**.

Boolean operators. Terms such as AND, OR, and NOT that allow one to fine-tune a database search.

Break-off rate. The proportion of respondents who fail to complete a survey once it is started.

C

CAQDAS. Computer-assisted qualitative data analysis software.

Categorical data. Data that fit into distinct categories such as zip code or academic major.

Categorical imperative. Philosopher Immanuel Kant's concept that a behavior is valid if one is willing to see it applied as a universal rule.

Categorial units. Content analysis units defined by having something in common or belonging to a researcher-defined class—for example, teachers, a specific cartoon character, or an event such as drinking coffee.

Categorization. The process of identifying an item of data as belonging to a category predetermined by the researcher or generated from the information provided by informants.

Causal relationship. A relationship between variables in which changes in one variable demonstrably result in changes in another.

Census. A study of every member of a population.

Central limit theorem. States, in summary, that the distribution of the average or sum of a large number of samples of a variable will be approximately normal, regardless of the underlying distribution.

Chicago. In the context of research reporting, refers to *The Chicago Manual of Style.*

Chi-square (χ^2). A statistical test for determining whether two groups differ significantly in their distribution of scores on the same variable.

Citations. The publication details of books, journal articles, or websites.

Closed-ended research questions. Questions which ask about the direction of the relationship between variables.

Code/coding. The process of transforming data into a simplified form, usually for computer processing.

Coding scheme. A systematic way of classifying or categorizing units of analysis.

Cohort. A group of people defined most typically by having an event in common.

Common Rule. The Federal Policy for the Protection of Human Subjects. Shared standards adopted by federal agencies for the protection of human research subjects.

Communicative act. In Hymes's ethnography of communication, the smaller units of speech within a speech event—for example, asking a question or telling a joke.

Communicative style. In Hymes's ethnography of communication, the speech style that is characteristic of someone—for example, formal or informal.

Conative function. One of Jakobson's semiotic functions. Establishes the sender's expectations of the receiver or what the receiver is expected to do as a result of receiving the message.

Concurrent validity. Concurrent validity is demonstrated when a measure correlates highly with other measures designed to measure the same construct.

Confederates. Participants in a study who have been briefed by the researcher to behave in a particular way.

Confidence interval. A range of values estimated from a **sample**, within which a value for a **population** is estimated to fall.

Confidence level. The calculated probability of a value being true. Typically, for communication research, a confidence level of 95 is used, meaning that a reported value is estimated to occur 95 times out of 100 if a population is repeatedly sampled.

Confidentiality. The assurance given to research participants that the researcher will not release any information that will identify them. The researcher can link information that participants provide to the identity of the person providing it.

Construct. Abstract idea or concept.

Construct validity. Construct validity occurs when the measures of one concept or construct agree with the measures of other related concepts.

Content analysis. Traditionally, a quantitative, systematic technique for describing the manifest content of communications.

Content validity: face, expert, or panel. The extent to which a measure fully represents a given concept, typically as judged by a panel of experts. See also **face validity**, **expert validity**, and **panel validity**.

Contingency table. A table that shows how scores for two or more variables are related—for example, gender by income. See also **cross-tabs**.

Continuous data. Data with incremental values between the minimum and maximum. For example, age can have values of years, months, weeks, days, hours, minutes, or seconds.

Contrast questions. Questions that ask respondents to explain the difference between two or more things or concepts.

Control. In experimental design, *control* refers to an experimental group that does not receive any experimental treatment in order to provide a baseline for measuring changes that might occur in other groups. As a goal of research, *control* refers to gaining information about human behavior in order to be able to predict and control it.

Control group. Experimental group not exposed to any experimental variable.

Convenience sampling. Sampling based on convenience to the researcher.

Convergent validity. Occurs where there is a demonstrable agreement between the concept or construct you are trying to measure and other related concepts.

Conversation analysis. A research approach that analyzes the rules governing conversational interactions.

Correlation. A statistical procedure for measuring the strength of association between two or more variables. More generally, the degree to which variables are related. See also **part correlation**, **partial correlation**, and **semipartial correlation**.

Correlation coefficients. Express the strength of the relationship between two variables, and range between -1.0 and $+1.0$ in value.

Covariance/covariation. A relationship between variables such that the values of one variable change as the values of another variable change.

Criterion validity. Criterion validity is demonstrated when a test or measure correlates highly with some tangible, external criterion.

Criterion variable. The variable whose value is predicted by the value of **predictor variables** in a **regression** analysis. See also **outcome variable**.

Critical analysis/criticism. Studies that explore the way in which communication establishes, reinforces, and maintains power structures in society.

Critical discourse analysis. Explores the relationship between language and power. The basic aim is to uncover the ideological assumptions behind public discourse and to link communication content with underlying power structures.

Cross-lagged surveys. Surveys that measure the relationship between a **dependent variable** and an **independent variable** at two points in time.

Cross-sectional surveys. Surveys taken at one point in time, as opposed to **trend studies**.

Cross-tabs. Short for *cross-tabulations*. A table that shows how scores for two or more variables are related. See also **contingency table**.

Curvilinear relationship. A relationship between two variables that, if plotted out, will show a curve rather than a straight line.

D

Data point. The recorded value of a variable for one individual.

Data reduction. The process of reducing "raw" data to a simpler form by using, for example, summary statistics, tables, or graphs.

Data set. All the data from a research project.

Database. In the context of bibliographic research, collections of (mostly) scholarly articles that can be searched electronically.

Debriefing. The process of ensuring that research participants receive a follow-up explanation of the research when it is completed.

Declaration of Helsinki. The World Medical Association's international ethical guidelines for medical professionals researching human subjects.

Deduction. Reasoning from a theory to defining the observations you will make to test the theory.

Degrees of freedom. A measure of the number of ways data could be combined and still produce the same value for a statistic.

Demographic questions. Questions pertaining to such variables as age, marital status, income, and occupation.

Dependent variable. A variable whose values change as a result of changes in another (independent) variable.

Description. An account or documentation of observed conditions. One basic goal of research is to describe communication phenomena in such a way that others can understand it.

Descriptive notes. The primary, detailed records of the human interactions, language, and settings that are the focus of the ethnography.

Descriptive questions. Questions that ask informants to describe a phenomenon.

Descriptive statistics. Statistics that describe and summarize the data for a sample.

Dichotomous questions. Questions that offer a choice between two possible answers—for example, "yes" or "no."

Diffusion. In experimental design, the problem of a treatment effect spreading from group to group as people communicate.

Disaffiliative responses. In conversation analysis, responses to a question or statement that break the link with the speaker.

Discourse. Generally, spoken or written communication. More specifically, a way of thinking about a topic or what can and cannot be said about it. See also **discourse analysis**.

Discourse analysis. Focuses on systems of meaning and how particular labels or concepts are developed and maintained by the use of language.

Divergent validity. Divergent validity is demonstrated when a measure of a construct or concept is shown to be unrelated to measures of unrelated concepts.

DOI. Short for *digital object identifier*. A string of characters used to uniquely identify a web-based document. Used in bibliographic citations.

Double negative. A combination of **negative wording** with a **double-barreled question**, almost guaranteed to confuse respondents.

Double-barreled questions. Questions that ask two questions simultaneously but allow for only one answer.

Dramatism/dramatistic analysis. Analyzing communication as performance, as actors acting out a drama. For example, Burke's dramatistic pentad asks, What act is taking place? Who is taking this action? How or by what means did the act take place? Where and when did the act take place? Why was the act done?

Dramatistic pentad. Kenneth Burke's core questions of *act, scene, agent, agency*, and *purpose* for analysis of motives.

E

Ecological isomorphism. The extent to which an experimental condition is similar to the real-world conditions it is attempting to simulate.

Editorial process. The process by which a manuscript becomes a published scholarly article or book. The three main phases are peer review, editing for style and accuracy, and production.

Emoticon. A typographic representation of an emotional state or mood, most often used to indicate the mood of a message's sender or how the message should be interpreted.

Empirical/empiricism. The view that knowledge should be based on experience and observation.

Ends. In Hymes's ethnography of communication, the goals of the communication being studied—for example, to persuade an audience on an issue.

Epistemology. The study or theory of knowledge. Epistemology addresses such questions as "What is knowledge?" and "How do we know what we know?"

Established measures reliability. A measure of whether the results obtained from an instrument that you are developing match the results obtained from a known, tested instrument designed for the same purpose.

Ethnography. The study of human social behavior, typically with emphasis on description.

Ethnomethodology. The study of how people make sense of their culture and communicate that understanding to others. Seeks to describe and explain cultural understandings in terms of the culture's own language and concepts.

Ethos. Aristotelian concept of source character or credibility in argumentation.

Ex post facto design. An "after the fact" experimental design in which there is no **control** over experimental conditions.

Experiment. A research design based on the technique of manipulating one or more variables in hopes of observing an effect. Typically, an experimental condition is applied to one group, and the results are compared with those from another group (**control group**) that has had no experimental treatment.

Experimental situation. The setting experimental subjects are placed in. May be a threat to external validity if it does not reflect external reality.

Experimenter bias. In experimental design, the problem of some kind of bias in an experimental group because of the way the researcher, knowingly or unknowingly, has selected its members.

Expert validity. Validity as judged by relevant experts. See also **panel validity**.

Explanation. An attempt to account for the relationships observed among phenomena. A basic goal of research is to explain how and why communication phenomena occur.

Exploration. "Mapping out" a new area of research before proceeding to study it more specifically. Research that may lead down unknown paths as opposed to testing a specific hypothesis.

Expressive function. One of Jakobson's semiotic functions. Describes or establishes the speaker's condition or emotional state.

External validity. Relates to whether an experiment has in fact captured the external world that the researcher is investigating.

F

F **value.** Denotes an analysis of variance value.

Face validity. A question or measure that appears to capture the concept it is intended to capture. See also **expert validity** and **panel validity**.

Facilitator. The leader of a focus group. Responsible for running the group's discussion and ensuring that it keeps "on topic." See also **moderator**.

Factorial designs. Experimental designs that manipulate two or more variables at a time.

Fantasy theme analysis. Fantasy themes are sagas, stories, or ideas shared by members of a group and that give members a common perspective and a shared understanding of the group's accomplishments.

Feminist criticism. A diversity of critical approaches centered on the problem of implicit and explicit male-oriented ideologies in communication content and processes. Feminist criticisms examine gender politics, gender representations, and the marginalizing implications of male-centered language.

Field experiment. A less sophisticated level of experimental design, where the effects of changes in one variable on another are observed under limited conditions of **control**.

Filter questions. Questions that determine whether a respondent is qualified to answer a question and that typically redirect them to another question if not.

Fixed coding. Assigning units of information to preassigned categories.

Flexible coding. Coding that allows new categories of data to emerge rather than using only preconceived categories.

Focus group. Small group of people brought together to discuss a topic of interest to the researcher.

Format. The structure of content required for a specific audience—for example, scholarly papers, news releases, and poster papers.

Frequency. The number of times a particular score or result occurs. Commonly reported in the form of a **frequency table**.

Frequency table. Table that shows categories of a variable by the number of times that category occurs.

Fully structured interview. Interview in which the researcher has determined what questions are important, the order they will be asked, and how they will be structured.

Funnel/inverted funnel. A set of questions that move from general to specific or vice versa.

G

Gatekeepers. Those who control access to research participants or the publication of research results—for example, employers and journal editors, respectively.

Genres. In Hymes's ethnography of communication, the traditional types of speech found in most cultures—for example, commencement addresses.

Grounded theory. A research approach that argues that theories should emerge from data analysis, not prior to data analysis.

H

Hawthorne effect. The effect that researchers themselves may have on an experimental group. Named after an organizational study in which employees were found to be responding to the perceived interest of management rather than the experimental condition itself.

Hermeneutic circle/Hermeneutics. The concept of understanding a whole in terms of its parts and vice versa.

Homogeneity. The degree of "sameness" in a population. Generally, the greater the homogeneity, the smaller the sample size required.

House style. The publication style of a specific journal or publisher.

Hyperlink. The web address embedded in a document that allows the viewer to open a second—linked—document.

Hypermedia. Web-based documents that link to other documents on the web.

Hypothesis. A testable statement about the relationships one expects to find among variables of interest. **Two-tailed tests** predict relationships between two variables but do not specify the direction of the relationship. **One-tailed tests** specify the direction of relationships between variables. A **null hypothesis** specifies that there is no relationship between variables.

I

IBM SPSS® Statistics. One of several statistical software packages used in the social sciences.

Ideology. A broad set of ideas that guide behavior and expectations. The body of knowledge and beliefs that guide groups and group members.

Idiographic. A research approach with an emphasis on understanding the subjectivity and individuality of human communication, rather than universal laws of human behavior.

Impact factor. In scholarly publishing, a measure of the number of times journal articles are cited by other scholarly articles.

Independent variable. A variable whose changes in values result in changes in another (dependent) variable.

Induction. Reasoning from observations to a theory that might explain the observations.

Inferential statistics. Statistics that estimate the values for a population from a sample of that population.

Informants. Interviewees considered capable of speaking on behalf of or about others.

Informed consent. The process by which potential research participants are informed of the nature of the research and given the opportunity to sign or not sign a voluntary agreement to participate.

Institutional review board (IRB). A panel established to review research proposals for their impact on human participants.

Instrumentality. In Hymes's ethnography of communication, the channels or methods used to communicate—for example, an online discussion group.

Interaction analysis. Research that seeks to document and understand group roles and interactions among members of a group.

Intercoder or observer reliability. A measure of the extent to which two different coders code the same phenomenon the same way.

Inter-item reliability. A measure of whether the individual questions in a question set are consistent in their results. See also **internal reliability**.

Internal reliability. A measure of whether all the questions in a question set are operationalizing the same concept and not different concepts. See also **inter-item reliability**.

Internal validity. Relates to experimental design. A study has internal validity when a cause-and-effect relationship between variables is clearly demonstrable, and observed changes can be attributed to a defined causal variable and not to any other possible variables.

Interpretive perspective. A research approach that seeks to understand how humans interpret or make sense of events in their lives. Interpretive studies can be understood as attempts to place oneself "in the other person's shoes."

Interquartile range. The range between the highest and lowest values for the middle 50% of values in a distribution.

Interval. Generally, the distance between points on a scale. In research terms, *interval* refers to a scale in which there is an assumption of equal intervals between points on the scale.

Interview. The process of asking questions of a respondent, usually face-to-face or by phone or video, to elicit information the researcher is interested in. See also **fully structured interview**, **semistructured interview**, and **unstructured interview**.

Interviewees. Individuals who are interviewed.

Intuition. Refers to arriving at an answer without quite knowing how one arrived there; a hunch or "gut instinct."

J

Judeo-Christian ethic. In the context of human subjects research, do not do to others what you would not want done to yourself. A concept shared by many religions.

Justice. A **Belmont Report** principle that the benefits and risks of research should be distributed fairly.

K

Key. In Hymes's ethnography of communication, the tone of speech. How the speech sounds—for example, formal or friendly.

Key informants. The individuals who are part of a community being studied and who can introduce the researcher and legitimize the researcher's work to their community.

KWIC. Key word in context. Content analysis term referring to display of a word and the words surrounding it.

L

Latent. Hidden; not apparent.

Leading questions. Questions worded to lead **respondents** to a particular answer rather than the one they might have genuinely given.

Lemmatization. Content analysis procedure for grouping words according to a common dictionary definition.

Leptokurtic. A distribution of values that is peaked or high relative to the **normal curve**. Values in such a distribution have a narrower **range**.

Likert scale. An interval scale on which **respondents** record their reactions to statements by checking their level of agreement between, for example, "strongly agree" and "strongly disagree."

Linear regression. A calculation of the value of one variable given the value of another. Assumes that the relationship between variables is linear. See also **regression**.

Literature. In the context of communication and other research, refers to **refereed** and published scholarly research reports.

Logos. Aristotelian concept of logic in argumentation.

Longitudinal studies. Studies that track people's changes in knowledge, attitude, or behavior over time.

M

Manifest. Apparent or observable.

Manipulation check. In experimental research, a check on whether the research participants interpreted the experimental conditions as the researcher intended.

MANOVA. Multiple analysis of variance. Used where there are multiple dependent variables. See also **ANOVA.**

Marxist perspective/criticism. The study of communication content aimed at assessing its political orientation or identifying messages that reinforce the ideology or vision of those in power.

Master analog. In **fantasy theme analysis,** a commonly understood theme or analogy that underpins a group fantasy—for example, space exploration, war, or detective work.

Master narrative. A covering story or fantasy that explains a group more readily or attracts more believers than other fantasies available to group members.

Maturation. In experimental design, the problem of individuals changing over time, most obviously by getting older.

Maximum. The highest value in a data set.

Mean. The average for a set of scores.

Measurement. The process of finding out whether people (or media content) have more or less of an attribute we are interested in. It is done by assigning numbers to the phenomena we are interested in.

Measures of central tendency: mean, median, and mode. Describe the central features of a data set rather than its outlying values.

Measures of dispersion: range, variance, and standard deviation. Describe the range and variability of values in a data set.

Median. The midpoint of a set of scores.

Metalingual function. One of Jakobson's semiotic functions. Establishes the agreed-upon meaning for words—for example, by establishing that *Rose* refers to the name of a girl, not a flower.

Metaphor analysis. Analysis of the analogies and metaphors used by group members to explain and interpret their group and to help simplify the complexities and ambiguities that are part of any group.

Method notes. Records of the specific methods researchers use to gather data—for example, direct observation and interviews.

Metric. A quantitative measure for a concept or activity—for example, the **impact factor** in scholarly publishing as a measure of influence.

Minimum. The lowest value in a data set.

MLA. Modern Language Association. In the context of reporting communication research, refers to the *MLA Style Manual*.

Mode. The most frequent score in a set of scores.

Moderator. The leader of a focus group. Responsible for running the group's discussion and ensuring that it keeps "on topic." See also **facilitator.**

Multimedia. Media that present audio and video content.

Multiple-choice questions. Questions that offer **respondents** a selection of answers from which they are instructed to select one or more.

Multiple regression. The use of more than one variable to predict the values for another variable. See also **regression.**

Multistage cluster sampling. Sampling based on first sampling large units such as states or provinces, then sampling smaller units such as towns, city blocks, and so on.

Multivariate. Pertaining to three or more variables, as in **multivariate analysis** or **multivariate statistics.**

Multivariate analysis/statistics. Analyses that examine the relationship among three or more variables simultaneously.

N

Narrative analysis. The study of the formal properties of stories that people tell. It generally attempts to identify such aspects as plot, setting, characters, and order of events.

Negative wording. Questions phrased using a negative rather than a positive (e.g., "don't" rather than "do").

Netnography. A specialized form of ethnography adapted to computer-mediated social worlds.

Network sampling. Sampling using members of a network to introduce a researcher to other members of the network. Also known as snowball sampling.

News determinants. Components of news stories such as timeliness, relevance, and proximity that make the stories newsworthy.

Nominal. A system of classification based on names rather than scales or rank ordering—for example, press, radio, and television.

Nomothetic. A research approach with an emphasis on measurement with a view to making generalizations about human behavior.

Nonparametric. Pertaining to data that cannot be assumed to have a normal distribution.

Nonprobability sampling. Sampling based on a judgment by the researcher.

Normal curve. Curve resulting from the plot of values with a normal distribution. Often called a bell curve because of its shape.

Normal distribution. Symmetrical distribution of values with the majority of scores "peaking" in the middle.

Norms. In Hymes's ethnography of communication, the rules governing speech and its interpretation—for example, students cannot ask questions until after the instructor has spoken.

Null hypothesis. The hypothesis that no significant difference will be found between groups or variables. See also hypothesis.

Numbers. Numbers assign value and relativity to phenomena. As contrasted with numerals, they can be calculated.

Numerals. Numerals are labels such as street numbers that cannot be computed.

Nuremberg Code. An international code emphasizing that research subjects must consent to the research in which they are involved and that the benefits of the research must outweigh the risks.

O

Observational study. A study based on observation of behaviors, not necessarily as in-depth as an ethnography.

Observer reliability. A measure of the extent to which observers are in agreement in their coding of observations. See also intercoder reliability.

One-tailed test. Proposing that any difference between two groups will be in one direction; that is, one group will score higher than another. See also two-tailed test.

Ontology. The study of the nature of existence and what it is that language actually refers to.

Open-ended research questions. Questions to which respondents can reply in their own words.

Operationalize. To define a concept in such a way that it can be measured.

Ordinal. Scales with some measure of progression such as "Freshman, Sophomore, Junior, Senior."

Outcome variable. The variable whose value is predicted by the value of predictor variables in a regression analysis. See also criterion variable.

P

Panel. A group of the same individuals retained to answer questions over time.

Panel presentation. A small group of researchers with shared interests presenting the results of their research.

Panel validity. Validity as judged by a group of relevant experts. See also expert validity.

Parameters. The values pertaining to a population rather than a sample.

Parametric statistics. Pertaining to data with distributions that approximate a normal distribution (i.e., have parameters). See also nonparametric.

Part or **partial correlation.** Shows the relationship between two variables with the effect of a third variable removed from one.

Participant. Any individual who has volunteered to be in a research project.

Path analysis. A method for mapping out causal relationships among interrelated variables.

Pathos. Aristotelian concept of emotion in argumentation.

Peer review. The process of having one's research reviewed by other researchers in the author's field prior to publication. See also refereeing.

Phatic function. One of Jakobson's semiotic functions. Keeps participants in communication "on track" by establishing how communication will take place.

Phenomenology. A research approach that attempts to understand human behavior and consciousness from the individual, subjective point of view.

Phrenologist. A practitioner of a now discredited "science" based on the assumption that people's personalities could be assessed from the size and shape of their skulls.

Physical units. In content analysis, physical units occupy an observable space in print media or time in audiovisual media—for example, an entire comic strip.

Pilot/piloting. A prototype or pretest. A small study conducted prior to a full-scale study to ensure that the full-scale study will work successfully.

Platykurtic. A distribution of values that is flat or low relative to the **normal curve**. Values in such a distribution have a wider **range**.

Poetic function. One of Jakobson's semiotic functions. The use of language for its own pleasure—for example, jokes or alliteration because they are pleasurable in their own right.

Popular articles. Articles published without a refereeing process, typically in newspapers and magazines, and targeted to a consumer public.

Population. Every individual or item of a type you want to study. The entire set of individuals or items from which a sample is drawn.

Positivism. The idea that phenomena are governed by, and can be explained by, rules based on objective observation and generalizations from those observations.

Poster paper. Scholarly research set out in poster format for display at conferences and meetings.

Prediction. One major goal of research; understanding human behavior in order to forecast the conditions under which it will occur.

Predictive validity. Predictive validity occurs when a measure successfully predicts a tangible outcome. For example, GRE scores should predict success in graduate school. See also **criterion validity**.

Predictor variable. Variable whose values are used in **regression** analysis to predict the value of **outcome** or **criterion variables**.

Primary source. An original article or book. See also **secondary source**.

Principle of utilitarianism. The principle of the greatest good for the greatest number.

Probability sampling. Sampling based on random selection of the sample units.

Professional reports. Reports written for groups with professional rather than scholarly interests.

Prompts. Questions that spark a response or further information from an interviewee—for example, "Why do you say that?"

Propositional units. In content analysis, propositional units are structures such as stories or dramas.

Proprietary. Pertaining to data or research tools that are privately owned and therefore may not be used without the owner's permission.

Purpose. In Burke's **dramatistic analysis**, the reason or motivation that explains an **act**.

Purposive/judgmental sampling. Sampling based on specific criteria the researcher may have.

Q

Q-Methodology. A research approach used to assess individuals' subjective understanding. Typically, participants rank a series of statements about a topic according to their perceived accuracy. Quantitative analysis of these rankings typically identifies a small number of factors that show the patterns of subjectivity within the participant group.

Qualitative. A research approach based on the use of language rather than numbers to understand and report human behavior.

Quantitative. A research approach based on measurement, counting, and, typically, statistical analysis.

Questionnaire. A set of questions to which **respondents** reply.

Quota sampling. Sampling that attempts to replicate in a sample the features that the researcher thinks are important in the population.

R

R. Open-source statistical software. Available at www.r-project.org.

r **value.** Denotes a correlation value.

Random assignment. The use of random selection to assign research participants to experimental groups.

Random digit dialing (RDD). A telephone survey method in which phone numbers are randomly dialed in hopes of reaching unlisted numbers.

Random numbers. Numbers that have an equal probability of occurring. Used to eliminate any researcher bias in selecting numbers.

Random numbers generator. A device for generating a sequence of numbers that has no pattern. Most typically a software program, but random numbers can also be generated by, for example, rolling dice.

Random sampling. Sampling in which every member of a population has an equal chance to be selected and in which selection is determined by "luck of the draw" rather than a decision by the researcher.

Range. The difference between the maximum value and minimum value in a data set.

Rank order/ranking questions. Questions that ask **respondents** to order items according to their perceived importance or preference.

Ratio. In measurement, refers to a scale which contains a "true" zero—for example, zero speed on a speedometer.

Ratio analysis. In Burke's **dramatistic analysis**, this means examining the relative significance of each pentad unit (**act**, **scene**, **agent**, **agency**, **purpose**) in any situation.

Rationalism. The view that knowledge is best acquired by reason and factual analysis rather than faith or emotion.

Refereed/ing. The process of having one's research reviewed by other researchers in the author's field prior to publication. See also **peer review**.

Referential function. One of Jakobson's semiotic functions. Establishes the communication context, dominant message, or agenda.

Regression. A statistical method for estimating the strength of relationships among variables.

Reification. Turning an abstract into a concrete thing—for example, assuming that because there are measures of intelligence, there is a unitary tangible entity called intelligence.

Reliability/reliability coefficients. A measure of the extent to which a test or measure performs consistently.

Repair mechanisms. In conversation analysis, repair mechanisms are the actions that restore a conversation when it is in danger of breaking down.

Repeated testing. In experimental design, a threat to internal validity due to participants becoming more and more familiar with a test.

Research question. The basic research interest posed as a question. **Open-ended research questions** ask simply whether there is a relationship between variables. **Closed-ended research questions** ask about the direction of the relationship.

Respondents. Interviewees or survey participants considered capable of speaking only on behalf of themselves. The individuals responding to **survey** or **interview** questions.

Rhetoric/rhetorical analysis. The study of the principles and means of persuasion and argumentation.

Rhetorician. One who studies **rhetoric**.

Root metaphor. A basic metaphor such as *war*, *family*, or *team* that shapes the way group members think and that they may or may not be consciously aware of.

S

Sample. A set of individuals or items selected from a wider population.

Sampling distribution. The distribution of values in a sample.

Sampling frame. The master list from which a sample is selected.

Sampling interval. The interval selected in **systematic sampling** (e.g., every 10th or 100th unit).

Sampling units. The units selected for study.

Scaled questions. Questions in which **respondents** are asked to mark their answers on a scale.

Scales. Measurement devices used to locate an individual's ranking on some attribute. Classic scales in communication research are the **Likert** and **semantic differential scales**.

Scene. In Burke's **dramatistic analysis**, the location where an **act** takes place.

Scholarly articles. Research papers that have been **peer reviewed** and published in academic journals.

Scientific method. A research approach based on developing specific hypotheses or propositions that can then be tested using specific observations designed for that purpose.

Search engine. A device such as Google or Yahoo that retrieves information from the web.

Search field. Searchable components of a database, such as *date, author,* and *title.*

Search term. The words(s) typed into a database or search engine when searching for information.

Secondary source. An author's interpretation or summary of an original source—for example, a literature review.

Selection bias. A problem in experimental design stemming from the experimental groups not being comparable.

Semantic differential. A scale anchored at opposite ends by opposing words such as "strong–weak" or "hot–cold."

Semiotic function. In Jakobson's model of communication, an attribute of language that allows communication to occur.

Semiotics/semiotician. The study of the relationships between signs and their interpretation and meaning.

Semipartial correlation. See **part correlation**.

Semistructured interviews. A set of interview questions that are largely predetermined but allow room for **interviewees** to add their own insights and views.

Sequence. The order in which questions are asked—for example from least to most difficult or general to specific.

Serials. Regularly published scholarly publications such as journals.

Significance. In general terms, importance or relevance, but see also **statistical significance**.

Situation. In Hymes's ethnography of communication, the setting where the activities take place and the overall scene of which they are a part.

Skew. Data distributions that, when plotted out, show an extended "tail." Skew is the "tail" of a distribution. Positive skew means the tail is in the high numbers; negative skew means that the tail is in the low numbers. For example, a quiz with a high percentage of scores in the 80's or 90s out of a possible 100 will produce a negative skew.

Slideware. Generic term for presentation software sucjh as PowerPoint and Keynote.

Snowball sampling. See **network sampling**.

Social scientists. Researchers who share the assumption that the methods of science can be applied to researching and understanding human behavior.

Solomon Four-Group Design. An experimental design using four groups. Two of these groups receive an experimental treatment; two groups receive no experimental treatment; two groups receive a pretest and a posttest; two groups receive only a posttest.

Speech community. In Hymes's ethnography of communication, a group of people who share a common language that differentiates them from other groups—for example, a group of communication majors.

Speech event. In Hymes's ethnography of communication, a specific speech activity—for example, an awards speech.

Speech situation. In Hymes's ethnography of communication, the overall scene of which activities are a part—for example, a college classroom.

Split-half technique. A way to determine **inter-item reliability** by correlating half the questions in a question set with the other half of the questions.

Spurious relationship. An apparent relationship between two variables that is actually caused by a third variable.

Standard deviation. A measure of the extent to which a set of scores vary on either side of their mean value. The square root of **variance**. See also **standard error**.

Standard error. For a **sampling distribution** (the distribution of scores for a **sample**), the standard deviation is called the **standard error**.

Statistical formulae. Formulae used to calculate statistics such as **mean, range**, and **variance**.

Statistical significance. The probability that a computed statistic such as a *t* test or correlation is not due to chance.

Statistics. Calculated numbers that summarize data and relationships among variables in a **sample**.

Stemming. Content analysis term for grouping different words by a common stem; for example, *fish* is the stem for *fisherman*, *fishy*, *fishtail*, *fishing*, and *fished*.

Stratified random sampling. Sampling in which randomly selected units from small or minority populations are forced into the sample to ensure that they are represented in proportion to their presence in the population.

Structural questions. Questions that ask interviewees to explain the relationships among different terms. For example, "Would you say that X is a part of Y?"

Structure. The extent to which an interview has a format. See also **fully structured interview**, **semistructured interviews**, and **unstructured interview**.

Style guide. A document detailing requirements for citation, heading levels, typography, and the like for such specific overall styles as **APA**, **Chicago**, and **MLA**.

Subjects. Individuals who participate in an experiment.

Survey. A research method in which predetermined, formatted questions are distributed to relatively large numbers of people. Typically, **respondents** respond by phone, mail, e-mail, or website.

Symbolic convergence. The condition of group members being in agreement on the organizational symbolism or stories that unite them.

Synchronous. Coordinated communication—for example, focus group members interacting with each other in "real time."

Syntactical units. In content analysis, syntactical units are units of language such as words or sentences.

Systematic sampling. Sampling by selecting every *n*th unit from a population.

t **test.** A statistical test for assessing whether the mean scores for two groups are significantly different.

t **test for dependent samples.** Test used where both groups consist of the same people, for example a pretest/posttest comparison.

t **test for independent samples.** Test used where two different groups are being compared.

T

Table. Data displayed and summarized by rows and columns.

Temporal ordering. Ordering based on a time sequence. To determine that A causes B, A must precede B in time.

Tenacity. A way of knowing based on accepting knowledge, correctly or incorrectly, because it has stood the test of time.

Test-retest. To determine the reliability of a measure by testing and retesting it under the same conditions. If the measure is reliable, it will produce similar results each time.

Thematic units. In content analysis, thematic units are broad topics within a structure—for example, relationships with a boss or peers.

Time series analysis. Analysis of a series of observations made over time.

Trade publication. A journal published for a particular industry. The articles are written by experts but not necessarily to the standards of an academic research publication.

Transitional relevance place (TRP). In conversation analysis, a transitional relevance place is the point in a conversation at which **turn taking** may take place.

Trend studies. Studies that measure the same items over time but draw different samples from the population to do so.

Triangulation. The use of two or more research methods to address the same research question. If results from different methods agree, researchers can have greater confidence in their findings.

Tri-modal distribution. Distributions of data having three values occurring with equal frequency.

Turn constructional unit (TCU). In conversation analysis, a sentence, word, or exclamation that signals a **transitional relevance place**—a point at which **turn taking** can occur.

Turn taking. In conversation analysis, the mechanism of who speaks next in a conversation and the mechanisms that indicate possible types of responses to a question.

Two-tailed test. Proposing that any difference between two groups will be in one direction; that is, one group will score higher than another. See also **one-tailed test**.

Type I error. Deciding wrongly that there was a significant result when in fact there was not.

Type II error. Deciding wrongly that there was no significant result when in fact there was.

U

Units. In content analysis, the aspects or components of content sampled for study. See also **physical units**, **propositional units**, **syntactical units**, and **thematic units**.

Univariate analysis/statistics. Statistics that describe only one variable.

Unobtrusive measures. Observations of people's behavior without them being aware of such observation.

Unstructured interview. An interview with broad questions and a loose schedule of questions so that **interviewees** have the freedom to volunteer information and to explain their responses.

Uses and gratifications theory. A theory of media use that proposes that individuals are proactive and selective in choosing media content to meet their specific needs.

Utterances. In conversation analysis, units of speech preceded by silence and followed either by silence or by another speaker.

V

Validity. A measure of whether a test measures what it is supposed to measure.

Variable. The aspects of a concept that are capable of being measured or taking on a value. The construct *academic performance* cannot be measured; the variable *grade point average* can.

Variance. A measure of the extent to which a set of scores vary on either side of their mean value. The square root of variance gives the **standard deviation**.

Veil of ignorance. Philosopher John Rawls's view that we take a dispassionate approach, reviewing all sides of a decision equally. We are asked to "wear a veil" that blinds us to all information about ourselves that might cloud our judgment.

Voice. The individual writing style of an author.

Volunteer sampling. Obtaining a sample by asking for volunteers.

W

Ways of speaking. In Hymes's ethnography of communication, the styles of speech that are characteristic of a culture or group; for example, at the beginning of a class, the instructor speaks before students do.

Within-subjects design. An experimental design in which participants are exposed to more than one experimental condition—for example, both democratic and autocratic managerial styles. See also **between-subjects design**.

Worldview. A major conceptual framework for understanding the world. For example, the view that humans are essentially similar and their behavior can be measured and predicted, versus the view that humans are individuals and unpredictable, and their behavior may be described but not predicted.

Z

z **score.** The number of units of standard deviation that any individual score is above or below the mean for a variable.

Index

Abduction, 24
Absent author, 267
Accuracy, in writing, 264–265
Acknowledgments, 44
Act in dramatistic analysis, 236
Action research, 12, 259
Acts of communication, 206
Address-based sampling (ABS), 149
Adjacency pairs, 241
Advertisements, 8–11
  content of, 10–11
  creators of, 11
  effectiveness of, 9–10
  feedback on, 10
Affiliative responses, 241
Agency in dramatistic analysis, 236
American Psychological Association (APA), 74
Analysis. *See* Content analysis, qualitative;
    Content analysis, quantitative
Analysis of variance (ANOVA), 129–130
Analytic notes, 205
Anomalous data, 98–100
Anonymity
  ethics and, 43
  on the Internet, 50
ANOVA (analysis of variance), 129–130
APA (American Psychological Association), 74
Appeals, 10
Aristotelian analysis, 235–236
Aristotle, 10, 235
Asynchronous communication, 203
Attrition, 187
Author, 259, 267
  voice of, 259
Authority, 28, 190–191
Autonomy, 47
Avatars, 204

Bales, Robert, 227
Bell curve, 119

Belmont Report, 46–47
Beneficence, 47
Bentham, Jeremy, 45
Bernays, Edward, 242–243
Between-subjects design, 186–187
Bibliographic research, 65
Bi-modal distribution, 105, 118
Bi-variate analysis, 101
Bi-variate data, and data reduction, 102–104
Boole, George, 68
Boolean operators, 68, 69 (exhibit)
Bormann, Ernest, 237
Break-off rate, 168
Burke, Kenneth, 11, 236

CAQDAS (computer-assisted qualitative data analysis software),
    210–211
Categorial units, 224
Categorical data, 103
Categorical imperative, 45
Categorization, 208
Causal relationship, 178
  and surveys, 158
  and cross-lagged surveys, 160
  and experimental designs, 181–183
Cause and effect, researching. *See* Experiments
Census, 118, 139
Central limit theorem, 119–120
Central tendency, measures of, 105
Champagne glass model of bibliographic research, 65
Chicago Manual of Style, 74
Chi-square test, 105, 110–112, 125
Citation management software, 71
Citations, 64
Closed-ended research questions, 32
Cluster sampling. *See* Multistage cluster sampling
Coded units and coding schemes, in content analysis,
    219–221, 224–227
Codes of ethics
  Belmont Report, 46–47

contemporary, 46–47
Declaration of Helsinki, 46–47
Nuremberg code, 46
Coding, fixed and flexible, 208–210
Cohort surveys, 159–160
Collaborators, 48
Common Rule, 48
Communication guidelines,
      268 (exhibit), 269
Communication research
   basic assumptions behind, 6–8
   decisions, 12–15
   getting started in, 1–2
   interest areas, 12, 13 (exhibit)
   participants, 7, 197–198, 259–260
   possibilities, 8–12
   problems, 16
   purpose of, 7
   situation, the, 2–6
   See also Content analysis, qualitative; Content analysis,
         quantitative; Descriptive statistics; Ethics; Experiments;
         Inferential statistics; Presenting research; Qualitative
         research; Quantitative research; Questions; Reviewing
         research; Sampling; Survey(s)
Communicative act, 206
Communicative style, 206
Computer-assisted qualitative data analysis software
      (CAQDAS), 210–211
Conative semiotic function, 244
Concurrent validity, 90
Confederates, 41
Conferences, presenting for, 265–266
Confidence interval, 123
Confidence level, 112, 124–125
Confidentiality, 43
Constant comparative method, 209
Constructs, 30–31
Construct validity, 89, 139–140
Contemporary codes of ethics, 46–47
Content analysis, qualitative, 234–254
   advantages and disadvantages of, 235
   conversation analysis, 240–242
   critical analyses, 246–248
   discourse analysis, 239–240
   metaphor analysis, 238–239
   narrative analysis, 238
   rhetorical analyses, 235–238
   semiotics, 242–245
   See also Qualitative research
Content analysis, quantitative, 216–233
   advantages and disadvantages of, 217–218
   basic, 218–222
   expanded, 222–227
   of human interaction, 227–229
   software, 229

units, 224
   See also Quantitative research
Content validity, 89
Contingency tables, 103
Continuous data, 103
Continuous variables, 84
Contrast questions, 202
Control, 26, 181
   designing experiments for, 181–182
   online surveys and, 167
   groups, 181
Convenience sampling, 139–140, 143 (exhibit),
      147 (exhibit)
Convergent validity, 89
Conversation analysis, 208, 240–242
   adjacency pairs, 241
   example, 243 (exhibit)
   repair mechanisms, 242
   turn taking, 241–242
   utterances, 241
Correlation, 86, 131–132
Correlation coefficient, 131
Covariance, 178
Criterion validity, 90
Critical analyses, 246–248
Critical discourse analysis, 247
Critical theorists, 27
Criticism, 27–28
Cross-lagged surveys, 160
Cross-sectional surveys, 159
Cross-tabs, 103
Curves, 118–120
Curvilinear, 132

Data, 14
   anomalous, 98–100
   categorical, 103
   computer-assisted qualitative data analysis software
         (CAQDAS), 210–211
   generalizing from, 119–125
   missing, 98–100
   patterns, reporting, 220, 221–222, 225–226, 227
   points, 98
   qualitative, 208–210
   reduction, 96, 100–104
   survey, capturing and processing, 171
Databases, 61–62
Data set, 96
Debriefing, 43–44, 51–52
Deception, and ethical decisions, 41
Decisions
   approach, 13–14
   data, 14–15
   field of study, 12
   priority, 14

report, 15
researcher, 12–13
sample size, 14
unavoidable, 12–15
See also Questions
Declaration of Helsinki, 46–47
Deduction, 23–24
Degrees of freedom (df), 111, 128
Demographic questions, 82
Dependent variable, 178
Description as a goal of research, 25
Descriptive notes, 205
Descriptive questions, 201
Descriptive statistics, 96–116, 118
    chi-square test, 105, 110–112
    data reduction, 96, 100–104
    measures of central tendency, 105
    measures of dispersion, 106–108
    missing and anomalous data, 98–100
    z scores, 109–110
Design-based approach, to Internet sampling, 151
Dichotomous questions, 161–162
Diffusion, 188
Digital object identifier (DOI), 70
Disaffiliative responses, 241
Discourse analysis, 239–240
Discrete variables, 84
Dispersion, measures of, 106–108
Divergent validity, 89
Dixon, Maria A., 66
DOI (digital object identifier), 70
Double-barreled questions, 165
Double negative, 165
Dramatistic analysis, 236–237
Dramatistic pentad, 236

Ecological isomorphism, 179
Editorial processes, 263–264
Electronic surveys, 170–171 (exhibit)
Emoticons, 207
Empiricism, 28
Ends of communication, 206
Epistemology, 28
Error, type I and II, 133
Established measures reliability, 87–88
Ethics, 40–57
    acknowledgment of others and, 44
    anonymity and, 43
    appropriate language and, 44–45
    codes of, contemporary, 46–47
    confidentiality and, 43
    debriefing and, 43–44
    deception and, 41
    generalizations and, 43
    history and, 46

honesty and, 42–43
institutional review boards (IRBs), 48
Internet and, 49–52
library research and, 60
literature review and, 44
money and, 42
of involvement, 48–49
peer review, 48
plagiarism and, 45
positions, classic, 45–46
regulations and, 48
relationships and, 42
research methods and, 34–35
sex and, 41
violence and, 41
Ethnographers, 14
Ethnography, 196
    methods, 204–207
    research principles, 204
    starting points, 206
Ethnomethodology, 33
Ethos, 236
Experimental situation, 189
Experimenter bias, 188
Experiments, 177–194
    advantages and disadvantages of, 178–179
    between-subjects and within-subjects design, 186–187
    control and, 181–182
    design, basic, 181
    ex post facto designs, 179–180
    factorial designs, 184–186
    field, 179–180
    one-group pretest-posttest design, 181
    random assignment and, 182–184
    Solomon four-group design, 183
    time series analysis, 184
    two-group pretest-posttest design, 182
    two-group random assignment pretest-posttest
        design, 182
    validity and, 187–190
Expert tour-guide author, 267–268
Expert validity, 89
Explanation, 24–25
Exploration, 24–25
Ex post facto design, 179–180
Expressive semiotic function, 244
External validity, 188–189

Facebook, 53, 133, 150
Face-to-face surveys, 171 (exhibit)
Face validity, 89
Facilitator, 202
Factorial designs, 184–186
Fantasy theme analysis, 237–238
Feminist criticism, 247

Field experiments, 179–180
Filter questions, 166–167
Findings, accepting or rejecting, 132–133
Finkelhor, David, 64
Fixed coding, 208
Flexible coding, 209–210
Focus groups, 196, 202–204
Format
    of scholarly and professional reports, 256–262
    of survey questions, 160-163
Framing questions, 165
Frequencies, 100
Frequency tables, 100
Fully structured interviews, 199–200
Funnel format, 166, 201
F value, 130

Gatekeepers, 205
Gates, Bill, 239
Geertz, Clifford, 197
Generalizations, making, 43
Genres of communication, 206
Goals of research, 24–28
    control, 26
    criticism, 27–28
    description, 25
    explanation, 25
    exploration, 24–25
    interpretation, 27
    prediction, 25–26
Gould, Stephen Jay, 92–93
Gray, Mary, 52
Grounded theory, 209
Groups, testing for differences, 125–131
    analysis of variance (ANOVA), 129–131
    t test, 125–129
Guidelines
    for communication, 268 (exhibit), 269
    for Internet research, 52
Guillory, Jamie E., 53

Hamel, Stephanie A., 66
Hancock, Jeffrey T., 53
Hawthorne effect, 189
Helsinki, Declaration of, 46–47
Hermeneutics, 34
Homogeneity of sample, 148
Honesty, 42–43
House styles, 257
How to Lie with Statistics (Huff), 134
Huff, Darrell, 134
Human behavior
    observation of, 8
    theories and generalizations, 7

Hume, David, 45
Hyperlinks, 262
Hypermedia, 256
Hypotheses, 24, 32, 123–124

IBM SPSS® Statistics, 98
Ideas and observations, 22–24
Identification, on the Internet, 50
Ideology, 247
Idiographic approach, 29
Impact factor, 63
Independent variable, 178
Induction, 23
Inferential statistics, 96, 117–137
    curves, language of, 118–119
    generalizing, 119–125
    groups, testing for differences, 125–131
    probability, 132–133
    significance, 133–134
    variables, testing for relationships, 131–132
Informants, 199
Information
    being skeptical about, 67–68
    identifying quality and relevant, 60–61
    must be recorded, 69–70
    should be recorded, 70–71
Informed consent, 47, 51–52
Institutional review boards (IRBs), 48, 248
Instructions, for surveys, 166–167
Instrumentality of communication, 206
Interaction analysis, 227
Intercoder reliability, 86–87
Interest groups, writing for, 261–262
Inter-item reliability, 87
Internal reliability, 87
Internal validity, 187–188
Internet, 49–50
    anonymity and identification on, 50
    guidelines and questions for research, 52
    informed consent and debriefing on, 51–52
    privacy on, 50–51
    sampling frames, 150–152
Interpretation, 27
Interpretive approach, 197
Interquartile range, 106
Interval, 82
Interval measurement, 83–84
Interview questions
    contrast, 202
    descriptive, 201
    ranking, 202
    structural, 201
Interview(s), 196, 199–202
    persona, 200

question prompts, 202
question types, 201–202
recording, 201
sensitivities, 201
sequence, 201
setting, 200–201
structure, 199–200
Interviewees, 199
Intuition, 28
Inverted funnel format, 166, 201
Involved author, 267
Involvement, and online surveys, 167

Jakobson, Roman, 244–245
Jobs, Steve, 239
Jones, Lisa M., 64
Journals, scholarly, 62–63
Judeo-Christian ethic, 45
Judgmental sampling, 140, 147 (exhibit)
Justice, 47

Kant, Immanuel, 45
Key, 206
Key informants, 205
Kramer, Adam D. I., 53
KWIC (key words in context), 229

Language
appropriate, 44–45
library research and, 60
survey wording and, 165–166
Latent content, 217
Leading questions, 164
Lemmatization, 229
Leptokurtic, 119
Lewis, Laurie K., 66
Library of Congress, and literature
searches, 67
Library research, 59–60
Likert scale, 84, 90–91, 92, 162–163
Linear regression, 132
Literature review, 44, 58, 72–74
questions, 74 (exhibit)
structuring, 73–74
style, questions of, 74
See also Reviewing research
Literature search
Library of Congress and, 67
relevance and quality, 60–61
saving results, 69–71
See also Reviewing research
Logos, 236
Longitudinal studies, 159
Lord Kelvin, 81–82

Mail surveys, 170 (exhibit)
Manifest, 217
Manipulation, 248
Manipulation checks, 189–190
MANOVA (multiple analysis of variance), 131
Marxist perspective, 247
Master analog, 237
Master narrative, 237
Maturation, 187
Maximum, 106
Mean, 105
Measurement
interval, 83
nominal, 83
ordinal, 83
ratio, 84
Measures
of central tendency, 105
of dispersion, 106–108
Median, 105
Metalingual, 245
Metaphor analysis, 238–239
Method notes, 205
Methods and epistemologies, 28
Metrics, 63, 109
Milgram, Stanley, 190–191
Mill, John Stuart, 45
Minimum, 106
Missing data, 98–100
Mitchell, Kimberly J., 64
MLA (Modern Language Association), 74
Mobile surveys, 168
Mode, 105
Model-based approach, to Internet sampling, 151
Moderator, 202
Multimedia, 256
Multiple analysis of variance (MANOVA), 131
Multiple-choice questions, 162
Multiple regression, 132
Multistage cluster sampling, 146–147
Multivariate analysis, 104, 184
Multivariate data, and data reduction, 104
Murphy, Alexandra G., 66

Narrative analysis, 238
Nathan, "Rebekah," 211
Negative wording, 165
Netnography, 207
Network sampling, 140–141, 147 (exhibit)
News determinants, 262
News media, writing for, 262–263
Newton, Isaac, 59
NOIR. *See* Research NOIR
Nominal, 82

Nominal measurement, 83
Nomothetic approach, 29
Nonparametric statistics, 124
Nonprobability samples, 139
Nonprobability sampling, 139–142, 147 (exhibit)
   convenience sampling, 139–140
   network or snowball sampling, 140–141
   purposive or judgmental sampling, 140
   quota sampling, 140
   volunteer sampling, 141–142
Normal curve, 119–122
Normal distribution, 118, 122–123
Norms of communication, 206
Null hypotheses, 32, 112
Numbers, 81–82. *See also* Content analysis, quantitative;
   Quantitative research; Surveys
Nuremberg Code, 46

Observational studies, 196, 207
Observations, capturing, 6
Observer reliability, 86–87
Observer roles, 198
O'Connor, Anahad, 64
One-group pretest-posttest design, 181
One-tailed hypotheses, 32
One-tailed test, 128
Online ethnography, 206–207
Online focus groups, 203–204
Online surveys, 167–168
Ontology, 30
Open-ended questions, 32, 161, 199
Operationalize, 30–31
Ordinal measurement, 83
Others, acknowledging, 44
Outcome or criterion variable, 132

Pacanowsky, Michael, 264
Panel presentations, 265–266
Panel studies, 159
Panel validity, 89
Parameters, 96
Parametric statistics, 124
Part correlation, 132
Partial correlation, 132
Participants, 206
   and ethics, 41
   and ethnographic methods, 206
   and experiments, 179-190
   focus group, 203
   in communication, 206
   relationships with researcher, 49, 197
   sampling, 141–171
   voices of, 259
Path analysis, 132
Pathos, 236
Peer persuasion, 16

Peer review, 48, 263
Phatic semiotic function, 245
Phenomenologists, 14
Phenomenology, 33
Phone surveys, 170 (exhibit)
Phrenologists, 81
Physical units, 224
Piloting, 148
Plagiarism, 45
Platykurtic, 119
Poetic semiotic function, 244
Politics, and publication, 75
Popular publications, 63
Population, 96, 139
   Internet, 50–51
   special, 152
Positivism, 28
Possibilities and decisions, 1–20
Postal sampling frames, 149
Poster papers, 265
PowerPoint, 266
Prediction, 25–26, 32
Predictive validity, 90
Predictor variable, 132
Presenting research, 255–272
   communication guidelines,
      268 (exhibit), 269
   conferences and panels, 265–266
   editorial processes, 263–264
   interest groups, writing for, 261–262
   news media, writing for, 261, 262–263
   popular media, writing for, 269
   PowerPoint, using, 266
   scholarly publics, writing for, 256–261, 269
   style and accuracy, 264–265
   web, using, 267–268
Pretest-posttest designs, 181–183
Primary sources, 64–65
Principle of utilitarianism, 45
Privacy
   online surveys and, 167
   on the Internet, 50–51
Probability/probabilities, 122–123, 132–133
Probability sampling, 142–147
   multistage cluster sampling, 146–147
   random sampling, 143–144
   stratified random sampling, 144
   systematic sampling, 144–146
Problem posing, 16
Problem solving, 16
Prompts, 202
Propositional units, 224
Proprietary, 44, 98
PSAs (public service advertisements), 8–11
Publication, and politics, 75
Publications, types of, 63–64

Public service advertisements (PSAs), 8–11
Purpose, 236
    in dramatistic analysis, 11, 237
    of research, 7, 35
Purposive sampling, 140, 147 (exhibit)

Q-Methodology, 15
Qualitative, 197
Qualitative research, 195–215
    advantages and disadvantages of, 196
    CAQDAS (computer-assisted qualitative data
        analysis software), 210–211
    data and, 208–210
    methods, 198–208
    researcher-participant relationships, 197
    versus quantitative research, similarities
        and differences, 196–197
    See also Content analysis, qualitative
Qualitative writing, 260–261
Quantitative, 197
Quantitative research, 80–95
    reliability, 85–87, 90
    research NOIR, 82–85
    scales, 82, 90–93
    validity, 85, 88–90
    versus qualitative research, similarities
        and differences, 196–197
    See also Content analysis, quantitative and Interview questions
Quantitative writing, 260–261
Questionnaire, 157
Quota sampling, 140, 147 (exhibit)

R, 98
Random assignment, 182–184
Random digit dialing (RDD), 149, 167
Random numbers, 183
Random numbers generator, 144
Random sampling, 143–144, 147 (exhibit)
Range, 106
Ranking questions, 202
Rankings, misleading, 112
Rank order questions, 83, 162
Ratio analysis, 237
Ratio measurement, 84
Rationalism, 28
Rawls, John, 45
Refereeing, 61
Referential, 245
Regression, 132
Regulations, and ethics, 48
Reification, 92
Relationships, and ethical decisions, 42
Relevant information, identifying, 60
Reliability, 85–88, 90, 217
    established measures, 87
    intercoder or observer, 86

inter-item or internal, 87
    test-retest, 86
Reliability coefficients, 86
Repair mechanism, 242
Repeated testing, 187
Report formats, scholarly and professional,
        258 (exhibit), 261
Research NOIR, 82–85
    in action, 85
    interval measurement, 83–84
    nominal measurement, 83
    ordinal measurement, 83
    ratio measurement, 84
Research questions
    firming up, 30–33
    first, 21–39
    framing, 165
    hermeneutics and, 34
    how, 28
    Internet research and, 52
    lack of, 33
    leading, 164
    questioning the, 33
    what, 22–24
    why, 24–28
    work, of others, 30
    worldviews and, 28–30
    See also Survey questions and Interview questions
Respondents, 199
Response rates, survey, 168–171
Responsibilities. See Ethics
Results, reporting, 221–222, 227
Reviewing research, 58–79
    bibliographic searches, 65–74
    databases, 61
    library research, 59–60
    literature review, 58, 72–74
    primary and secondary sources, 64–65
    publications, types of, 63
    relevance and quality, 60–61
    scholarly journals, 62–63
    search engines, 61
Rhetoric, 235–238
Rhetorical analyses, 235–238
    Aristotelian analysis, 235–236
    dramatistic analysis, 236–237
    fantasy theme analysis, 237–238
Rhetoricians, 234
Richardson, Brian K., 66
Root metaphor, 239

Sample, 96, 139
Sample size, 14, 124–125, 148–149
Sampling, 138–156
    convenience, 139
    distribution, 123

ethics and, 135
frames, 143, 149–152, 223
future of, 152
Internet, 150
interval, 144
methods, advantages and disadvantages of, 147 (exhibit)
mulstistage cluster, 146
network or snowball, 140
nonprobability, 139 -142
postal, 149
probability, 142 -147
purposive or judgmental, 140
quota, 140
random, 143
sample size and, 148 -149
special population, 152
stratified random, 144
systematic, 144
telephone, 149
units, 143
Scaled questions, 33
Scales, measurement, 80, 90, 93
introduction to, 82
Likert, 84, 90–91, 92
semantic differential, 84, 91–93
Scene, 236
Schmidt, Benjamin, 229
Scholarly articles, 63–64
Scholarly databases, versus search engines, 61–62
Scholarly journals, 62–63
Scholarly literature, 72–73 (exhibit)
Scholarly publications, 63, 257–258
Scholarly publics
presenting for, 265–266
writing for, 256–261
Scientific methods, 28
Search
engines, 50, 61–62
fields, 62, 65–66
Library of Congress and, 67
results, 69–74
strategies, 65
terms, 60, 65–66
Secondary sources, 64–65
Selection bias, 187
Selectivity, in statistics, 134–135
Semantic differential scale, 84, 91–93, 163
Semiotic functions, 244–245
Semioticians, 244
Semiotics, 242–245
Semiotic thinking, 242–244
Semipartial correlation, 132
Semistructured interviews, 199
Sequence, of an interview, 201

Serials, 30
Significance, 117, 133–134
Simplification, in statistics, 134–135
Situation of communication, 206
Skew, 118
Slideware, 266
Snowball sampling, 140–141, 147 (exhibit)
Social scientists, 13
Software
CAQDAS (computer-assisted qualitative data analysis software), 210–211
citation management, 71
content analysis, 229
Solomon Four-Group Design, 183–184, 188
Special population sampling, 152
Speech community, 206
Speech event, 206
Speech situation, 206
Split half technique, 87
Spurious relationships, 187
Standard deviation, 106, 107–108, 120–122, 124 (exhibit)
Standard error, 123, 148
Stanford prison experiment (Zimbardo), 191
Statistics, 96. *See also* Descriptive statistics;
Inferential statistics
Stemming, 229
Stratified random sampling, 144–145, 147 (exhibit)
Structural questions, 201
Structure, of an interview, 200
Style
guide, 257
in writing, 264–265
library research and, 60
Subjects, 46
and research ethics, 46–52
and experimental design, 186
Survey(s), 157–176
advantages and disadvantages of, 158–159
data, capturing and processing, 171
ethics in, 172–173
filter questions and instructions, 166–167
guiding respondents through, 166
language, 165–166
methods, advantages and disadvantages of, 170–171 (exhibit)
mobile, 168
online, 167–168
other people's, using, 171–172
questions, writing and formatting, 160–163
response rates, improving, 168–171
sampling, future of, 152
types of, 159–160
wording, 163–167
Survey questions, 160–163
demographic, 160

dichotomous, 161–162
double-barreled, 165
inverted funnel, 166
Likert scale, 162–163
multiple-choice, 162
open-ended, 161
rank order, 83, 162
semantic differential scale, 163
Symbolic convergence, 237
Synchronous communication, 203
Syntactical units, 224
Systematic sampling, 144–146, 147 (exhibit)

Tables, 97
Technology, and online surveys, 167
Telephone sampling frames, 149–150
Temporal ordering, 183
Tenacity, 28
Test-retest reliability, 86
Thematic units, 224
Time series analysis, 184
Trade publications, 63
Transitional relevance place, 241
Trend studies, 159
Triangulation, 15
Tri-modal distribution, 105, 118
t tests, 105, 125–129
Turn constructional unit, 241
Turn taking, 240–242
Tuskegee medical studies, 46
Two-group pretest-posttest design, 182
Two-group random assignment pretest-posttest design, 183
Two-tailed hypotheses, 32
Two-tailed test, 128
Type I error, 133
Type II error, 133

Units, 218
Univariate analysis, 100
Univariate data, and data reduction, 100–102
Unobtrusive measures, 42, 196, 207–208

Unstructured interviews, 199
USA PATRIOT Act, 51
Uses and gratifications theory, 200
Utterances, 241

Validity, 85, 218
construct, 89
content, 89
criterion, 89
measurement and, 88–90
Variables, 31
continuous, 84
dependent, 178
discrete, 84
independent, 178
outcome or criterion, 132
predictor, 132
testing for relationships, 131–132
Variance, 106–108
"Veil of ignorance," 45
Voice, 257
Volunteer sampling, 141–142, 147 (exhibit)

Ways of speaking, 206
Web
information on the, 67–68
writing and presenting with the, 267–268
Within-subjects design, 186
Wolak, Janis, 64
Wording, survey, 163–167
Words. *See* Content analysis, qualitative; Qualitative research
Worldviews, 29
Writing
for interest groups, 261–262
for news media, 261, 262–263
for popular media, 269
for scholarly publics, 256–261, 269
qualitative and quantitative, 260–261

Zimbardo, Philip, 191
z scores, 109–110, 120–124

About the Author

Donald Treadwell earned his master's degree in communication from Cornell University and his PhD in communication and rhetoric from Rensselaer Polytechnic Institute.

He developed and taught communication research classes in classroom and online settings and also taught courses in organizational communication, public relations, and public relations writing. He is the coauthor of *Public Relations Writing: Principles in Practice* (2nd ed., Sage, 2005).

He has published and presented research on organizational image, consumer response to college names, health professionals' images of AIDS, faculty perceptions of the communication discipline, and employers' expectations of newly hired communication graduates. His research appears in *Communication Monographs, Journal of Technical Writing and Communication, Public Relations Review, Journal of Human Subjectivity,* and *Criminal Justice Ethics*.

He is professor emeritus, Westfield State University, and has international consulting experience in agricultural extension and health communication.